Digital Intermedia and Video

Digital Intermediates
for Film and Video

Jack James

AMSTERDAM • BOSTON • HEIDELBERG • LONDON
NEW YORK • OXFORD • PARIS • SAN DIEGO
SAN FRANCISCO • SINGAPORE • SYDNEY • TOKYO
Focal Press is an imprint of Elsevier

ELSEVIER

Acquisitions Editor: Angelina Ward
Publishing Services Manager: Simon Crump
Assistant Editor: Rachel Epstein
Marketing Manager: Christine Degon
Cover Design: Eric DeCicco

Focal Press is an imprint of Elsevier
30 Corporate Drive, Suite 400, Burlington, MA 01803, USA
Linacre House, Jordan Hill, Oxford OX2 8DP, UK

Library of Congress Cataloging-in-Publication Data
James, Jack (Jack M.)
  Digital intermediates for film and video / Jack James.
      p. cm.
  1. Photography—Retouching. 2. Digital video—Editing. 3. Video recording. 4. Scanning systems. 5. Photographs. I. Title.
   TR310.J36 2005
   778.5'293—dc22   2005020379

British Library Cataloguing-in-Publication Data
A catalogue record for this book is available from the British Library.

ISBN 13: 978-0-240-80702-7
ISBN 10: 0-240-80702-2

For information on all Focal Press publications

visit our website at www.books.elsevier.com

05 06 07 08 09 10   10 9 8 7 6 5 4 3 2 1
Printed in the United States of America

CONTENTS

1

THE DIGITAL INTERMEDIATE PARADIGM

The phrases "never been done before," "pushing the envelope," and "attempting the impossible" crop up rather often in the film industry, particularly in post-production. But the methodology used to finish HBO's "Band of Brothers" mini-series in 2000 involved a completely new work flow, justifying the frequent use of these comments to some extent. Every scene of the production was shot on 35mm photographic film (with the exception of a number of computer-generated visual effects and a few seconds of 16mm footage), but by the time of completion, the entire, edited series existed only as a bunch of data stored on a number of hard disks and digital tapes. This wasn't anything new in itself. Disney's *Toy Story* had been an entirely digital production, and the film *Pleasantville* involved scanning and digitally color-grading a cut film to a set of digital files, before recording back onto film.

What was unique was the unprecedented level of control made available to the filmmakers. The series' editors, who were themselves working with separate video references of all the film footage, were able to make adjustments to their cuts, and see the changes implemented into the final version almost instantly, the existing sequences rearranged, and any new material added. At the same time, the cinematographers and directors would oversee the color correction of the production interactively, at the highest possible level of quality, complete with visual effects and titles, and synchronized to the latest audio mix. They had the ability to jump to any particular scene and even to compare the look of multiple scenes to ensure continuity. Further, the level of control of color grading enabled a unique look that would be extremely difficult to obtain (some might say impossible) using traditional photochemical processes. Meanwhile, other departments composited titles, dissolves, and other optical effects with a similar degree of interactivity and control, and others used digital paint tools to remove defects such as dust and scratches from the scanned images, resulting in images of extremely high quality.

This process wasn't completely smooth-running: a lot of things didn't work as theorized, a great many things broke completely, and some days it seemed that we were attempting the impossible. But many lessons are learned the hard way, and envisioned ideals soon gave way to practical fixes and workarounds. And to some degree, that philosophy still prevails throughout this rapidly growing digital intermediate industry.

For this reason, the aim of this book is not just to present a technical discussion of the theoretical possibilities, the "wouldn't it be good if everyone did approach"; the aim is also to cover current working practices, and explain why certain things have to be done the way they are—even though it can seem inefficient or irrational at times—and, of course, to list possible methods to improve them.

There is also a website that accompanies the book, which details new advances and changes in the industry, as well as points to other helpful resources. Find it online at www.digitalintermediates.org.

1.1   WHAT IS A DIGITAL INTERMEDIATE?

If you have ever worked with an image-editing system, such as Adobe's ubiquitous Photoshop (www.adobe.com), then you are already familiar with the concept of a digital intermediate. With digital image editing, you take an image from some source, such as a piece of film, a paper printout, or even an existing digital image (if using a digital camera for instance), bring it into your digital system (by using a scanner or by copying the file), make changes to it as required, and then output it (e.g., by printing onto photographic paper or putting it on the Internet). Your image has just undergone a digital intermediate process, one that is in very many ways analogous to the process used for high-budget feature films (albeit on a much smaller scale).

The digital intermediate is often defined as a digital replacement for a photochemical "intermediate"—a stage in processing in which a strip of film (either an "interpositive" or an "internegative") is used to reorganize and make changes to the original, source footage prior to output—and is often regarded as only applicable to Hollywood-budget film productions. It is true that the digital intermediate fulfills this function; however, it potentially fulfills many others too. First, any material that can be digitized (i.e., made digital) can be used as source material, and the same is also true of output format. For this reason, it is somewhat arrogant to presume that digital intermediates are only used for film production, as the digital intermediate paradigm has already been used with video production for many years. Second, the budget is something of a nonissue. More is possible with a larger budget, less compromises need to be made, and a higher level of quality can be maintained. But footage that is captured using consumer-grade DV camcorders as opposed to 35mm film cameras is still a candidate for a digital intermediate process. Possibly one of the most interesting features of the digital intermediate process is that it can be used for almost any budget or scale. So, perhaps for a better definition of what a digital intermediate is, it's a paradigm for completing a production by digital means, whether it's the latest Hollywood epic or an amateur wedding video.

1.2   DIGITAL INTERMEDIATES FOR VIDEO

Video editing used to be a fairly straightforward process, requiring two video cassette recorders (VCRs), one acting as a player, the other as a recorder. Shots are assembled onto the recorded tape by playing

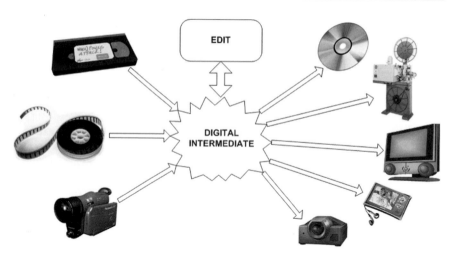

FIGURE 1-1 With a digital intermediate pipeline, it's possible to work with a number of different media

them in the desired sequence. This simple, yet efficient "tape-to-tape" system was excellent for putting programs together quickly, but it limited creativity and experimentation because you couldn't go back and change something at the beginning without re-recording everything again. Video editing was a linear process (unlike film editing, where editors could happily chop up bits of film at the beginning of a reel without having to rework the whole film).

The nature of video also meant that creating effects, such as split-screens or dissolves, was possible but required dedicated hardware for each function. Suddenly a fully equipped video-editing suite was crammed with various boxes, each of which required specific training to use, not to mention cost to install and maintain.

With the advent of nonlinear editing systems, computer technology brought a digital intermediate of sorts to the video world. Rather than record video from one tape to another, it was captured onto a computer system, which then was used for editing in a nonlinear fashion, allowing video editors to work with far greater flexibility. Once the virtual editing (or "offline" editing) had been completed, there were two possible routes for output. In some cases, the details of the edit could be sent to a linear system, and the original tapes were used to recreate the desired cuts in what was termed the "online" edit. Alternatively, the offline version could be output directly to tape from the digital system, complete with dissolves and other effects. Over time, the possibilities grew, such that it became possible to perform sophisticated color-grading of footage, along with numerous other effects. Now, much of the same technology is available to the amateur videographer as to the professional.

1.3   DIGITAL INTERMEDIATES FOR FILM

Back in the "golden era" of film production, perhaps thousands of feet of 35mm negative (the same stuff you put in a nondigital stills camera) would be generated every day of a shoot. All this film would have to be soaked in numerous chemical baths, and then it would all get printed onto more film—this time 35mm "positive" (or "reversal") film. This process allowed a light to be shone through, projecting the image onto something (e.g., a cinema screen) in the correct color for viewing.

So, at the end of shooting a production, you would have maybe a million feet of celluloid, at which point would come the editors to sort through it all, which had to be done by hand. But because the negative is so fragile and yet so valuable (each bit of original negative retains the highest level of quality and represents all the set design, acting, camerawork, and lighting invested in it), there was constant risk of damage to it, particularly during editing but also during duplication and printing.

More copies of the negative were created for the editors to work with, and once they had decided how it was going to cut together, they would dig out the original and match all the cuts and joins they made (and they really used scissors and glue to do it) to the original.

So now there would be a cut-together film, which consists of hundreds of valuable strips of film, held together by little more than tape. Woe unto any filmmaker who decided they wanted to make changes to it at this point.

Other problems still had to be dealt with. First of all, you don't want to keep running a priceless reel of film through a duplicator every time you want to make a cinema print (especially bearing in mind that you might need to make some 10,000 or more prints for a distribution run). Second, different scenes might have been shot on different days, so the color would need adjusting (or would require being "timed") so that the different colors matched better.

Hence the internegative and interpositive copies of the original, cut-together film. Creating these additional reels allows for color timing to be done too, and so the result is a single piece of film with no joins. So now everyone is happy, even after running it through the copying machine 10,000 times.

Well, almost. See, the internegative is of significantly lower quality than the original, and all the color timing is done using a combination of beams of light, colored filters, and chemicals, which is a bit like trying to copy a Rembrandt using finger paints. But until the digital intermediate process gained a degree of authority, filmmakers (and the audience) just lived with the limitations of the photochemical process.

Things improved a little with the advent of nonlinear video editing. It basically meant that rather than having to physically wade through reels of film to look at shots, copies of all the film could be "telecined" (i.e., transferred) to videotapes and edited as with any other video production, finally matching the edit back to the individual strips of film. But many of the quality issues remained, and filmmakers were still unable to match the degree of stylization achieved in video production without resorting to visual effects (and at significant cost).

At least, not until the advent of the digital intermediate process for film came into use, offering significant advantages over the traditional, optical process.

1.4 THE ADVANTAGES

A digital intermediate work flow provides lots of wonderful advantages to a production. The most immediately obvious is that in addition to its nonlinear nature, it also offers "instant seek"—the capability to jump to any point in a sequence without having to spool through the footage to get there (this was one of the features that drew many consumers to adopt DVD technology and dump VHS videos). As well as saving time, digital intermediate work flow has practical implications: two shots at different points in a program can be checked easily for continuity.

It offers a more flexible approach. Changes made to the production can be automatically synchronized with the digital version, so that if, for example, changes to the edit are made, the digital version reorganizes (i.e., reconforms) itself to match the new edit. Rather than editors having to manually search through reels of film or hours of video, they can match digital files to offline edited versions using information such as timecode or keycode numbers. In addition to the nonlinear editing capability, almost every aspect of the digital intermediate process is nonlinear, and so productions can be completed in a more convenient order, rather than having to be completed chronologically.

Digital systems enable a degree of intelligence to be imparted to the images used, meaning that images can be tagged, sorted, and indexed as needed. Specific digital processes can provide a form of image analysis, allowing objective quality measurement, filtering to increase sharpness or reduce noise, and enabling options such as feature tracking.

Digital images are just numbers, and so may be copied accurately and easily. Unlike analog formats, digital media doesn't suffer from "generational loss," meaning that each copy is a perfect duplicate of the original. This single fact means that a superior level of image quality can be maintained throughout the digital intermediate process, allowing for greater experimentation and disaster recovery (as back-ups of the original images can be made without risking damaging them). With film and video processes, even with a tightly controlled work flow, the final version of a production would already have undergone a number of copies (or generations) and be inferior in quality to the original.

In many situations, digital image processing can be much faster than its analog (nondigital) counterparts. Many operations, such as resizing or repositioning images happen almost instantly, compared to analog systems that may require setting up complex optical systems to accomplish the same thing. This speed allows for a great deal of inter-active feedback, particularly with color grading, where changes to the color of an image can be adjusted by turning dials and the like, and seeing the changes instantly reflected in the full-quality version. This affords the filmmaker a much greater level of creative control and more freedom to experiment with different options (or to make tweaks).

Finally, digital systems have the potential to add increased security and protection to stored data. Use of encryption and digital rights management technology can ensure that only authorized people have access to the images in the first place. This can be used to help com-bat piracy and to prevent the making of unauthorized copies, as well as to allow a greater number of (authorized) people to access the pro-duction with ease.

Is the digital intermediate system a perfect one? Not by a long shot. Anyone who has used a computer for five minutes instantly becomes an expert in all the things that can go wrong—accidental file deletion, hardware failures, software crashes, and so on. Now, take into account that a typical digital intermediate needs around 150,000 individual frames, which typically amounts to 1.5 terabytes (which is 1.5 million megabytes) for film material, and you don't have to have be a profes-sor to realize that things can and do go wrong. Having said that, as time goes by, the associated equipment is getting faster and more reli-able, and more people are using it, which means that it's also getting easier to use. There are many possibilities for exploiting this technol-ogy that haven't properly been explored, and the potential is certainly there to create productions far exceeding even the quality of film.

In addition, parts of the process tend to be very slow. Data transport in particular can take significantly longer than video systems, and many digital systems require time-consuming rendering and check-ing processes to be factored into the overall completion schedule.

There are also issues that arise from a general lack of standardiza-tion throughout the industry, such as the problem of the best method of long-term storage. Many of the potential advantages of a digital work flow are dependent on the system they run on, meaning full-quality playback, or any of the other bells and whistles of a rival system may not be available due to performance and other factors.

Finally, data is not an inherently visual medium, and so it's not as easy to look at a disk to work out the contents as it is to, say, play a tape in a VCR or put a strip of film on a lightbox.

1.5 THE FLEXIBLE APPROACH

A digital intermediate is not just for feature films. It is a paradigm that can be used on any number of source and destination media, be it, film, video, or digital. There are already a number of established digital intermediate pipelines that aim to solve different problems.

1.5.1 Telecine

Getting film transferred to video has been necessary for many applications for a number of years. For example, creating video releases to coincide with theatrical releases of films (for rental or sale) previously required converting the film to a video format. This is accomplished by using a "telecine" process.

A typical telecine process involves using a dedicated machine to convert photographic film directly to video. Although analog telecines exist, they have recently all but been phased out by digital ones. Nevertheless, the basic idea is the same: in goes the film, out comes video. The limitation is that this is something of a linear process, in that the film must be output in the same order as it is fed in.[1] Moreover, although it's possible to modify the output to change the color components of the images, these modifications must be done in real time and may therefore be more limited and more expensive to implement than those provided by a digital intermediate process.

---

[1] There are methods for getting around this limitation, but they involve video editing to some degree.

Using a digital intermediate process, digitizing the film to data, such as by using a scanner instead of a telecine, the scanned film may be processed in whatever way is necessary, and then the modified data may be output to video. This makes all the features of the digital intermediate available, such as the ability to remove dust and scratches from the film image, to reorganize scenes or shots, and to apply color grading in a nonlinear fashion. Moreover, multiple reels may be processed together, in any order. The downside is that the digital intermediate process may ultimately take longer than a direct telecine approach.

FIGURE 1-2   A typical telecine work flow

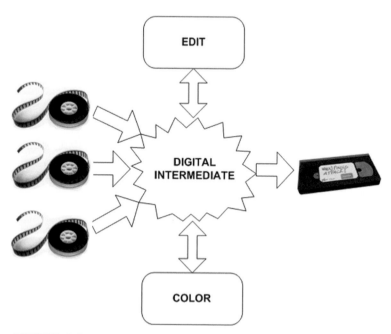

FIGURE 1-3   Adapting the telecine process to a digital intermediate pipeline

1.5.2 Film Production

The usual method for finishing a feature film is to telecine all the "dailies" (film footage produced during shooting, sometimes called "rushes") and then import the resulting video footage into a nonlinear editing system until a final cut is produced. This final cut is then matched back to the original film negative. It is then cut together (a process referred to as a "negative cut," or "neg-cut") to match the final edit before being color-timed and duplicated for distribution. More recently, an additional telecine process of the edited, color-timed film is used at the end to generate video deliverables for television, airline, and consumer release.

A digital intermediate work flow streamlines this process somewhat, but there are numerous ways of doing it. Ideally, the rushes could be scanned rather than telecined, with digital copies sent to the editing team (or videos output from the digital scans). The edited version could then be sent for digital color timing, digital restoration (e.g., to repair dust and scratches on the scanned images), and effects. Finally, the finished, digital production can be output back onto film and simultaneously to other formats, such as video or streaming Internet media.

Practicality (not to mention expense) places some limitations on this idealized pipeline, however, and the reality is that the production is

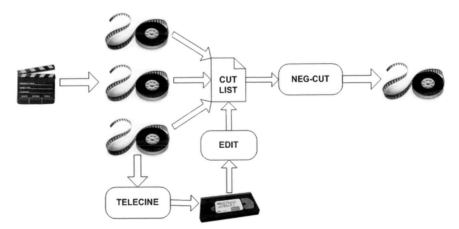

FIGURE 1-4   A typical film post-production pipeline

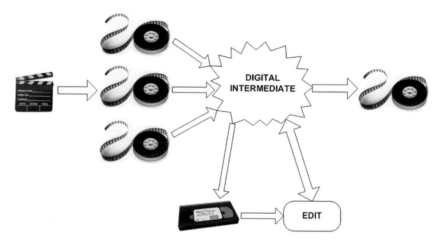

FIGURE 1-5   An ideal digital intermediate work flow for film post-production

normally edited before any scanning is done, using telecined rushes (as with a nondigital pipeline). The edited version is used to determine which footage needs to be scanned (rather than scan everything), and to help automatically conform the scanned material to create the desired program in a digital form.

Much of the problem with a digital intermediate approach is that the volume of data required to complete a single film is enormous, which

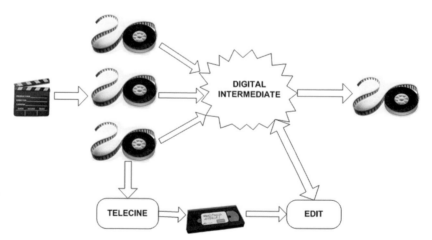

FIGURE 1-6   A typical digital intermediate work flow for film post-production

in turn means it can be slow to transport and process and can require a lot of storage space. In addition, color-management issues have to be addressed: film is very different from video in terms of color and dynamic range, and so accurate color management is essential, particularly when outputting to both film and video, and especially for ensuring that digital color timing looks as it was intended.

1.5.3 Video Production

Video production already makes use of a digital intermediate pipeline almost exclusively, with the exception of linear (tape-to-tape) video production. The simplest (and ideal) method is to digitize all video footage, edit and process it digitally, and then output it directly back to video, as used by many broadcast news organizations. This is not only fast, but it's also inexpensive and allows the production to enjoy all the benefits of the digital intermediate work flow, such as effects and color grading.

In some instances, a slightly different approach is needed, such as when working with the slightly unwieldy high definition (HD) video formats. Under these circumstances, it may be more efficient (and less expensive) to use the offline/online approach, such that the editing process is done "offline," typically at a lower quality than the original source, focusing on cutting individual shots and sequences, rather than on the specific effects to be applied. The final cut is then saved as a list of edits (or EDL), which is used to assemble the original, full-quality material during the "online" editing stage, where the necessary effects and image processing is applied, and the sequence is output.

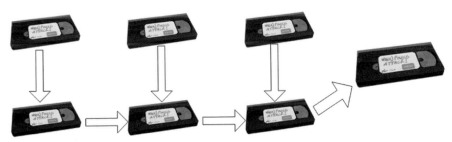

FIGURE 1-7   A linear video-editing work flow involves making edits sequentially

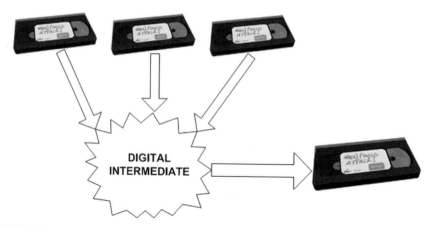

FIGURE 1-8   A digital intermediate work flow allows edits to be made in any order

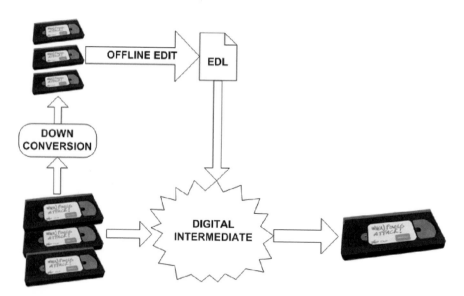

FIGURE 1-9   An online/offline digital intermediate paradigm

The only real downside to using a digital intermediate pipeline in this way, as opposed to a tape-to-tape system, is that additional time may be needed to digitize video material before it can be used. Even so, many productions are able to even eliminate this disadvantage by performing the digitization during the initial recording of the source material.

FIGURE 1-10 A video-to-film work flow

1.5.4 Video-to-Film Conversion

A digital intermediate process is essential to taking video footage and outputting it to film. Generally speaking, video footage is of inferior quality to film.[2] However, it's sometimes necessary to print video images onto film—for example, to show televised commercials in cinemas or for short films that may have originally been shot on a video format. By far the best way to do this is to digitize the video footage, process it, and then record it onto film. Several digital processes may be necessary for this to happen successfully, including resizing and repositioning the images (as video is usually too small to fill a frame of film), as well as color-space conversion (to correct for color differences between video and film), and possibly de-interlacing them (to correct for video motion artifacts).

1.5.5 Live Production

Provided that the data can be processed fast enough, it may be possible, or even desirable to use a digital work flow for live broadcasts. In the simplest instance, this may mean a "webcam" that processes and outputs footage directly to the Internet, potentially without even keeping a recorded copy of the footage. At the other extreme, such as for sports event coverage, video footage can be captured, processed, and output as quickly as it is received, allowing the use of digital effects to be applied, such as a digital zoom, text, or some form of filtering. However, such a system is prone to digital defects such as image

---

[2] Many estimate that HD video is of equivalent quality to super-16mm film however.

FIGURE 1-11 A digital intermediate work flow can be used for live productions

artifacts or corruption because there is not enough time to correct or repair such problems. In addition, the entire system is limited to digital-processing techniques that can be applied faster than the images are received.

1.5.6 Digital Production

It is entirely feasible to work with footage that originated in a digital form, created on a computer system. In fact, this process is used to create completely digital productions such as Disney's *The Incredibles* and Dreamworks's *Shrek*. Scenes are generated within a virtual environment and are rendered to produce digital footage. This digital footage can be referenced within the digital intermediate pipeline exactly as if it were digitized video or scanned film, with a multitude of processing options available.[3]

As new shooting methods gain prominence, such as recording video footage directly to digital media, the available processing options will increase, as will the ease of use and integration of a digital pipeline. Note that audio does not factor into any of these pipelines, though it will represent a significant part of most productions. This is because audio content tends to be treated separately from visual content and is only combined with visual elements at the output stage.

---

[3] In fact, such a pipeline affords even more options, particularly as computer-generated images can be encoded with additional image information, such as relative depth and separation of different elements into layers.

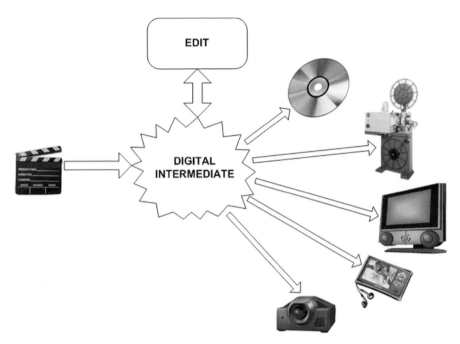

FIGURE 1-12   A completely digital production provides many possibilities

1.6 THE CREATIVE OPTION

A digital pipeline enables the filmmaker to have an unprecedented degree of creative control over the visual content of a production. The most obvious benefit is the significant amount of control with respect to color-grading digital images. Whereas nondigital grading is usually limited to adjustments that affect the overall content, digital grading allows precise control over the color of individual elements within a scene. It's a lot like the difference between a chain saw and a scalpel.

Creative options are not just limited to altering the color content however. Numerous digital filters are available to stylize footage further, as well as correct problems or enhance camerawork. All of these effects can be controlled as precisely as the color-grading process, using masking and keying techniques to isolate specific regions within the images, and tracking and animation techniques to adjust each effect over time.

1.7 THE ASSURANCE OF QUALITY

Use of a digital intermediate pipeline is not necessarily a guarantee of quality, as there are many factors to consider, which will be covered throughout this book. Done properly however, a digital pipeline can ensure that the production is processed at the highest possible level of quality, and that this level is maintained through to final output.

Copying a digital file creates a duplicate that is mathematically identical to the original. It doesn't matter if the file in question is a webpage accessed from the Internet or a complete digital feature film copied between file servers; the content, and by extension the quality, remains the same.

This is different than copying other media, such as film and video (and to some degree, digital video), which inevitably undergo some degradation (both physically and in terms of the diminishment of signal strength) with each copy.

FIGURE 1-13   With film formats, each new copy degrades the image further

FIGURE 1-14   With video formats, each new copy degrades the image further

FIGURE 1-15 With digital formats, each new copy is identical to the last

1.8 THE PATH TO DIGITAL CINEMA

Perhaps what will prove to be the biggest selling point of the digital intermediate pipeline is that it offers the easiest transition to digital cinema. Digital cinema (or D-Cinema) involves the projection of images and audio in a theatrical context from a digital source. The aim is to provide a cinema experience that maintains a level of quality and flexibility that at least matches traditional cinema without increasing the associated cost. At the present time, the vast majority of cinemas do not have digital projection capability, and so output for digital cinema is rare. But as this changes (which is expected within the next few years), the need to output to a digital format will grow, and this need will be fulfilled easily through use of the digital intermediate process.

1.9 SUMMARY

The digital intermediate is a paradigm for completing productions, able to suit a number of different work flows and requirements, and universally conferring a greater degree of creative control and flexibility, maintaining a higher level of image quality, and allowing simultaneous output of many different formats.

Regardless of the specific work flow required, all digital intermediate pipelines share various key components that are covered in subsequent chapters. Chapter 5 covers the requirements for bringing image and other components into the digital realm. Chapter 6 describes how to manage the volume of data used by a typical pipeline, while Chapter 7 deals with ways to assemble the data into meaningful shots, scenes, and programs. Chapters 8, 9, and 10 examine the creative options available to a digital pipeline, in terms of color grading, retouching, and effects, respectively. Chapter 11 looks at the options available for outputting the finished, all-digital production, while Chapter 12 covers ways to ensure a high level of quality. Chapters 13 and 14 look at the future of the digital intermediate and ways to better take advantage of the available features.

The next few chapters will focus on the three main media involved in production: video, film, and digital images.

2

VIDEO

Video is one of the most widely-used formats for creating moving images, by both amateurs and professionals alike, and it's surprising how strictly standardized it is, considering the numerous manufacturers in constant competition. Take, for example, the lowly VHS cassette. Despite the many different makes and models of VHS cassette recorders, and the multitude of different VHS cassette manufacturers, any standard VHS cassette can be used in just about any VHS recorder. It's a similar story with playback—intercontinental issues aside (you can't necessarily play a European VHS in a U.S. recorder, for reasons that will be covered later)—a VHS recorded on one machine will play as intended on any other machine.

There are many different video formats though, which are constantly undergoing revision. The current crop of HD, DV, and DVD formats will gradually replace VHS and Betacam SP formats, just as previously popular M-II and U-Matic formats were replaced in mainstream video production. Of course, today's formats will eventually give way to future formats, and in time, the use of video may give way entirely to the use of completely digital systems.

2.1 A BRIEF HISTORY OF TELEVISION

The way that modern video systems work is determined to a large degree by the systems that were created decades ago. Video technology stems from the invention of television, and color television is built upon the principles of black-and-white television. The fundamental building block of electronic television is the cathode ray tube (CRT). Put simply, the CRT is a beam of electrons fired down a vacuum tube at a screen. The screen is coated with a phosphorescent material, which glows when struck by electrons. The basic setup allows a glowing dot to be produced on the screen. By using a combination of magnets and electrical current, both the intensity and position of the beam can be altered. And because the phosphors continue to glow for a short period after the beam has moved, the beam can rapidly sweep out patterns on the screen.

This concept was adapted to form complete images by sweeping the beam across several rows. During the trace of each row, the intensity of the beam can be varied to form a monochrome picture.

For this to work for television, the path of the beam had to be standardized, so that the picture area and timing of the beam was the same regardless of the particular television set used for display. In essence, the television signal received consisted of the intensity component only. This process was tested in the 1930s, resulting in the first television broadcasts in 1936.

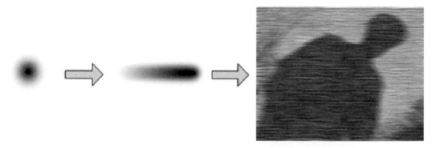

FIGURE 2-1 A single beam can be used to trace intricate patterns on a phosphor screen

In the 1960s, color television became a reality. Importantly, the color television signals could still be seen on black-and-white televisions, a feat achieved by encoding the color components separately from the luminance. By then, the resolution of the image had improved greatly, and numerous technical innovations had resulted in televisions sets and broadcast systems that created and displayed images with increasing clarity, at reduced cost.

Around this point, national standards were defined. The NTSC standard was used for U.S. broadcasts, but the PAL standard was adopted by many other countries, as NTSC showed problems trying to replicate certain colors. The completion of these standards led to widespread manufacture of commercial televisions and the use of video casette recorders (VCRs).

2.2 VIDEO IMAGE CREATION

In many ways, video cameras generate images in much the same way as digital cameras. Video cameras are essentially an optical system built around a detector, typically a CCD (charge coupled device), which exploits the photoelectric effect to generate an electrical signal.[1] This electrical signal is then recorded to magnetic tape for later playback. The basic idea is that the more light received by the detector, the stronger the electrical signal. Because an electrical signal can be measured continuously, the changes in light can be recorded over time. That's nice if you want to keep track of the amount of light at a single, specific point in space (and in fact, this forms the basis of most light meters used in photography), but it's not much good for recording recognizable images.

So rather than having a single light detector, video cameras have a grid (or "array") of them. Provided there are enough elements in the grid, a detailed gray scale image can be formed. And, as before, the image constantly updates over time, resulting in the formation of a moving image. To record a color image, the light received must be separated into spectral components (typically red, green, and blue—RGB—which recombine to form white)—for example, by splitting the incoming

---

[1] The photoelectric effect is one where light hitting certain materials produces an electrical current.

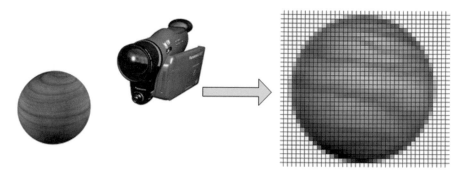

FIGURE 2-2 Video images consist of individual picture elements arranged in a grid

beam into three beams and diverting each beam to a CCD array that is sensitive to a particular component.

There are some limitations to this process. The main problem is the system bandwidth (i.e., the maximum amount of information the system can carry at a given point in time). Especially with color video of a reasonable resolution (i.e., level of spatial detail), a large quantity of signal information is generated, in many cases more than the format allows for (or the components of the system can handle). There are several ways to minimize the bandwidth requirements, which include limiting the maximum resolution and the color space, splitting the recording into fractions of time (frames and fields), and using compression, each of which is covered in this chapter.

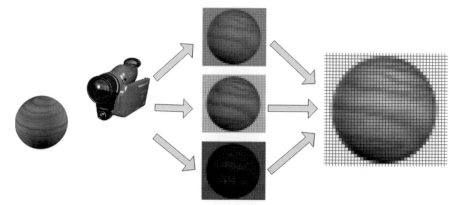

FIGURE 2-3 Color video images are formed by separating red, green, and blue components of the image and recording each separately. (See also the Color Insert)

Video images aren't created by video cameras exclusively. Many computer systems are able to directly output video signals (e.g., outputting exactly what is seen on a monitor), which can be recorded to tape as needed (this also applies to DVD players and video game consoles). In addition, other types of devices may generate video signals, such as pattern generators used to test and calibrate video equipment.[2]

2.3 ANATOMY OF A VIDEO IMAGE

Video images are just a single continuous electrical signal (with the exception of component video images, which are covered later). This means that part of the signal carries image information and part of it carries special "sync pulses" to identify where each part of the image begins and ends (although the timing of the signal is also critical in ensuring this happens).[3] Video images are constructed from the signal line by line, field by field, and frame by frame.

2.4 VIDEO STANDARDS

For various historical reasons, different geographic regions use different video standards that are incompatible. The United States and Japan, for example, use the NTSC standard, while Australia and most of Europe, use the PAL video standard. Other parts of the world use the less-common SECAM standard.

The choice of video standard defines many of the attributes of the video signal, such as the resolution and frame rate (see the Appendix

---

[2] Also worth noting is that video signals can be generated in a sense by using television antennae or satellite receivers. Although this process could technically be considered a form of transportation rather than creation, it is a perfectly reasonable way to record a signal consisting of nothing but random noise.

[3] These sync pulses, when taken cumulatively, create a "vertical interval" of the signal where no image information is present. The vertical interval can be used to carry additional information, such as the "teletext" or "closed captions" that can optionally be encoded during broadcast and displayed on the receiving television. The vertical interval may also be used to carry certain types of timecode for editing purposes.

for details on the different systems). Each system is incompatible with the others, which is why European video tapes won't play on U.S. VCRs (although they can still be used for making new recordings), and vice versa. However, it is possible to get around this limitation by using "standards converters," which are devices that alter video signals, changing them from one standard to another.

2.4.1 Definition

Similar in concept to the difference between different video standards, a recent development is videos of different definition. Originally, all video types could be categorized in what is now known as "standard definition" (or SD), with fixed frame rates, resolutions, and so on, as determined by the standard used. However, now a new generation of high definition (or HD) video formats have arrived that deliver greater resolution than standard definition formats, are in many ways independent from the different video standards, and are typically defined by their resolution and frame rate.[4]

Other formats, such as the broadcast HDTV or the new HDV formats, offer improved quality over SD formats and fall under the high definition umbrella, although they may not be of the same level of quality as other high-end HD formats. For more details on different SD and HD standards, refer to the Appendix.

2.5 RESOLUTION

In broad terms, resolution determines the level of detail in an image. In video signals, the resolution is the measure of the number of horizontal lines used to build a picture. The higher the number of lines, the higher the resolution, and the higher the level of detail that can be "resolved," and hence, the greater the quality of the image.

In practical terms, the resolution of a video image is determined by the standard. For example, PAL videos have 625 lines of resolution,

---

[4] Most HD formats match the frame rate of SD systems to ease conversion, but there is no such thing as an NTSC HD tape.

and NTSC 525. In practice, however, some of these lines are not used for image information, so the actual picture resolution is slightly lower.[5] Each high definition format also has a specific number of lines associated with it. For instance, both the 1080p30 and 1080i50 formats have 1080 lines of picture (and unlike SD formats, all the lines are used for image information).

FIGURE 2-4 An image at HD resolution (top) and an equivalent SD resolution image. © 2005 Andrew Francis

---

[5] The horizontal resolution of a video image is determined by part of the signal, the "subcarrier" frequency, which also is determined by the video standard.

2.6 TEMPORAL FREQUENCY

Like most moving picture media, video gives the illusion of motion by showing multiple images in rapid succession. Each image is known as a "frame," and the frequency of the frames being displayed is known as the "frame rate," usually measured in frames per second (or Hertz). As with resolution, the frame rate is determined by the video standard. PAL and SECAM systems use 25 frames per second, while NTSC runs at 29.97.[6] Humans are not particularly sensitive to differences in frame rate faster than 20 frames per second (fps), so a higher frame rate does not necessarily impart a greater degree of visual quality to a sequence. The most important aspect about frame rate is that it should be consistent throughout a project to ensure accurate editing later on. It is possible to "retime" or change the frame rate digitally, either keeping the apparent speed of motion constant between two formats or to allow for temporal effects, such as slow motion.

FIGURE 2-5   A sequence captured at 30fps

FIGURE 2-6   The same sequence at 25fps. Although the 30fps sequence has more frames during the same time period, the two sequences are perceptually the same

---

[6] This somewhat awkward number leads to problems that will be covered in Chapter 7.

2.6.1 Fields

To confuse issues further, video systems (with the exception of newer "progressive scan" formats) divide each image frame into two "fields," Each field consists of half of the lines of the original image, with one field containing all the even-numbered lines, and the other field containing the odd-numbered lines. These are "interlaced" to form the complete frame.

Interlacing is done to limit the bandwidth during recording. Most video cameras record imagery using a "line transfer" method, whereby each line of a frame is sent from the CCD to the recording mechanism sequentially. The problem was that video cameras could not do this fast enough (because the bandwidth was insufficient to allow it), and so a significant amount of time passed between transferring the first line of a frame and the last line. The last line of the image actually happened a significant amount of time after the first, meaning that the top part of the picture was "older" than the lower part. The result is that strange streaking and other visual artifacts will appear, particularly in regions with lots of motion.[7]

FIGURE 2-7 Two fields are combined to form an interlaced frame

---

[7] There was also a problem with televisions trying to display full frames, in that the top half of the picture started to fade from the screen while the lower half was being traced, creating a flickering effect.

Frames are therefore displayed a field at a time—so quickly (close to 60 fields per second for NTSC video) that individual frames are perceived as entire frames, which are in turn perceived as continuous motion. Most video cameras are designed so that each field is recorded independently, so that each is an accurate recording of that moment in time, rather than recording a complete frame and dividing it into two fields.

Interlaced HD formats denote the interlacing with an "i" preceding the field rate (as in 1080i59.94), whereas progressive formats use a "p" (as in 1080p29.97).[8] There are also references to "progressive segmented frames" (or PsF), which are essentially progressive frames that have been split into two fields for encoding purposes only.

When recording video for display directly on television sets, the issue of fields is somewhat irrelevant. Provided that the correct video standard is adhered to, a video recording will play back as intended, without requiring any knowledge of the composition of the fields and frames of the images. However, digital intermediate environments

FIGURE 2-8   Interlaced formats record sequences a field at a time

FIGURE 2-9   Progressive formats record sequences a frame at a time

---

[8] It is actually more correct to always refer to the frame rate for both interlaced and progressive types, but the vast majority of manufacturers adopt the convention used here.

are almost exclusively based around progressive image formats, which allows for easy conversion between various formats, layering of elements, and repositioning and resizing of footage, among other options. Use of interlaced imagery in a frame-based environment, be it digital, film, or progressive scan video, can result in visible artifacts being produced. For this reason, it is advisable to work with progressive scan (full-frame) formats or to utilize some de-interlacing methods (discussed in Chapter 9) on interlaced video footage to be used in a digital intermediate pipeline.

2.7   COLOR

We've established that, in order for a color image to be recorded, the light received by the camera must be split into separate components. Typically, these components are red, green, and blue light, which recombine in various proportions to form the full spectrum of color.

The majority of video formats do not record color information as separate red, green, and blue components though. Instead, the color information is stored according to the luminance component (the level of brightness or darkness), with color information stored separately. For PAL systems, a YUV color system is identified (Y being the luminance component, and U and V being chromacity components), and for NTSC systems, a YIQ (Y is again the luminance component, and I and Q the chromacity components).[9] Black-and-white televisions are able to extract the Y component (and ignore the color components) to produce a decent black-and-white image. For color televisions, the three components may be recombined to form full color images. In addition, the organization of the three components allows for some specific advantages to transporting the video signals.

---

[9] YIQ and YUV are similar in principle, although the associated mathematics for deriving each of the components from an RGB image is slightly different. However, it is fairly easy to convert between the two.

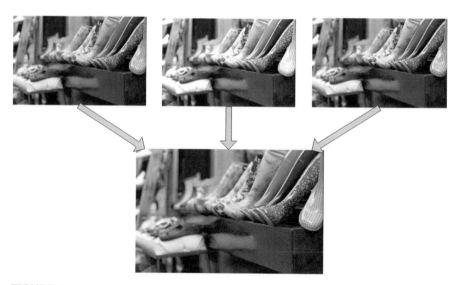

FIGURE 2-10 Color video images are made up of one luminance channel and two chromacity channels. © 2005 Andrew Francis. (See also the Color Insert.)

2.7.1 Gamma

The Y component of a digital video signal (which includes most modern video cameras) is not a true measure of luminance (the absolute light level in a scene) but is actually a nonlinear, weighted average of the RGB values received by the camera, created by converting the received RGB values to Y'IQ (or Y'UV).[10] The difference is subtle and requires the received light to be "gamma corrected" before being encoded.

A nonlinear response to light is one where twice the amount of light does not necessarily result in a corresponding signal that is twice as strong. Many different media exhibit this nonlinearity, such as film projection, and even the image displayed on a monitor. Digital images, on the other hand, encode luminance (or in this case, "luma") values on a linear scale. This means that they will not display as intended if output directly to a monitor.

---

[10] A similar process occurs when video images are displayed on an RGB monitor (such as a computer monitor).

Gamma correction attempts to solve this problem by altering the luminance of the RGB values in a nonlinear way, which better matches the response of a monitor. The result is that the recorded image looks correct when viewed on a monitor. Different video standards (and therefore different video cameras) use different gamma values, which are used during recording to encode the image values.

2.7.2 Video Compression

The human eye responds better to changes in luminance than it does to changes in chromacity. This fact is used to reduce the amount of information that a video signal needs to carry. It means that for a typical YIQ signal, the Y component is far more important than the I and Q components and suggests that the Y component should carry more information than the other two. To limit the required bandwidth of the signal, the color information is made smaller (or "compressed") by discarding some of it. This allows signals to be broadcast much more efficiently and greatly simplifies the electronics associated with decoding and displaying video signals.

Different video formats (specifically, different video tape systems, such as Betacam or VHS) use different levels of compression, which results in different levels of quality (but also different inherent costs). The level of compression is often described in terms of a "sampling ratio," with the relative quality of each component. For example, a sampling ratio of 4:4:4 (either for Y:I:Q or Y:U:V) indicates no color compression, as each component contains the same amount of compression. On the other hand, a ratio of 4:1:1 means that almost no color information is present at all (although the luminance level is intact).[11] Such a low level of color information may be imperceptible to the human eye in many cases; however, as discussed further in Chapter 8, even the imperceptible color information is used during image editing, in particular during color-grading processes.

---

[11] The exact method of reducing the color components is a function of the camera, which may use sophisticated sampling techniques or may introduce color artifacts.

In addition, some video formats further reduce bandwidth requirements by discarding some of the spatial information, which means
reducing the stored resolution. For example, a PAL VHS stores
around only 275 lines (compared to the broadcast standard of 625),
which are then "up-sampled" (i.e., duplicated or blended) to fill the display, again resulting in an inferior-quality image. Refer to the Appendix
for the compression levels of the most common video formats.

2.7.3 Composite and Component

Video signals may be recorded (as well as transported) either as
"component video" signals, such that each of the Y, I, and Q components are recorded and transported separately, or as "composite
video" signals, where the components are encoded as a single signal.
Component video signals are generally of higher quality by being
kept separate (because doing so prevents the different signals from
contaminating each other and reduces the chance of noise and other
distortions affecting the signal) but are more expensive, requiring
additional electronics to process each signal, as well as additional
cables for transport.[12]

2.7.4 Precision

Another aspect to video color quality is the maximum precision of
each point recorded. Compression discards color information to
reduce the bandwidth of the signal, but even where no compression
is used (or when looking at only the luminance part of the signal),
there is a limit to the accuracy of the measurements or recordings. For
the most part, distinguishing between light areas and dark areas of an
image is easy, but regions where the difference is more subtle may
cause problems.

Suppose you have an apple pie. You could be fairly confident of dividing it into two halves. You could further divide each of these into two

---

[12] Generally speaking, component video signals have a much better signal-to-noise
ratio than composite video equivalents.

more halves, and so on. But at some point, you could not confidently subdivide the pie without risking it falling apart (or some similar culinary *faux pas*). One possible solution is to start with a bigger pie.

In the same way, the full range of light in a video image may be divided into luminance values, like dividing a ruler into millimeters or inches. But there is a limit to the number of divisions that may be made, and that limit is due to the maximum precision of the video system. Higher levels of precision result in more accurate tonal rendition and therefore higher-quality images.

Precision is usually measured in bits per sample (in much the same way that digital images are, as covered in Chapter 4), so that 10 bits per sample (which is used by digital Betacam formats) represents greater precision than 8 bits per sample (as used by DVCAM formats).

Note that color precision can only be accurately measured for digital video formats because the precision of analog formats depends on a large number of factors, such as the condition of the tape and VCR used.

2.7.5 Headroom

At what point can a paint stroke be considered white rather than gray? How bright must a shade of red be for it to be considered bright red? These are not necessarily deep philosophical questions, and the answer is simple: it depends. It depends upon the context of the scene, and it depends upon the will of the person creating the image.

The human eye is very versatile. After around 30 minutes of being immersed in a completely dark environment, the eye develops night vision, allowing it to see under extremely low levels of light. Objects that were previously invisible might suddenly appear very bright. And this is true of pretty much any situation. To determine the brightness of a particular point in a scene, you compare it to every other point in the scene. Put a gray cat in front of a black curtain, and it will appear much brighter than the same cat in front of a white curtain. We can look at a photograph of a scene and perceive the light and dark values similar to our experience when we are actually at the scene, because the person taking the photograph (or indeed, the camera itself) defined explicit boundaries as to the locations of the light and dark regions. The photographer sets the exposure so that bright areas are recorded as such (or conversely, so that dark areas appear dark).

Different mediums respond differently to luminance range (or "dynamic range," which is covered in Chapter 5), which means that film can capture greater differences between light and dark regions of a scene. Nevertheless, the basic concept remains: a point is set for every scene where a specific level of illumination can be considered white, and a point where a lower level of illumination is considered black.

Video systems define these regions in terms of signal voltage. By definition, any point in the signal that falls below a certain voltage is considered black, and anything above another voltage is considered white. This is also true of most digital image formats, where a pixel value of 0 is considered black, and 255 is considered white. The key difference between video and digital formats, however (and in fact, one of digital imaging's key failings), is that video signals that stray outside these boundaries are still recorded. They still display as black or white respectively, but there is a degree of "headroom," from which the luminance can be rescued by reprocessing the signal. The amount of headroom depends on the video tape quality and the specifics of the video format. It should also be noted that the integrity of the video image in the headroom regions is not as secure as it is

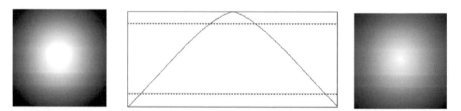

FIGURE 2-11 A video image can contain more information than is within the visible boundaries (shown by the dashed lines on the graph). The image on the left is the image as it would be displayed on a monitor, while the graph shows the "hidden" information (as seen on a waveform monitor). The full detail can be rescued even after the recording, as shown in the image on the right

within the predefined luminance ranges and may be more susceptible to noise and other degradation.

2.8 TIMECODE

To make video editing easier, most video formats carry "timecode"
information alongside the picture. Timecode is a numeric method
for identifying each frame in a sequence. The most commonly used
timecode format is the SMPTE/EBU timecode, which has eight digits denoting hours, minutes, seconds, and frames. For example, a
timecode of 10:33:04:12 is 10 hours, 33 minutes, 4 seconds, and 12
frames.

During recording, suitably equipped video cameras inscribe a timecode on the first frame of video, and it counts upward, much like
a clock. Timecode can be set to start at any arbitrary value, such as
00:00:00:00 or 07:21:55:04, but it will always count upward.
Timecode can be provided by external devices, which is especially
useful for synchronizing to audio, for instance. For example, if you
are shooting a music promotional video, the music track can be
playing on the set, and the track time can be fed from the music
player to the video camera. This enables the video elements to be
easily assembled into the correct part of the song during editing. It
is also possible to generate timecode based on the time of the day
(called simply "time of day" recording), so that footage recorded at
1:03 pm might have a timecode of 13:03:00:00 and so on, which is
useful for live recordings. This means however, that the recorded
timecode will be discontinuous every time the recording is stopped.
For example, if a recording stops at 15:06:07:04 and then starts 10
minutes later, the recorded timecode will jump from 15:16:07:04,
which can cause problems with some video systems later on. This is
known as "free run" recording.

Many video productions adopt the practice of using continuous timecode on all recordings. A day of shooting will start with video recording on a timecode of 01:00:00:00, which continues without breaks.
Anytime a recording is stopped in the middle of a tape, the next
recording picks up the timecode from where it left off (a process
known as "record run" recording), so the tape is free of timecode

"breaks."[13] When the tape is filled, a new one is started at a new time-code, such as 02:00:00:00 (assuming each tape lasts for approximately 60 minutes). This practice allows footage to be accurately identified during editing and playback. It is also considered good practice to allow an extra few seconds of recording at the start and end of each recording session to compensate for the "pre-roll" and "post-roll" mechanisms of many editing systems, which use this extra time to position the tape in the right place and accelerate the tape transport to the correct speed (or decelerate the tape upon completion of the transfer).

Timecode is usually recorded to tape using a combination of vertical interval timecode (VITC), which writes the information into the unused lines of the video signal, and longitudinal timecode (LTC), which is available on certain tape formats and writes the information to a physically separate part of the tape as an analog signal. The main difference between the two timecode types is that VITC can be set only during the recording process, whereas LTC can be modified without affecting the image. VITC tends to be accurately read when running a tape slowly (such as when "jogging" through a tape frame by frame to find a particular frame), while LTC works better at high speed (such as when rewinding a tape). Because both types of timecode can exist on a single tape, conflicting timecodes can cause editing problems. Should any such problem arise, it is recommended that the LTC be adjusted to match the VITC.[14] In general, anytime dubs (i.e., copies) of tapes are made that contain timecode information, this information is usually carried over to the new tape, which can ease tracking and editing.

2.8.1 Drop-Frame & Non-Drop-Frame Timecode

Timecode runs slightly differently depending on the video standard. PAL systems run at 25 frames per second, so the seconds of the time-code are incremented every 25 frames. This means that the timecode

---

[13] Many cameras are able to perform this function as long as they do not run out of power.

[14] It is important to note that some nonprofessional video systems do not support true timecode, but instead use a frame "counter." While it can be used to get estimates of the duration of a particular sequence, the counter is reset with each tape and does not help to identify specific frames.

of the frame that follows 00:00:00:24 will be 00:00:01:00. For NTSC video formats, the timecode runs at 30 frames per second, which means that the timecode of the frame after 00:00:00:24 will be 00:00:00:25 and so on, up to 00:00:00:29 at which point the next frame becomes 01:00:01:00.

There is a problem with this method though: NTSC video does not actually run at 30 frames per second. It actually runs at 29.97 frames per second. This is also true for the 29.97p and 59.94i HD video formats, although 30p and 60i formats run at exactly 30 frames per second (which in turn makes 30p and 60i formats incompatible with most NTSC systems). This tiny discrepancy (of 0.1%) may not seem significant, but it will accumulate, resulting in a difference (or "drift") of about 3.6 seconds for every hour recorded. Clearly this drift creates an issue when using time-of-day timecode continuously, or when broadcasting—you may suddenly find you have an extra 3.6 seconds of material to broadcast every hour. (PAL systems do not have this issue.)

To solve this problem, NTSC drop-frame (DF) timecode may be used. To ensure that the timecode does not drift, the timecode "drops" (or discards) 18 frames every 10 minutes. In doing this, no content is lost; the timecode just skips a number. The way that DF timecode is usually implemented is that two frames are dropped on the minute, every minute, except for every tenth minute. This means that the timecode will go from 00;00;59;29 to 00;01;00;02 (rather than 00:01:00:00), but also from 00;29;59;29 to 00;30;00;00.[15] This method ensures that the timecode is perfectly synchronized to "real" time every 10 minutes.

Where such accuracy is not important, it may be desirable to bury your head in the sand and just pretend that this drift in timecode does not exist for the sake of simplicity. In this case, non-drop-frame (NDF) timecode can be used, which provides a more continuous, logical method to count frames, such that 00:00:59:29 does in fact lead to

---

[15] Note the use of semicolons (;) rather than colons (:) to denote the use of drop-frame timecode.

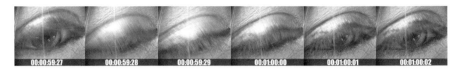

FIGURE 2-12   A video sequence recorded with NDF timecode

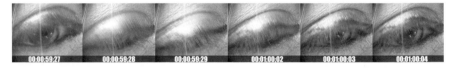

FIGURE 2-13   The same sequence as shown in Figure 2-12, this time recorded with DF timecode

00:01:00:00 (but that 01:00:00:00 of footage is in fact only 59 minutes and 53.4 seconds in length). Regardless of the system used, consistency is essential. Mixing DF timecode with NDF timecode can cause problems when editing or assembling video footage.

It should also be noted that 23.98p HD formats, designed to ease the transition of material shot at 24fps to NTSC formats, do not support the use of DF timecode and therefore cannot be used to make time-of-day recordings.

2.8.2   Burnt-in Timecode

With editing systems, the timecode information can be extracted from the video tape and displayed onscreen alongside the video image. In some situations, it is also desirable to display timecode onscreen even if a suitable editing system is not being used—for example, when a recording was made onto a Betacam tape (which supports different types of timecode) and is then dubbed across to a DVD for playback on a TV (which does not usually allow for timecode to be displayed alongside the picture). In this case, timecode may be "burnt-in" to the video image. With burnt-in timecode (BITC), each frame is visually printed with corresponding timecode, and the timecode will remain through copying to other formats (although it cannot be later removed).

2.9   LIMITATIONS OF VIDEO

Video is certainly one of the cheapest moving picture formats to use. At the low end, miniDV cameras are very inexpensive and are able to produce reasonable quality images. At the high end, HD cameras produce images that approach the quality of 35mm film, but cost slightly less when taking production factors into account.

One important issue is that color rendition of video images is inferior to those produced by other formats. The dynamic range (a measure of the brightness and contrast abilities of a system, discussed in Chapter 5) of video images is much lower than the dynamic range of film images (although new cameras are emerging that have a nonlinear response to light, which is more like film), and color compression ultimately degrades the video image (although some cameras have a sampling ratio of 4:4:4 and do not discard color information). Even where color compression is not noticeable when viewing the footage, subsequent processes, such as color grading and duplication, can exacerbate even small artifacts.

All video formats suffer from "generational loss." This means that every time a copy of any video footage is made, the copy will be of lower quality than the original, because during the dubbing process, additional errors and defects are introduced into the signal, particularly noise. The effect becomes more pronounced with each generation, meaning that a twentieth-generation video will be particularly degraded compared to the original.[16] With a digital intermediate pipeline however—even one that simply digitizes the footage and outputs it straight from the digital version—all copies can be made digitally, and so generation loss becomes less of an issue. With such a pipeline, the video undergoes less degradation, and so the overall quality remains higher.

---

[16] Ironically, this fact reduces the availability of high-quality pirated video material.

Finally, there is the question of speed. All video runs in real time, meaning it takes an hour to transport (i.e., play or copy) an hour of video footage. In some respects, this speed is faster than other formats, but in time, digital equivalents will perform operations many times faster, meaning it might take 10 minutes to copy an hour of digital footage across the world.

2.10 DIGITAL VIDEO

Digital video formats, such as DVCAM, DV SP, and the various HD formats (and to some extent, DVD-video) can be treated the same as analog formats for most purposes. The key difference has to do with the way that digital video images are stored. Unlike analog video recorders, which inscribe the electronic signal directly onto the magnetic video tape, digital video recorders first digitize the video signal (refer to Chapter 5 for more on the digitization process) and then record the images to tape as a series of digits. Doing so retains the quality of the images better than analog recordings because there is less chance of noise affecting the signal.

For the most part, however, digital video systems behave like analog ones. Output is typically made using analog cables (either component or composite cables) in real time, which means that noise or other errors can still be introduced and that each copy is still prone to generation loss (although at a much lower level).[17] The color components of the images are usually handled in the same way as with analog counterparts, with chromaticity separated from the luminance components and possibly compressed.

Digital video formats also have the advantage of recording additional, nonimage information. For example, as well as recording continuous timecode, digital cameras can record time of day as a separate data stream. The separate time-of-day recording can be used during editing to quickly separate shots. The additional data that can be

---

[17] With some digital video systems, it is possible to use digital cables (such as firewire cables) to directly transport the digital data rather than the analog data, although this must still be performed in real time and is thus vulnerable to playback errors.

recorded onto tape can also include the camera settings, such as the aperture and shutter settings. In the future, it may be possible to encode even more information digitally, such as production notes and take numbers, providing easy access later on.

The line between video and native digital formats is getting increasingly thin. We already think of digital still cameras as producing entirely digital images. In addition, there is very little difference between digital still cameras and modern digital video cameras that can record directly to a digital storage device, such as a hard disk.

2.11 SUMMARY

There are several different standards for video images, each varying in quality, and they tend to be incompatible. Even within a given standard, different video formats can affect the final quality of recorded footage. The reasons for this are largely historical, because video itself stems from the progress of television. In coming years, this trend may change, with new high definition video systems setting the standard for future television broadcasts.

Though video lacks the resolution and color range of photographic film, notable features such as the ability to track footage through timecode assignment, and the huge advantage of being able to view video footage as it is recorded, and with significant ease at any point later, make it a very useful format. Further, the available headroom that allows for extra color information to be squeezed into a recording makes video preferable to digital images in some instances.

Video is a very hard medium to understand conceptually, but it is very easy to use in practice. You get a VCR, push in a video tape, and press Play. However, to integrate video into a digital intermediate pipeline, it is important to be aware of factors such as interlacing and compression, to ensure the maximum possible level of quality. The similarities with completely digital systems mean that video is highly suited to a digital intermediate work flow. Photographic film, on the other hand, is much easier to understand but has many more practical considerations that have to be addressed.

3

PHOTOGRAPHIC FILM

Since the end of the nineteenth century, people have been able to watch moving pictures through the medium of photographic film. It's a medium that has changed surprisingly little during the past century, particularly compared to the progress of video and similar technologies, but film is still widely considered to produce the highest-quality images in the motion picture industry.

3.1   FILM IMAGE FORMATION

A length of photographic film consists of light-sensitive crystals bound together in a transparent material. There are other aspects to most common film formats, such as "sprockets," "dye layers," and "key numbers" (each of which will be covered later in this chapter), but the crystals and binding agents are the only requirements for image formation.

Film consists of silver halide crystals that are sensitive to light. When light falls on the crystals, they become chemically activated. At this point, there is no visible change to the crystals. However, the chemical changes mean that it is possible to use further chemical processes to separate the crystals that have been exposed to light from those that have not.

With regards to imaging, this process works when the light reflected from a scene is focused on a piece of film using an optical system (i.e., a combination of lenses, mirrors, and so on). There will be more light in brighter parts of the scene, and so the equivalent bright areas imaged on the film will activate the crystals at those points quicker than those that are less bright. If the combination of the brightness of the scene and the length of time the light from the scene is in contact with the film is balanced correctly (or, to use photography terminology, if the film is correctly "exposed"), a "latent" image is formed on the film. This latent image consists of groups of film crystals that have been chemically activated and is therefore invisible. If you were to take the piece of exposed film and examine it carefully, even with the aid of a microscope, you'd be unable to find any evidence of any of the features in the scene that was photographed. But the paradox is that you couldn't put exposed film under a microscope without exposing it further. Even after the latent image has formed, any additional light that hits it, even a barely perceptible amount, will still affect the film. This means that the film must be kept in complete darkness before and after the desired image is exposed. To make the latent image visible (not to mention permanent), the film must undergo a development process.

Development involves putting the film through a number of different chemical baths, which contain the developing agents necessary to convert the activated crystals to metallic silver and to remove them from the film. Because the crystals are so small, a detailed image with a large tonal range remains as the negative image of the original scene.

This "negative" can be used as the basis for creating a print, by acting as a filter between a light source and another sensitive material. To create an image on paper, for example, an enlarger is used to project the negative image onto photographic paper, which in turn undergoes a chemical development process, resulting in an image that is

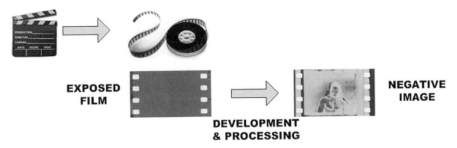

FIGURE 3-1 Photographic image formation involves many stages before the image is even visible

the negative of the negative. Alternatively, the image can be projected onto another piece of film, which is developed to form a positive image that can be projected onto a screen.

The film itself usually consists of individual "reels" or lengths of celluloid several hundred feet long, which have "sprockets" running along one or both of the edges. The sprockets (or perforations) are holes in the film that are used to hold the film in place in the camera (or other equipment) and advance it a frame at a time.

The most significant aspect of all film material is that it is highly standardized, in terms of the size and positioning of the various elements (i.e., the sprockets and the actual frame locations), and these standards have changed very little during the entire history of the motion picture industry. Film created for theatrical release decades ago can be easily viewed even in today's modern cinemas.

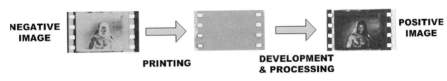

FIGURE 3-2 A positive film image is produced by developing a print of a negative

FIGURE 3-3 A reel of film (left) and a closeup of an undeveloped negative, with sprockets running down the sides

3.2 FILM STOCK

Many of the properties of a film image are determined by the composition of the film material, or "stock." The film stock affects the level of detail in each image, the way that colors are recorded, as well as how sensitive the film is to light. Different stocks are created for different situations. For example, certain film stocks may be optimized for shooting subjects lit by tungsten light (i.e, they are "tungsten balanced") and others for daylight scenes ("daylight balanced"). Also, different film manufacturers create film materials using proprietary formulas, and so the various stocks produced by each manufacturer may be considered different from each other.

The differences between stocks are due to differences in a number of properties of the film material, in particular differences in the size, shape, and distribution of the silver halide crystals, which in turn determine many aspects of the material.

3.2.1 Tonal Range

The tonal range of the image is determined by the build-up (or density) of opaque crystals in the film during development. Areas of higher density block out more light, and the difference between the opacity of the areas with highest density possible (or "D-max") and the completely transparent (or "D-min") indicates the tonal range of the image.[1]

Photographic film has a nonlinear response to light (rather like human vision), meaning that doubling the amount of light in a scene will not necessarily result in an image that is twice as bright. In fact, most types of film have a "characteristic curve," a graph that can be plotted to show the film's response to an increase of light. The curve follows an S-shape, with the exact shape of the curve determining in part how the image looks. Much of the somewhat ethereal quality of film images is due to the characteristic curve of the film.

The nature of the curve means that the mid-tones of the image are compressed (i.e., less detailed in terms of luminance differences), while the shadow and highlight regions have a much higher level of

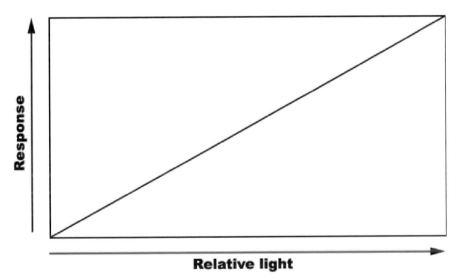

FIGURE 3-4 Graph showing a linear response to light

---

[1] The minimum density will never be completely zero because the base material inevitably provides some degree of opacity. In addition, there may be some slight light exposure to seemingly unexposed regions. For this reason, D-min is also referred to as "base + fog."

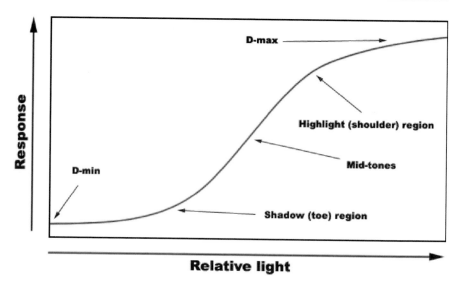

FIGURE 3-5 Graph showing the characteristic curve of a typical film material's response to light

FIGURE 3-6 The characteristic curve of film determines in part how the resulting image will look. © 2005 Andrew Francis

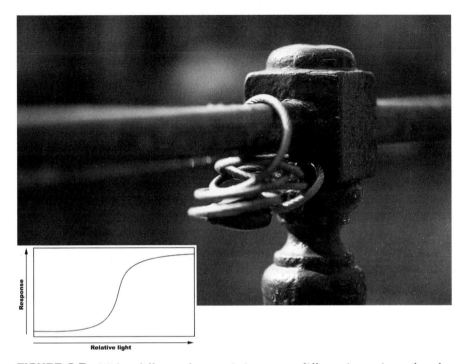

FIGURE 3-7 With a different characteristic curve, a different image is produced

detail than linear formats. The nature of the curve also means that film tends to have a much greater "exposure latitude" (which is the overall luminance range that can be recorded for a scene) than other formats. This extended latitude grants a lot more flexibility during color grading, because scenes can be adjusted to increase or decrease the effective exposure within the recorded image.

Different stocks will have different maximum and minimum density levels and different characteristic curves, reflecting differences in the way that tones are reproduced.

3.2.2 FILM SPEED

Different film stocks are given a speed rating. This is a numerical value that can be used in conjunction with a number of other factors to determine the optimum exposure of the film material. In broad terms, the speed of a film is a measure of its sensitivity to light. A "faster" film (i.e., one with a higher speed value) requires less light (either in terms of the intensity of the light, or the length of time the film is exposed to the light) to provide a satisfactory image and is typically comprised of larger crystals. A number of external factors can also affect the speed of a piece of film, such as the type of light in the scene and the development process.

Measuring the speed of a material in a useful way is a complex issue, and several different methods attempt to do this. The most widely accepted speed rating system is the ISO system. Each film stock is assigned an ISO speed rating, and this value can be used in conjunction with a measurement of the amount of light in the scene (typically determined by using a handheld light meter) and the camera settings (notably the aperture and shutter angle) to achieve a correctly exposed image. Even so, the reported speed rating of a film stock is not applicable to every lighting condition, and so the cinematographer often has to adapt (or ignore) it for each situation.[2]

3.2.3 Graininess and Granularity

Although each silver halide crystal is microscopic in size, film images tend to have visible patterns of "graininess," made up of randomly sized and shaped grains. This grain pattern is caused by individual silver halide crystals forming "clumps" (or by appearing to do so because of the way they are distributed within the material). The perceived size of the clumps (or the level of graininess of the image) is completely subjective, determined by the film stock and the visual contents of the image. Sharper images tend to be less grainy than blurred images (or those with fewer small details). It is also worth noting that enlarging images tends to make the grain more pronounced.

Similar to this is granularity, which is a more objective measure of the crystal structure in a photographic image. The granularity is deter-

---

[2] Manufacturers may offer an "exposure index" rating in addition to (or instead of) an ISO rating. This rating is the effective speed rating under the most probable lighting and development conditions.

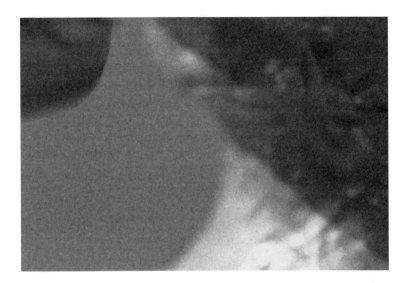

FIGURE 3-8 Close up, the grain patterns can be seen, particularly in regions of solid color

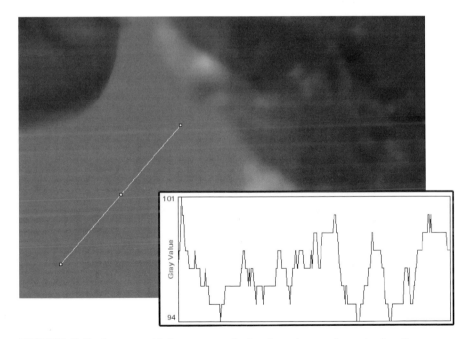

FIGURE 3-9 Images with lower granularity show less variance in density

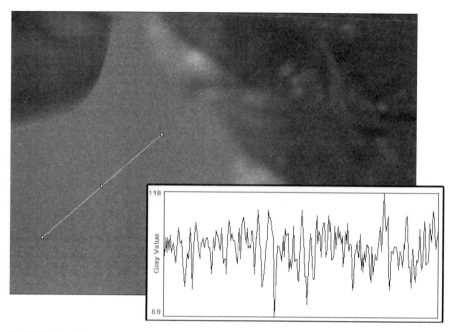

FIGURE 3-10   Images with higher granularity show a greater degree of variance in density

mined by measuring the fluctuations of density in a developed image of a uniform tone (such as a gray card). The amount of granularity depends upon the film stock, the development process, and the amount of light exposure.

3.2.4   Color Reproduction

As with many imaging technologies, film can record images in color by combining several monochromatic images. Modern film achieves this by combining multiple "dye layers." Each layer is sensitive to a different part of the spectrum and only records light of a particular color. Typical color film has a red-sensitive layer, a green-sensitive layer, and a blue-sensitive layer, so that white light will affect all layers. During development, the layers are dyed so that each layer filters light through in the appropriate color. For negative images, this means the dyes are cyan, magenta, and yellow, and for prints, they are red, green, and blue. Thus, projecting white, unfiltered light

through a print creates an image that is an accurate, full-color recon-
struction of the original scene.

Different film stocks may reproduce colors in slightly different ways and
may be aimed toward capturing color accurately or more aesthetically.

3.3   FILM FORMATS

Film, and in particular, motion picture film, is rigorously standardized.
This means that every aspect of the film image is strictly defined in terms
of its size and position. Other, nonimage elements are also standardized,
such as the positioning and size of the sprockets. This standardization is
irrespective of the stock type or manufacturer, which is why footage can
be shot on any particular film stock and still be projected.

There are several different formats though, each existing for different
applications, each with their own standards. The formats differ in two
main ways: the gauge of the film material and the aspect ratio of the
image.

3.3.1   Gauge

A larger piece of film can record a larger image. This in turn determines the maximum level of detail that can be recorded within an
image. All things equal, a larger piece of film (i.e., a larger gauge)
implies the ability to record an image of higher quality. It does not
imply, however, the capability to record more of the scene but simply
to better resolve small features and details. When the images are projected onto the same screen, the images shot on larger gauge film will
appear sharper and the apparent graininess will be much lower.

Gauge is measured as the width of the film material. The most common
gauges are 16mm, 35mm (which is also a commonly used format for
still photography), and 70mm. Of these, 35mm is the most popular for
motion picture production, striking a suitable compromise between
manageability and quality when projected onto the average cinema
screen. Films with 70mm formats are used for productions intended for
much larger screens, while 16mm film tends to be used by productions
on a lower budget (or those that are not destined for cinema projection).

3.3.2   Aspect Ratio and Framing

The shape of an image on a piece of film is determined by its "aspect ratio," the ratio of the width of the image to its height. Different film formats have different aspect ratios, and when certain aspect ratios are combined with certain gauges, these characteristics determine the exact size of the image. For example, the "full aperture" 35mm film format has an aspect ratio of 4:3 (or 1.33). It spans the usable width of the film (with some allowance given to the sprockets), of approximately 25mm. Therefore, the height can be calculated as roughly 19mm.[3]

In practice, the entire width of the gauge is rarely used. This is because part of the film area is used for optical sound tracks and because cinematographers (and audiences) prefer images that have rather wide aspect ratios (such as 1.85), probably because such images give a greater sense of psychological immersion when viewed.

This issue is compounded somewhat by the mechanics of the projector and the film camera. Rather than maximize the available film area when recording images so that each frame is placed directly next to another, every frame must occupy a fixed number of sprockets, depending upon the gauge. For example, 35mm film formats almost always use four sprockets (and are referred to as "4-perf" formats). With the 4-perf format, much of the film area is wasted, particularly with wide images. However, there are very good reasons for using this format. Most importantly, it allows a single projector to be used for projecting films of different aspect ratio; the only difference is that a mask (or "gate") has to be used to block out light that is outside of the image area. The same is also true for film cameras because each frame is advanced by a number of sprockets. This ensures that the different 4-perf formats, for example, are compatible to some degree.

All of this means that the different film formats depend on the gauge of the material but also on the shape and positioning of the images on the film. Fortunately, because the parameters for each format are rigidly defined and maintained throughout the motion picture industry, problems with projection are rarely encountered.

---

[3] The exact dimensions are 24.89mm horizontally and 18.67mm vertically.

FIGURE 3-11   A full aperture framing

FIGURE 3-12   An academy aperture framing

FIGURE 3-13   Super 35 with center framing

Special consideration should also be given to anamorphic (or CinemaScope) formats, which use special lenses to compress very wide images (typically with ratios greater than 2:1) onto much narrower film areas. In practice, anamorphically squeezed film formats may be handled in the same way as formats that are not squeezed, although the squeezed formats will appear distorted when viewed under normal projection (or on such devices as lightboxes). To view the images correctly, they must be unsqueezed, using projectors equipped with suitable lenses. Note that most cinema projectors are able to rotate between two or more lenses for this purpose, without requiring additional screening rooms.[4]

FIGURE 3-14   A cinemascope image as it appears on film, and as it is displayed when unsqueezed

[4] An interesting characteristic of shooting anamorphic images is that light reflections on the lens, such as flare, tend to be seen as large streaks of light when projected.

FILM IMAGE QUALITY

The quality of a film image is difficult to quantify, especially compared to digital and video formats. Certainly the definition (or resolution) of a particular stock can be determined, such as by photographing a high-contrast edge and then measuring the recorded thickness of the edge. The same can be said for color reproduction, where test patterns can be filmed and then measured from the developed material later.

In more pragmatic terms, film quality is largely a subjective issue. Film images may appear sharper than they actually are because edges, particularly high-contrast edges, are exaggerated somewhat. In some cases, color reproduction may not be accurate, but many audience members (and a great number of cinematographers) prefer the look of film images to those that are more realistic. Similarly, graininess might be one of the more important factors in determining quality, but it is a completely subjective one. Granularity can be measured, but it tends to be inconsistent, with different amounts of granularity seen at different levels of brightness. Grain size—and to some degree, the resolution of film—cannot be directly correlated to video or digital images because the grains are not uniformly distributed or shaped like video and digital images. This becomes even more significant when you consider that film is a moving image. Because the grain position and size changes every frame, it's likely that even in watching footage of a still scene, the grain differences are averaged out perceptually, and so a moving image sequence may be subjectively higher quality than a single still image taken from the sequence. Only one thing is certain: each successive generation (i.e., copy) of a film image is of lower quality than the preceding one. (Chapter 5 examines methods of analyzing film images.) Most likely, the most significant issues of film quality concern processing or exposure problems, copying, and the accumulation of physical damage, such as dust, scratches, and mold.

3.4 FRAME RATE

As with most moving picture media, film imparts the illusion of motion by displaying still images in rapid succession. In most cases, this rate is taken to be 24 frames per second (although some areas in Europe use a rate of 25 frames per second to maintain easy conversion between film and PAL video formats).[5] For this reason, film footage is usually photographed at a rate of 24 frames per second.

In some instances, different frame rates are used. For example, time lapse and other fast-motion effects can be created by photographing a scene at a much slower frame rate. If, for example, a scene is photographed once per second, then the scene will appear 24 times faster when viewed. Alternatively, slow-motion effects can be produced by recording at faster frame rates, a technique that is used often for special effects or heightened drama. (There are other methods for changing the apparent speed of a shot, several of which are covered later in this book.) In terms of producing slow-motion footage at least, film remains the best option for capturing a scene.

3.5 KEY NUMBERS

A typical feature film production will generate many miles of film footage that must be sorted through prior to editing. After editing, the final cut must be matched back to the original negative. This requires careful indexing and meticulous comparison of every frame of every strip of film. Fortunately, an efficient method of doing this has evolved—the use of "key numbers."

Key numbers (or keycodes) are serial numbers printed along the edge of every strip of film. The idea is that every single frame of motion picture film ever produced has a unique number to identify it.

The numbers are necessarily long and can also be used to identify the manufacturer of the film material, as well as the stock type and batch number. Key numbers on most modern films are also machine readable, which is useful when film is telecined to video tape for editing

---

[5] During projection in a cinema, each frame is actually presented twice in rapid succession, which reduces the visible flicker caused by the projector switching frames.

purposes and when converting film footage to digital images in digital intermediate environments. (More information about the layout of key numbers can be found in the Appendix.)

3.6 FILM MEDIA PROBLEMS

Film media can produce images that are superior to many other imaging methods, and the infrastructure for film production is so highly controlled that it is easy to generate footage that can be viewed across the world on equipment that may be many years old. However, this comes at a cost. Film is notoriously expensive to work with, partly because of manufacturing costs and also because of all the support that is required to utilize it successfully.

Film is at constant risk of contamination by light. Unlike a video tape, which can be protected from accidental re-recording, film must be kept in absolute darkness from the moment it is manufactured to the point where the image is exposed. After the image is exposed, it must be protected from any additional light until it has been processed. Furthermore, film is physically fragile, susceptible to dust and scratches, and any number of factors that can damage it. All of this means it must be handled carefully, which of course, also costs money.

There is no degree of interactivity with film image formation, unlike with video formats, where the image can be viewed as it is recorded, allowing changes to be made, and the results seen instantly. With film, the actual results are not available until after a lengthy processing phase, which at best takes a number of hours to complete. The shooting process therefore requires a great deal of estimation on the part of the crew. It is possible to use a "video tap" to view a video representation of the image through the camera, but this method provides an incomplete picture, particularly because film's generally predictable response to light breaks down at extreme levels of illumination (either very bright or very dark scenes).[6]

Finally, film quality decreases steadily with every copy made. There are many reasons for this degradation; it is a function of all analog media and is also a function of the accuracy of the chemical process.

---

[6] This condition is termed "reciprocity law failure."

Film images cannot be adjusted as flexibly as video or digital images can. It is possible to change the color and shape of film images using a number of optical and chemical processes, but these processes are neither as versatile nor as accurate as other methods. In addition, they usually depend on the creation of one or more generations of the film.

3.7 SUMMARY

Film produces higher-quality images than any other medium currently being used. The images are formed by groups of light-sensitive crystals, which determine the appearance of the final image, in terms of detail, color reproduction, and granularity. Film can record images across a great range of frame rates, which is useful for slow-motion and fast-motion effects, and generally produces better results than other formats.

Film must go through a lengthy development and processing phase before the recorded image is visible, and it must be protected from physical damage and accidental exposure to light. It may undergo additional color processing during development, but these methods tend to lack accuracy and may degrade the image quality.

Although different film stocks produce different results in the way a scene appears and in the length of time required to make an exposure, very strict definitions govern the placement and size of the image on the film material. Such strictures have made it possible for modern cinemas to present films made decades ago.

Film has the potential to capture and display moving pictures with unrivaled quality. It is limited in terms of editing and copying, which are processes that are easily accomplished on both video and digital images. (Digital images are especially easy to edit and copy.) For these reasons, film productions, with material shot on film and ultimately projected on film, benefit immensely from a digital intermediate process, which provides additional advantages to the film-production process. In the long term, the advantages of digital-imaging technology may overtake even those of film in terms of quality, speed, and expense.

4

DIGITAL MEDIA

4.1 DIGITAL IMAGES

A fundamental requirement of the digital intermediate process is that all images involved in the process must be digital. Because of this requirement, the entire digital intermediate pipeline is prone to exactly the same limitations and potential pitfalls inherent in digital media. Just as a cinematographer needs at least a basic understanding of the photochemical process, so people using the digital intermediate process need to have a basic understanding of the properties of digital images.

The concept of the digital image has been around since the early days of computing. Back in the 1960s, getting a computer to display even a small picture took incredible resources. Nowadays, we are so overwhelmed with digital images that we barely notice them. From pictures on websites, photos from digital cameras, to interfaces on mobile phones, digital imaging helps us interact more intuitively with technology, as well as provides perfect copies of pictures that can be transmitted across the world almost instantly or stored on disks for future use.

4.2   CREATING DIGITAL IMAGES

Digital images may be created in a number of ways. Perhaps the most common method—converting (or digitizing) images from another media (such as photographic film)—is covered in Chapter 5. Another common method is to use a digital camera to photograph something that can provide a set of digital images. Finally, it is also possible to create images from scratch, completely within a computer. Images created in this way are called "computer-generated" (CG) images.

4.3   THE ANATOMY OF A DIGITAL IMAGE

All information that can be processed by computer technology (i.e., data) is binary. This means that if you were to look at a piece of computer data in its simplest form, it could be described as a combination of ones and zeros—for example, 10110010. It can also be thought of as a bank of switches, each of which can be either "on" or "off." This is true for any type of information that flows through any digital computer system. Given the correct context, the computer knows how to interpret this stream of numbers, whether it is a digital image, a spreadsheet, or even a piece of software code. The combinations of ones and zeros form the building blocks of any type of data. In theory, digital images could be represented in a multitude of different ways; however, in practice, almost all digital images comprise the same basic features.

BITS AND BYTES

The smallest unit of computer data is a bit (short for "binary digit"). Each bit can be either a zero or a one. The most common unit of data is a byte, which is a group of 8 bits. Each byte of data can have 256 (2^8) possible combinations of ones and zeros. Therefore, each byte can have any of 256 different values. These values can refer to anything, such as letters of the alphabet in a text document. The kilobyte (KB) is 1024 bytes. Most simple

(continues)

BITS AND BYTES (*continued*)

text documents are several kilobytes in size. One megabyte (MB) is 1024 kilobytes (approximately one million bytes). A floppy disk can hold around one-and-a-half megabytes of data, enough for most documents, or small or compressed digital images. One gigabyte (GB) is 1024 megabytes (approximately one billion bytes), which is enough to contain about five minutes of DV (digital video) footage. Finally, the terabyte (TB) is 1024 gigabytes (approximately one trillion bytes). It takes approximately one-and-a-half terabytes to store a 90 minute film at 2k resolution. Refer to the Appendix for a list of file sizes for common applications.

4.3.1 Pixels

The most common type of digital image is bitmap (or raster) images, which are conceptually similar to video images. With this type of digital image, each image comprises a number of building blocks known collectively as "pixels" (short for "picture elements"). Each pixel is a binary number, representing a single square of a solid color. Put enough of them together, and you have a picture, in the same way a detailed mosaic is made from many small ceramic tiles.

FIGURE 4-1 Individual pixels can be seen when an image is viewed close up

Most imaging systems work in a similar way. You can see the individual grains that form a photograph when you view it close up. Because the grains in photographs are randomly shaped, they are harder to distinguish than pixels of the same size, but the concept is the same. Pixels are regularly shaped and arranged in a gridlike manner for the sake of efficiency, making them easily displayed and simplifying all the "behind-the-scenes" mathematics performed by the computer (and making these processes therefore faster).

Digital images have square-shaped pixels, and so do most devices for viewing digital images, such as computer monitors. When a computer monitor displays an image, it traces a small spot that corresponds to each pixel.

In broad terms, increasing the number of pixels in an image also increases the image's level of detail and increases the file size, because more bytes of information are needed to record each pixel. Doubling the number of pixels in an image will double its file size. Doubling the width and height of an image will quadruple its file size (by doubling the length and width, you quadruple the area, and hence the number of pixels).

4.3.2 Pixel Aspect Ratio

Although it's not very common, digital images can have nonsquare pixels. This means that rather than being perfectly square, each pixel is meant to represent a more rectangular shape. There are a few reasons why you might want to do this, but the most common is to match pixels to the CCD elements in video cameras, which are rectangular rather than square. The actual shape of the pixel is described by a pixel aspect ratio, which is simply the ratio between the height and width of the pixel. Square pixels have a pixel aspect ratio of 1.0. PAL DVCAM images have a pixel aspect ratio of 1.07, indicating that each pixel is 7% wider than it is tall.

Where the ratio becomes relevant is in displaying the images (e.g., on a monitor). Almost every digital display device is configured to display square pixels only. Displaying nonsquare pixel-based images becomes more of a problem the bigger the image is. To compensate for this, the display device must add (or remove) a proportion of pixels to the image (for display purposes only) so that the overall image has the correct proportions. The Appendix includes a list of pixel aspect ratios for different imaging formats.

4.3.3 Print Resolution

Some digital images encode a "print size" or the number of dots per inch (dpi) or pixels per inch (ppi). Even more confusing, this is often referred to as the "resolution" of the image, which is a somewhat unnecessary (and confusing) measurement. It basically means that if the image is printed, there is some way to correlate each pixel to real-world measurements. For instance, a 100×100 pixel image, printed at 100dpi (meaning that 100 pixels are in an inch, or alternatively, that each pixel is 1/100 of an inch in diameter), will be exactly 1 inch by 1 inch in size. Reducing the dpi to 50 will result in a 2 inch by 2 inch printed image. However, the amount of information (and hence the detail) is unaffected by differences in the dpi value. Whether there are 10 pixels per inch, or 10,000, makes no difference to the total number of pixels, and hence the spatial detail and file size of the image. The dpi value is an arbitrary figure used in reproducing an image in print form. Therefore, the dpi value of an image usually can be ignored (unless you need to print the image, of course).

THE PROBLEM OF FILE SIZE

Increasing the file size of an image has a variety of side effects. When you increase the file size of any piece of data, you are increasing the amount of information contained in that file. The result is that it takes longer to access a bigger file, longer to move or copy it, and more disk space is needed to store it. In addition, computers use memory known as "random access memory" (RAM) to perform operations (such as displaying or resizing) on an image. Like disk space, RAM is a limited commodity and can only hold a finite amount of data at any one time. Also, regardless of disk space or RAM limitations, more computations are

(continues)

THE PROBLEM OF FILE SIZE (*continued*)

needed to modify larger files (which means that larger files are manipulated more slowly).

A useful analogy is that of a library. Imagine that your computer is a library, and your images, rather than being pictures, are books, with each book describing a picture. A bigger book (or a larger file) contains a more detailed description of the picture and requires more pages to do so. That's why the book is physically bigger. If you imagine that the shelves in the library are analogous to storage space (such as disk drives) within a computer, you can see that bigger books require more shelf space to store them. Similarly it takes longer for someone to read (or access) the bigger books, and because they are heavier, it takes longer to move them around.

Now imagine a table in the library, where you can spread out all the pages from the books and look at them all at once (in the same way that files can be loaded into the RAM of a computer system). Again, your table only has so much space, and thus it can hold a limited number of pages. If you want to reorganize, make corrections, or copy any of the books into a new book, it will take physically longer to write out each new book.

This analogy also provides clues as to methods that can solve some of these file-size issues. For example, a library may have a vault or similar external storage facility for infrequently used books. In the same way, a computer system might have an offline archive device, such as a tape backup system, so that infrequently used files can be stored externally. You can build one or more additional libraries, move some of the books to the new libraries, and mail books between them. With computer systems, you can do something similar; network separate computer systems via cables (or even wireless transmissions).

Ultimately though, there must be a balance between speed, capacity, and cost in any digital intermediate pipeline. Many facilities aim to choose file sizes that are optimal for the color-correction system, and they then base the rest of the pipeline around that size, because color correction is by far the most interactive stage of the process.

4.3.4 Tonality

Every single pixel has a color assigned to it. A group of pixels can all be the same color, but a single pixel can't have multiple colors associated with it. In a very simple image, each pixel has a choice of being either black or white. This limitation is necessary, for example, for LCD displays on mobile phones, which can only display pixels as black or white (i.e., each pixel has a binary value for color—0 or 1, black or white, respectively). While this may not seem like much, with a high-resolution image, it is possible to get a fairly detailed black-and-white image.

However, for images with a wide tonal range, describing color in terms of black or white pixels isn't terribly efficient (or accurate). Each

FIGURE 4-2 This image uses a combination of about 650,000 black or white pixels to simulate tonality

FIGURE 4-3   This image has the same number of pixels as the one in Figure 4-2 and each pixel has 256 shades of gray to choose from

pixel could be any shade of gray. So, in most monochrome (or gray scale) images, each pixel is given a value between 0 and 255, of varying intensity (for a total of 256 shades of gray). Each pixel actually could be given any number of shades of grey, but having 256 possible values (or levels) makes it convenient to store as an 8-bit number in a computer. Because each pixel in the image has an 8-bit number associated with it to describe the shade of gray (or the brightness or luminosity of the pixel), the image is said to have 8 bits-per-pixel, or a bit depth of 8 bits. Increasing the bit depth allows for a greater number of possible shades, and thus a greater tonal range.

Theoretically, there is no limit to the bit depth of an image. However, increasing the bit depth also increases the file size, because more information is needed to encode each pixel. An image with a 10-bit-per-pixel depth allows 1024 shades of grey and would result in a file that is 25% larger, compared to a file with 8 bits per pixel.

4.3.5   Color

When painting, you can make new colors by mixing different primary colors together. For example, mixing yellow and blue paint makes green. This process is known as the "subtractive method of color mixing," because the more colors you mix in, the closer you get to black. To produce color images on a monitor, different amounts of red, green, and blue light are mixed together. This process is based on the "additive system of color mixing," where the primary colors are red, green, and blue, and the more colors you mix together, the closer you get to white. Any color can be made by mixing different quantities of red, green, and blue light, which is the process used to display color images on monitors, televisions, and so on.

A color digital image contains a number of channels. Each channel is a single, monochrome image. Most color digital images have red, green, and blue channels, which are mixed together to form the full-color RGB image. Each channel contains a possible number of color values (in the same way that gray scale images do), which provides the possible color range for each channel. In a sense, three separate grayscale images are mixed together to make a color image, so there might be three separate 8-bit-per-pixel channels in every image. In most cases, each channel shares the same characteristics of pixel dimensions and bit depth as the others, to enable them to be combined in a fast and meaningful way. For instance, in a typical 400 by 400 pixel color image, there will be three channels (one each for red, green, and blue), having 400 by 400 pixels at 8 bits per pixel. The entire image will therefore have 400 by 400 pixels, with an effective overall bit depth of 24 bits per pixel (or 8 bits per channel). The resulting file will be three times bigger than its monochrome counterpart and have a total of approximately 16.8 million possible colors available to the image.

In addition, other paradigms combine channels in ways different from RGB images. For example CMYK images combine four channels (one each for cyan, magenta, yellow, and black) in the same way that the printing press combines inks on paper to form color images (using a subtractive color model). A HLS model uses three channels, one each of hue, luminosity, and saturation. Other color models use one channel to describe the luminance, and two for the color content, such as the Lab model or the color models used in high dynamic range (HDR) formats (see Chapter 13 for more on HDR images). For the most part, different models can be used to produce the same digital image, but there may be differences in terms of the color space of the image, meaning that certain models can produce colors that others can't reproduce. This topic is examined further in Chapter 8.

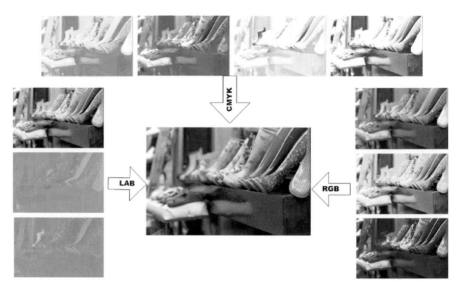

FIGURE 4-4   Digital images can use any of a number of different models to reproduce colors. © 2005 Andrew Francis. (See also the Color Insert)

4.3.6   Alpha Channels

It is also possible for an image to have extra, nonimage channels. The most common fourth channel is known as the "alpha" channel and is usually used as an extra "control" channel, to define regions of an image that can be used when modifying or combining images. For example, a pixel with an alpha channel of 0 may mean that the pixel shouldn't be modified at all, with an alpha channel of 255, the pixel would be affected fully, and a value of 127 might mean that the pixel would be affected at 50%. There may be additional channels to perform specific functions for color correction, masking, and so on. Each additional channel will increase the file size—doubling the number of channels will typically double the file size. Alpha channels aren't generally displayed as part of the image and won't affect its appearance.

4.3.7   Transparency

Digital images need not be opaque. By encoding separate transparency information, each pixel in the image may have a degree of transparency.

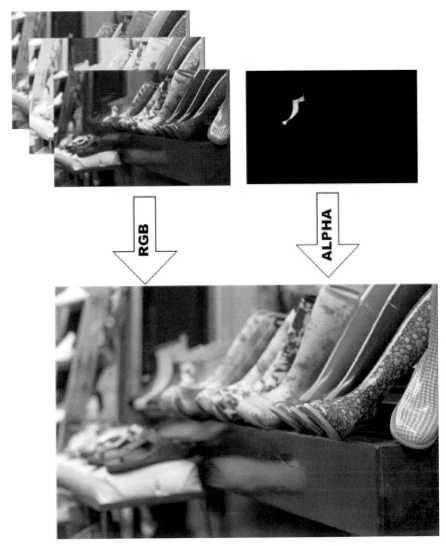

FIGURE 4-5 The alpha channel is separate from the color channels and doesn't affect the appearance of the image. In this case, the alpha channel might be used to mask one of the boots. © 2005 Andrew Francis

Transparency can be encoded in several ways. The most common way is to simply use an alpha channel to define the amount of transparency. The value associated with each pixel in the alpha channel defines the level of transparency for that pixel.[1] Another way to encode

---

[1] Conventions vary as to whether black or white pixels in the alpha channel represent full transparency.

transparency is to nominate a specific pixel value to indicate transparency. Using this method, every pixel of the specified color is taken to be transparent. A final way is to make use of vector graphics (which are covered later in this chapter) to specify regions of transparency.

4.3.8 Layers

A layered image is one that contains several separate images combined or stacked together. Layers allow superimposing (or compositing) images on top of each other, animation, or other special effects. While each layer is a separate image, it typically shares qualities such as pixel resolution, bit depth, and number of channels per image.

4.3.9 Motion

There are a few ways to turn a digital image into a moving image. The simplest is to vary one of its parameters over time—for example, by cycling through the colors in an image. In an image with multiple layers, each of the layers might be moved about over time, independently from each other. These methods are fairly limiting but result in small

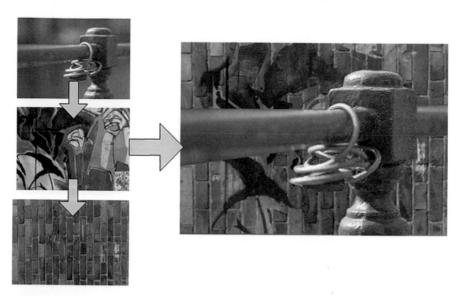

FIGURE 4-6 Layers may be combined using transparency, alpha channels, or other methods to produce a composite image

file sizes, as effectively, only one image (with perhaps several layers) must be stored, along with a small amount of data describing the motion. Displaying the motion correctly depends on the ability of the display system to provide the correct motion when the file is viewed. This method is suitable for special situations and is commonly seen in flash animations on some websites. However, to efficiently display high-quality images, the same method is used for video and film— a series of images is presented to the viewer in rapid succession.

Using this method, a number of frames are shown at a predetermined frame rate. As with video and film, this method of working with digital media produces the illusion of motion to the viewer. Unlike video and film, however, digital media isn't subject to a specific frame rate. Digital media can be played at 24fps to match film projection, 29.97fps to match NTSC video, 10 million fps, or 1 frame per day. Most of the time, the frame rates used in a digital intermediate pipeline are determined by other factors, such as the frame rate of the original or output media, or the limits of the playback system.

It's also worth noting that unlike other media, digital images can be played in a nonlinear fashion. With video and film formats, footage can be viewed only in sequence (although it is sometimes possible to alter the speed or play a sequence in reverse), whereas with digital media, frames can be accessed and displayed in any order, depending upon the software used.

4.4 DIGITAL IMAGE OPERATIONS

One of the main advantages of digital technology is that manipulation and analysis of the underlying data is very simple, compared to analog equivalents. Because digital images are simply numbers, it is possible to affect underlying parameters just by doing simple math. For example, to increase the brightness of a pixel, you increase the corresponding level of the pixel. To increase the overall brightness of an image, you increase the level of all pixels by a fixed amount; to darken them, you just lower the values. Many more operations are possible, by performing simple or complex calculations on individual pixels or convolving regions with a matrix (which is discussed in the following section).

FIGURE 4-7   Increasing the values of the pixels results in an increase in brightness.
© 2005 Andrew Francis

FIGURE 4-8   A convolution matrix can be applied to a selected area—in this case, sharpening the image. © 2005 Andrew Francis

4.4.1 Convolution

Convolution is a process where a digital image is modified using a mathematical matrix of numbers to transform the image. One of the more common convolution matrices is for sharpening an image. Changing the size or values of the convolution matrix will increase, reduce, or alter the effect.

Many other options are available, usually referred to as digital image "filters," that can be used for a variety of artistic, analytic, or special effects. Many digital-image-processing applications are available that allow a vast number of different operations across an image, or even to just a localized area.

4.5 ALTERNATIVES TO RASTER IMAGES

In addition to the many types of raster images, there are other paradigms for representing images digitally, such as vector graphics. Vector graphics are basically mathematical representations of shapes, such as rectangles and circles. They can be filled shapes, can be transparent, and can overlap. The advantages of vectors is that they are resolution independent, meaning that you can zoom into or out of them without having problems such as aliasing. A vector curve is always going to be perfectly smooth, and edges will always be perfectly sharp. Vector graphics typically require less information to store, resulting in smaller file sizes than equivalent raster images.

A disadvantage is that vectors can't easily represent the complex details that a photograph or pixel-based image can. Also, vector graphics are difficult to generate. You couldn't, for example, make a vector image by scanning a photograph. It is important to remember that even a vector image must be rasterized (i.e., converted to pixels) before it can be displayed; however, this rasterization needn't be permanent and is for display purposes only. Although vector graphics don't intrinsically support the use of color, many applications assign colors and patterns to the edges and contents of the shapes.

Several vector-based imaging programs are available, and many imaging programs combine vector graphics with pixel-based imagery. Many digital intermediate systems use vectors to define regions for selective editing of images.

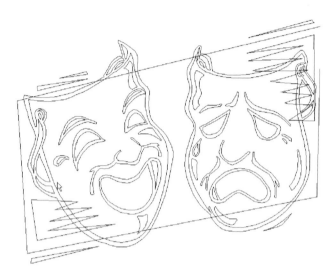

FIGURE 4-9   A vector image is made up of mathematical coordinates that form shapes

FIGURE 4-10   Even when the vector image is zoomed into, the sharp edge is retained

FIGURE 4-11 In some cases, it's possible to apply colors and patterns to the individual shapes

FIGURE 4-12 A fractal image has detail no matter how far you zoom in

FRACTAL IMAGES

Similar to vector images is the idea of fractal images. Fractals are complex formulas that generate infinitely complex, resolution-independent patternse. In a fractal image file, only parameters that describe the formulas must be recorded. For this reason, the file sizes can be incredibly small, smaller even than vector-based images, and yet the information they contain can be very detailed. However, it is very difficult to generate anything other than strange patterns with fractals, and intense computation is required to display them. For these reasons, fractal images are less common than vector graphics. Fractal technology is applied to other aspects of digital imaging, such as special types of image compression.

4.6   FILE FORMATS

As there are so many different ways to represent a digital image, there are literally hundreds of different digital image file formats that can be used for different purposes. The formats can vary based upon the number of channels and layers, the bit depth, and the color space. Some formats are highly standardized, and thus are guaranteed to work with a large number of applications; some are less standardized but still highly popular. (The less-standardized formats can cause headaches when you try to move them between various applications.) Some have been optimized for various functions, such as the ability to load a small part of an image at a time. Some formats are even more flexible, allowing any number of options to be determined separately for each file; however, these formats are normally limited to being readable by a specific application.

For moving picture images, each frame can be stored as a separate digital image file, or an entire sequence can be saved as a single, self-contained file (which applies to video tapes and reels of film). Again, there are many different formats for storing such media, some of which have a high level of compatibility with a great number of processing applications.[2]

The file formats that are relevant to the digital intermediate process are covered in later chapters.

4.7 COMPRESSION

One of the main problems with digital images is large file sizes. The size of a single raster image is roughly

number_of_pixels × number_of_channels × bit_depth_per_channel × number_of_layers

It is easy to quickly produce large files. For example, a film-quality image is typically taken to be 48MB. This size is too large to put onto a website or to email. Furthermore, the high volume of images produced for feature films (typically 50–100 million frames per film) means that even relatively small images require a large amount of disk space.

One of the ways to solve this problem is to reduce the amount of data. For example, you can lower the resolution of an image by a process known as "interpolation," which merges or discards a proportion of pixels to produce an image with fewer pixels. (Interpolation typically involves the use of some form of anti-aliasing to preserve detail and maximize quality.) Other methods may be to limit the color palette to a much smaller number by using an "indexed-color" image.

Indexed-color images have a preselected palette of colors available to use in the image. Rather than assume that you need 16.8 million different colors in a single image, a much smaller number of colors is chosen from the 16.8 million possibilities, and the pixels are assigned a color from this palette. This process results in a much smaller file size but at a cost of a reduced number of available colors in each image. For example, GIF files allow a color palette of about 256 colors, preselected from a range of about 16.8 million, thereby reducing the file size to a third of the original size.

---

[2] Even the highly standardized DV format can be saved on a computer in a number of different ways.

The most common method for reducing file size is to use a form of compression. There are two main ways of compressing a digital image. The first, known as "lossless" compression, simply rearranges the saved data in a more efficient way (e.g., by indexing all the colors in such a way that the most popular colors have a smaller index number), using less disk space.[3] On average, it is possible to reduce the file size by half (without any alteration to the content or quality of the image), but doing so is dependent on the content of the image. For all intents and purposes, a file compressed with lossless compression is identical to its uncompressed counterpart.

An alternative way of compressing digital images is to use "lossy" compression. This method optimizes image size by discarding some of the data—ideally, data that is superfluous. For example, JPEG (the popular format for the distribution of photographic images over the Internet) compression works by reducing the number of colors based on the color response of the human eye. In theory, it discards colors the eye wouldn't detect easily anyway. Other methods are even more esoteric—for example, converting areas of the image to equivalent fractals.

4.7.1 Visually Lossless Compression

The term "visually lossless compression" is something of a buzzword among manufacturers. Essentially, it refers to compression methods, such as the JPEG compression method, that reduce quality, based on the human eye's limits of perception. In theory, there is nothing wrong with using visually lossless compression because the imagery is perceptually the same, which is why it's very suitable for consumers. However, its strength lies in the assumption that all you are going to do with images compressed in this manner is view them. In the digital intermediate pipeline however, this assumption is incorrect because frames undergo many mathematical operations, such as resizing, color-correcting, and so on, all of which benefit from the available quality outside of the perceptive range of the human eye.

---

[3] In certain situations, some types of lossless compression can create a larger file size than the original!

By way of an analogy, let's say you have a scene containing a stack of gold bullion on a table. If you were to set up a camera and tripod to photograph the scene from a specific angle, you might find that some of the gold would not be visible through the lens. You could safely remove those extraneous gold bars from the scene and take the photograph, and no one would know the difference. However, doing so means that you can't change the camera setup without revealing the missing gold. In the same way, visually lossless compression removes parts of the image that aren't seen but inhibits editing ability later on. The destruction of information by the compression method becomes clear as you make changes to it, such as by color grading.

Each compression method introduces different artifacts into the image. You can often get a better understanding of how a particular compression method affects an image by loading a digital image and then saving it with maximum compression. This pushes the compression algorithm to such extremes that the quality reduction becomes visibly apparent in many cases. This problem is often further exacerbated by repeatedly recompressing files.

In addition, many compression artifacts become apparent only when watching the footage at speed. Any form of lossy compression is, by

FIGURE 4-13   Too much compression can lead to visible artifacts

definition, a destructive process, and its use is therefore recommended only as a final process before displaying the image.

4.7.2   Motion Compression

With a large number of stills, a lot of data has to be moved around to view the files in real time, without any lagging or dropped frames. With low-end computer systems and/or high-quality images, compression becomes very important for the viewing of such images. For example, a typical 90 minute program at SD video resolution requires approximately 150GB of space to allow it to be stored uncompressed. However, a consumer DVD can only store up to 9GB, and consumer equipment can't move around such a high volume of data at speeds fast enough for real-time playback.

DATA CORRUPTION

When a piece of film is damaged, it can become scratched or torn. With video tapes, the noise level may increase, or drop-out or interference may occur. When a digital file is damaged (i.e., corrupted)—either due to physical damage to the storage device, or a software error in accessing or creating the files), individual pixels, lines, or even frames are destroyed—they are inaccessible or otherwise randomized—partially dependent upon the file format used. Chapter 9 details ways of correcting some of these problems. Data has one significant advantage over other media though, which is that a backup copy is always as good as the original.

For digital moving picture formats, compression methods can work across a range of frames. Lossy motion compression typically works by comparing the content of each frame to the previous or next frame (or both frames in bidirectional compression) and looking for differences. Because a relatively small amount of difference exists between adjacent frames, space can be saved by only storing the differences, rather than storing each individual frame. The degree of sensitivity in detecting these changes can be adjusted and combined with lossy still image compression. To aid playback of these files, a parameter can be

RENDER ARTIFACTS

A whole class of problems can occur during the process of rendering images. Rendering is the process of converting one set of (usually computer-generated) data into another, suitable for display. Rendering is commonly used to convert a multilayered, composited image or shot, or a 3D scene, into a single-layered (i.e., flattened) sequence of images. In fact, almost all color-grading systems will involve rendering to output the color-graded footage. During this process, many errors can occur—errors caused by a lack of precision in calculations, glitches in the rendering software, or even sporadic hardware faults. Such faults can create noise or corruption artifacts. Fortunately, most rendering processes aren't destructive—they create new files rather than overwriting originals—so if spotted early enough, re-rendering the images will usually fix the problem. This is why it is important to carefully check every rendered image as early as possible in the digital intermediate process.

set on certain types of files to provide a fixed bit rate of each file, so that one second's worth of images occupies a fixed amount of disk space (the quality level being continuously adjusted to meet this target), resulting in smooth playback. Variable bit rate compression methods continuously adjust the footage's bit rate, so that more detailed images lose less information than less detailed images.

4.8 ENCRYPTION AND WATERMARKING

Another option granted by digital media is the use of encryption. This allows each digital file (each image frame or video stream) to be encrypted or scrambled with a special code. A user or system then supplies the correct code, and the file is decrypted (i.e., unscrambled). Without the code, the encrypted image doesn't display properly. Other implementations, such as watermarking, stamp a hidden pattern over an image. The hidden pattern can contain information about the origin of the image, for instance, which can be used to trace transferred images or prevent operations such as editing or copying the image. As with lossless compression, most image-encryption methods shouldn't affect the quality of an image.[4] However, it may affect the performance of the system because additional computation is required to decrypt files each time they are accessed. Encrypted images tend to share the same disadvantages of lossless-compressed images. Further, encryption may also exclude the use of lossless compression as well. In some cases, it is possible to use an encryption method that allows lossless compression to be used in conjunction with encryption, but in most situations, it's a case of one or the other (or most frequently, neither). Encryption and watermarking techniques will probably see more usage as the performance of imaging systems improves (and thus the additional computation involved in working with and encrypted images becomes negligible), and so does the awareness and paranoia of filmmakers and distributors toward the threat of computer hackers and piracy.

4.9   METADATA

Finally, it is worth noting that almost all digital image formats or storage methods have some proviso for encoding additional information (or metadata), such as a text comment, along with each image or group of images. This functionality is entirely dependent upon the software and file formats used. Even where the use of metadata isn't natively supported, it can be augmented in other ways, which is covered further in Chapter 6.

4.10   PROBLEMS WITH DIGITAL MEDIA

By their very nature, digital images are prone to a number of problems, or artifacts. These problems may be invisible except under certain circumstances, or they may significantly degrade and distort the image. Artifacts are generated either during the digitization process, or through image processing, such as compressing or color-grading the image. The most common digital artifacts are covered in Chapter 12.

---

[4] Watermarking an image alters the image slightly, although it does not normally introduce significant degradation.

Pretty much all of the problems with digital media have to do with the "quantization" of information. Unlike analog sources that record continuous streams of information, digital images (by definition) contain discrete (i.e., separate or distinct) units of information. Most of the failings of digital images can be directly attributed to this characteristic.

An important requirement of moving pictures is that the images are processed (and displayed) at a regular, usually predetermined rate. Analog video systems are designed to work in real time when recording or playing back. This means that one second of recorded footage takes exactly one second to display or copy. With digital media however, this isn't necessarily the case. Computer systems have a lot of variables attached to them (e.g., the specifications of the system, the software running on them, network conditions, and cabling quality) that all affect the playback. Displaying a series of frames on a computer system may result in a different experience each time. Computer systems can suffer from "lag," which is when a queue (or line) of frames to be displayed builds up, making a fixed-length sequence take longer than real time to display completely (although at no loss in image quality). Alternatively, digital images may be prone to dropped frames, where certain frames are discarded to maintain the real-time speed of playback. Conversely, if the host computer system is displaying frames too quickly, stuttering may occur as some frames are held on the display for longer than others. Dropped frames and stuttering

FLICKER

The human eye can detect changes of illumination at a much higher rate than it can discriminate motion. When film is projected on a cinema screen, a visible "flicker" occurs when the projector shutter closes and advances to the next frame. To overcome this issue, each frame is usually flashed onto the screen twice, resulting in the shutter opening 48 (or 50) times every second, thus eliminating any visual flicker. Televisions and monitors use a similar approach, although flicker is strictly a display-related issue and therefore doesn't affect the creation or manipulation of digital media at all.

are purely display issues and don't affect the quality of the data saved in any way (unless you are recording the output of the display, e.g., to video).

4.11 SUMMARY

Digital media offers many advantages over other types of media, such as the capability of making perfect duplicates quickly. However, lots of variables must be considered. Generally speaking, as the quality of an image increases, so do the associated costs. While a larger file might contain more pixels, and therefore more detail, it also becomes less practical to work with, requiring more storage space and additional processing and transmission time.

There are no specific standards when working with digital images. They may be encoded in a variety of different file formats, each suitable for specific purposes. Digital files may have additional options available for tracking and protecting images, or they can be compressed to reduce storage requirements. Lossless compression can reduce the size of each file without compromising quality; lossy compression can produce much smaller files but may degrade the image.

However, digital images can suffer from the lack of sufficient information to produce colors or details, thus exhibiting a number of artifacts. Some artifacts may only become noticeable late in the digital intermediate process (e.g., when performing color grading).

In the next chapter, the journey into the digital intermediate process begins. The first stage in the process is getting digital and analog material into the chain, while maintaining the highest level of quality.

5

ACQUISITION

Any digital intermediate process begins with the acquisition of media (sometimes referred to as the "ingest" of media). In many cases, the digital intermediate process is the final stage of a production, following shooting and editing. In these cases, the type of media required can be worked out before the digital intermediate process begins. Typically, there is footage for the final cut and there can also be audio and textual elements, such as titles and dialog. The focus of the majority of this book will be on the visual component of the digital intermediate, because the audio is almost always mastered independently and added separately at the end.

5.1 CRUNCHING NUMBERS

Computers don't understand analog information (which includes printed images, reels of film, people talking, and so on). This means you can't just show a film, edited or otherwise, to a computer system and get it to create a color-graded digital master (not yet anyway).

It is important to remember throughout the intermediate process that from the moment you begin, all you're doing is crunching numbers. Even though a skilled colorist can turn a blue sweater red, or selectively add or remove colors throughout a scene; to the computer systems involved in the process all that is happening is that one long number is converted into another long number. The system works because of the innovative software involved and the experienced operators who can predict how the system is likely to react to changes and can understand the limitations and shortcuts.

Computers can do very complicated mathematics very, very quickly compared to humans. Computers are able to take a digital image with the same amount of detail as a piece of film and almost instantly produce a perfect copy. However, all they are doing is performing some repetitive calculations at very high speed. This strength can also be a weakness. Because the computer has no knowledge of what the image contains and can associate no meaning to it, it cannot tell which parts are important. For this reason, defects such as noise, dust, and scratches are treated with the same care as desirable parts of an image. For this reason, you must always assume the golden rule: what you get out of a digital system will only ever be as good as what you put into it.

Actually, that rule isn't strictly true. Some methods for automated processes can perform feature analysis on images and sequences of images, can estimate which parts of an image or sequence of images are important and use that information to enhance the images—"estimate" being the keyword. Also, at every stage of the digital intermediate process are operators who are able to make subjective decisions about the processing and quality of the images, ensuring the highest possible standard throughout.

5.2 DIGITAL IMAGE QUALITY

The fundamental advantage that digital media has over analog materials is that digital information can be transferred across large distances with no loss of quality. A digital image looks exactly the same whether you're accessing a digital camera directly, or from the other side of the world, or accessing the image via the Internet, bounced off of satellites, or through some other transfer method. As long as the data remains unaltered, it's as good as the original. Sadly, the same cannot be said for video and film, which are both analog formats and therefore subject to many forms of degradation, the most significant being "generation loss."

5.2.1   Generation Loss

Every time you copy an analog source, such as a video tape or a reel of film, it degrades quality. In fact, every time you even view certain analog sources (including both film and video), it suffers a loss of quality. This is because most analog-viewing devices are mechanical and have moving parts that can damage the source. Viewing (or even handling) film prints or negatives can cause scratches or dust and other damage to them.[1] Video tapes risk decay or becoming demagnetized every time they're moved across a video head.

Each copy of an analog source introduces additional, lasting damage to the copy. A copy of a copy retains all the errors so far and then adds more errors. Errors are caused by effects such as noise (in the case of video) and chemical stains (in the case of film), among others.[2] Each successive copy is called a "generation." A fifth-generation copy is therefore typically of lower quality than a second-generation copy. To maximize the quality, it's preferable to work from original material whenever possible.

5.2.2   What Is Quality?

This book includes discussions of various factors that influence the somewhat esoteric criteria of "quality." As we know, quality, especially picture quality, can be a very subjective thing. For example, a well-lit

---

[1] Celluloid is particularly susceptible to static electricity, which effectively attracts tiny particles to stick to the film.
[2] Video tapes may also lose other information, such as timecodes, which are encoded directly on the tape. However, many video tape machines have mechanisms to reduce or prevent the likeliness of such loss occurring.

scene recorded on DVCAM video might be considered of superior quality to a poorly lit scene filmed on 35mm negative. There are ways to measure image quality objectively though; if you assume all other things (such as lighting, set design, and so on) to be equal, then "quality" can be defined as "how closely an image matches the original content," which is how the term is used throughout this book. There is another issue at stake though. What if you don't want the final project to closely resemble the original? After all, part of the "magic" of filmmaking is in creating imagery that looks far removed from or even better than real life. However, even in those situations, you want to produce images that are of high quality—with as much detail as possible—so that you selectively control what stays and what doesn't later on.

In the digital intermediate pipeline, the aim is to maintain the highest possible quality throughout, with the material prepared for supervised sessions with the filmmakers, who then make decisions about how to affect the images and control the subjective level of quality. For example, if you want a shot to look blurry in the final production, it can be argued that it doesn't matter if the scene is transferred at low quality, making it visibly blurry. However, in this case, there is no way to "unblur" the image later on (even digital sharpening techniques won't create as good an image as the original footage), and the level of blurriness can't be adjusted interactively, in context with the scene. Chapter 14 contains information about using digital processes to help define the aesthetics and style of a production.

5.2.3 Resolving Power

Resolving power is one objective method for measuring the quality of an image. It is found by measuring how much detail is crammed into a given area. The simplest way to measure is to capture an image of a chart of lines that alternate between black and white and get increasingly thinner. When the lines are too thin for the recorder, they are recorded as gray. The point where this occurs is used to calculate the "resolution" of the recorder.

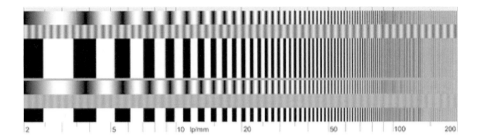

FIGURE 5-1 A chart such as this can be used to determine the resolving power of an imaging system. © Norman Koren, Available at www.normankoren.com

With film, the resolution depends upon the average grain size, and the resolution of video tape depends upon the properties of the type of signal received. Other factors can also play a part in influencing the resolving power, such as the optical system (i.e., lenses). In reality, the derived resolving power is actually a measurement of the entire imaging system.[3]

Ultimately though, to get the most relevant result, the resolving power, and thus the maximum resolution of any system, should be measured by looking at the final output.

5.2.4 Spread Function

Further evaluation of any optical system can be made by determining its spread function. The spread function is essentially a measurement of how different a single point of light (or a line or a hard edge) appears when recorded and demonstrates many different characteristics of degradation in a system.

---

[3] In the case of digital cameras, the resolving power can be calculated from the output resolution only if the optical components (such as the lens and CCD array) themselves have at least the same resolving power as the recorded resolution. Unfortunately, in many cases the resolving power of the optical components isn't the same as the recorded resolution, and the resolution is "cheated" by "up-sampling" the captured image.

5.2.5 Modulation Transfer Function

An even more useful result is the modulation transfer function (MTF). In simple terms, MTF is a measurement of the response (or accuracy) of any system across varying frequencies (which amounts to the level of detail). You would expect that the accuracy of reproduction for most systems would be directly proportional to the level of detail, so that, for example, an image of large squares would be more faithfully reproduced than an image of very thin lines. However in practice this often isn't the case. MTF measurements and graphs serve to illustrate exactly how the systems respond to different frequencies, thus highlighting potential problems, as well as serving as a useful method for making objective comparisons of systems and components.

One of the reasons the MTF measurement is useful is because certain systems respond better than others under certain conditions. For example, some types of photographic film exhibit greater granular-

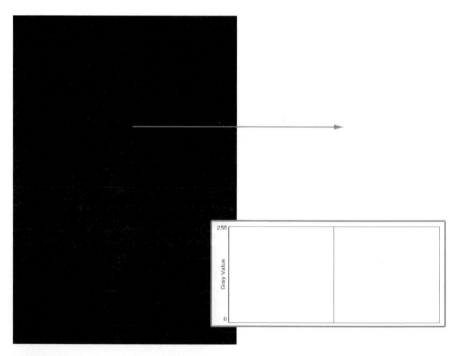

FIGURE 5-2 A perfect hard edge is plotted with a vertical line

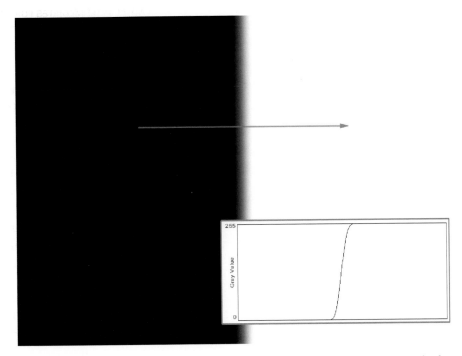

FIGURE 5-3 With a blurred (more realistic) edge, the transition is more gradual

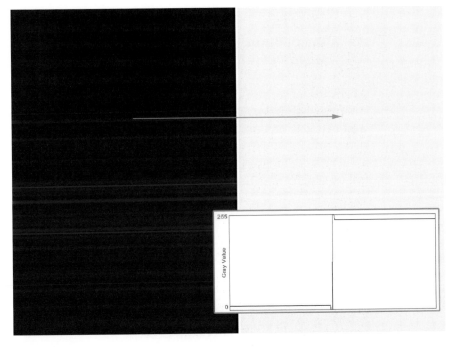

FIGURE 5-4 An artificially sharpened edge may exaggerate the edge

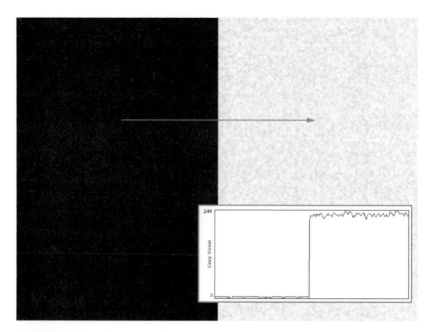

FIGURE 5-5 Factors such as film grain may also play a part in the measurement of an edge

ity in the mid-tone regions than in shadow or highlight areas. An MTF can provide an objective measurement of these types of effects.

MTFs are measured by imaging a special chart (which displays a series of sine wave patterns) and performing various measurements and calculations on it.

5.2.6 Signal-to-Noise Ratios

Another useful measurement of the quality of a system is its signal-to-noise ratio. This is calculated by dividing the signal strength of a system by the inherent noise. Every system, or signal (such as a video signal) has some degree of noise inherent, which comes from a variety of sources. Every time the signal is amplified, the noise is amplified along with it. A higher signal-to-noise ratio indicates a higher quality system than a lower ratio, because it means the effects of noise are less pronounced.

5.2.7 Detective Quantum Efficiency

Modulation transfer functions don't take into account the effects of noise in a system, and signal-to-noise ratios don't tell us anything about the accuracy of a system's response to light (i.e., its contrast performance). A method that combines these two measurements is the detective quantum efficiency (DQE). A low signal-to-noise ratio, combined with high-contrast performance results in a high DQE (and a superior image). As with the other methods, a system's DQE is typically measured across a range of frequencies input (such as by using a standard resolution chart), and the results allow direct comparison between different systems.

5.2.8 Compression Ratios

Certain digital and analog compression methods (such as video compression or JPEG digital compression) discard a set amount of information (and by extension, reduce quality by a proportional amount). While some of these methods are designed to discard information that is imperceptible to the human eye, the image is still considered degraded. Digital systems tend to measure compression as a percentage of the available information, so that a lower percentage is more degraded than a higher compression. The same is also true of video compression, which describes compression ratios in terms of YIQ or YUV levels. Video compression is discussed in Chapter 2 and digital compression is discussed in Chapter 4.

LOSSLESS COMPRESSION

Interestingly, "lossless" digital compression isn't a particularly popular method for storing digital images in the digital intermediate environment, despite the fact that it reduces each file's size without any quality degradation whatsoever. There are several reasons to explain this:

(continues)

LOSSLESS COMPRESSION (*continued*)

1. Corruption. If a digital image that uses lossless compression is damaged, even by a single pixel, the damage can be propagated over a much larger area, potentially destroying the entire frame.

2. Budgeting. The size of files that use lossless compression vary depending on the information contained within them. For this reason, it can be impossible to predict how much disk space is required for a given number of digital images that use lossless compression, which, of course, makes it difficult to budget disk space for a project.

3. Speed. Additional computation must be performed to compress and decompress digital images. The performance difference might be insignificant for a single frame, but when trying to display a sequence of images at a rate of 25 frames per second (or higher), the computations can add up and can be an unnecessary usage of computer resources. What is unclear is how this performance hit may be offset by the associated gain in transfer speed (i.e., the files are smaller and can therefore be transferred faster).

4. Compatibility. Use of any compression method makes the file format more complicated. In general, it can be relatively simple to extract image data from simple file formats, particularly when they're stored using the RGB color model, even if the specifics of the format are unknown. However, as soon as compression is used, the exact specification of the file format must be known before the image data can be accessed. The reason this is an issue is because all the software used in the pipeline must be able to process files according to the exact specification. Given that it's possible that a file format (such as TIFF) might support multiple compression methods, it becomes likely that at least some of software won't be able to access a given compressed file format. Furthermore, it means that long-term storage of compressed files may not be accessible in the future, particularly if the compression standards change (or are made redundant). The most efficient use of lossless compression probably lies in transferring dig-

(continues)

> ### LOSSLESS COMPRESSION (*continued*)
>
> ital files over relatively long distances. For instance, if a shot needs to be transferred across an Internet link (such as by virtual private networking—VPN—or file transfer protocol—
>
> FTP), then the system can be designed to take each frame, compress it via lossless compression, transfer the file, and then uncompress it at the other end (probably combined with some form of digital verification method, which is covered in Chapter 6). Also, lossless compression is ideal for short-term data backups because it can reduce the time both to store and to retrieve a backup, as well as the amount of storage space required.

5.2.9 The Eye of the Beholder

With all this discussion about image degradation and quality, it's important to remember that the human eye itself isn't a perfect optical system. Many of the shortcuts used by video- and digital-imaging devices are based upon inaccuracies in the human eye. For example, the human eye is much more sensitive to red and green light than blue.[4] Also, due to the large number of rod (luminance-sensitive) cells compared to cone (chroma-sensitive) cells, humans can more readily detect changes in luminance than in color. For this reason, many devices (in particular, video systems) are optimized for these parameters. Because of this, it's important to remember that even if some degradation occurs, it may be within the parameters of degradation experienced by the human eye anyway and is thus undetectable to end users.

There are two main reasons why you might want to keep information that is imperceptible to the human eye. The first is machine vision (which is less relevant to the entertainment industry) and the second is image manipulation, such as digital color grading (which is covered later in Chapter 8). Ultimately, it's desirable that a pipeline not suffer any degradation at all, whether or not it's perceptible. In fact, selective information loss can be more of a problem than overall

---

[4] This is due to a concentration of red- and green-sensitive cells at the center of the retina, known as the macula lutea, or "yellow spot."

degradation—first, because it means an image may not look as degraded as it is, and second, because it degrades the affected parts of the image more (which then means that those parts of the image don't respond well to manipulation).

5.3 MEDIA ACQUISITION

There are two distinct ways to acquire media for inclusion within a digital intermediate: by electronic transfer or by analog-to-digital conversion. These methods vary in efficiency, speed, and quality.

If the source material is already in a digital form, it simply needs to be transferred from the original storage device into the storage devices used for the digital intermediate pipeline. If the material exists in some other form, then it must first be digitized (or converted to a digital format).

5.4 DATA TRANSFER

A data transfer involves taking a set of images that are already in digital form (or taking some other data such as audio tracks or timecode information) and copying or moving the associated files from one device to another. For example, if you've shot something on a DV (digital video) camera, you can just pop the tape in a DV tape deck connected to a digital-editing system via a firewire cable, and all the data can be copied digitally from the tape, ready for editing.[5]

This process becomes complicated because there are many different ways to store, or encode digital information. In the same way that

---

[5] Although some sources are listed as being digital, they may commonly be transferred by analog means. For instance, high-definition video is an inherently digital format, and yet it's not unusual for HD tape decks to be wired into a video-switching matrix (a device that allows video to be routed to many different places at the same time) via analog means. Many facilities are actually set up to acquire HD video via analog means, rather than transferring the raw digital data.

A PERFECT COPY EVERY TIME?

Just because a transfer is made digitally, doesn't mean it isn't subject to quality loss. In many cases, a bit-for-bit copy is made in the same way that files can be moved about on a hard drive. However, this may not be the case in several cases, such as copying files between different operating systems (although even in this instance the data should have the same content) or when transferring data between different software packages or devices. In some of these cases, the information may be "transcoded," potentially resulting in a loss of quality. Always be sure to check that data transfers are bit-for-bit whenever possible.

different languages can be used to describe the same things, different images can be recorded in a variety of different ways. It's often necessary to perform additional data management, such as file format or color-space conversion during or after transfer. The transfer method might use a transcoding process, which effectively reinterprets the images from scratch, and thereby subjects them to further degradation.

Data conversion notwithstanding, digital transmission allows data, such as images or video streams, to be copied or moved over long distances, with no loss in quality at all. For this reason, data transfer is preferable to every other acquisition method. However, everything is ultimately sourced from analog media, so the ideal scenario is to keep everything digital beginning with the step of analog-to-digital conversion and continuing onward. Whether the analog-to-digital conversion happens in the camera, as in the case of digital cameras, or after shooting, as when scanning film negatives, everything should be digital from that point onward.

An interesting factor affecting data transfer is speed. Video is always copied in real time (i.e., it takes one minute to copy one minute of footage, and so on). Video also has an advantage because it can be copied to many tapes at the same time (to as many recorders as available) through a process of signal amplification. Film can be duplicated at a rate of hundreds of feet per minute.

Data, however, is transferred at varying speeds. The transfer speed completely depends on a number of factors, such as bandwidth, network traffic, type of cabling, speed of the host computer, and so on. In some cases, it's possible that a digital video sequence can be copied or moved faster than real time, and in others, it may be much slower than real time. It's also possible that a transfer may begin rapidly and then slow to a crawl. The important thing is that each copy is identical to the original. Further, a single piece of data can be accessed by multiple devices at the same time, which is a (theoretically) more efficient way of working. Given a reel of film or a video tape, only one person can modify the contents at a time. But the digital equivalent allows each frame to be treated and modified independently, and in some highly specialized applications, even a single frame can be modified by different people at the same time. There are some pitfalls though. Certain applications "lock" files so that they cannot be accessed by others, to avoid reducing the speed of throughput. Locking files is especially common on software-based grading systems, which prevent frames that are in use from being copied or modified from outside the grading system. Although file locking is sensible, it can cause problems (e.g., when data transfers overrun their allotted time, as when the process of copying a number of frames overnight hasn't been completed by the time the colorist starts work the next day), or when the system contains software errors, requiring it to be rebooted to "unlock" certain files.

Some digital media formats (e.g., DV or Internet streaming) are specified to work at a preset speed. In the case of DV video, for example, transfer from a DV tape to a capture system always occurs in real time. If the transfer speed drops during the capture process, the process might halt, normally reporting "dropped frames" or some other error, and have to be restarted. Internet streaming is designed to work at a given transfer speed (normally significantly lower than the maximum transfer speed) and will continue to transfer video at speeds above that rate—although the end user may experience viewing problems (e.g., slow downs or dropped frames) if the average transfer speed falls below the target rate.

A computer accessing its own files uses data-transfer operations. For example, displaying a digital image on a screen typically involves several processes: the data is transferred from the source storage device to the computer system through a number of cables and junctions, into the computer's RAM. From there, it's transferred to the computer's graphics subsystem, which in turn transmits the data to the monitor through another cable. This description somewhat oversimplifies what exactly happens; in practice, even more factors play a part—for instance, displaying an image from a network location rather than a local disk drive necessitates even more transfers, through more cables and numerous network routers.

Data-transfer operations are normally used only for computer-generated or digital video productions, because most footage is generated using analog means, such as shooting on film, which is unfortunate because it's the most convenient method for acquiring images. As digital filmmaking matures and gains popularity, the data-transfer method of acquisition will become more common. Until that time, the majority of footage will be fed into the digital intermediate pipeline using digitization methods.

5.5 DIGITIZATION

Digitization is the first step in converting an analog source to a digital format. It is currently the most common method for image acquisition in filmmaking. Almost everything is sourced from an analog format at some stage, with the notable exception of computer-generated imagery.[6]

To produce a digital version of anything analog, an analog-to-digital conversion must be made. Without question, this event ultimately has the most impact on quality in any digital pipeline (coupled, of course, with whatever was shot in the first place). From this moment on, you can only reduce quality—purposefully in many cases, but irreversibly nonetheless. How you go from an analog source to a digital source has a bearing on every subsequent stage, and therefore this process must be planned carefully in advance based upon the requirements of the film.

---

[6] Although even CG imagery may contain some elements from analog sources.

5.5.1   Sampling

The process of digitization is a statistical reduction of information. Analog sources effectively have an unlimited level of detail. The closer you examine any analog source, the more detail you find. Some of that is "useful" detail, providing more of the image content, and some of the detail is just a factor of defects, such as noise. The first step in digitization is to decide how much of this detail you actually need. It isn't possible to capture absolutely everything, but in most cases, it isn't necessary. In the same way that the attitudes of an entire population can be determined by interviewing a small, carefully selected "sample" of individuals, an analog source can be sampled to build a complete picture. An entire branch of mathematics, sampling theory, is devoted to methods for doing this, but the basic idea is that if you make enough samples of an image at regular intervals, you'll be able to re-create the original faithfully.[7] This means that you start with an analog source, which has an infinite level of detail, and you split it into parts.

Imagine, for instance, that you're painting a scene that includes a tree. Let's say you use a large paintbrush, one that can cover the entire canvas in a few strokes, and a pot of black paint. After maybe four strokes, you might have a vague impression of the tree. Now let's say you use a smaller brush (or a bigger canvas). It takes a lot more strokes to paint a picture of the tree, but now you can paint more of its subtle details. But it's still not an exact image of the tree. Let's now assume that you start the painting again, but this time with a few different colors of paint. You can even mix these colors to create new colors. This provides an even more accurate image of the tree.

What you've done, in a very loose sense, is digitized the tree onto the canvas. Even with a very thin brush, you can't replicate all the detail of the scene. The more carefully you inspect the scene, the more details become revealed. But at some point, you decide that

---

[7] Even some analog devices use sampling techniques, such as telephones and faxes, which sample an analog source and then re-encode it as an analog electrical signal.

the level of detail is close enough to make no visible difference. For example, make the canvas as big as a cinema screen, and the level of detail high enough that your eyes can't actually perceive all the detail from a few feet away. Then say that you don't want to be able to perceive specific points where one color of paint begins and another ends. Maybe now you have something that approximates a projected photograph.

Anything analog has to be digitized somehow so it can be replicated in another form. Take photographic film, for instance. The detail level of a scene imaged on a photograph is determined by the grain size (among other things) of the film. You can think of taking a photograph as an analog-to-analog process, which digitizes a scene at the level of the grain size.[8]

As another example, consider the way that the moving picture actually works—by projecting a series of stills at a rate of around 24 frames a second. What has happened is that time itself has been digitized by this process, breaking down a continuous (analog) motion into discrete (digital) parts. But when a moving picture is played back, we perceive the motion as smooth, because it occurs at a slightly higher rate than our eyes can detect.

You can use many different ways to digitize an image, but the most common method is to break down an image into regularly arranged, repeating squares. There are many reasons for doing it this way, but the main reason is that it allows the data collected to be identical to how digital images are stored and displayed, resulting in no necessary further degradation of the image.

In the simplest case, a single point of a source is sampled, which then corresponds to a single pixel of the digital image. This process is repeated at regularly spaced intervals, horizontally and vertically, until the entire image is digitized.

---

[8] Actually it's more like an analog-to-digital process, if you think of it in terms of the huge (but finite) number of photon and grain interactions on a piece of film, but thinking about it like that can be unnecessarily confusing and misleading.

ARE PIXELS BEST?

Surprisingly, the use of a grid of square-shaped pixels is a bad way to create a representation of an image. One study has shown that digital images have a higher MTF when rotated 45 degrees during digitization (but the downside to this method is that rotating the image back for viewing purposes degrades it, so destroying the quality gain of rotating it in the first place). However, a so-called "honeycomb" structure of digital images, where the pixels are diamonds rather than squares, produces visibly sharper results (both objectively and subjectively) than a regular pixel arrangement.

The main reason that pixels are square is because it simplifies the mathematics involved in displaying and manipulating digital images. And now, everything, from software to monitors, is designed to work with square-pixel images, so it's unlikely to change in the near future. The notable exception is that it's possible to have nonsquare (meaning rectangular) pixels in some cases. Images with nonsquare pixels work on the basis that you can just add or remove a certain proportion of square pixels to enable them to be viewed at the correct ratio on square-pixel devices. (See Chapter 4 for more information about nonsquare pixels.) One of the reasons that grain-for-pixel, film still produces a superior image is because photographic grains are randomly shaped and randomly distributed, making them less vulnerable to effects such as aliasing.

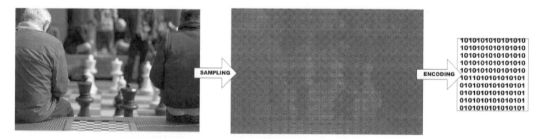

FIGURE 5-6 Digital images may be created by sampling an analog source and then encoding it into a digital format

5.5.2 Interpolation

Digital images can change resolution as required, through a process called "resampling."[9] For example, a 200×200 image can be resampled to a 100×100 image or to a 400×400 image. Increasing the number of pixels is referred to as "upsampling" (or "uprez'ing"), while decreasing the pixel count is "downsampling" (or "downrez'ing"). Resampling is used for a variety of reasons, often so that different footage is processed at the same time (so that video footage can be recorded onto film, it must first be upsampled to match the film image resolution). However, increasing the pixel resolution in this way won't increase the image's level of quality (though decreasing the resolution will cause a reduction of quality). This is because you can never get additional quality from a digital image that wasn't captured in the first place.

To resample an image, a calculation must be made to work out what the new pixels look like. This process is known as "interpolation." There are different interpolation methods (or algorithms) for different situations, which are explored in Chapter 10. Interpolators merely estimate how additional detail would look (in the case of upsampling) based upon existing pixels. When downsampling, estimation is less an issue, because a reduction in quality doesn't have to estimate detail that doesn't exist. However, upsampling should be avoided whenever possible.

DIGITAL ZOOM

Certain digital-imaging devices have a digital zoom function. This function is just a method of upsampling parts of an image, to make those parts appear larger. However, there is no quality benefit to using such features, especially because they can be replicated later in the digital intermediate pipeline, using higher quality interpolation algorithms.

---

[9] This term is a little misleading because the process does not actually go back to the original source and sample it again. It merely uses the information already available.

FIGURE 5-7 Upsampling artificially increases the resolution of an image, while downsampling decreases it. © 2005 Andrew Francis

QUALITY AND WINE

Digital image quality is analogous to a bottle of wine. Imagine that your original scene is a vat of wine, and you fill a bottle with a sample. The size of that bottle is equivalent to the quality of the imaging format, so that 35mm film is equivalent to a large bottle, whereas VHS video is a much smaller bottle. Between the time the wine is in the vat, and the time you get to pour yourself a glass, the wine might have been transferred to many different bottles. Anytime it's transferred to a smaller bottle (or put through a quality-reducing process), some of the wine will be permanently discarded. Similarly, transferring the wine to a larger bottle doesn't give you any more wine, but you don't necessarily lose any either. Interpolation is like watering down the wine: you can use it to fill a larger bottle, but it won't give you any more wine.

5.5.3 Color Space

So far, we've mainly looked at the RGB model of digital images, because the most common types of digital image are of this model and are ideally suited to being viewed on an RGB display device, such as a computer monitor. However, there are many different ways of using digital images, other than displaying them on a monitor. Digital images can be printed on paper, put on video, recorded by lasers onto photographic film, or even just analyzed by machines without ever being looked at.

Each of these different methods understands color in a different way. For example, many colors that can be seen on projected film can't be displayed on video (and vice versa). The range of colors that a system is able to reproduce is known as its "color space" (or "gamut"). Most of the time, the color spaces of different systems overlap, and the systems can show the same color. So, for example, an image displayed on a (properly calibrated) monitor will look exactly like the color print. However, where areas of color don't match, the colors are said to be "out of gamut" and may look wrong.

Even the human eye has its own gamut. For example, some video cameras can detect infrared or ultraviolet, which is outside of the gamut of the human eye. However, the color space of the human eye is much larger than most color-reproduction systems, which is why we can easily detect differences between colors viewed in different mediums.

Digital images are often optimized for a specific color space. This means that the images may be interpreted a certain way, depending on their application. For example, the common three-channel RGB color image discussed earlier, aims to be suitable for viewing on most computer monitors. Printing houses may adopt the four-channel CYMK color space, which is interpreted in a similar way to the cyan, yellow, magenta, and black inks used for printing on paper. Images for photographic film typically use a three-channel RGB color space but by using a logarithmic scale. This is done for efficiency because film responds to light differently at the extremes of color than in the mid-tones. This topic is covered in Chapter 8.

5.5.4 Nonlinear Color Space

Certain materials, including photographic film, don't respond to light in a linear fashion. That is, adding twice as much light to a photographic material won't necessarily result in an image that is twice as bright. For this reason, digital images can be stored in a nonlinear fashion. With linear-color-space images, pixels are encoded with brightness values on each channel. Nonlinear color spaces work this way too, but the difference is that the values are mapped onto another scale, so that values of 0, 1, 2, 3, etc. might be mapped to brightness values of 0, 1, 4, 9, respectively (in this case, an exponential color space is used) instead. This method makes it possible for very high values and very low values to be stored together in the same image, resulting in more efficient use of disk space.

Where problems occur with nonlinear-color-space images is in trying to convert data between different spaces, because it can be difficult to correlate colors from one color space to another. Color-space conversion is covered further in Chapter 8.

5.5.5 Gamma

Although RGB provides a suitable model for displaying images on a number of devices, such as televisions and computer monitors, there is no direct correlation between the brightness of a pixel of an RGB digital image and the corresponding brightness of a point on a monitor. Part of the problem is that monitors have a luminance range that is nonlinear, but another problem is that there is so much variance between monitors.

The first problem is resolved by applying gamma correction to the image. In gamma-correcting an image, the luma signal sent to the monitor for display is adjusted so that it's represented on a nonlinear scale, compensating for the response of the monitor (so that the image looks as it should, at least in theory). Gamma is a specific scale that combines both contrast and brightness. The amount of gamma to be applied is variable, with a value of 1.0 making no difference to the input and output of the pixel values, and higher and lower values increasing or decreasing the gamma correction, respectively. This is complicated somewhat by the use of different standards for different applications. For example, older Macintosh computers use a gamma of 1.8, whereas Windows computers typically use a value of 2.2.

Because of the variance between different monitors (and lighting conditions), the gamma correction must be adjusted for each monitor for accurate results. The most common way of doing this is using a gamma-calibration system. Using such a system, a series of readings of the response of the viewing device to different images and luma values is made, and the optimum gamma correction is determined. Many digital images may also have additional gamma information encoded into them, so that they can be displayed more accurately on other calibrated systems (although such embedded information is useful only if the originator of the material was working with a calibrated system). During acquisition, gamma correction may be applied automatically to certain types of media, such as video or digital images from elsewhere, and can affect the images' colors. Many digital intermediate pipelines try to avoid altering color content in any way prior to the color-grading stage because such alterations may degrade the images. Color-grading and calibration are covered further in Chapter 8.

5.5.6 Dynamic Range

The intensity range of an image is the ratio of its brightest point to the darkest point. The density range of a photographic image is the ratio of the highest density on the film (the D-max) to the lowest (the D-min). Either of these terms can be taken as the dynamic range of an image. In terms of digital image formats, the dynamic range of the image can be derived from the bit depth: an 8-bit image, having 256 values per pixel, has a dynamic range of 256:1. A (linear) 10-bit image has a dynamic range of 1024:1. The dynamic range of the human eye is roughly 10,000:1, whereas most CRT displays are approximately 100:1. Televisions are around 30:1 or 40:1. Where this becomes important is in trying to capture the available intensity range from another source (either analog or digital). If the dynamic range of the capture device (such as a film scanner or digital camera) is lower than the dynamic range of the scene being imaged, some tonal information will be lost. If the dynamic range of the image format being used is lower than the information being captured, some information will be lost. Similarly, using a file format with a high dynamic range doesn't necessarily mean that the image itself will have a high dynamic range.

There's a subtle difference between dynamic range and color precision. Color precision is a purely mathematical concept, determined by the bit depth of an image. A 10-bit file has greater precision (and is therefore less prone to color artifacts) than an 8-bit file. On the other hand, a nonlinear 8-bit image might have a greater dynamic range than a linear 10-bit image, meaning it could reconstruct a greater range of luminance but at a lower degree of accuracy.

COLOR VERSUS RESOLUTION

If you look at the specifications for most digital-imaging devices, the pixel resolution is always the most predominant factor. However, it isn't necessarily the most important. As discussed previously, resolution is theoretically equivalent to the system's resolving power, although this isn't necessarily the case. In practice, the question of image quality relies on two main factors— the (true) resolution of the image and its color range. It's not clear which of these two values is more important, although there seems to be an upper limit on the "useful" color range. Essentially, if the color range is high enough to allow color grading without introducing banding or other artifacts, then increasing the color range further has no benefit. Current tests determine this limit to be about 16 bits per channel for RGB channels, giving approximately 280 trillion possible colors for each image. All things being equal, this means that if the image-capture device already has a sufficiently high color range, the determining factor is going to be resolution; images can always benefit from extra sharpness. However, too often, a high resolution is quoted alongside a substantially low color range, especially in the case of digital cameras.

Another caveat to this argument is that the color range is inherently limited by the viewing device. Even the best monitors are configured to display a maximum of 10 bits per channel, which means that anything higher can't even be displayed properly. Similarly, other output devices such as film recorders may have a maximum color range on a similar scale. Therefore, even an

(continues)

COLOR VERSUS RESOLUTION (*continued*)

image with 16 bits per channel may have to be reduced to a lower color range before printing (but the higher range will still help to reduce color artifacts). On the other hand, there isn't really an upper limit on useful pixel resolution. Even if an image has more pixels than can be displayed at once, it still has the benefit of being able to be viewed at different scales. For instance, you can look at a large image, viewing it at the full level of quality (one pixel of image occupies a single pixel on the display) so that you only see a quarter of it at any time, or you have the option to zoom out the image, reducing the number of pixels displayed but enabling you to see the entire image. In terms of color range, there is no real equivalent. You could opt to view a section of the color range at once, such as having a virtual exposure control to expand the highlight or shadow areas as needed, but such controls aren't particularly common.

This limitation is a bit of a setback for the digital intermediate pipeline, because if devices were able to register or print a greater color range, it would contribute to a higher level of detail in an image with a reduced number of pixels. If you consider the edge of an object being imaged, such as the leaves on a tree, a capture device would better reproduce the veins on the leaves if the sample pixel count was increased. However, it's also feasible to assume that a more accurate color sample would also improve the rendition of detail, because each pixel would be afforded a slightly more accurate "average" of the color of the pixel. Clearly this isn't a perfect solution, because you would also benefit from a reduction of aliasing artifacts by having a higher pixel count. However, it's worth noting that in terms of file size at least, doubling the number of colors (e.g., going from 256 colors per pixel to 512 colors) requires only a 12.5% increase in file size (the increase of 8 bits per pixel to 9 bits per pixel is 12.5%), whereas doubling the number of pixels doubles the file size.

(*continues*)

COLOR VERSUS RESOLUTION (*continued*)

For moving images, a third factor is also relevant to quality: time, or the number of images per second. Currently, this factor doesn't really undergo significant change during the intermediate process (with the exception of format conversion or motion effects), because there isn't as much stretching and squashing of time as with colors or pixels. There may be a point in the future where filmmakers experiment more with the process of manipulating the speed of a shot during the digital intermediate process, which may require scenes to be filmed at a higher frame rate to allow for this possibility to work well. For now though, such shots are usually planned well in advance, or the filmmaker uses interpolation methods.

What tends to happen is that the digital intermediate process uses the same frame rate as used by the majority of the source material (such as 24fps for film productions, or 29.97 for NTSC video productions), and everything else is changed to match it. Ultimately, the use of this method will normally be decided by the lead editor on the project.

5.5.7 Acquisition for Digital Intermediates

The aim of acquisition for the digital intermediate pipeline is to obtain, whenever possible, digital images whose quality isn't compromised in any way. Current technology dictates a trade-off between speed and quality, particularly in analog-to-digital conversions. However, most digital intermediate facilities believe that quality must take precedence over speed at this stage, especially when dealing with the high-quality demands of cinema or (to a slightly lesser extent) high-definition video formats. The quality level set at the stage of image acquisition will have a profound effect on the quality through the pipeline, regardless of the target quality of the final product. This is true of many mediums—for instance, a VHS video originated from a HD video source will look superior to a VHS video originated from a VHS source, even though the content might be the same. There are other considerations—for example, the quality level shouldn't be so high that it impacts the performance of the playback system. Most facilities require that all screenings for the production team, or any interactive sessions (such as color grading) be done at the maximum level of quality in real time.

5.6 ACQUISITION FROM VIDEO SOURCES

Acquisition of digital images from video sources is actually a fairly straightforward process. All that is required is a video playback device, an analog-to-digital converter, and a data storage device. The quality of the conversion depends entirely upon the analog-to-digital converter (ADC).

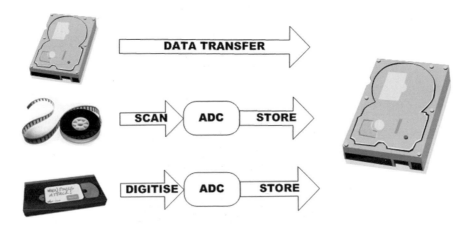

FIGURE 5-8 Digital media may be acquired easily using a data-transfer method, while analog sources must undergo a digital-to-analog conversion

Video signals are formatted in a way that translates to digital images very easily. Depending upon the video format, the necessary resolution can be derived that corresponds exactly to the number of lines in the image. In this case, no additional benefit is derived from digitizing the video to a higher resolution (because there will be no additional information to record, unlike for photographic sources). Both YIQ- and YUV-encoded colors can be converted to RGB-encoded ones, although some RGB color spaces have different gamuts than the video ones.[10] A higher bit depth may provide a quality advantage in terms of color precision, because a wider variety of colors can be sampled, although this will inevitably depend on the precision of the source video. However, many video formats inherently use color compression to reduce the transmission overhead, and so the benefit may be slight. In most cases, it's unlikely that any benefit will be gained from using more than 10 bits per channel RGB images.

In any case, provided the file format is appropriate, any reduction of quality will largely be due to noise added by the ADC and its subsystems. With most ADCs, the noise introduced will be negligible; otherwise, a noise-reduction technique, such as image averaging, can be used (see Chapter 9 for more on this technique). A table of digital resolutions for various video formats is included in the Appendix.

A simple, effective system for digitizing video sources is a dedicated computer workstation with a video capture card. The source deck (or video matrix, in facilities with a large number of video decks) connects to the capture card, and software within the computer saves the incoming video as a series of still images onto a local disk or network. Video is normally transferred in real time, meaning it takes one hour to digitize an hour's worth of video.

5.6.1 Digital Video

With digital video formats (such as DV, DVCAM, and HD video), the video is already stored in a digital format. Therefore, acquiring video of this type requires no analog-to-digital conversion and is

---

[10] The Adobe 98 RGB color space is similar to the NTSC color space, while the sRGB color space is similar to the PAL color space.

usually facilitated by directly transferring the data from the tape
deck to the host computer (such as with a firewire connection).
When transferring digital video this way; there will be a much
lower degree of quality loss compared to transferring video using
analog means.

DIGITAL TAPE DAMAGE

In the event that the tape has been damaged too much, rendering
some of the data inaccessible, portions of the footage will also be
damaged, or corrupted. This problem is commonly seen when
large blocks of the picture are missing (called "picture dropout"),
or when playback isn't smooth (in this case, frames are said to have
been "dropped"). Digital formats are inherently more robust than
analog ones. However, there is a point where errors can cause digital formats to suddenly break. This is entirely dependent upon the
ability of the system to access the data correctly.

FIGURE 5-9 When using digital tapes, a single tape error can impact a
sequence of frames

Certain digital formats, especially those with a high level of
compression, have a further weakness in this area, where a single data error could destroy an entire image or movie sequence.
This problem occurs because some formats work by using interframe encoding, storing the data with references to past or future

(*continues*)

> ## DIGITAL TAPE DAMAGE (*continued*)
>
> data. In this case, if some data is damaged, some or all of the data referencing the damaged data may become damaged as a result.
>
> As an analogy, imagine that you stored your reels of film in a number of locked vaults. If one of the keys to the vaults became damaged, you wouldn't be able to access any of the film within that vault. It's important to remember that just because something is stored digitally, it isn't impervious to physical damage.

The process isn't exactly the same as copying a set of digital images from one disk to another, however. Digital video is always transferred in real time, and thus, any read errors can't be corrected by attempting to re-read the data from the tape, which is why some errors may be introduced during capture. However, this disadvantage is the only real weakness of digital video capture, and in general, very high-quality transfers can be achieved. In the event that the errors are significant, problems may be corrected by redigitizing the tape (assuming the tape itself is not damaged).

5.6.2 Timecode

Video timecode is often used to determine the parts of a video tape that have to be captured. For example, a video tape may contain 90 minutes of footage, but only 2 minutes are actually needed. In this case, the capture system might allow for the capture of video starting at a timecode of 01:00:00:00 (the "in point") and ending at 01:02:00:00 (the "out point").

To enable video footage to be referenced correctly later on, it's often desirable to capture this timecode information along with the image content for every frame. Capturing this information is usually done by using a simple cable between the capture system and the VCR, but the information somehow must be tied with the image data. Certain digital file formats, such as MXF, allow time-code to be embedded within the file, but for less-sophisticated formats, a common method is to convert the timecode to a frame number, as covered in Chapter 6. Even for systems that have no capability for capturing timecode, the frame-numbering method can be used to retrospectively attach timecode to captured footage by renumbering the data.

In some cases, it may be necessary to include additional information, such as the tape reel number or the date of shooting.

5.6.3 Frames versus Fields

One stumbling block in video acquisition is that many standard definition video formats are interlaced, which means that each frame of video actually consists of two interlaced fields. Typically, each field is recorded with a slight delay in between. This means that a frame of a fast-moving object might be at a slightly different position on each field of a frame, and that visually, the object will appear to be shifted horizontally on alternate lines (which can look similar to aliasing

PROGRESSIVE SCAN

Many modern video cameras (especially HD cameras) have the capability to capture video in a "progressive scan" mode. Rather than record two separate fields for each frame, a single whole frame is recorded. This is a preferable capture method for digital imaging as it eliminates the need to later de-interlace them. Progressive scan video formats are often denoted with a "p" following the frame rate, such as "24p" (interlaced formats are followed with an "i", such as "50i". It is also worth noting that interlaced formats don't necessarily have interlacing—for example, a set of (progressive) digital stills can be output to a 50i video format, simply dividing each frame into two fields. Effectively, each frame is identical to a 25p equivalent; it's just stored in a different way.

artifacts). If the final output is a video format anyway, this doesn't necessarily matter (because it would be split back into fields anyway). But often, especially when mastering to film or other formats, it's desirable to remove the interlacing motion artifacts on each frame. The methods for doing this are covered in Chapter 9.

5.7 ACQUISITION FROM PHOTOGRAPHIC SOURCES

At present, an undeveloped piece of film can't be digitized. For this reason, the initial step in the digital intermediate chain is to develop the photographic material. This is an inherently chemical process and should be done as soon after exposure as possible, to prevent the risk of "fogging" or otherwise spoiling the film.

Once the film has been processed, the bulk of image acquisition involves using specialized film scanners to digitize reels of film, creating a series of stills that correspond to each frame on a reel. Depending upon the particular digital intermediate pipeline you're using, you may wish to scan everything that has been shot as soon as the negative is developed, or (if the film has already been completed in a chemical lab environment) to scan a theatrical release print (e.g., for transfer to video or digital master). A common method at the moment is to scan "master negative reels," which are reels that comprise only the selected takes that are to be used in the final edit.

5.7.1 Film Scanners

Regardless of the paradigm, the process of digitizing film is the same. The basic methodology of a scanning process is that a reel of film is loaded onto the film scanner (in a way similar to using a projector or an ultrasonic cleaner).[11] The film is scanned by illuminating the surface, usually with a very intense light source (such as a metal halide lamp). The light is then measured in terms of transmittance (i.e., how much light passes through to the other side),

---

[11] In most cases, it's advisable to previously clean the film with a dedicated film cleaner, therefore ensuring that the reel is as free from defects as possible.

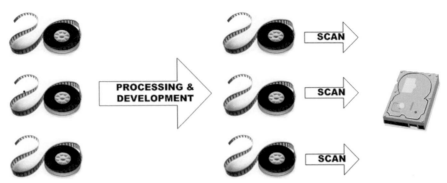

FIGURE 5-10 Film material must be developed and then scanned before it can be used in a digital intermediate process

typically a line at a time by a trilinear CCD array (a single line of photosensitive CCD elements for each channel of red, green, and blue light) or by some other method, depending upon the scanner configuration. Each point measured, or sampled, along the line corresponds to a single pixel in the image, with separate measurements for the red, green, and blue light. Motors in the scanner advance the film to the next line, and the process is repeated. Finally, when the entire frame has been scanned, the image is saved, and the scanner advances to the next frame. It can take anywhere between 4 and 320 seconds to scan a foot (i.e., 16 frames) of film, depending upon the resolution and type of scanner.[12] It is interesting to note that the maximum color precision (or bit depth) of the scans doesn't affect the scanning time at all but is instead dependent upon the sensitivity of the scanner.

Most high-end film scanners are made to exceptionally high optical standards and don't introduce any significant artifacts, such as noise. In addition, scanners don't capture motion; they merely record a sequence of stills. The distinction is important because it means that they don't introduce (or remove) any additional temporal artifacts (such as motion blur) that weren't originally recorded. However, spatial and chromatic artifacts may still be introduced as a result of the analog-to-digital conversion. If the sensitivity of the scanner to color

---

[12] Not including the time to load the film and set up the scanner's parameters.

or if the scanned pixel resolution is too low for the type of film, artifacts such as banding or aliasing may occur.

With current systems, the color information contained on a frame of film is higher than can be captured by most scanners. Most film scanners capture 10-bit (linear or nonlinear) Cineon or DPX files (see the sidebar, "Cineon/DPX Images," later in this chapter). Ideally, nonlinear log (or logarithmic) files are preferable because they provide a better representation of film color space. If the color-correction, conforming, and finishing systems aren't designed to handle log files, it may be better to scan to linear color space files, avoiding problems later on. Even with log files, it isn't possible to capture the entire dynamic range of film with most image formats.

Either way, the scanner process should be set up to maximize the contrast range of the images captured, so that the brightest point on the film (i.e., the white point) is set to a value just under the maximum brightness value of the file, and the darkest point on the image (i.e., the black point) is just above a value of pure black. Note that values that are outside the picture area (and therefore irrelevant) can safely be ignored. Maximizing the images' color ranges ensures that no clipping or crushing of colors will occur and affords the maximum possible flexibility and quality levels later on in the process. Most scanners have this capability, and settings can usually be made on a shot-by-shot basis.

The usual work flow for the scanner operator, having loaded the film onto the scanner, is to create black-and-white point settings for each shot on the film, while playing through the reel at high speed. (These point settings are typically stored as a small "grading list" that can then be saved if needed later—e.g., for rescans. Most scanners are able to display the film on a monitor at a faster rate than the time required to digitize the film to data files.) While it's possible to set these levels visually (in a properly calibrated environment and with a highly experienced operator, at least), it's preferable to use more objective means to determine these settings. The most common method is to use a vectorscope, which can measure the intensity of the video signal generated by the scanner and match the peak white level to the white point of the output image (and do the same for the black point). Some scanners provide this

FIGURE 5-11 Filmlight's Northlight scanner is able to calculate the scanning parameters by analyzing the film

information automatically, by taking density readings across an image.

Once the levels have been set, the scanner returns to the start of the reel and digitizes each frame, applying the point settings, typically generating a series of digital images to a local disk drive. With certain scanners, such as Filmlight's Northlight scanner (www.filmlight. ltd.uk), shots don't have to be set up this way. Instead, such scanners employ an "unattended scanning" paradigm, which means that once the film is put onto the scanner, the scanner identifies the base density of the film (either by matching stock presets from the key numbers or by taking a reading in between frames), calibrates itself, and digitizes the film without having to set up grading parameters for each shot. This capability is ideal because it guarantees that the film is captured quickly, with the maximum possible color range for the film stock. This system may fail, however, when scanning a reel made up of different film stocks spliced together.[13]

---

[13] Another interesting feature of the Northlight scanner is that the film is scanned horizontally rather than vertically. Combined with a slightly downward air pressure, this feature supposedly reduces the amount of dust on the film during the scanning process.

5.7.2 Scan Dimensions

Unlike video, there is no perfect translation between the dimensions of photographic film and digital images. Photographic grains are randomly shaped and randomly arranged, unlike the precisely structured video image. It is therefore reasonable to suggest that

CINEON/DPX IMAGES

Cineon and DPX files are currently the most popular formats in the digital intermediate environment. The two formats are almost identical (i.e., the information they contain is exactly the same, they're just structured slightly differently); the Cineon format is a slight modification of the Digital Moving Picture Exchange (DPX), SMPTE-specified format.[14]

Cineon and DPX files are typically 8 bits or 10 bits per channel (the latter is more common) of three-channel (RGB) data, which can be encoded as either linear or nonlinear RGB and are uncompressed. The linear color space has applications for storing video, while the nonlinear color space is more suitable for representing film. This duality makes the two formats very useful to a digital intermediate environment, which frequently switches between film and video sources. The nonlinear color space is designed to match the characteristics of photographic film by modeling transmission density as the brightness component of each channel. Photographic film doesn't respond in a linear way to light; it responds logarithmically, so that more of a brightness (or contrast) range is at the extremes (blacks or whites) of a negative. Images saved in this logarithmic (or log) color space are a much more accurate representation of the film image they were digitized from (i.e., having a higher dynamic range); however, they won't display properly on a linear device, such as a computer monitor. To compensate for this, applications working with log Cineon or DPX files must employ special lookup tables (or LUTs) to alter the way the images are displayed on a monitor (but without actually affecting the data).

---

[14] SMPTE is the abbreviation for the Society of Motion Picture and Television Engineers.

HDR IMAGES

High dynamic range (HDR) images can overcome many of the problems of moving between different color spaces. HDR images encompass a very large and very precise color space (some implementations are large enough to include every useful color space that exists) and utilize tone-mapping functions to correctly translate between different display devices. At the present time, the digital intermediate pipeline is concerned only with the color spaces of photographic film, of the Cineon/DPX image format, and of the RGB model (for computer monitors), but as this expands to include more applications, HDR images and tone mapping will play a more important role. HDR images may also preclude the need to perform a "one-light" grading pass on scanned film, because the format has sufficient precision to make this stage redundant, which will reduce the scanning time somewhat. (HDR images are discussed in Chapter 13.)

scanned images can be any resolution. It can also be suggested that the ideal image resolution should be as high as possible, while remaining practical to work with (i.e., not taking too long to process, copy, or display). Other considerations include the possibility that the film scanner color-correction and conforming system may be limited to working with images of a specific or optimum size.

Of the several accepted standards, the most common is 2k and 4k resolution for 35mm negatives. This value refers to the number of pixels along the horizontal edge. A typical, full frame of a 35mm negative scans at 2048 pixels (the width) by 1556 pixels (the height), making it a 2k image (i.e., having approximately 2000 pixels along the width). A 4k image is 4096 by 3112 pixels in size (resulting in a file size that is four times larger for each frame). Different specifications apply to different formats (e.g., when you want to scan only the Academy area). These specifications are listed in the Appendix.

5.7.3   Nyquist Frequency

The Nyquist frequency (also called the "Shannon sampling frequency") is a simple mathematical equation used to determine the amount of information required to successfully reproduce a signal (i.e., an analog source). It is used to determine the point where all the relevant information is captured (and so recording any more will have no benefit).

This equation—Nyquist frequency = 1 / (2 × sampling interval)—can be used when digitizing an image to determine the maximum useful resolution, using a measurement of the resolving power of the image. For example, for a typical 35mm negative, the resolving power is around 150 lines per millimeter.[15] The Nyquist frequency, in this case, is equivalent to the resolving power (because no more information can be successfully recorded beyond this amount). Putting this value into the equation gives us a sampling interval of 0.0033, meaning that a pixel must be sampled every 0.0033mm (or that there must be 300 pixels for each millimeter of film).[16] In practical terms, given that the height of a full frame of 35mm negative is 18.67mm, a completely accurate representation of a frame of 35mm film requires approximately 5600 lines of resolution. Assuming the resolving power of film is the same horizontally as it is vertically, our desired image size is approximately 5600 × 7500 pixels per frame, which is required to completely capture all of the

---

MEGAPIXELS

A trend in digital camera manufacture is to talk about "megapixels," which is a somewhat arbitrary measurement and refers to the total number (in millions) of pixels in an image. To calculate image size in megapixels, multiply the width of the image by its height, and then divide by one million. A 2k image is thus equivalent to a 3.2 megapixel image, and a 4k image is 12.7 megapixels.

---

[15] This result will vary, depending on the type of film stock. Also, different film stocks have different resolving powers, depending upon factors such as exposure.
[16] A quicker way to get this result is to simply double the resolving power.

detail in a frame of film. At 10 bits per channel, it would make each frame about 150MB.

Unfortunately, current technology simply cannot store or process files that large in a practical manner. However, this limit is theoretical; in reality the difference in quality between an image that large and a 4k image, for example, may be negligible. It is questionable whether that much detail really can be perceived, given factors such as film grain; and in any case, the ultimate question is whether an audience in a cinema is able to perceive any difference. The bottom line, at the moment at least, is to aim to try to capture as high a resolution as possible.

5.7.4 Punch Holes

Many scanner systems require that each reel of film includes a "punch hole" (or a marker frame at the beginning of each reel). The easiest way to make a punch hole is to literally punch out a hole in the negative at the beginning of the reel (before any useful images!). The reason for doing this is to provide an arbitrary sync point that will allow each frame of data to be matched back to a specific frame on the reel. In simple terms, each frame scanned is given a frame number, so

ENHANCED 2K

In many cases, film scanners can scan images that are much larger than is practical to work with. For instance, many scanners can scan 4k images, but the constraints of the rest of the system might require images no larger than 2k. In this situation, it may seem more efficient to scan at 2k and keep everything at that resolution. However, tests have shown that the quality improves when the film is instead scanned at 4k and resampled down to 2k. Provided that the appropriate resampling method is used, the so-called "enhanced 2k" footage appears almost as sharp as 4k footage and is a vast improvement over a regular 2k scan.

that the punch hole is frame 0, and every frame after goes up by one. For example, the thirty-first frame after the punch hole is simply frame 31.

SCAN EDLS

Lengthy reels of film, especially those with many shots, can require a long time to set up, even before anything is scanned. One of the reasons for the prolonged setup time is that the scanner operator has to go through the entire reel first, marking cut points to divide each shot. One way to speed up this process is through the use of a scan edit decision list (EDL), which essentially is a list of cut points for every shot on the reel. Using scan EDLs isn't usually an option when the film has just been developed, but in productions where each reel of film has been telecined already, scan EDLs may be available and can reduce the length of time required to scan each reel. EDLs come in many different flavors and are discussed in Chapter 7.

5.7.5 Splices

When scanning film, you may encounter a problem if the reel contains splices. When a film splice runs through certain scanners, it can cause the frame to "bounce," meaning that the image shifts vertically. This problem is less likely to happen with pin-registered scanners. Even when using scanners that are not pin-registered, the problem of bounce can be corrected digitally, but doing so is usually an operator-controlled procedure (rather than an automatic one) and as such can add to the cost and duration of the project. Perception of bounce is much greater on monitors than on projected images; therefore, bouncing shots may not be noticeable on cinema releases.

Additionally, the materials used to make a splice may intrude into the image area, damaging the image and requiring its restoration. For all of these reasons, it is preferable for productions to minimize the number of splices made to film material intended for scanning.

5.7.6 Datacines

In addition to film scanners, telecines are used to convert film reels to other media (typically to video). Telecines, particularly older machines, may perform an analog-to-analog conversion rather than an analog-to-digital one and work in real time. Film scanners traditionally differ from telecines in a number of ways. An important advantage of using scanners is that they have the capability to output to a digital format. On the other hand, telecines traditionally enable color grading and the viewing of film material in real time. However, in recent years, the differences between the two have become more subtle. Some telecines, such as Thomson's Spirit 4K (www.thomsongrassvalley.com), can directly output high-quality data and are referred to as "datacines," whereas some scanners provide rudimentary color-grading and display options. At the present time, the main difference between scanners and telecines seems to be that telecines are operated by experienced colorists, while scanners operate almost automatically.

Color grading performed at the acquisition stage may have less of a destructive effect on the quality of the images because most high-

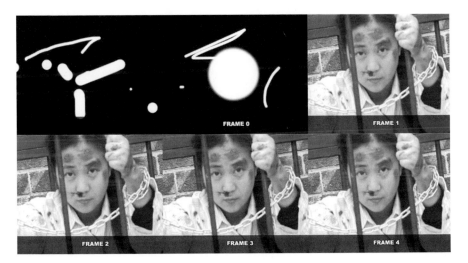

FIGURE 5-12 Film frames are generally counted beginning with the first frame that follows a punch hole frame

end scanners perform color grading prior to actually capturing the image, effectively recalibrating the scan parameters to maximize the captured dynamic range within the new color parameters. In fact, this paradigm is a perfectly viable one for the digital intermediate pipeline. Even so, most pipelines prefer to leave color correction to a later stage because doing so allows more flexibility and makes it possible to view changes in a more useful context, with all the material available at the same time.

Telecines are routinely used by the film industry to allow the viewing of rushes (or dailies) of film that has just been developed,

FIGURE 5-13   Thomson's Spirit 4K can scan film as well as telecine it

although this practice eventually may be replaced by the advent of digital dailies.

5.7.7 Digital Dailies

One of the advantages of digital media is that it can be viewed simultaneously from a number of places over a great distance. When shooting film, filmmakers typically send the day's filmed material to be developed and then printed or telecined, or both (depending on their preference and the budget). The developed negative is stored, and the filmmakers watch the telecine or print to assess their work. However, as more filmmakers turn to the digital intermediate pipeline, the idea of digital dailies may become more attractive. As soon as the film negative is developed, it can be sent to the digital intermediate facility to be scanned. The scanned data can then be made available for viewing and copying. The negative can be stored safely (and theoretically is never needed again), and the data can be archived for post-production. The copies can be manipulated (e.g., compressed or encrypted) in many ways that don't affect the original data, and they can be transmitted across the Internet, providing them to filmmakers, editors, and any number of people who may require an instant copy.

THE DEATH OF FILM?

Ever since the boom of the digital image industry in the early 1990s, people have been wildly proclaiming an end to celluloid. However, these claims seem to be unfounded, at least for the time being. While it's true that sales of consumer photographic film have fallen in recent years (reflecting the widespread use of digital imaging devices), sales of film for the motion picture industry haven't fallen.

It is feasible that technology eventually will reach a point where digital imaging becomes technically superior to film in every

(continues)

THE DEATH OF FILM? *(continued)*

way, but that point is still a long way off. In the immediate future, it's likely that celluloid will still be used on the set as a general purpose recording device, although digital capture devices may be preferable for certain types of shots, such as effects shots. At the present time, photographic film produces subjectively better imagery than its digital counterparts. The current thrust of technology is to try to maintain the quality recorded on film from the point of digitization onward. In the motion picture industry at least, nothing suggests that film, as a shooting format, is due to be retired any time soon. Furthermore, photographic film is more reliable—experienced filmmakers know what is and what isn't possible to do with film and are highly aware of the necessary precautions that must be taken when working with film. In the time-pressured environment of the set, producers cannot afford to take unnecessary risks, such as having a digital-imaging device fail for any number of reasons. In fact, when digital counterparts fail within the digital intermediate pipeline, producers are often relieved that they can fall back on the camera negative or source video tapes. In these early stages of digital film, a reel of film certainly has a greater lifespan than the latest digital storage device. A properly stored negative will last longer than a hard disk, because film is highly standardized as compared to computer components. Some computer hardware that is only a few years old already is incompatible with new systems. The same cannot be said for film, which relies on the correct positioning of the images, a constant frame rate, the size and shape of the perforations, and little else.

Digital photography is much more appropriate with many applications than chemical photography. A great cost and speed advantage is associated with digital cameras as opposed to film cameras, particularly if the images are ultimately used for websites, emails, or small prints. In these cases, there is absolutely no reason to go through the time-consuming (and

(continues)

THE DEATH OF FILM? *(continued)*

relatively expensive) processes of chemical development, printing, and the scanning of the negative, when you ultimately end up with a picture that is marginally different from a digital equivalent. But the motion picture industry is highly specialized, and it requires a massive volume of imagery be recorded over a short, intense time frame. The motion picture process benefits greatly from having the luxury of a post-production phase, so it's here that the digital advantages come into effect. Finally, as digital cameras get better and cheaper, so will film scanners; thus it may become feasible to shoot on larger formats than 35mm, resulting in a corresponding increase in overall quality. So if you shoot on film, you'll still be able to take advantage of the improvements in technology for many years to come.

In any case, the digital film process eventually will probably stop trying to emulate the look of photographic film and instead explore an exciting new range of possibilities now available, in exactly the same way that some digital photographers are doing with still photography. When that happens, lots of people will just prefer the methodology, techniques, and output that photographic film provides. And more than this, lots of people will use both.

Digital dailies aren't presently a popular option, mainly because the speed of the technology is much slower than a traditional telecine process, and the space requirements for storing a high volume of scanned film (especially when most of it will never be used) are too large to be practical. (There is certainly a positive element to limiting the number of people who have access to production material as well). However, as the technology becomes faster, the need for digital dailies will increase. Digital dailies may even be generated using more automation to produce footage that is displayed by a single piece of equipment, and may also include the means to apply some basic color grading to the footage.

5.7.8   Scanner Gauges

Although 35mm film is by far the most common gauge of film that is scanned, some film scanners accept a variety of other gauges, such as 16mm or 70mm. In addition, many scanners can capture specific regions of each frame, such as the "Academy aperture" region (which has a 1.37 aspect ratio). Capturing film of different gauges normally involves replacing the scanner gate to allow the different size of film to run smoothly through the machinery. It may also be necessary to change scanning parameters, such as the scanned image dimensions, to accommodate differences between formats.

ORIGINAL FILM NEGATIVES

A scanner normally works just as well using a film positive (or print) as a negative. However, the process of making a print from a negative, and then a negative from the print, and so on, results in generation loss for each successive copy. Therefore, it's always advisable to scan the original negative that was shot on the set. Even when a copy might look better (e.g., when it has been processed and color-timed in a lab), it's still going to be of a lower quality than the original. Finally, because the original negative can be damaged just as easily during the scanning process as during the duplication procedure, it might be advisable to duplicate the negative after it has been scanned. Ultimately though, the possibility of damaging the negative depends on whether the scanning facility takes appropriate precautions to protect original materials (and fortunately, most of them do).

5.7.9   Anamorphic Film

Anamorphic images have a ratio of 2.35 to 1, which is much wider than the 1.33 to 1 ratio of full-aperture 35mm film. Rather than waste film area, anamorphic images use a special lens to "squeeze" the picture horizontally to make it fit much more comfortably on the film area. When projected, the film is "unsqueezed" to give it the proper dimensions.

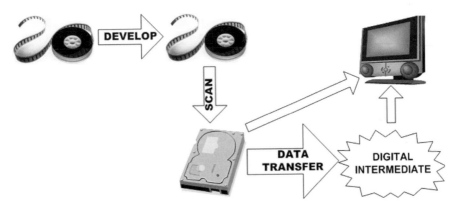

FIGURE 5-14   The digital dailies paradigm allows film to be scanned for viewing and simultaneously acquired into the digital intermediate pipeline for later use

In the digital intermediate pipeline, anamorphic images can either be unsqueezed at the time of scanning and then saved as images with a wide aspect ratio, or be saved as narrower, squeezed images (with a wide pixel aspect ratio). The latter method has the advantage of saving disk space (and removing the need to resqueeze the images if out-

HANDLING FILM MORE THAN ONCE

One much-touted advantage of the digital intermediate process is that it requires a reel of original negative be handled only once. After development, the negative only has to be loaded onto the film scanner, scanned, and then stored away—it need not be handled again and thus isn't subject to potential damage. That's the theory. While this is the case for the majority of film that is scanned, there are a variety of situations that require the film be removed from storage and go through the scanning process again. Data corruption, scanner faults, missing frames, and a myriad of other problems can occur and necessitate the film being rescanned. Although there is not usually an impact on the image quality if a reel is rescanned (particularly with pin-registered scanners, and those that allow the calibration settings to be saved), it is worth recognizing that even after a reel has been scanned, it may be needed again.

putting back to film) but requires that each device used to view the images (e.g., the conforming and color-correction systems) be able to automatically unsqueeze the images for display purposes. However, for images that have been squeezed in this way , the effective horizontal resolution (and by extension, the quality level) is halved compared to the vertical resolution. Superior quality images may be obtained by unsqueezing the images optically at the scanning stage (or by scanning twice the number of pixels horizontally than normal) and saving the images with square pixels.

5.7.10 Pin Registration

Pin registration ensures accurate positioning of each frame of film. Essentially, precisely positioned pins or "teeth" position film using the perforations along its edge, in the same way that a film is loaded into a camera. Using pin registration is necessary for two reasons. First, it reduces the possibility of the images "weaving" (i.e., moving up and down or from side to side in the frame) when played back in a sequence.[17] Second, if any frames have to be rescanned at a later date, they're more likely to match the originals exactly in terms of positioning and can therefore transparently replace the original scans. These effects become more pronounced at higher image resolutions.

The disadvantage of using pin registration is that it somewhat increases the scanning time because pin-registered scanners have to pause between each frame to ensure the frame's correct positioning, whereas those scanners that aren't pin-registered can continuously run the film over the scanning laser without stopping.

For nonpin-registered scanners (which includes most telecines), it's possible to compensate for the lack of pin registration by using a digital process known as "motion stabilization" (or image stabilization), which is covered in Chapter 9. However, having to run this process on every scanned frame may be considered an extravagant waste of computer resources (and probably justifies the additional cost of a pin-registered scanner).

---

[17] Unless, of course, the film was weaving during shooting.

FORWARD PLANNING

Because the scanning process can be time consuming, several things can be done concurrently to save time later. For example, many color-correction systems use proxy images (or "proxies") that are simply downsized copies of the scanned frames. Because it's (usually) quicker to resample a file than to scan it as each frame is being scanned, the previous scan can be copied and resized. That way, by the time the scan is completed, a set of proxies is also saved alongside it. Beware, this process can actually impair the performance of faster scanners, because destination disks are being accessed more often, which can cause the scanner to stall.

Also, many conforming systems require that the data be assigned specific frame numbers. Normally, the film scanner saves the frames (starting with the punch hole) from 0 and then just increments the count for each frame. After that scanning, all the frames can be renumbered appropriately. To save time (and possibly prevent confusion later), some film scanners enable you to specify the numbering system to be used, which requires no extra time and has no impact on performance.

Finally, when presented with a high volume of film to be scanned all at once, it's worth working out the order in which the reels will be needed. For instance, complex sequences may have to be conformed sooner if the filmmakers prefer working with particular sections of the film first, to define or experiment with specific "looks" during the color-correction process.

5.7.11 Key Numbers and Timecodes

A useful component of motion picture film is the key numbers. Every few frames of film negative manufactured is pre-exposed with a unique serial number, so that every frame can be independently referenced. These numbers were originally introduced to allow the use of cut lists, which specifically refer to individual or ranges of frames. The cut lists were useful because they enabled film editors to cut together sequences from prints of negatives (making it possible to avoid handling the original negative and subjecting it to possible damage) and then easily match each frame in the cut back to the corresponding negative frame.

More recently, a machine-readable code (or "bar code") is included alongside each number. Some film scanners incorporate a key number reader that reads the bar code as the film is scanned and then embeds the corresponding number into the image file. This procedure is necessary for productions where the data will be conformed digitally, using a key-numbered cut list (see Chapter 7 for a discussion of conforming projects using key numbers).

Similar to key numbers is the idea of timecodes. Most video sources contain a timecode track that makes it possible to reference a particular frame. In some cases, it's possible to record timecode information onto film for the same purpose. While timecodes aren't unique like key numbers (i.e., two reels of film might contain the same timecodes but never the same key numbers), they're useful for synchronizing film with other devices. For instance, when filming a music promotion, the timecodes might be linked to the soundtrack, so that the audio can be quickly matched to the picture. Sometimes this linking is performed with a "timecode slate" or a clapperboard containing timecodes, which is filmed at the beginning of each take, or alternatively, the timecode information can be embedded on the outside edge of the film in a machine-readable format. When the latter method is used, film scanners equipped with a timecode reader embed the timecode information into the scanned image.

DIGITAL CAMERAS AND SCANNERS

Digital cameras, camcorders, and image scanners are all analog-to-digital devices. They each take an analog source (i.e., with cameras, the source is reflected light from a scene) and convert it to a digital format. However, many of these devices try to "improve" picture quality by applying a set of post-processing filters on the digitized images. In many cases, these filters can be

(continues)

DIGITAL CAMERAS AND SCANNERS (*continued*)

beneficial—for instance, when compensating for CCD defects within the device. All too often however, the device automatically applies digital sharpening and color-correction filters, which degrade the image. When using such a device, be sure to disable color grading or sharpening that can be done later. Some newer digital cameras provide access to the "raw" data of the camera, providing the image information in the form it was received from the CCD array and allowing you to apply the filters. This also has the effect of acquiring images that are at the maximum possible quality level, provided all the software can correctly interpret the file.

However, in some cases (especially on high-end cameras and scanners), devices utilize optical filters that don't degrade the image quality at all but just alter the way the information is captured prior to digitization (which is kind of like positioning actors where you want them in the first place, rather than positioning them later by editing the images). For example, applying a "one-light" grade to film on certain film scanners provides a quality gain in the captured data, with no loss of information.

IT DOESN'T LOOK RIGHT!

Acquiring media for use in the digital intermediate pipeline has something of a pitfall, which is that you intuitively expect a properly captured, accurate representation of the source media to look as good as it should. That is, you naturally assume that a scanned reel of film, when viewed on a monitor, should look equally as good as (if not better than) a projected print of the same film. However, this assumption isn't always correct, especially with scanned film. The aim of the acquisition stage isn't necessarily to get the best-looking scanned data of a particular reel of film; it's to ensure that the maximum level of quality is available to be used later down the line. Correctly scanned film,

(*continues*)

IT DOESN'T LOOK RIGHT! (*continued*)

even when perfectly exposed, might look flat and colorless. This is because the colors may have been optimized to accommodate as wide a contrast ratio or dynamic range as possible, so that there are a greater number of possibilities for color grading and the other phases, without having to compromise image quality. It may also be that a lookup table must first be applied to the data so it can be correctly displayed on a monitor. In some pipelines, until this color-correction phase begins, you may not even be able to see the potential output of the images in terms of color. Some facilities, on the other hand, such as those offering digital dailies services, may be able to generate two types of images: one for viewing purposes and one for processing purposes (although both images would come from the same source data).

5.8 SUMMARY

Before any material can be used in the digital intermediate environment, it must first be ingested. With digital source material, this ingestion may be as simple as transferring the source data by copying files between devices.

With analog material, such as film and video, analog-to-digital conversion, a largely mathematical process, must be used. Film material may be digitized using a digital film scanner, or a suitably equipped telecine, while video sources require a video capture device. In general, analog-to-digital conversion should be performed at the highest quality possible, working from original material whenever feasible, capturing as much useful information as practicable, to benefit later stages in the pipeline.

In theory, data transfer can occur at much higher speeds than video or film, but in practice, data transfer can be a very slow process. For this reason, a balance must be achieved between image quality and file-size considerations, which in turn impact the pipeline's performance and relative cost.

The image quality of acquired footage depends on a number of factors, such as the color space, the precision, and the resolution, and there are methods for measuring each factor throughout the pipeline. The digital acquisition process typically generates a large volume of data, and the organization of this data is the subject of the next chapter

6

ASSET MANAGEMENT

6.1 DATA IS VOLATILE

Imagine you are carrying a reel of film to a vault when all of a sudden, it spontaneously combusts, bursting into flames and leaves behind a pile of ash. Imagine you are watching a video, and some of the frames suddenly are missing or duplicated or completely randomized.

Although these events sound far-fetched, the equivalent situations can (and do) happen frequently in the digital realm. Data gets moved and reorganized far more than video footage or reels of film. Data is easily duplicated and just as easily deleted, permanently lost at the click of a button. Even limited experience with computers can show how easy it is for things to go wrong. A system crash might destroy the last thing you were working on; a hardware failure could prevent access to entire reels of film.

In the typical digital intermediate pipeline, because each frame corresponds to a single digital file, a large number of files must be managed.

New data is generated constantly, by the acquisition of new source material, from making changes to edits, and through conforming and grading frames produced for output processes. Files can be reordered within a sequence or relocated into another sequence. They might have to be replaced with new or updated versions. More often than not, data storage space is limited, and redundant images must be removed to save space.

Accidents can happen, and managing data successfully is a result of considerable planning, organization, and establishing and enforcing conventions (which inevitably change between projects). Successful data management requires knowledge of the processes behind every other step in the pipeline, the ability to prioritize and make last-minute changes, as well as having an awareness of the limitations of each system used.

6.2 COMPUTER SYSTEMS

The digital intermediate process uses any number of computer systems to process data. Each computer system comprises a number of different components, each of which fulfills a different function. Each component contributes to the system's overall speed, although the amount of data that can be moved at one time between components (i.e., the system bandwidth) is also a crucial factor.

6.2.1 Processors

Computers are simply glorified number crunchers, processing vast amounts of data using simple, repetitive mathematics, or long, complex calculations. The speed at which a computer can perform calculations depends on a number of factors, most notably the "clock speed" of the central processing unit (CPU), typically measured in millions of cycles per seconds (MHz) or millions of instructions per second (MIPS). Generally, the higher the clock speed, the faster the system's processing capability.

Other factors are also in play. For example, a single computer can contain multiple processors, each of which can process an individual set of calculations concurrently, multiplying the system's overall speed.[1] Many modern CPUs use a layered caching mechanism, which stores solutions to recent calculations for quick retrieval, eliminating the need to recalculate complex equations; the caching mechanisms can vastly accelerate the system's processing capability.

Newer systems may also have a graphical processing unit (GPU), which can accelerate image-manipulation processes, such as resizing or repositioning images or performing color-grading tasks. While using the GPU can be quicker than using the CPU to perform the same calculations (or it can free the CPU to perform other tasks), the results it produces may differ among systems.

6.2.2 Temporary Data Storage

Computers need access to a data store, for example, to load an image for modification or display. In many cases, the data stored isn't permanently needed and is used only for processing purposes. Most computers have a fast random access memory (RAM) store for this purpose, and the contents of the store are cleared each time the computer is switched off. Higher amounts of RAM make it possible to quickly process larger images or a larger number of images.

In the digital intermediate pipeline, much of the data transfer involves moving data between the temporary data store for processing and a permanent data store for copying and saving material.

6.2.3 Permanent Data Storage

All data used during a digital intermediate pipeline, whether scanned images, edit decision lists, project files, even image manipulation software, has to be stored somewhere permanently. On a typical computer system, such as a PC in an office, data is stored on a hard drive, a magnetic storage device. Take, for example, a spreadsheet. The software used to create the spreadsheet is stored on the

---

[1] This is not always the case because the ability of the system to efficiently use multiple processes will also depend upon the software.

PC's hard disk and accessed from there whenever the user needs to run it (or "execute" it). The spreadsheet that is created is also stored on the hard drive as an individual file. It might then be transported (e.g., emailed), converted, or output to another format (e.g., converted to a file readable in a different application or a file printed on paper), or it might be copied to another device (e.g., a floppy disk or CD-ROM). There might be one copy of the spreadsheet or several. The spreadsheet might be in several versions, exist in different formats, and reside on several different devices in several different locations. The same is true for any type of computer data. Simply copying data between different digital storage devices doesn't alter the content of the data. Copying a file from one hard drive to another results in identical files being stored in two places at the same time.

Permanent data storage isn't an essential component of a computer system and may be supplied as an external device, such as on a network. For example, computer used just to perform signal-processing (for example, to convert between video standards) can be set up to receive data, process it in RAM, and output the result to another system, without having to store the data internally.

6.2.4 Communication

Many computer systems can communicate with other systems. A number of different technologies can do so—technologies from cable-based interfaces such as RS-422, USB, Firewire, Ethernet, HIPPI, fiber-channel, and GSN to wireless methods such as infrared, Bluetooth, and 802.11 (Wi-Fi). Each varies in reliability and bandwidth. Communication between systems is made by transmitting data across various channels. For example, an image file can be sent from a scanner to a storage system via a GSN cable, or configuration instructions can be sent from one system to another using infra-red beams.

6.2.5 Input and Feedback

Computer systems typically comprise a method for inputting data and providing feedback about the operations performed on them.

Input methods include keyboards, mice, graphics tablets, joysticks, touch screens, and trackballs, while feedback can be provided through attached monitors, printers, or even simple indicator lights. Differences between input methods vary mostly by convenience or personal preference. The expense of feedback mechanisms usually increases with greater accuracy in reproduction. For example, many people prefer to use an elaborate input system, comprising trackballs and switches, to perform color grading, although the same functions can largely be performed using a mouse and keyboard. A higher-quality monitor may provide more accurate feedback in terms of resolution and color when working with digital images, although it inevitably is more expensive than a lower-quality one.

6.2.6 Operating Systems

The operating system (OS) is the software that controls fundamental aspects of the computer, such as data organization, communications with different hardware components, and software execution. At present, the main operating systems (which are also referred to as "platforms") used by most digital intermediate facilities are UNIX, Linux, Windows, and Macintosh. Each has its strengths and weaknesses in terms of data storage and the availability and reliability of compatible hardware and software components. Furthermore, copying data between two different systems can have undesired side effects. For instance, while Windows allows filenames to contain spaces (e.g., my file), files named this way can cause problems on UNIX systems (which prefer my_file). Similarly, Windows prefers files to be named with an extension after each filename to reflect the file type (e.g., a JPEG file being named my file.jpg), whereas other operating systems don't use this convention.[2]

---

[2] This book doesn't assume the use of a particular OS, but instead offers strategies that can be used on any of them (e.g., recommending that files be named without spaces and filenames always include an extension). This convention also reduces the problems faced when transferring data between different systems.

6.3   FILES AND FOLDERS

A data file is a self-contained unit of information. Typically, each file is a separate document, such as a spreadsheet or digital image. Each file can be accessed and manipulated independently from the others. For example, in a sequence of images that make up a shot, each frame can be stored as a separate file and can be copied, modified, and deleted without affecting the others.

Having a load of files pooled together isn't a very good system of organization, and so the use of folders becomes important. Folders (also called "directories") are containers for files, which can be used to create different categories for files. In addition, folders can be "nested," meaning that you can have folders within folders.

There is a caveat, however: each file (within a folder) must be given a unique filename. You can't have two files both called my_file.pic (even if they contain different data) in the same folder, but you can place them into separate folders.

6.3.1   File Manipulation

The majority of data management involves the manipulation of files and folders, either individually or in groups. Table 6.1 describes the common file manipulation processes. These processes can be applied manually (by interacting with the OS) or through automated, software-driven processes (such as scheduled backups). The operations can be performed "gesturally", such as by selecting files and clicking buttons with a mouse, or with typed commands, depending upon the operating system.

The processes shown in this list also apply to folders. Operations performed on a folder will (normally) also affect its contents, such that deleting a folder will delete any files or folders within that folder.

6.3.2 File Attributes

Each file may be assigned one or more file attributes by the operating system. These are digital tags that define the file in some way. For instance, the file may have a read-only attribute, meaning it can be opened and looked at (i.e., read) but the contents can't be changed (i.e., written). Most of the time, the possible attributes are determined by the host operating system. File attributes aren't standardized between operating systems, and so copying files between devices may not retain the attributes (although the content and filename may be unchanged). However, in a more controlled environment (such as a specialist digital intermediate facility), it's possible to take advantage of file attributes by generating ones that are specific to the digital intermediate process. For example, an image may be set with

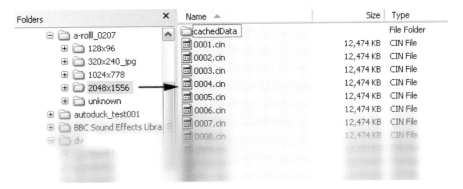

FIGURE 6-1 Folders can be used to organize files and other folders

TABLE 6-1 File Manipulation Processes

Process	Result
Copy	Creates a duplicate of the file and its contents, either with a different filename in the same folder, or with the same filename in another location.
Delete	Erases the data, removing the file (and typically relinquishing disk space).
Move	Copies the file and then deletes the original.
Rename	Changes the filename but doesn't affect the data.

attributes such as ungraded, original, or archived. Such a system would be useful for generating a list of images meeting relevant criteria (e.g., to compile a list of files that haven't yet been archived). Doing so may require a degree of computer programming however, and so a more practical solution may be to use a database-driven asset management tool, which is covered later in this chapter.

6.3.3 File Access

Accessing, or opening a file enables you to view and/or edit it with a specific program. Files can be accessed locally (e.g., when stored on the computer's hard drive) or remotely (e.g., across a network, such as a web page). In most cases, a file can be viewed simultaneously from several places (both locally and remotely). So, an image on a hard drive can be opened and looked at by someone sitting at that machine, and someone able to access the file via a network link can view the same image on their machine. However, each time a file is accessed, the performance of the host system (i.e., the system that actually stores the file) is impacted slightly. This impact becomes a problem is when there is high throughput of data on the host system.[3] The process of opening a file requires resources on the host computer (once a file has been opened, no more data is accessed). If someone is viewing a sequence of images at high speed (which requires multiple files be opened in rapid succession), and someone else views the same sequence on another machine, the playback in both cases will suffer, causing it to stutter or stall.[4]

When editing a file directly in an application (as opposed to just viewing it), the operating system or application normally locks the file. This prevents anyone else (or any other process) from accessing the file, to ensure that it isn't moved or altered outside of the

---

[3] "Denial of service attacks" on web servers exploit this technique to cause the web server to crash. The attack involves making an extremely high number of simultaneous requests for a specific file. This overloads (and crashes) the system.

[4] To a large extent, to create a performance hit, the same data doesn't have to be accessed; even accessing different data from the same disk can reduce the overall performance.

application. The downside to locking files is that if the file is due to be copied somewhere (or backed up), the copy may fail. Some applications lock files even just for viewing purposes. For instance, a real-time playback system that has loaded an entire film may lock all the required files, to prevent performance issues caused by other running processes.

6.3.4 File Caching

A common technique that computer systems use to gain faster data throughput is caching operations and files. A cache is a readily available, recent store of data. In its simplest form, a cache might hold the solution to some complex calculation. If the same calculation must be performed again (which occurs rather often in the digital realm), the system can just consult the cache for the answer, avoiding the need to recalculate it. The same process applies to files; frequently accessed files are cached, so that the next time the file is requested, it can be pulled directly from the cache, resulting in a faster turnaround. Grading systems (especially software-based ones) tend to cache modified images separately from the original ones, so that the changes can be played back as smoothly as the original.

It's important to remember that the image you see onscreen isn't necessarily an exact copy of the one that is saved to disk. If the application you're using to view files employs a caching mechanism, it may be necessary to rebuild (or refresh or flush) the cache when you're about to perform an operation that requires looking directly at the stored data (e.g., when you check a sequence prior to making a backup); otherwise, you may miss problems that are there (or conversely, see problems that aren't there).

6.3.5 File Permissions

The notion of attaching permissions to files is somewhat Orwellian and, in practice, can be both a blessing and a curse. Basically, file permissions (variously referred to as "access rights," "privileges," or "file security") determine who is able to access or modify a file.

Typically, when you log into your computer, your login (or user-name) identifies you to the computer, which in turn allows you to access certain files (or you may be denied access to others). Permissions can be beneficial; after all it's logical to reason that if you're working with a group of files for viewing purposes only, restricting your permission so you're allowed only to view those files prevents you from accidentally altering (or deleting) them. Consideration must also be given to the notion that malicious individuals, such as trespassers (or computer hackers) who lack the necessary credentials, are restricted access. The permissions-granting process can be extended somewhat, so that each user can be a member of a user group, which is assigned its own set of permissions and rules.

However, problems can arise that are caused by setting file permissions incorrectly. For example, a backup application (software programs are normally given their own access rights as well) might have unlimited read permission, so it can back up every file on the system. But when creating files, the software may be assigned different permissions. So, when restoring a previously backedup file, the original permissions may not be correctly retained, and files that were previously accessible to everyone may now be restricted to a specific group (and vice versa).

QUOTA MANAGEMENT

One option for controlling the flow of data is to utilize quota management for each user or user group. Whereas file permissions limit access to particular files or folders, quota management limits the amount of storage space available to each user or user group. When users reach their limit, they are unable to use any more space until they delete some of their other files. Judicious use of this option can help to prevent storage space being consumed by nonessential processes, but it can cause problems in practice, such as when you're trying to move data to make way for something else and that results in the quota limit being reached.

6.4 FILE FORMATS

Computer data is just a bunch of ones and zeros. To make sense of it, each file is encoded, or formatted, in a specific way. The particular method used for each file is known as the "file format." Literally thousands of different file formats, for documents, operating system files, programs, and so on, are in existence. For digital images alone, the number of different formats is in the hundreds.

The Appendix lists and compares some of the more common digital image file formats. File formats vary in a few key ways, which are discussed in the following sections.

6.4.1 Compatibility

Broadly speaking, the more popular a file format, the more applications that support it. That a particular file format is compatible with a given operating system and application is of paramount importance to the digital intermediate pipeline. While it's possible to convert between most digital image formats without any loss of information, it requires resources (e.g., the time spent to convert a sequence of frames) that might be better spent on other things.[5]

Desired file formats should be cross-platform, meaning that they should be usable regardless of which operating system they're loaded on. Each operating system normally uses an internal file format (e.g., the Windows Bitmap format on the Windows operating system). These formats tend to be widely supported by applications that run on that operating system, but problems can arise if the file must be used by an application on a different operating system.

6.4.2 Efficiency

Although many digital image formats contain image information that is common to all of them, the method used to store it might vary, to address specific uses. Thus, the disk space requirement for different

---

[5] With the exception of lossy-compressed formats, or those requiring color-space conversion, which alter the information and can lead to degradation of quality.

file formats varies. The efficiency of a particular file format can be described as its ability to encode information while minimizing another factor (most commonly disk space). In practical terms though, a more disk-space-efficient file might not be as useful as a less-efficient one if the computational costs required to decode the file are higher. For example, an image that is compressed using lossless compression is much more efficient in terms of disk space than an uncompressed file, but the uncompressed one might be faster to display (and thus more efficient in terms of speed). Certain formats are simply more efficient by restricting data. For instance, the CompuServe GIF format, popularized by the Internet, preselects a palette of 256 colors (8 bits-per-pixel) from a much larger spectrum (typically 24 bits-per-pixel), resulting in a much smaller file with the same color information (as long as no more than 256 different colors are in the original image).

6.4.3 Robustness

Files have to be able to withstand changes in imaging technology. Many image formats are designed by hardware and software manufacturers who wish to showcase a particular feature they've developed. For example, some digital camera manufacturers have designed specific image formats, such as the FlashPix format, which allows a layered image to contain a compressed JPEG image layer that can be accessed quickly for display, and a more detailed, uncompressed raw data layer. The problem is that these particular formats don't tend to be supported for long and are quickly superseded by other formats.

On the other hand, several open-source formats are available, which are kind of a shared project among programmers around the world. The programmers are free to contribute improvements to the computer code, which may then form part of the specification. Open-source formats that are properly managed, such as the TIFF file format, have been around for a long time and endured many changes and benefits. The downside to open-source formats is, of course, applications must keep up with the changes.[6]

---

[6] The TIFF specification actually allows the use of any of several different encoding methods. While this can be a good thing, in terms of keeping up with changes in technology, the problem arises when two separate TIFF files are incompatible, with some applications being able to read one type but not the other.

Moreover, the specifications for certain file formats (especially open-source ones) have a tendency to change over time. Therefore, it's important to work with a format that is supported through all its various incarnations (i.e., are backwards-compatible), including those that haven't been developed yet (making them future-proof). Otherwise, a situation may arise in which archived files are unusable after five years.

As a final note, some file formats include provisions to prevent data corruption, such as including a checksum or some degree of redundancy, making them even more robust (but possibly requiring additional computation or disk space).

6.4.4 Color Model

Each color model usually requires a separate encoding method. The RGB color model is the most popular for digital images and is used by a large number of formats. But to use a photographic film color model, another file format (such as the log Cineon format) is required. Typically you use the format that is relevant to the color space you require. However, confusion can arise when a single file format can incorporate any of several color spaces (such as the Cineon and DPX formats, which can be linear or logarithmic and either 8 bits or 10 bits per channel), requiring the user to determine which color space is used.[7] A common solution for avoiding this confusion is to restrict the usage of the file format to specific color models (e.g., only allowing the use of 10-bit logarithmic Cineon files perhaps with linear RGB files encoded using the DPX format).

6.4.5 Additional Features

A file format may include other options, many of which are specific to particular applications. One example is the inclusion of timecode

---

[7] Most of the file formats that can utilize a number of color models usually have some kind of information in the "header" (i.e., the area of data before the image data) to determine which model is relevant; however, the usage of the header is in turn dependent upon the application that created the file in the first place.

or key number data in the file, so that digitized material can be traced back to its origin. An extension of this option is including some kind of bar code or unique serial number to allow tracking (either of the original material or of the file itself). Many file formats have at least some provision for including textual information in the file (and unlike metadata attached to files by an operating system, these files should survive being copied across devices or to another operating system), but getting applications to correctly read or save this information can be a problem (i.e., including text in an image file is considered optional and is therefore ignored by many image-processing and image-manipulation applications).

Even more complex data can be stored in certain image formats. The Adobe Photoshop file format, for instance, has provisions for storing multiple image layers, each with their own transparency information, along with vector- or text-based layers, and even layers to modify the appearance of other layers. Of course, all these additional features come at some cost—usually increased storage space requirements. The important point is to select a format that has all the options you'll need.

Ultimately, the file formats that the digital intermediate applications (such as the color-grading and conforming systems) can work with will dictate which file formats are adopted.

6.5 NAMING CONVENTIONS

However you plan to implement a digital intermediate pipeline, it's important to establish naming conventions, a set of rules governing how files in the pipeline should be named and organized. Naming conventions are a good way to create consistency throughout the project and help with tracking data later. Everyone involved with the creation or manipulation of any of the data should be aware of the project's naming conventions. One popular convention is to include for each image the shot name, frame number, and image resolution (as well as the file extension to differentiate between file formats), naming a typical image file something like:

132_035_tk1_2048_1556.0135.cin

Although this name is quite long, it contains a lot of information about the file that would otherwise be accessible only by opening it.[8] Other possibilities are to encode a frame number (e.g., 001222.dpx) or to name a scanned film image by its corresponding key number (e.g., kz_23_1234_5677+14.cin). The latter filename is somewhat unwieldy but has the advantage of guaranteeing that each frame has a unique filename.

6.5.1 Timecodes and Frame Numbers

Although timecode seems to be a suitable paradigm for naming a sequence of digital image frames, in practice it's unusable. A frame with timecode of 01:22:13:04 cannot be stored as 01:22:13:04.pic, because most operating systems prevent the inclusion of colons (among other symbols) in a filename. The name could be 01.22.13.04.pic or even just 01221304.pic, but these names can be confusing when mixing them with files that don't have an associated timecode (e.g., computer-generated shots) and instead carry only a frame number (e.g., 442.pic). The problem of frame rate must also be dealt with; digital images don't have an inherent frame rate, and so it can be difficult to identify the frame rate in the timecode number of a frame in a sequence.

Fortunately, for each timecode, an equivalent frame number can be derived, and many digital intermediate pipelines (and the associated applications) prefer timecode to be encoded as a frame number. To convert a timecode into a frame number, you simply add the number of frames from zero, so that a timecode of 00:00:00:00 becomes 0000000.dpx and 01:22:13:04 becomes 0123329.dpx (at 25fps). Several software timecode calculators are available; they can perform the conversions for you, but to do it manually, you can use the following simple formula:

$$H \times R \times 3600 + M \times R \times 60 + S \times R + F$$

---

[8] Although the image size may seem like a strange attribute to encode in the file-name, in reality, it can be difficult to remember what the image's exact resolution is without opening the file. In addition, in many instances, there may be multiple versions of the same image at different resolutions.

Where H is the number of hours, M minutes, S seconds, F frames, and R is the frame rate For example, the timecode 01:22:13:04 (at 25fps) becomes the following:

$$1 \times 25 \times 3600 + 22 \times 25 \times 60 + 13 \times 25 + 4 = 123329$$

Of course, this process is reversible, so you can derive the timecode given a frame number (but the math gets a little more complicated).

It's recommended that non-drop-frame timecode should be used wherever possible, because the conventions seem to break down with drop-frame timecode. When working with drop-frame timecode, you can either convert each drop-frame number separately (which is preferable but will result in gaps in the frame numbering of a sequence, so that a sequence becomes 0107999, 0108002, 0108003, etc.), or you can derive the frame number for the first frame of an image and then just increment the frame numbers, so that a sequence beginning at 0107999 continues as 0108000, 0108001, and so on.

6.5.2 Number Padding

Computers don't count in the same way as people count. It sounds crazy, but it's true. If you were to put the following files in order:

12.dpx, 011.dpx, 9.dpx, 1.dpx

you would expect to end up with the following:

1.dpx, 9.dpx, 011.dpx, 12.dpx

A computer, however, would usually sort them this way:

011.dpx, 1.dpx, 12.dpx, 9.dpx

People read numbers from right to left, whereas most computer systems treat them the same as letters when they form part of a filename, reading from left to right. To prevent a sequence that is encoded purely in frame numbers from being re-ordered, the numbers must be padded with zeros. The filenames must have a predetermined number of digits, smaller numbers having one or more zeros placed before the number. The number of required digits can be worked out ahead of time; for example, for a sequence that is less than 100 frames, the filename requires only two digits, from 00, 01, 02 . . . 99. For frame numbers derived from timecodes, seven digits are necessary (or six if the timecodes are unlikely to be higher than nine hours). Determining the number of required digits prevents problems occurring later by applications trying to (incorrectly) sort frames in order.

COLLAPSED FRAMES AND DISCONTINUOUS NUMBERING

Because of the sheer number of files being managed, it's sometimes more useful to list files in groups than individually. If frames are appropriately named, rather than listing a group of files as

    shot_01_0001.dpx
    shot_01_0002.dpx
    ...

It's more useful to display the frame range as

    shot_01_[1-200].dpx
    shot_02_[1-317].dpx
    ...

Some operating systems have methods for displaying files in this "collapsed" format, as do some applications. Also useful is the ability to simultaneously perform data operations on a range of files in the same way (although this process also can be handled by manually selecting the group of frames to be processed).

Another issue with listing files is that sometimes frame ranges have gaps, so that there might be a frame range from 1–32, and then from 50–75—for example:

    ...
    shot_01_0032.dpx
    shot_01_0050.dpx
    ...

(continues)

> ## COLLAPSED FRAMES AND DISCONTINUOUS NUMBERING (*continued*)
>
> Gaps usually occur when only a select part of a sequence is required, to save transfer time and storage space. In this situation, it's useful to display frames as follows:
>
> shot_01_[1-32,50-75].dpx
>
> It might also be useful to display a count of the resulting number of frames (58 in this case). Also important to bear in mind when renumbering filenames with numbering gaps, an automated way of renumbering is required to preserve the gaps with the new numbering. For example, the range might be
>
> shot_01_[11-42,60-85].dpx
>
> Unless, of course, you intend to eliminate the discontinuity.

6.6   DATA ORGANIZATION

You can approach asset management, digital or otherwise, in many ways. Each digital intermediate facility does things in a slightly different way, depending on its internal configuration requirements and experience.

6.6.1   The Data Pool

The simplest method of organizing files is to use a single location that contains all the digital intermediate files, without using folders. This situation is useful for small projects because it's much easier to keep track of the files. Using this method, it's easy to tell at a glance whether the file you're looking for exists in the pipeline (either it will be there or it won't).

However, this approach has several disadvantages. First, each file must be named carefully to reflect its contents. Second, the more files are stored in the pool, the longer it takes for the operating system to

FIGURE 6-2 By organizing material into a single pool, all the files can be viewed at once

sort through them. With a large number of files, simply browsing the pool to display the contents can take significant time. Saving each frame as a separate file becomes impractical. However, storing entire image sequences as single files (e.g., with DV stream files, where sequences that are potentially hundreds of minutes long are encoded as single files, such as tape01.dv, tape02.dv, etc.) might be more suitable.

You can store a number of files inside a single container file (e.g., such as ZIP, TAR, or SIT files)—possibly also using lossless compression methods to store the data more efficiently. In this way, hundreds of still images may be grouped together. This approach may be more appropriate for archival purposes or for storing infrequently used files, because accessing or modifying files stored within a container file requires first extracting the required files and then injecting the modified files back into the container, which can require a significant amount of time, particularly if compression is used.[9]

---

[9] Modifying files within a container can cause the entire container file to be re-created, so even if the file you modify is small, it can still take a long time to store the modification.

6.6.2 Folder Organization

Perhaps the most common method for organizing files is to use folders to separate files into groups. Folders work in the same way as the file containers paradigm discussed previously, but there is no delay when accessing files inside folders. Furthermore, folders can be nested, so folders can contain other folders. This approach allows you to organize files in a variety of ways. For instance, you can divide files into categories, such as "film_scans," "video_transfers," "rendered_effects," and "color_graded_finals." Each of these folders can then be further subdivided, for instance, by reel number or shot name. Further divisions might differentiate between files of different formats or image sizes. A typical file using this method might be

film_scans/reel_018/shot_239/2048 × 1556/cin/01222.cin

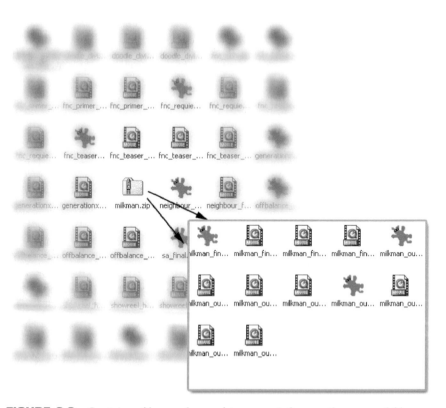

FIGURE 6-3 Container files can be used to group infrequently accessed files

FIGURE 6-4 Folders can be used to effectively aid naming conventions

Working in this way can make it very easy to organize and track data throughout the pipeline, using a simple hierarchical structure. However, there are some disadvantages. First, it takes extra time to create the folder structure for each group of data. It doesn't necessarily take a long time, but generally speaking, the more subdivisions you create, the more folders have to be created, which can be time-consuming overall. The process can be especially time-consuming if the folders have to be generated manually (by someone typing commands into the operating system). This process in turn increases the possibility that folders may be misspelled or put in the wrong place. Second, it's easy to become reliant on the folder structures to provide information about the files, thus neglecting to properly name the files themselves. Because files are independent from folders, files can be moved around without moving the folders that contain them. Copying, say, a range of frames to another location, without also copying the associated folder structure, might result in files losing this associated identity.

It can also be difficult to know exactly which data exists without looking through all the folders on the drive. Finally, some operating systems place restrictions on the depth and length of a folder structure.

FIGURE 6-5 Copying files without copying the folder structure can result in the loss of the files' identities

6.6.3 Layered Data

One activity that can quickly cause data management to become a logistical nightmare is trying to track different versions of an image or shot. For each shot in the finished production, you might have several versions—for example, one or more raw scans (with film sources), "dust-busted" raw scans, color-graded versions, and any number of edited versions. Each version of a single shot might require a set of images. In this case, a much better option is to use layered data.

As mentioned earlier, a single file can store images in layers, each with its own transparency settings. A single image file can contain the original scanned image and "cleaned" scaned image layers, successive color-graded layers, and text layers (the latter have transparency, allowing them to be composited over any of the images).

Use of layered images has the advantage of keeping together all versions for a specific image, with the ability to turn specific or redundant layers "off" without actually deleting them. A single layered file can be rendered to easily produce final output for a number of different situations. However, each layered file can get quite large and therefore may not be as efficient to manage as individual single-layer files. It can also be difficult to see which layers a file contains without opening it. Additionally, few digital intermediate applications currently support the use of layered images.

6.6.4 Automated Data

A further option is to hand over the data micromanagement to dedicated asset management systems. The system can name and store files using unique identifiers, serial numbers that are meaningless to people looking at the files directly on the disk (e.g., filenames like as375tjsa000.cin) but allow the system to track and index each file individually. Alternatively, the system may track existing files according to already established conventions.

With many data management systems, attributes (e.g., source and shot name) can be explicitly specified. You can group or regroup the files in

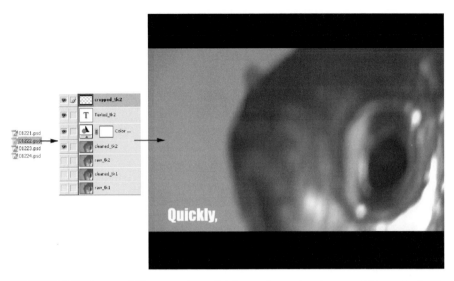

FIGURE 6-6 Layered files contain multiple versions of an image within a single file

any number of ways, sort the data according to various parameters (e.g., by date or shot name), and even perform searches for specific files, without actually affecting the data itself.

The downside to using an asset management system is that you can become dependent upon it, and therefore vulnerable to software glitches, incompatibility issues, or other faults. It can be very difficult to regain access to the raw data if the system fails. Also, many implementations of these tracking systems inevitably involve some kind of caching mechanism, and it's possible that you may not be viewing the data as it actually is (e.g., if a managed file is deleted outside of the system).

Successful data management strategies will undoubtedly involve some combination of the previously discussed options, depending upon the specifics of the pipeline. However, the paradigm that you use will inevitably be determined by factors that can't be controlled, such as application or system requirements. Consideration must also be made to the storage devices.

6.7 DATA STORAGE

All computer data must be stored on physical media if it's to be accessed a number of times or by different systems. Different types of storage devices can be used with computer systems, and they vary in terms of performance, reliability, and price.

6.7.1 Hard Drives

The most common data storage device is the hard drive. As stated earlier, hard drives are magnetic drives connected to a host computer system, which can store a large amount of information relatively cheaply and can be accessed by the host quite quickly. Some removable hard drives can be easily disconnected from the host system and plugged into another one, allowing the contents to be transferred quickly. So-called "hot-swappable" drives can be removed while the host computer remains switched on. This also includes devices such as floppy disks (though they're typically limited in terms of storage capacity). It's also possible to install multiple hard drives in a single computer system to increase the overall storage capacity. Hard drives are mechanical devices, and as such they're prone to mechanical failures. A significant drive failure may cause the loss of the entire drive's contents, making all the data stored on it irretrievable.

6.7.2 Write Once, Read Many

Write once, read many (or WORM) drives come in many varieties, the most popular being optical CD-ROM and DVD-ROM drives. These allow data to be stored on portable disks (such as CDs or DVDs). Generally, WORM drives are slower to access and of lower capacity than hard drives, but they're highly portable and tend to be extremely cheap. However, WORM disks have a disadvantage compared to other disks: once data is written on a WORM disk, it isn't possible to delete files to make room for anything else; you must instead use a new disk.[10]

---

[10] There are CD and DVD "rewritable" disks, which do enable you to erase all the contents and start again, although they may require specific hardware.

Optical storage devices are thought to have a shelf life of up to 100 years, making them ideal for archival and backup purposes; however, the actual lifespan of CDs and DVDs remains to be seen.

6.7.3 Linear Storage

Linear storage devices are designed to store a large volume of data on a spool of tape, in a way similar to conventional video tape recorders. However, the access time is extremely slow because the tape has to be spooled backward and forward to locate a specific data sector. Thus, tapes are usually used only for backup purposes. Typical data tapes store around 200GB of data (or more if combined with a compression algorithm) and are reusable. However, as hard drives become larger and cheaper, tape storage may become obsolete.

6.7.4 Arrayed Storage

Disk arrays, such as RAID (Redundant Array of Independent Disks systems, take advantage of the low cost of hard drives by linking together several to act as one large drive. Data is striped (i.e., written) across all drives simultaneously. When a file is read from the array, each disk works simultaneously. Because the amount of data on each disk is only a fraction of the whole file, the file is read much faster. Therefore, the overall data rate is much higher. RAID arrays also allow redundancy—that is, one of the disks in the array may contain error-correcting data, which makes it possible for data to be recovered in case of failure. If one of the disks in the array fails, it can quickly be replaced with a new one, and the damaged data is recovered. In the (somewhat unlikely) event of two or more disks in the array failing at the same time, the data would likely be irrecoverable. RAID arrays can be configured in a number of different ways, either to maximize performance or to minimize the risk of data loss.

There are many variants of data storage devices, such as flash drives or magneto-optical drives, but they're equivalent to one of the storage options mentioned previously in this section, and they vary only in terms of speed and capacity. It's also possible to utilize dedicated network storage devices, which aren't connected directly to the host computer but instead are accessible to a group of computers.

6.8 NETWORK PARADIGMS

In many situations, it makes sense to link together several computer systems, creating a networked environment to easily share and distribute data. Several different network models can be used, each with its relative strengths and weaknesses.

6.8.1 Workstation

The simplest paradigm is the workstation. A single computer system, detached from any network, does everything. It stores all the data locally (i.e., on the system's disks), and all the applications required (e.g., for conforming and color correction) are run on that machine. A workstation typically has an attached backup device (e.g., a tape backup system), and all backups are made directly from that computer. Similarly, the workstation can be used for all acquisition and output.

The workstation model is inexpensive to set up and maintain; it's also the most reliable model because no additional communication or compatibility issues need be worried about. Another advantage is that the data-transfer speed of such a system is maximized, because data transfer happens without having to send information long distances along network cables. However, an upper limit exists on requirements such as storage and processing power. A single workstation can hold only a finite number of disk drives and processors and as such may not be able to cope with the volume of data associated with feature film mastering, for example.

Second, and perhaps more importantly, only one person can use a workstation at a time, which isn't efficient and isn't practical for larger-scale productions that require a degree of multitasking. Although a workstation paradigm allows multiple processes to run simultaneously on the host system, it can impact the overall system performance. As discussed earlier, multiple processes (or people) accessing the same data all at once can cause performance issues, which applies to the systems themselves. Accessing data from a workstation requires some degree of processing on the computer's part. If several processes are simultaneously accessing data stored on one system (even when accessing different data), the overall system

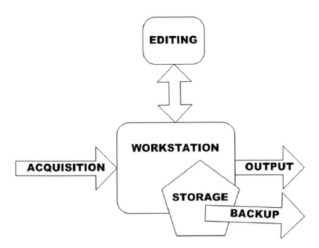

FIGURE 6-7 With a workstation paradigm, only a single system is used

performance is degraded. Therefore, for larger projects at least, some distribution of data may help to relieve the burden.

6.8.2 Client/Server

An extension of the workstation is the client/server. A client (essentially a workstation) accesses data from the server via a network link (usually a network cable) and runs processes on it locally. A server is a computer system that is dedicated to distributing (or "serving") a resource such as computer files (but resources can include any kind of data—e.g., weather reports or the local time).[11]

The client/server network is accessed when you view a webpage. In this case, the webpage is stored on a server, and your computer acts as a client, downloading the page and displaying it on your monitor. In the digital intermediate pipeline, a server might store all the project's images, and a client would access the files for conforming, color grading, and so on.

---

[11] A server can also be used as a workstation; however, the trend is to avoid doing this because it can degrade system performance (and hence its ability to serve data), and also because it increases the likelihood of something going wrong with it.

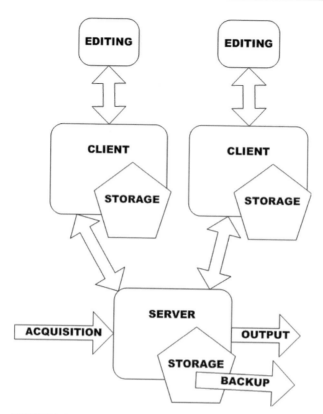

FIGURE 6-8   Multiple workstation clients can simultaneously connect to a server that contains the relevant data

With the client/server model, there can be multiple clients, which could include a client for doing backups, another for color grading, another for organizing the data, and so on. Servers are usually capable of managing access rights and can provide advanced features, such as choosing which clients have priority over data access (in the event that several clients are simultaneously accessing a single piece of data).

The client/server model is more expensive than using a single workstation, because you have to factor in the price of each additional machine, as well as the communications infrastructure. It can also be much slower to access files, because the transfer speed is dictated almost entirely by the type of network links (which themselves vary in price and performance capabilities). The system also becomes more prone to failure; with multiple computers (and their respective links), the more systems are involved, and the higher the probability of failure. Failure isn't necessarily a problem with multiple clients; when a client fails, you can switch to another one. In reality though, client machines are often configured for specific purposes (such as color-grading workstations having specific peripherals attached for the sole purpose of color grading), and the loss of a client machine might cause severe problems. Further, a server failure can be catastrophic, because all data required by every client becomes inaccessible.

6.8.3 Local Area Network

The local area network (LAN) is a much more flexible approach to networking computers. Basically, every computer within the network

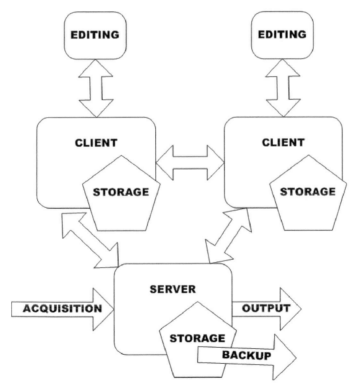

FIGURE 6-9 In a LAN environment, every computer system can access every other computer system

is able to access every other computer. In effect, every computer acts as a client and a server, although it's possible to establish machines as dedicated servers.

The downside to a LAN is that it costs money, particularly for all the additional hardware, routers switchers, and cables. In addition, trying to track data across a number of different systems in addition to tracking it through files and folders on each disk can become messy. The increased likelihood of systems failures increases or performance is degraded when a lot of people are accessing the same data, although system failures and performance hits can be reduced by investing in higher-quality network systems.

6.8.4 Wide Area Network

A wide area network (WAN) takes the concept of a LAN and spreads it across a larger distance. The Web is an example of a WAN, because it involves a huge number of computer systems across the world being networked. In the case of the Web, each server might be considered equally relevant, whereas a WAN in a digital intermediate pipeline would probably involve a central core of computer systems (e.g., those that store and process images) with some long-distance clients that connect to access the core computers.

WANs are used for a variety of reasons. People with portable computers outside of the digital intermediate facility (e.g., individuals on a shoot) require access to a WAN, or a facility with departments located throughout the world uses a WAN to connect them.

A WAN typically includes computer systems that aren't always connected. For example, a WAN includes computer systems that connect using a dialup modem, connecting periodically to download or upload a portion of data and then disconnecting (normally because a long-distance network connection costs money, especially when using phone lines). Further, the long distances that data sometimes has to travel, across many connections of varying bandwidth, means that the transfer speed of long-distance clients may be far too slow for some practical applications (e.g., copying an entire reel of film).

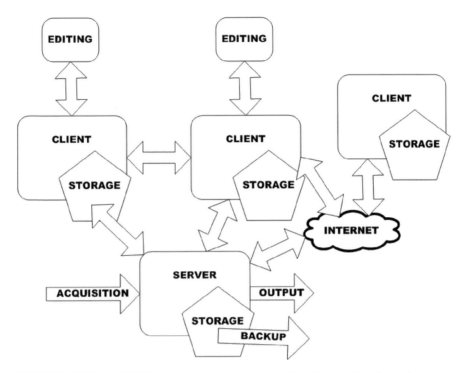

FIGURE 6-10   A WAN network can make use of the Internet to share data over long distances

Coupled with these disadvantages, the cost of establishing a functional WAN can be very expensive (especially without using leased lines). However, there are ways around this expense. Most WANs now make use of the Internet as a transport protocol, which means that anyone with access to the Internet can theoretically access the digital intermediate servers (of course, this kind of access in turn means that security becomes a more prominent issue).

6.8.5   Storage Area Network

One of the best ways to have a networked environment, while maintaining the speed advantage of a workstation paradigm, is through the use of a storage area network (SAN). With the SAN paradigm, storage devices (e.g., hard drives and tape backup devices) are treated independently from computer systems (both clients and servers). With a SAN, you effectively have a pool of these storage devices, all linked together by the SAN interface, which typically uses high-speed connections to link the devices. The net result is that all the devices are available directly to each other, which means files can be copied or moved between devices at high speeds. Further client machines can access the data without having to first access a server, which makes it seem as if the storage devices are attached directly to the client computer.

The speed at which a client machine can access files on a SAN depends entirely upon the system components and type of connections, but devices within the SAN tend to use fiber-channel connections, which can theoretically transport data as fast as the devices can read it (i.e., approximately 200MB per second across a distance of up to 100 kilometers). Using multiple fiber-channel connections makes it possible to move around even more data.

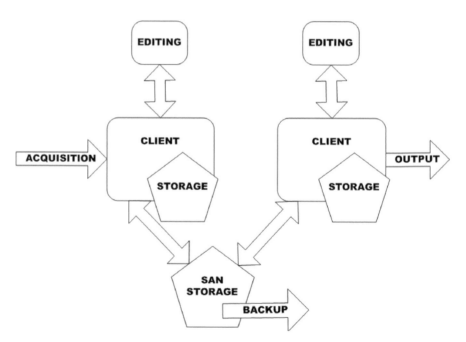

FIGURE 6-11   A SAN network provides stored data to every connected system

The benefits of a SAN network come at a price. It costs a lot of money to implement a SAN paradigm (on top of the cost of creating a LAN network). Each component involves very sophisticated technology, including the use of lasers and fiber optics. In addition, most SANs are designed for other applications, such as distributing a large number of small files to a large number of destinations. The digital intermediate pipeline typically requires much larger files to be transmitted at high speed to fewer clients, and only a few SAN designs are optimized for this type of delivery.

6.8.6 SneakerNet

A very simple, yet highly effective network model, is to physically transport the storage devices to a new location. Doing so can save a lot of time and effort, because the contents of the device become instantly accessible to the new system. A SneakerNet may prove to be the most practical solution in many cases. The downside is that the original machine (and any devices connected to it) will lose access to the data while the components are elsewhere. Second, compatibility issues may be involved between the original system and the newly connected one, issues that cause problems when trying to access the data.

6.8.7 Clustering

A cluster is a group of (usually inexpensive) computers that are linked together as a single unit to provide a high degree of processing power. Rather than having a single machine process 100 images, a large number of machines (e.g., 20) can each render five frames. Until recently, the way to maximize processing power was to use a single dedicated machine (sometimes referred to as a "slave"), containing a high number of CPUs. The problem with this paradigm was that such machines could be incredibly expensive, and pipelines would become dependent upon them. Thus, a hardware failure would be catastrophic.

Although each machine in a cluster must process an individual file (you can't have a number of machines each processing a single file, unlike a single machine with multiple CPUs), the number of files

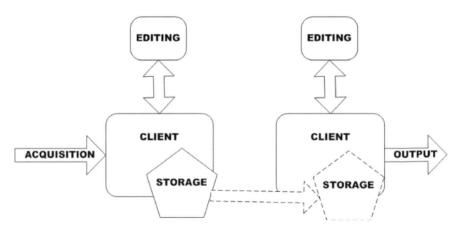

FIGURE 6-12   If all else fails, the storage device can be disconnected from one system and connected to another to quickly share data

required by a digital intermediate pipeline (especially in instances where each frame is a separate file) is so high that clusters become feasible. The downside to clustered machines is that they cost money (and aren't really useful for any other purpose), and they require some management in terms of scheduling. Finally, if a machine inside the cluster fails, the cluster as a whole will still work (at a proportionally reduced capacity), but if the interface for the cluster fails, the whole cluster becomes inaccessible.

WIRELESS NETWORKING

While not strictly a network paradigm in its own right, wireless (or Wi-Fi) networking deserves some attention. A wireless network uses short-range radio waves to transmit information (eliminating the need for physical cables to connect machines). Each machine is fitted with a transmitter/receiver, which communicates with a central, wireless bridge (or hotspot). An advantage of wireless networks is that the computers in the network can be easily moved about (within the range of the bridge), making them ideal for use with portable computers.

(continues)

WIRELESS NETWORKING (*continued*)

However, a few issues make wireless networks inferior to cabled networks. First, anyone within range of the bridge is able to access the network, which can quickly become a security issue compared to more secure cabled networks. However, some wireless networks enable the encryption of signals, so that only someone with the correct pass code can access the network. Second, the bandwidth is very limited. The demands of the digital intermediate pipeline might require that several hundreds of megabytes of data be transmitted every second; currently, the fastest wireless technology (802.11g) can reach only around 100 megabits, which is roughly 10MB per second. In addition, the actual coverage in the real world tends to vary and depends upon a lot of factors. So in practice, a wireless network may have an even lower bandwidth than is indicated by the specifications for wireless.

MULTITASKING

A benefit of modern digital systems is their ability to multitask. Multiple processes can be simultaneously executed from a single workstation. In reality, multitasking data processes may cause them to each run at a reduced level of performance. In certain situations, multitasking can be advantageous. For example, several processes that require different computer resources can be run at the same time. Using a workstation to process image operations (e.g., resizing) on the local disk (using CPU resources), while transferring a different set of files across a network (using network resources) and displaying another set of frames (using memory and disk resources) can be done simultaneously without any significant impact on performance. Multitasking in this way can help reduce the overall time for completing a project, without having to install additional workstations.

6.9 DATA TRACKING

Most operating systems can provide some fundamental information (in addition to the filename) about each file and folder, regardless of the content, which can be useful in tracking a file or folder's origin.

6.9.1 Date and Time

The single most reliable method for determining a file's origin is to examine the file's timestamp. Most operating systems record several different timestamps for each file.

First, the creation time is recorded. Simply put, it's the date and time when the file was first created, and (theoretically at least) the creation time will never change. File creation in the digital intermediate process occurs almost exclusively through acquisition (e.g., scanning a frame of film) or rendering (e.g., when producing color-graded versions). If you have a record of when a particular reel of film was scanned, for example, you can look for files whose creation timestamps match the time and date of the scanned file.

Second, each file has a modification time.[12] This timestamp is the time and date that the file was last written (or saved from within an application) to disk. Comparing the modification timestamp to the creation timestamp usually reveals whether the file has been altered since it was created. Note that the process of overwriting a file (i.e., creating a new file to replace an original file, as in the case of rescanning a range of frames) doesn't necessarily reset the creation timestamp. To ensure that the creation timestamp is reset, first delete the original files.

The last timestamp is the accessed time of a file. It shows when the file was last accessed, which normally means when the file was last opened (e.g., for viewing or copying). In terms of data tracking though, this information may not have any practical use at all.[13]

---

[12] If only one time and date is shown for a file, it's usually the modification time.

[13] In some operating systems, obtaining the accessed timestamp of a file is considered a file access in its own right and will actually reset the timestamp to the current time!

Each timestamp is generally determined by the host computer's internal clock. If the file is created on a machine whose internal clock is off by an hour, for instance, each time a file's timestamp changes (as when it's modified), the timestamp will be wrong by an hour. For this reason, it's highly recommended that all machines in the pipeline have their clocks synchronized regularly.

You should be aware of a few things when dealing with timestamps. Although timestamps can be altered manually (e.g., when you need to make a file to appear to have been modified), in practice manual alteration isn't usually done (due to the sheer number of files associated with the pipeline). Also, when copying files, the new file's timestamp may be different than the original's (although in all other respects, the file will be exactly the same). May be the creation or modified times (or both) are changed to reflect the time that the copy was made. The way in which the timestamp is affected depends entirely upon the operating system and the software making the copy. It's recommended that you use copying software that preserves the original dates, because there usually is no need to differentiate between a copied file and the original (the distinction is somewhat meaningless).[14]

6.9.2 Ownership

Most operating systems record the user that created each file as the creator and/or the file's owner. This process can be used for automated processes as well as users—for instance, the creator of a file can be recorded as "film_scanner" instead of "joe." Depending on the operating system, both the user who created the file and the one who last modified it can be designated as owners.

As with timestamps, file ownership can be changed manually. Again, copying files may result in the user who copied the files, instead of the original creator, being designated owner.

---

[14] Similarly, when restoring files that have been backed up to an archive system, the backup software may record the timestamps as the time of restoration, rather than recording the timestamps of the originals.

6.9.3 Metadata

Files can also contain ancillary data, known collectively as "metadata," that is stored with the file (but without altering the file's content). This metadata might be stored by the operating system or as part of the file format (e.g., certain image files allow metadata, such as timecode or key numbers, to be stored within the file), or the metadata may be stored in an external file or database. Metadata can include any kind of textual information (e.g., a description of the file's contents or statistical information) and may be entered automatically or manually.

6.9.4 File Size

A slightly less obvious piece of information that can be used to assist with tracking is the size (in bytes) of each file. Because digital intermediate files are usually generated in autonomous and fairly predictable ways, the file size can be used by an experienced manager to quickly calculate the pixel dimensions and number of channels within an image (which will be a fixed file size for uncompressed files), without having to open the file. Examining the size of a particular file can reveal more information about the file than just the amount of disk space it uses.

As an example, a method to quickly check images for corruption (e.g., when a copy process fails) is to examine the file size. When dealing with perhaps 10,000 images, the corrupt file usually stands out as being significantly smaller than the others (particularly when no compression is used), sometimes even being listed as occupying 0 bytes. Being able to access this information is clearly a lot quicker than scrolling through all the files to pinpoint the corrupted one.

6.9.5 Image Thumbnails

Graphical operating systems (or graphical file management programs) may have the capability to display thumbnails for image files.

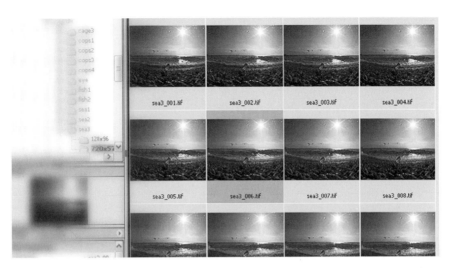

FIGURE 6-13 Image files may be displayed as thumbnails, as a means of previewing the file contents

Activating this mode displays each file as an image showing the file contents. Depending on the system, the thumbnails might be generated each time the files are listed (which can be a very slow process, especially with thousands of frames), or they might be cached (the cache typically is saved to an additional file). Thumbnails can be useful in quickly determining the pictorial content of a set of files. It can be especially useful in locating a particular image where a number of number of different images are located (e.g., reference images taken from key points in a sequence). However, because some image thumbnails might be cached and because they don't contain much image detail, they aren't an infallible indicator of a file's contents. In addition, certain image formats might not be supported by the operating system or file management application.

Although many of the parameters listed previously, such as the timestamp or metadata, can be entered manually, in the digital intermediate pipeline, manual entry can be somewhat impractical because typically hundreds of thousands of files must be managed. In general, many of these details may not be carried across when transferring files between different operating systems (e.g., between Linux and Windows), and so tests should be conducted prior to using a cross-platform pipeline.

REAL-TIME DATA

With video tape, pretty much every operation, such as playing and dubbing, is done in real-time, meaning that copies of video tapes are made at the same speed at which the material was originally recorded. So, if you were to record on video tape a sequence featuring a clock ticking, every time you played or dubbed the sequence, the clock would appear to be ticking at the right speed.

Data, on the other hand doesn't work this way. Transfers simply occur as fast as possible, governed by the limitations of the host hardware and software. For many applications, this speed is faster than necessary. Theoretically at least, an email message can be transmitted from one side of the world to the other in less time than it takes the recipient to read it. However, the digital intermediate pipeline requires a much higher volume of data than is contained in a few email messages. Even with images of 2k resolution, most machines struggle to move 24 frames of image data each second. The result is that copying image data frequently takes longer than displaying it. Even displaying images in real-time requires dedicated equipment, and this hardware tends to be devoted to supervised grading sessions.

Clearly, as the hardware performance-to-price ratio improves, data transfer will get faster. However, this increase in transfer rates will probably result in filmmakers wanting to work with larger, higher-quality images rather than a boost in the speed of existing data. So (for now at least), copying image data remains a slower option than copying video.

6.10 DATA OPERATIONS

When all your data has been scanned, digitized, organized and correctly named, it's then available to the various conforming and color-correction programs. Well, in theory it is. In reality, some data will probably have to undergo several processes before it can be used. Some or all of these processes may be done automatically, or even on the fly (i.e., processed in real time by the conforming and grading systems). These operations typically produce a new set of files, which may have to be renamed to stay in line with the established naming conventions.

6.10.1 File Format Translation

Data is commonly acquired in a file format different from the preferred pipeline format (e.g., a film scanner may produce files that can't be used by the conforming system). Depending upon the type of translation required, the data may or may not be altered by this process. For example, translating a Cineon file to a DPX file requires changes to the header (nonimage) data only. However, going from a JPEG file to a TIFF file requires a degree of "transcoding," the process of reinterpreting image data from one encoding paradigm to another. Be warned though—differences in encoding paradigms mean that some image information can be lost at this stage. For example, transcoding a 10-bit file to an 8-bit file inevitably results in the loss of the 10-bit file's extra precision (i.e., the accuracy afforded by the extra information). Further, even if the new format is superior to the old one in terms of encoding precision, no quality gain is realized. For example, imagine a DV file that has been transferred directly from a digital video camera. With the DV file format, all frames in a sequence are stored in a single file that utilizes lossy compression. However, suppose a color-grading system in the pipeline works only with individual TIFF image frames. Therefore, the DV file has to be transcoded into TIFF images. Although the quality of the TIFF image format is superior to the DV file format, the quality isn't improved, but neither is it diminished. On the other hand, performing the reverse process, transcoding a sequence of TIFF images to a DV file degrades the overall quality.

Sometimes this degradation is inevitable. Constraints within the pipeline (or the requirements of a specific output format, such as a DVD master) may necessitate the step of transcoding to an inferior format. As with the "enhanced 2k" scenario described in Chapter 5, delaying this transcoding step until as late in the pipeline as possible can significantly boost the overall image quality.

Format conversion typically takes only slightly longer than the process of making a copy of a file. Transcoding a file can take longer than simply converting formats, as it typically involves much more complex processing. Furthermore, certain transcoding methods yield higher-quality results than others, and possibly make use of edge or color-enhancement algorithms.

6.10.2 Image Scaling

Some applications or output methods (notably film recorders) require images of specific pixel dimensions. For this reason, images can be "upsampled" (i.e., the image size is increased) or "downsampled" (i.e., the image size is reduced). It seems that downsampling an image would reduce the image quality, while upsampling would at least keep the quality level the same. Unfortunately, both processes reduce the quality somewhat. This result involves the "point spread function" discussed in Chapter 5 (see the section "Spread Function," in Chapter 5).

A single point, or even an edge, might be infinitesimally small from an imaging point of view. Imagine a digital image of a green leaf against a plain white background. If we were to zoom right into the picture so we were looking at the individual pixels making up the edge of the leaf, we would see that some of the pixels comprise a mixture of both the green leaf, and the white background (making the pixels light-green). This is caused by anti-aliasing of the image, where the resolution of the digital image is not high enough to distinguish between where the green leaf ends and the white background begins. Nowhere on the image is there a spot that includes both the leaf and background. In the digital realm, that scenario doesn't happen. To reduce aliasing, an image of a green leaf against a white background might contain pixels on the leaf's edge that are rendered as both leaf and background (and that appear as a lighter shade of green). There's nothing inherently wrong with this; it's both a necessary and useful device, as it presents a more coherent of the image (the alternative would be an image that contains aliasing arte-facts), and it means that each pixel represents the point-spread function of the image. The issue is that when an image is resampled, this problem is amplified—that is, the pixels that are on the edge of the leaf, containing a mixture of green leaf and white background, describing an edge are treated as any other pixels and are resized as well. The result is that the edges in the image can appear to lose sharpness (i.e., the point spread function grows with the image as it's resampled). And, of course, the situation worsens when the image is downsampled because it loses both sharpness and its small details.

There are several ways to reduce the side effects of image scaling. The most common way to use a resampling algorithm (many different types exist) that utilizes an interpolation method that incorporates edge detection to calculate the probable locations of edges and keeps them as sharp as possible. A good upsampling algorithm can maximize the sharpness of the original, creating a new image that may even appear to be perceptually sharper than the original (with more pixels to describe an edge, the edge might "appear" to be more distinctly defined), although the image details aren't increased. (The details can be increased only by re-imaging a scene at a higher resolution.) And, as we've seen in Chapter 5, downsampling an image under the right conditions can produce perceptually superior results than re-imaging a scene at a lower resolution.

Resampling images is normally a computationally intensive process, especially when using more sophisticated algorithms, and can be time consuming. Each of the many different resizing algorithms is suitable for a specific situation, and some of them are discussed in Chapter 10.

6.10.3 Color-Space Conversion

Moving an image between two different color spaces is one of the most complex data operations involved in the digital intermediate process. In some instances, it may not even be possible, or at the very least, it may require configuring conversion parameters on a shot-by-shot basis. The most common type of color-space conversion in the digital intermediate pipeline, especially when dealing with images sourced from film material, occurs between logarithmic and linear RGB color spaces. Conversions are made to enable accurate color correction for different output formats. A logarithmic image, sourced from film, outputs accurately back onto film without requiring any conversion. To output a logarithmic image to video, or display it on a monitor, it must first be converted to a more linear color space.[15] In terms of color grading, a logarithmic image might have to be converted to a linear one to be displayed on the color-grading system's display; after that, the color grading is applied to the image, and then it's converted back into logarithmic space to be output back onto film.

Color-space conversion requires colors within the original color space be "mapped" onto equivalent colors in the new color space, using a specific lookup table (or LUT). On top of that, different color spaces have colors that are unique to that color space. For example, a particular shade of red in film color space has no exact match in linear color space. Therefore, colors are rearranged to achieve the closest match, but rearranging can cause banding effects, where colors are "clipped" at a certain point, which can be seen in the image as regions of color that change in visible "steps." A possible way around this problem is to change all the color in the scene to accommodate such clipping problems (in a process known as "chroma scaling" or "luma scaling"), but doing so will inevitably result in less accurate color conversion (although no perceptual difference may be detected). It's also possible to restrict this scaling effect to the extremes of the luminance range (i.e., the shadows and highlights), performing a "soft clip."

A more advanced method is to use a 3D LUT, which can provide more accurate results. The fact that the color-space conversion issue has many different solutions is part of the problem. Different LUTs are appropriate in different situations, and many different parameters must be adjusted in each instance. It's a highly subjective process and producing a usable image can require several attempts.

Because of this issue's complexity, many pipelines incorporate the use of additional hardware or software-driven devices to perform this conversion in real time, affecting only the way the image is displayed. The color-grading system then has to modify only the original (logarithmic) data, thus minimizing the required number of conversions, while maximizing the overall quality. Color management issues are discussed in Chapter 8.

---

[15] More precisely, a gamma-corrected linear color space.

With all data operations, consistency is paramount. Using images of different resolutions, color spaces, or even interpolation methods can produce profoundly disturbing images when they're played back in real time (or at least, something approaching real time). Objects may appear to go in and out of focus, sudden color changes (i.e., grading flashes) may be apparent, random noise might be produced, or images may even be slightly distorted. An image that looks acceptable when viewed as a still might become unacceptable when played as part of a sequence.

A PICTURE IS WORTH A THOUSAND WORDS

In many instances, the most useful tool in digital asset management is simply the ability to view a file. Looking at an image often reveals problems that can't be easily detected by software processes—problems such as lack of sharpness or incorrect coloring. Further, the ability to play back a sequence of images in real time (even if playback occurs at a lower resolution than the original images) can reveal problems that would otherwise be undetectable (but which, ultimately, the audience would see).

6.11 MULTIPLE RESOLUTIONS

In some instances, it's useful to keep multiple copies of a shot, each at a different resolution. Probably the most popular use is for proxy images (or proxies), downsampled copies of the full-size images. Proxies are substituted for the full-size images in some digital intermediate applications. Doing this provides all the benefits of working with smaller images—namely, faster throughput, which gives operators the ability to work at real-time speeds without expensive hardware. Presently, the common practice is for color-grading and conforming processes to use proxies for playback but retain the option to switch to full-size images for detailed work and checking. Use of proxies works only with systems that use a control-file paradigm (covered in Chapter 8)—that is, those systems that don't apply changes to the images directly until the option is selected to "render" out the new images. In this way, the application applies all the control file's parameters to the full-size images, producing results of the maximum possible quality (and doing so when speed is less critical, such as overnight).

This approach has several drawbacks. The first affects detail work, such as the careful positioning of mats; proxy images might not include enough detail to allow accurate work. In this case, being able to switch between proxies and the full-size images is necessary. Coupled with this drawback is the fact that proxy images (unless they're constantly updated) may not completely reflect the way the full-size images look, particularly when restoration work has been done on the full-resolution images. Then there is the psychological drawback: working with higher-quality images can inspire higher-quality results.

However, these drawbacks are nonissues for most pipelines. The significant issue is that additional disk space is required to store proxies alongside the full-size images.[16] Proxies are usually generated automatically—during acquisition, for example, or by the conforming or color-grading systems themselves, or by downsampling full-size images.

You might want to store multiple resolutions of images, particularly for output purposes. Each medium—for example, film, standard definition (SD) and HD video, and web delivery—has different resolution requirements. It's common practice to render final versions of a production to resolutions suitable for each of these mediums (or to make downsampled copies from a single render). On top of this, final versions might be output to different color spaces for different purposes.

VIDEO PROXIES

At times, all the data-tracking systems in the world can't help you find a particular shot or sequence (e.g., a shot that is described as "that shot with the man crawling through the tunnel"). For this reason (and countless others), it can be invaluable to have a video

(continues)

---

[16] Some pipelines, especially those using a LAN or WAN network solution, choose to leave the full-size images on the central server and store proxies on local machines, which can greatly enhance the data throughput rate.

VIDEO PROXIES (*continued*)

proxy of associated data. One option for creating proxies is to output copies of all image data onto video tape, which can be easily and conveniently accessed. Another option is to render sequences to some kind of digital video file, such as a QuickTime movie file, that could be stored on a central server, accessible to everyone who needs it and accessed at a rate much faster than playing through a stream of files. Additional information, such as each file's filename, can also be burnt-in to the image to make it possible to find. When browsing for footage, many digital-image-editing systems, such as Autodesk's Combustion software (www.discreet.com), can display image sequences as video thumbnails.

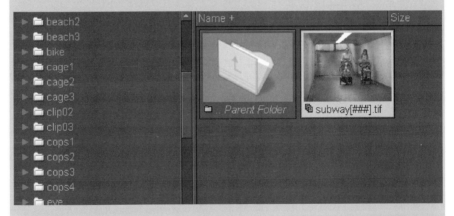

FIGURE 6-14 Using a graphical image browser, such as the one in Autodesk's Combustion, you can play through footage before opening it for editing

DIGITAL SLATES

One of the more useful aspects of using computer technology is the ability to record additional information to a separate file. For example, a log sheet, with information about a sequence, such as when it was shot, can be included with a video sequence. It's perfectly possible (and perhaps even useful) to encode this information for reference later—for example, the information can be encoded into a separate text file, accompanying the digitized images in the shot. It's also possible to put this information inside "slate" frame, which is an image displaying text, such as "Scene 1, shot 8, take 4" or any other information. Using slate frames make such information accessible to operators who are working purely with images.

FIGURE 6-15   Adding a single slate image frame to the beginning of every sequence can help to quickly identify its contents and purpose

6.12   COLLABORATION

The larger the production, the more people tend to be involved with it. While it's perfectly possible (in some situations at least) for one person to complete the entire digital intermediate process on a project, several people usually are involved. Many individuals usually work on a high-budget feature film: several digital color timers, one or more online editors, one or more restoration artists and scanner operators, and a team of digital asset managers. The result is that a number of people access the data at the same time for different purposes. Scheduling becomes an important issue because, as mentioned earlier, each separate access of data reduces each user's transfer speed. Certain processes (e.g., color-grading sessions with the director of photography of the production) must be given priority, which of course means that other operators are left with fewer resources. On top of that, it's all too easy to lose track of which shots have been completed in the rush to meet deadlines and be hindered in dealing with crippling problems when they arise (and they will). Clearly, experienced and efficient management of the overall work flow is important, and a number of project-management options are available to make things run a little smoother.

6.12.1 Versioning and Overwriting

What should you do when you make alterations to an image or image sequence? Should you save the modified version separately from the original, or should you replace the original? There are arguments in favor of both approaches. Saving new versions of images has the advantage of making it possible to return to a previous version if a problem is encountered with the new one. For example, the process of restoration (covered in Chapter 9) involves the use of digital paint to repair a set of images, to repair damage or remove unwanted elements from a shot. However, in some instances, the restoration process can inadvertently increase the damage to a shot, such as by introducing new artifacts into an image. For this reason, you can revert to a previous version of a shot and perform the restoration again. In other similar instances, having previous versions can prove useful—such as when a scene must be rescanned from film. However, this process can soon become a logistical nightmare because ensuring that all systems are using the most up-to-date versions of the shot can require a lot of work. (Most automated processes in the digital intermediate pipeline use the filename of an image from a control file to determine which images to use, and so the control file must be manually updated each time a new version of an image is produced.[17] In addition, obligatory disk space requirements must be considered, because every new version consumes more disk space.

---

[17] Incidentally, implementing new versions of control files (such as new grading lists or EDLs) usually presents less of a problem, as there is usually only one person using them at a time, and most applications are designed to "remember" which the last version used was.

Simply replacing (or overwriting) the original versions with newer ones has the opposite effect: changes are permanent, and no additional space is required. The only factor that needs to be considered with regards to propagating the changes to the rest of the pipeline is that cached files or proxy images might have to be regenerated (but see also the sidebar "Dependencies," later in this chapter). An additional down side to this approach is that the system becomes more vulnerable to errors. When a sequence is created, each original file is systematically replaced with the new one (i.e., first the original is deleted, and then the new one is created in its place). So, if anything, from a network error to a power failure, disrupts this process, you can end up with a sequence of images that are part new version, part old version. Further, the file being processed when this happens might become corrupted. Because creating new versions of a sequence can take a long time, the probability of such failures is greater. And if the sequences take a long time to process, it's likely they're processed at a time when no one is working on them (such as overnight), which means the errors could go unnoticed for long periods of time. As if that weren't bad enough, there's another problem too: if anyone happens to be using an image at the time it's being overwritten, the file might be set to read-only and not be replaced, meaning some of the frames in a sequence are new versions and others are not. A similar situation can arise where two separate people are editing the same sequence at the same time.

The simple solution to these issues is to vigorously and continuously check all the data for possible problems. However, doing so just isn't practical when dealing with hundreds of thousands of images, with new versions constantly being created. A more workable situation is to periodically back up data, such as after the initial acquisition of images into the system, so the backups can be restored later if necessary. An even more useful (but slightly slower) option is to save new versions of sequences separately from the originals, then compress the original sequences (e.g., using lossless compression, storing the sequence in a ZIP file), delete the original frames, move the new version to the location where the original ones were stored (giving them the same filename), and add a slate indicating the latest changes. Then, when the new versions can be thoroughly checked and approved, the ZIP file containing the original images can safely be deleted, relinquishing the disk space.

Another solution is to use a software data management system that automatically tracks changes to files and automatically archives older versions.

DEPENDENCIES

Although many operations in the digital intermediate pipeline can be performed concurrently, a fairly structured flow of data still must be maintained from one particular application to the next. For example, one particular pipeline might demand that the final output come from the color-grading system, which means that the data must have already been conformed, restored, and had effects applied to it. Each step in the chain, to some degree, can be said to be "dependent" upon previous steps. For instance, whatever the specifics of the pipeline, all operations on the data must have been completed prior to output. On top of that, some pipelines require that the color-grading stage be done with the program completely conformed, so as not to spend unnecessary time color-correcting shots that are ultimately not used. Conversely, the attitude might be taken that the restoration process should be done on all the data when this approach provides an overall increase in the turnaround speed to the pipeline. In this case, the restoration stage is dependent only on acquisition. Knowledge of the various

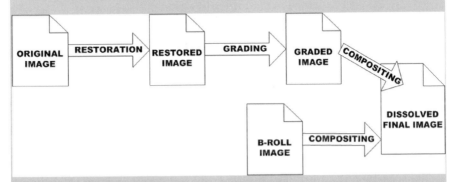

FIGURE 6-16 In this example, there are several steps that lead to a dissolved image, each of which produces new images. Modifying images early in the chain may affect images output further down the chain that are dependent upon them

(continues)

DEPENDENCIES (*continued*)

dependencies of each process can assist greatly in successfully managing and scheduling the data flow.

If any of the data is replaced, the changes must be propagated forward to any other processes that are dependent upon it, so that if a show is reconformed, those changes are updated in the color-grading system.

6.12.2   Check In, Check Out, Roll Back

A software system data management system can provide an easy way of knowing who is working on a particular section of data. Users of such a checkout system can choose to indicate a particular file or sequence to edit, which would then become assigned or checked out to them. Other users can still view the sequence but can't edit it. When the assigned operator has completed making changes to the files, they're checked in, and the software automatically replaces the original version (usually including an annotated description of the changes that were made) with the new one, which then becomes available to everyone again. More sophisticated software can take dependencies into account, so that users are prevented (or at least warned) from altering files with dependencies on other files being edited by someone else.

IN-PLACE EDITING

Some applications allow in-place editing of images, which means that changes made while editing a file are saved immediately as they happen, rather than the changes being explicitly saved by the user, or the changes being saved when the file is closed. In-place editing can significantly reduce the risk of files getting corrupted; however, it negates the users' ability to retain the previous version separately from the new one—unless of course you make a copy of the original prior to editing it.

A more powerful extension of this approach is to include a rollback feature. This feature archives redundant shots automatically, as protection against their being deleted. Then, if it becomes necessary to revert to a previous version, the corresponding sequence on disk can be rolled back to the archived version. Alternatively, if the original version is no longer needed, it can be deleted to conserve disk space.

6.12.3   Checksum Verification

One common problem with file transfers (i.e., copying from one device to another) is knowing whether the transfer was successful—that is, the copied file is, in fact, identical to the original. Although a benefit of digital media is that copies of originals are identical to the original, in practice files can be corrupted. If a lot of transfers are occurring, some might fail. Failure could be due to a hardware or software error, or to the concurrent transfers getting entangled. It's rare, but it happens. Similarly, when restoring an archive from an older storage device, such as a digital tape, the tape may have decayed, introducing errors when the files are being read. Precautions, such as storing each frame as a separte entry on the tape or using the highest quality tapes available, can be taken to prevent this problem from becoming an issue, but when it does occur, it may go unnoticed for a significant period (usually until someone tries to use the files)

There are options to verify the integrity of a file without having to view it. The most common of these options is to use checksums. The checksum of a file is simply a number generated by adding all the digits in a data file. This measurement is first made when you know the file is intact (e.g., just before copying it) and can later be compared to the checksum of the file in question (i.e., the newly copied file). If the checksums match, then generally speaking, the files are identical.[18] You can record each file's checksum within a folder in the digital intermediate pipeline. The checksum is recorded to a small, separate file using additional (freely available) software. The software both records the original file's checksum and later uses the recorded checksum to verify the integrity of the files, or copies of the file.

---

[18] More robust variants of this technique, such as MD5 verification, provide fewer false positives, but they generally take longer to process.

6.12.4   Database-Driven Asset Management

Many of the processes described previously can be simplified and automated by using a database-driven asset management system. Such a system tracks all digital assets within a database, which can record any number of factors relating to the files, such as who accessed and modified them (and when); in addition, the system can store comments—for example, a director's feedback concerning a particular shot. Such systems can be very useful for determining at a glance, the overall state of the production. Many of these applications have options for checking files in and out and rolling files back to previous versions, and many even handle tasks such as thumbnail and video proxy creation and checksum verification.

Systems such as NXN's Alienbrain data management software (www.alienbrain.com) enable you to perform all the usual data processes, such as copying files between storage devices and deleting files, while handling versioning and automatically checking files in and out of the database.

FIGURE 6-17   Asset management systems such as NXN's Alienbrain can help track different versions of shots

6.13   IMAGE MEASUREMENT

Many of the problems that can occur with digital images can be detected by eye, either by scrutinizing a still image on a screen (or printout) or by watching a sequence of images in real time. However, in some instances, problems might not be detectable onscreen and become apparent when you're actually looking at the raw data. Conversely, at times, something might look like a problem onscreen, but your analysis of the data indicates this isn't the case. Such an analysis requires appropriate image measurement software, such as the freely available, multiplatform ImageJ (rsb.info.nih.gov/ij), which can accomplish several tasks.

6.13.1   Statistical Information

Basic information about an image, such as the type of file (regardless of what the file extension says it is), its pixel dimensions, bit depth (or precision—i.e., the degree of accuracy in reproducing colors), and color space, as well as the maximum, minimum, and average pixel values (which can help you determine how balanced the image is overall), can all be determined fairly easily and have practical uses.

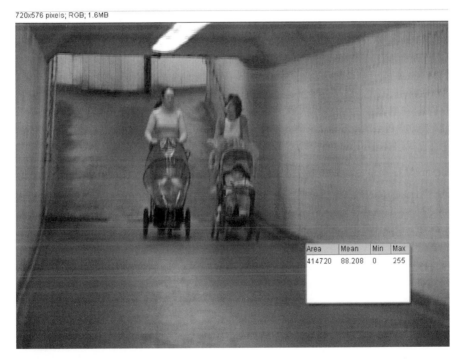

FIGURE   6-18   Basic Statistical Information can reveal a lot about the image content

If an image appears to be very dark, it can be confirmed by checking the average pixel value (it's considered low when it's under 50% of the maximum). You may also determine that the peak white (i.e., the maximum level of the pixel value) is low, possibly indicating that the image wasn't captured correctly (or it was originally underexposed).

6.13.2 Pixel Information

Information can be obtained about specific pixels in the image, too. Everything you can possibly want to know about pixels usually can be found by selecting the appropriate mode and pointing the mouse at the pixel in question. Some image-analysis programs enable you to take this functionality further and provide average readings for an area (or selection) of pixels.

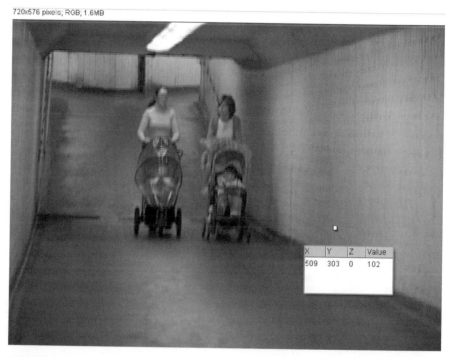

FIGURE 6-19 Analysis can be constrained to a single pixel or a region within the image

6.13.3 Histogram

It can also be useful to see information about an image in the form of a graph. Probably the most useful type of graph is the "image histogram," which displays the distribution of an image's pixel values, displaying the frequency of each level. This information can also provide a sense of tonal range, such as when an image is too bright (e.g., indicated when the majority of the graph is skewed toward the high values) or the overall contrast (indicated by how evenly the values are distributed). The histogram can suggest other factors are in play, such as over-sharpening (which appears as small spikes in the graph), banding (indicated by gaps in the graph), and clipping (indicated when the graph shows a disproportionate number of pixels at its extreme edges). With some applications, a histogram can be plotted for a specific part of an image, allowing you to focus on that specific area.

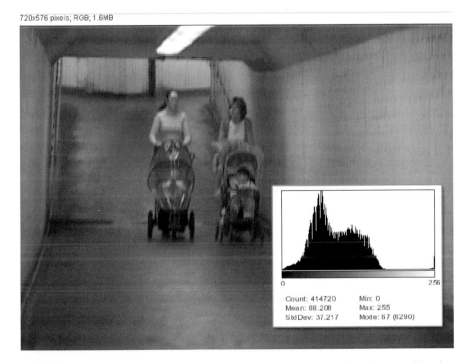

FIGURE 6-20 A histogram provides information about the distribution of brightness within an image. This histogram shows evidence of banding and clipping and indicates the image, on the whole, is rather dark

For images with high bit-depths, it may not be possible to display the complete range, and the histogram might be displayed in a "zoomed-out" manner.

6.13.4 Surface Plot

An extension of the histogram, a surface plot shows a 3D representation of the pixel values. Each pixel in the image is mapped onto a third dimension, which is determined by the pixel's value. A surface plot can provide a more detailed presentation of the distribution of an image's pixel values, but it provides essentially the same information as you can acquire by just viewing the image in gray scale.

6.14 WHEN THINGS GO WRONG

Anyone working on a production set knows the adage "if it can go wrong, it will go wrong." Similarly, anyone who has used a computer for more than five minutes knows they can behave erratically. Naturally, combining a production with computers tends to result in the worst elements of both. The bigger the production, the greater the potential of things going wrong.

Problems such as locked files, hardware failures (including damaged cables, power cuts, or someone pulling the wrong plug), software crashes (which always seem to be completely random and perfectly timed to cause maximum inconvenience), data loss, and even "finger trouble" (i.e., accidentally pressing the wrong button) when combined can each produce bizarre, unpredictable, and frustrating problems. Storage devices become erratic when they're close to maximum capacity, and most data operations simply fail when the disk space is insufficient. Compounding the issue somewhat are the ambiguous error messages that may (or may not) be displayed in the event of such a problem. A team of people working around the clock may inadvertently overwrite or undo (or unnecessarily redo) work done by a supporting team, which can result in mass confusion. The net result is that frames get lost or mixed up, or they're otherwise unusable, to say nothing of the time that may be wasted in trying to resolve problems.

720x576 pixels; RGB; 1.6MB

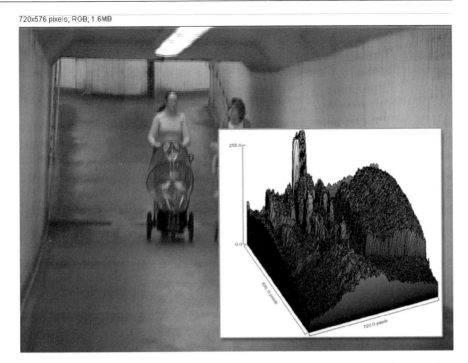

FIGURE 6-21   A surface plot shows a 3D representation of the distribution of an image's pixel values

More nefarious situations can arise: data can be deliberately destroyed (or stolen) by viruses, hackers, and other malicious entities. The problem isn't just limited to software-based attacks. Physical theft or damage of equipment is just as much of a problem.

While it's not always possible to anticipate and prevent such situations, measures can be taken to reduce the likelihood of problems occurring, as well as the problems' potentially destructive impact. Data-based disasters are more likely to happen when the system is under stress—when many people are constantly accessing a set of files, a problem is more likely to occur. This situation can also arise when a specific workstation or device is constantly used. Generally speaking, if you don't use a computer, it's less likely to break. Similarly, if the number of people working on a project is kept to a minimum, it's less likely to develop problems. However, that approach isn't a very practical one for completing a project within a tight deadline. There are other ways to reduce a system's burden—for example, by making multiple copies of files that may be needed by numerous different departments. Similarly, having multiple workstations for each task means that when one workstation breaks, you simply switch to another (which is known as "hot seating").

VALUABLE DATA

Given that data stored on computers is essentially a long string of numbers, it's strange to think that some files are considered more "valuable" than others. This is the case, however; some files simply require a lot more effort to re-create. In the same way that you might regard a shooting script's only copy to be priceless, certain files—in particular, the project files (e.g., the "grading lists")—are the result of many man hours of labor, and re-creating them would require a long time should anything happen to the originals. Clearly, these valuable files must be identified at the start of any project and protected as much as possible.

6.15 BACKUPS

Probably the most important fail-safe that can be implemented in a digital intermediate pipeline is simply making backups of all the relevant files. Making a backup (especially when backing up files to an external location) ensures that even if the worst-case scenario imaginable occurs, there is still a point where all the work performed (at the time of the backup) can be recovered. Acquired images can be restored without the often lengthy and sometimes complicated procedures of redigitizing the original material (and preventing original material from additional exposure to potentially damaging processes). Project files for conforming the mass of data, control files for color-grading settings, and so on also can be restored without having to repeat painstaking creative and technical processes. Similarly, files destined for output can be recovered without the need to re-render them from the source data.

To create successful backups, you must have unrestricted access to the data, sufficient data-transfer speed, and sufficient storage capacity. Of the three, access to the data usually proves to be the most problematic in practice. Data is constantly being shifted around, accessed, and modified by the various facets of the pipeline. It's common practice to have supervised sessions (with production team members overseeing and directing the editorial and creative efforts of the digital intermediate facility) during the daytime, which means that the data is almost exclusively prioritized for the production team's needs. Secondary operations (e.g., restoration, rendering, and other data operations) are performed at night, when the impact on data-transfer rates is of secondary concern. For this reason, backups are typically done after-hours, but of course the backups are then in competition with all the other night time operations for access to the data. The other two factors, speed and capacity, inevitably are determined by the hardware and networking paradigms. Each of the several different ways of approaching the issue of production backups is suited to a specific situation.

6.15.1 Regular Project File Backups

Creating a backup copy of the project files should be considered essential by any size production facility. Even if you're working with a single DV file on one workstation, creating backups of the essential files at key points in the production is worthwhile and invaluable if the backup is ever required. (Most project files are small enough to fit onto an inexpensive rewritable CD.)

Larger-scale productions should make regular backups of color-grading lists, effects project files, EDLs, conform lists, as well as any data management databases. These backups can be made on a weekly "rolling" basis, so that they're made every day and are replaced each week. In addition, some data management software may have provisions for backing up the rollback files, allowing multiple versions of each project file to be saved in addition to the current version. In addition, at least one backup copy should be kept at an external location, to allow recovery in the event of a major disaster (such as a fire).

6.15.2   Image Data Backups

Most large productions routinely create backups of image data at key points in the pipeline. For smaller productions, especially video-based ones, this approach may be unnecessary. In a small production, if any of the source image data must be replaced, it can usually be redigitized (or retransferred) from the original source media, typically with no discernable difference in the images. Other images might have to be re-rendered, but providing the project files are intact, this process shouldn't present any problems. Making backups of all the image data (including multiple versions of specific shots) requires a lot of data storage and typically takes a long time.

Regardless, for large-scale productions, making backups of all the images is considered essential for several reasons. First, the issue of quality, especially for film-originated material: having to rescan any reels requires handling the film again, potentially exposing it to damage. Second, the associated costs of the additional scanner time might far outweigh the costs of creating and implementing a backup system. Finally, it's likely that in some cases, restoring images from data backups is faster than re-creating it (which may also be true for rendered image data). In addition, a large production's image data usually goes through many transformations. Rescanning film requires it be "dust-busted" (i.e., the process of digitally removing the dust scanned along with the film) once again, because some of the dust inevitably is in a different position, which is a very time-consuming process. Other factors, such as the "registration" (i.e., positioning) of the frames may change between scans, which potentially could create conflicts with work already done (such as color grading). For all of these reasons, it's recommended that all image data derived from a film source be backed up after creation. For image data derived from video sources, the main variable between captures is random noise. Ultimately, having to redigitize a video source won't lead to many issues. The decision to back up video-derived footage likely is determined by speed and cost implications.

FIREWIRE BACKUPS

A recent development in backup systems is the use of consumer-grade data storage devices. Although few applications require as much data storage as feature film imaging, disk drives aimed at the average computer user now store up to around 500GB of data (which is sufficient storage for around 30 minutes of 2k image data or around 8 minutes of 4k data). Many of these devices can be used externally, meaning they can be connected to a workstation, usually by a Firewire interface. While the Firewire interface doesn't have the bandwidth to allow 2k images to be manipulated in real time, they make ideal candidates for short-term backups, as well as for certain SneakerNet scenarios. However, most Firewire disk drives are less-suitable for long-term storage because they are inexpensive and highly portable—they're designed to be under constant use and may fail if left unused for extended periods of time.

6.15.3 Mirrored Storage

One of the main advantages of video footage compared to photographic film is that a single video signal can be simultaneously copied to multiple destinations. When playing a video tape, the video signal can be split into multiple signals, and each signal is amplified and transmitted elsewhere.[19] Thus, you can watch the tape's contents on a monitor while it's recorded to several other tapes.

Image data can work in a similar way. Multiple copies of image files, each identical to the original, can be simultaneously created and sent to different devices. This advantage is utilized with the "mirrored storage" paradigm. With mirrored storage, a duplicate

---

[19] Although each amplification introduces additional noise into the signal, the difference is negligible in most cases.

storage system (such as a set of hard drives) is created, and the duplicate system is identical to the original storage system. The operating system (or a dedicated hardware device) ensures that the contents of both storage systems remain identical, so that each contains the same set of data. When changes are made to any of the files, those changes are propagated to the mirrored files. In the event of a hardware failure in one of the storage devices, users are diverted to the mirrored system with no discernible interruptions. A mirrored storage system can be crucial in ensuring that users are unaffected by hardware failures in the storage devices; however, such a system can be an expensive option. Most digital intermediate facilities prefer to have additional disk space available for practical use, rather than as a backup device. An additional problem is that such a system won't help if the problem isn't hardware related: when a file is accidentally overwritten (e.g., when a user makes unwanted changes to a file by pressing the wrong button), it will be overwritten on both systems.

6.15.4 Delayed Mirrored Storage

Perhaps a more useful paradigm than simply mirrored storage is a mirrored system that updates after an adjustable delay (e.g., delayed by one hour or by one day). This way, any data faults that occur that aren't hardware related can be replaced from the mirrored data, provided that the replacement occurs before the mirrored data is updated. Similarly, such a system still can be used to recover from storage hardware failures, but all the changes to the data that weren't copied to the mirrored disks at the time of the failure are still lost. Therefore, successful use of such a system requires careful balancing of the delay intervals.

As with many other paradigms associated with the digital intermediate process, delayed mirrored storage systems can be combined to create a specific backup solution for each production. It is even possible that an exceptionally proactive pipeline may be able to put all of the options in place, making real-time backups of every version of every file, but this approach would be a costly one and might negatively impact the pipeline's overall performance.

DATA RECOVERY

When all else fails, when data is lost and no backup is available, several possible avenues for recovering data are still available. When deleting files, most operating systems don't necessarily erase all the data from the disk, but instead the operating system "marks" the file as deleted, hides it from the user, and recycles the storage space when it's needed. Therefore, it's sometimes possible to "undelete" files that have been recently deleted (provided they haven't yet been overwritten by other files).

In more extreme situations, it's possible to send storage devices to dedicated data recovery facilities. This approach can be an expensive and time-consuming process, but it may be the only option.

6.16 ONLINE AND OFFLINE STORAGE

Many tasks within the digital intermediate environment don't necessarily require constant access to the original data. Restoration typically requires access, at any one time, to a small portion of the entire film—the portion can be cached on a local machine and rendered separately. Conforming can usually be achieved using low-resolution proxy images, with changes to the full-size data made later. Even though a large amount of data is needed to make up an entire, conformed, and corrected production, it's very rare for all of it to be needed at any one time. Even output is typically done on a reel-by-reel basis.

For this reason, it may be possible, or even desirable, to use an offline storage paradigm. With such a system, unneeded data is taken offline—that is, it's copied to an external storage device and removed from the system (or replaced by a placeholder, such as a proxy image or a generic "File offline" message). When needed, the offline files are brought back online by restoring them from the backup device.

However, it's important to remember that the decision to make specific offline files must be decided in advance, because bringing offline files back online can be a time-consuming process. Producers and directors might not want to decide in advance which part of the film they want to work with—after all, one of the great advantages of the digital intermediate is its flexibility. Further, just because an offline file is backed up to some other device, there's no guarantee that it's safe there. Portable disks are especially prone to wear and tear, and files are more likely to suffer from corruption if they're constantly transferred to and from such devices.

The offline storage paradigm can be extended for other purposes. In a networked environment, a system having access to the data (e.g., through the Internet) can make a copy of only the data needed for a specific task, copying it onto local storage, with all other data marked as being offline. The system can then disconnect from the network if needed (which is especially convenient when using a laptop) and be set up elsewhere—e.g., on the set of a production. When the system is returned to the network, changes are synchronized, so that files modified on the external machine are copied back to the main server, and modified files on the server are copied to the external machine. This approach might cause problems if the same file is modified on both the server and the external workstation between synchronizations.

6.16.1 Nearline Storage

A popular compromise between the low cost of offline data storage and the high performance of online storage systems is the nearline storage paradigm. This paradigm uses a collection of inexpensive storage disks. Generally speaking, the performance from nearline systems cannot compete with online storage systems, and most facilities that use nearline storage rotate the data between the online storage and the nearline storage, copying it from online storage to nearline to recover storage space on the online system, and copying the data from the nearline to the online storage when fast performance is paramount.

SYSTEM SECURITY

In addition to protecting against data loss by misadventure, digital intermediate facilities also can (and should) protect data against malicious attacks. Software- and hardware-based solutions are available to protect against viruses and hacking attempts. Most companies with systems connected to the Internet have some form of firewall that determines whether access to the Internet is allowed.

An extreme (some may say "paranoid") form of protection involves the use of electromagnetic (EM) shielding. Electronic interference such as EM radiation can damage data storage devices, causing data loss. Stronger radiation can completely destroy all electronic components within range, including microchips.

6.17 MANAGING OTHER ASSETS

It's easy to forget that the majority of materials handled during a production aren't in digital form. Physical reels of film, video tapes, and lots and lots of paper are also used, all of which need to be logged and tracked. One way to integrate the management of these materials with the management of digital assets is by using a digital-tracking system, such as a barcoding system. Affixing a unique barcode to each nondata item allows it to be logged and tracked in a computer database just like any digital file. The barcode can be scanned each time the associated details must be updated, such as when transporting a can of film.

Even more exotic possibilities are available, for example, by using radio-frequency ID (RFID) tags that respond to specific radio waves. Equipping room entrances and exits with transmitters allows the tagged items to be automatically tracked. Thus, when a tagged item is carried outside of the building, a transmitter can automatically log the item as being off-site in the tracking database.

6.18 SUMMARY

Working with computer data isn't the same as working with images. When working with images directly (particularly nondigital images), you can clearly see what you're working with data. When working with data, you're manipulating digits contained within files and folders, which means that a carefully planned management strategy is essential.

A number of tools can track and organize files—tools such as file attributes and folder structures, and features such as file permissions and quota management can help prevent problems, such as running out of storage space or the accidental deletion of a file.

Files can be named in many ways, and they can be spread across any number of disks or even networked computers. For this reason, it's important to establish proper naming conventions prior to starting a digital intermediate production and ensure that everyone involved is aware of them.

Even the most basic systems can provide information about digital image files, such as when they were last edited and who made the changes, but more advanced information, such as statistical analysis or notes stored in a database, may be attached to individual files.

Digital images, along with any other types of computer data, are susceptible to corruption and other faults. These problems can be easily detected through checksum verification, and the impact can be minimized by implementing an appropriate backup system.

Chapter 7 discusses ways to form the data that has been sorted and organized into something meaningful.

7

CONFORMING

In the previous chapter, we saw how a well-executed asset management system ensures that all the data for the digital intermediate—the digital images and the files supporting them—are intact and accounted for. However, the data doesn't yet have any structure, coherence, purpose, or meaning. It must be organized to form the fully edited final piece. This is achieved by assembling the required sequences, shots, and frames, as determined by the production's editor, in a process known as "conforming."

In this chapter, we examine the conforming process's capability to recreate a program that matches the production editor's cut. We'll discuss the various methods for conforming a program digitally, and the digital intermediate pipeline's features that make this process a smooth one. But first, we'll take a look at the way conforming is conventionally done for video and film productions.

7.1 PULLING IT ALL TOGETHER

In most productions, especially large-scale productions, the editor rarely directly creates the finished product. What usually happens is that the editor (or editing team) works with a copy of all the footage to make a final edit. Because editors don't normally have to work with footage at maximum quality to edit the program, they tend to work with lower-resolution copies, which greatly reduces the cost and time that is incurred by working with maximum quality images.

Almost all editing systems in use today are "nonlinear," meaning that projects don't have to be edited in chronological order. With linear-editing systems, edits must be made in the order that they will be shown. To cut a scene at the end of the show and then go back and work on the beginning, you use a nonlinear system. In addition, most editing systems are video-based or digital video-based, even when shooting and finishing on film, because greater creative and productive effort is possible. Video is easier to manipulate than film, and it's much cheaper to run off copies. The downside is that the quality is significantly lower, but by conforming, you can simply use the edit made to the video version and apply it to the original film, which results in a maximum quality version that matches the video edit frame for frame.

7.1.1 Conforming from Video

It's perfectly feasible to edit original video material directly and produce a video master without including a separate conforming stage. The requirement to conform video arose because certain editing systems used internal compression to increase storage space and make editing video a smoother, more interactive experience. This compression significantly reduced the quality of the footage within the editing system; when the edit was completed, the editing system's output wasn't of sufficient quality to be suitable for the creation of the video master. A separate editing process was born, that of the online edit. The purpose of the online edit is to match the final cut produced by the editor during the offline edit, the process of cutting the show from the raw footage, to the original, high-quality source tapes, resulting in a maximum-quality, conformed version that perfectly matches the offline edit. Additional processes can then be applied, such as color grading, titling, and adding effects—processes that can't be applied to the lower-quality offline version or can't easily be translated between the two editing stages.

For the online edit to accurately match the offline edit, we have to know several things about the offline edit. For each frame in the edit, we need to know which tape it originated from (i.e., the source tape), where it's located on that tape (i.e., the source position), and where in the final program it's going (the record position). For the purpose of the offline edit, we assume that each program is to be output onto a single tape.[1] This may seem a very simple way to describe a final edit, especially when it may take several months to complete the offline-editing process, but it's usually sufficient to re-create the entire edit from the source tapes. After all, the ultimate purpose of the offline edit, in terms of the visual content, is to determine the footage's order and timing.

The process of going through the source material and matching it to the offline edit is actually very simple, provided that the correct procedures were followed by the production crew in creating the source material. Every source tape should be given a unique identifier, typically a reel number, such as #1033. Adding the number can be done after the footage is recorded onto the tape or before the editor captures the footage in the editing system. The offline-editing system itself must have a way of identifying each tape upon capturing from it. This is normally achieved by asking the editor for a reel number each time a new tape is inserted. The offline-editing system is thus able to track, for each frame of footage, the tape it originated from.

When tracking each frame to a precise location within a tape, editing systems rely on the video timecode recorded along with the picture. The timecode is essentially a system for counting frames, but it usually divides the frames into hours, minutes, and seconds, as determined by the format's frame rate. For instance, a tape that is 250 frames from the start, in PAL format (at 25 frames per second) is

---

[1] In actual fact, long-form productions are often divided into reels of approximately 20 minutes each; however, for the purposes of the offline edit, each output reel is treated as a separate program.

10 seconds long. The timecode for this frame would be recorded as 00:00:10:00.

When recording a tape, the timecode can be arbitrarily assigned. That is, the timecode can be set to start at 00:00:00:00 or 12:00:00:00. It can be synchronized to another source, such as a timecode from a music track or even the time of day. The only requirements are the timecode must run continuously (in a regular, linear fashion), and it must be unique within that tape (so that no given timecode occurs twice on the same tape). Video productions also tend to shoot each new tape with hourly increments to the timecode, so that the first tape starts at 01:00:00:00, the second at 02:00:00:00, and so on. Timecodes with hourly increments are useful in tracking and checking, because it complements the reel number assigned to the tape (which is much easier to change or misread).

The editing system also tracks the timecode for captured footage, as it does with the reel number. Most offline-editing systems do this automatically by reading the recorded timecode directly from the tape. The online-editing system actively "seeks" a desired timecode on a tape by reading the timecodes as it spools through the tape. Together, the timecode and unique reel number information attached to each frame make every single frame in the production individually accountable.

With the steadily increasing power and capacity of modern editing systems, many video productions eschew the need for separate online- and offline-editing systems and can edit throughout at a maximum (or at least acceptable) level of quality. Many higher-end productions, such as music promos or commercials, have an online-editing stage purely to take advantage of the sophisticated effects and titling tools available. At the present time, however, the need to separate the offline and online edits is growing as more productions turn to high-definition video creation. HD editing requires a much higher level of resources than SD video editing, so many productions are choosing to offline edit the HD material at a much lower resolution, typically at SD video quality, before online editing from the original HD source material.

OFFLINE EDITS FROM DUBBED TAPES

It's likely that the offline edit wasn't created from the original tapes but instead from copies (or dubs), which may also have gone through a down-conversion or format-conversion process. It's vital that these dubbed tapes retain all the timecode information in the originals, and that they're given the same reel numbers as the originals. This ensures that the footage is correctly tracked during the offline edit.

In addition, all tapes used for both the online and offline edits should be free from timecode "breaks," where footage loses timecode information or the timecode goes out of sync with the picture (but the picture content remains intact) and should have sufficient run-up time before (known as "pre-roll") and after ("post-roll") each recording. Problems with either timecode breaks or insufficient pre-roll or post-roll can usually be corrected by dubbing the footage onto a new tape.

7.1.2 Conforming from Film

Film material is almost never edited directly. The overriding reason, out of several possible ones, is that handling an original negative tends to degrade it (the more you handle film, the more you subject it to damage such as scratches) and places it at risk. There's a risk that you can damage original video tapes by handling them excessively, but the overall risk with video tapes is much lower than with film. Because of this, editing film always involves two separate processes: creating the desired cut and applying that cut to the original negative.

Before the rise of video-editing systems, film editors first made copies of the original negative. Duplicating film is usually done optically, exposing a new piece of film by shining light through the original. Exposing film usually involves inverting the picture, black becomes white and vice versa—hence, the term "negative."[2] Therefore, copying a negative produces a positive (i.e., a print), and copying that positive produces another negative. Due to generation loss, the new

---

[2] With the exception of slide film and Polaroid film.

negative is of lower quality than the original. A limited number of positives (usually just one) are created from the original negative to avoid handling the original more than necessary. All other prints used for editing and viewing purposes (i.e., work prints) are usually created from a negative that is created from this positive, just as an offline-video edit normally produces a lower-quality picture than the original source video.

A film editor makes cuts using scissors and glue, either with prints (which can be viewed directly on a projector or a desk-based viewing device, such as a Steinbeck) or negatives (in which case a print is created from the cut negative). As with offline video-editing, once the final cut is complete, the edits are matched back to the original negative, which is cut in the same way to produce the finished movie. For this process to work correctly, there must be a way to relate the cuts made to the copies back to the original, without having to rely on an editing machine to track changes. Fortunately, motion picture film provides an easy way to do this.

Every frame of motion picture film created for use in cameras has an associated serial number called a "key number." The key number is simply a number that runs along the outside edge of the film that denotes the film stock and batch number, but most importantly, it assigns a completely unique code to every frame of film ever produced. Unlike video tapes, where two different tapes can share the same timecode, key numbers give each frame a value that distinguishes it from every other frame. You could compare all the film footage shot for the entire "James Bond" series and not run into a duplicate key number. And because key numbers are exposed onto the film (just like the actual image), they survive being copied onto new reels of film.

So, for a film editor to accurately match the final edit to the original negative, the editor creates a list of key number values for the cut. The same cuts can then be made to the original negative, ready for processing and duplication for cinema release. However, cutting film in this way, although simple, isn't particularly fast or efficient. It's a non-linear process (i.e., you can make changes to previously made edits), but it requires careful organization. When you want to find a particular shot, you either have to know exactly where it is or have to wade through large bins of film reels. And thus, the film-editing paradigm is merged with the video-editing paradigm to some degree. Rather than generating new reels of film for editing, the original negative is telecined to a video format suitable for editing, usually as soon as it has been processed.[3] Then the negative is safely stored away, and the editor can use a video-based editing system to cut the movie together.

Modern motion picture film normally includes machine-readable key numbers stamped next to the printed key numbers, so suitably equipped telecine machines can "burn" it into the picture and thus it's permanently displayed over the footage. In addition, a log file can be created to marry the video tape's timecode with the film's key numbers. The editing system reads in the log file when capturing the corresponding video footage and ties the footage to the key number internally. Once editing is complete, the editing system produces a list of cuts with corresponding key numbers. The original negative can then be cut together using this list to produce an identical cut at the highest possible quality. Clearly many parallels exist between using this system and using the offline/online video-editing process.

However, there are a few issues with this method. First of all, key numbers aren't necessarily accurate to exact frames. This is because key numbers are only marked every four frames, and it may be impossible to determine the precise frame for small edits. The biggest problem concerns the difference in frame rates between film and video.

7.1.3 Pulldowns

Film runs at 24 frames per second, whereas NTSC video runs at 29.97fps. Effectively, the video version runs 25% faster than the film version, which causes problems, especially when trying to sync sound to picture. So that the picture plays back at the same speed on video as on film, you must make a frame-rate conversion. The most common method for doing so is the 2-3 pulldown. Using this method,

---

[3] The same video is sometimes used to watch the dailies of the developed film, when the production team doesn't require the dailies to be viewed on film.

five frames of video are used for every four frames of film, so that the first frame of film is recorded onto one frame (i.e., two fields) of video, and the next frame of film is recorded onto three fields of video; this process is repeated for subsequent frames.[4] The order of this cycle is known as the "cadence." The net result is that the video's effective frame rate becomes 23.976 frames per second.[5] Although this process may not seem too complicated at first, it can be difficult to work out exactly which frame of video corresponds to the same frame on film by the time the final edit has been completed. That's because it's perfectly possible to cut on a frame that actually corresponds to two frames of film or the previous or next frame from the one expected, depending on the cadence. The process of working out how a video frame corresponds back to the film is known as an "inverse telecine" and is normally handled automatically by the editing system. The output of the editing system may, however, require some tweaking by the editor. It's likely that this problem will be greatly reduced by new 24p video-editing systems, which run at the same speed as the film (and without any interlacing).

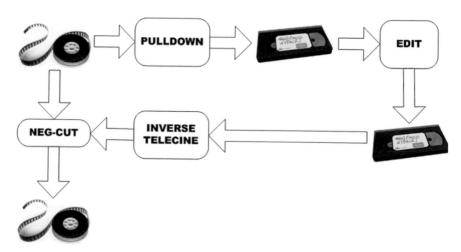

FIGURE 7-1 Film material must go through a pulldown to allow editing on video and an inverse telecine to match the edited video back to the original negative

---

[4] The alternative is to do a 3-2 pulldown, where the first frame of film equates to three fields, the second frame to two fields, and so on.

[5] Working with PAL video systems makes this process easier, because the video format runs at 25fps, which is only a 4% difference. To compensate, the sound is simply run slightly faster during editing.

7.1.4 EDLs and Cut Lists

Both video and film final cuts can be described as a simple list of "events" (i.e, individual, uninterrupted elements of footage, such as a shot that runs for five seconds before another one is cut to). For video, these events are edit decision lists (EDLs), which contain source reel, source timecode, and record timecode information for each event. For film, a cut list contains the key numbers for the first and last frame of each edit. It may contain additional information, such as the camera reel number, the scene and take numbers, and the equivalent video timecode. Each list is designed to be machine readable as well as human readable. Each edit is described in plain text on one line. As with many components of post-production, dozens of different formats are designed for use with different systems. A system usually is able to interpret specific formats, which can potentially lead to compatibility issues. Fortunately though, by their nature every EDL format is normally structured fairly simply, so it's usually a trivial matter to convert between formats, even if this must be done manually.

The entire feature's final cut can be expressed in a thousand lines or so (depending on the number of edits), which makes the EDL perhaps the smallest piece of data in the whole filmmaking process, as well as one of the most important pieces.

THE SONY CMX 3600 EDL FORMAT

Since EDLs are so crucial to post-production, it's important to be familiar with them. Although many different formats are available; the Sony CMX 3600 is probably the most widely used. The Appendix contains an example of a CMX 3600-formatted EDL, as well as a breakdown of its structure.

7.1.5 Transitions

Transitions are used to bridge two different shots together. The simplest and most common type of transition is a cut. A cut involves the first shot ending on one frame, followed by the new shot starting on the next frame. Skillful editing hides this somewhat harsh transition. The audience accepts the drastic change in the picture without even realizing it.

At times, a cut doesn't work or may ruin the pacing of the picture. Editors have at their disposal several alternatives to using a cut, whether working on a film-based project or a video-based one. A fade-in (or fade-up) involves gradually raising the level of the shot over the length of the transition. At the start of the shot, the picture is completely black, and the level increases until the complete picture is visible, which occurs at the end of the transition. At that point, the shot continues playing normally. The opposite occurs in a fade-out: as the shot nears its end, the image level decreases, reaching black on the last frame. An extension to this process and the most common type of transition after a cut is a dissolve.

A dissolve gradually drops the level of the outgoing shot while raising the level of the incoming shot. The result is that the first shot seems to blend into the second. The duration of the dissolve can be varied, providing that there is enough footage for the overlapping area. The longer the dissolve, the more footage is required at the end of the outgoing shot and at the beginning of the incoming shot.[6]

Wipe effects (or wipes) are similar to dissolves in that two adjacent shots overlap. Whereas a dissolve blends together two complete images, a wipe superimposes one shot over the other using an animated pattern. Over the course of the wipe, the incoming shot increasingly dominates the overall picture. For instance, using one of the simplest wipe effects results in the new image appearing to "slide in" over the previous shot.

Most transitions can be encoded into an EDL and should carry over from the offline edit to the online edit. In addition, the online-editing system invariably has methods for fine-tuning the transition. For example, dissolves may use different methods to blend together two shots, and you can adjust the rate at which the images dissolve. Wipes are usually specified by SMTPE-standard codes to determine the pattern used, but they too can normally be manipulated during the online edit to create more specific patterns.

---

[6] A "soft cut" is one where a very short dissolve, usually a single frame, is used in place of a cut. In theory soft cuts are more pleasing to the eye than regular cuts, but in practice, they're rarely used.

FIGURE 7-2 A dissolve effect smoothly blends two shots

FIGURE 7-3   A wipe effect gradually slides in one image over another

The reason dissolves and wipes are normally fine-tuned during the online edit rather than the offline edit is because such detailed settings don't get conferred into the EDL. The EDL records only the transition type and duration (and the base pattern number in the case of wipe effects).

7.1.6 Motion Effects

In addition to changing transitions, editors also have the capability to adjust the speed of a shot; this process is often referred to as "speed changes." A shot can be set to run slower or faster than its original recording speed. For instance, film footage that was recorded at 24fps can instead be played back at 48fps (200% speed), making the footage appear to move twice as fast. Or the film can be played back at 12fps (50% speed), making the footage appear to be moving in slow motion. It's also possible to completely reverse a shot. The actual mechanics of this process vary according to the online-editing system. The simplest method for performing a speed-change operation is to repeat or drop, as required, a proportional number of frames from the shot. So, a shot at 24fps that is speed-changed to 200% might drop every other frame, while the same shot at 50% speed might repeat each frame once.

Changing the speed of a shot need not be linear. Rather than just applying a constant speed change to a sequence of frames, it's also possible to apply acceleration or deceleration to footage. This process, known as "time-warping," gives the editor greater control over the way a shot progresses. Using time-warping software, it's possible to start a shot in slow motion, gradually build up its speed until it's playing faster than originally recorded, and then even reverse it.

When performing a speed change, the resulting motion might not look smooth, especially when the scene contains a lot of fast motion. A more suitable option under these circumstances is to use motion interpolation software to generate new frames. Motion interpolation can be performed using several different options. The simplest involves blending frames. The amount of blending can be controlled to "weight" the motion and in doing so, can approximate motion between frames. A more advanced method involves the use of a motion analysis solution, such as RE:Vision Effects' Twixtor software (www.revisionfx.com), which can provide an even greater level of accuracy by breaking down and analyzing the movement of objects within a frame.

Another simple motion effect is the freeze frame (or frame hold). This effect is created by repeating a single frame for a predetermined length of time.

It's possible to combine motion effects with different transitions—for example, a freeze frame might be combined with a fade in, or a speed change with a dissolve. Again, the EDL contains only a limited amount of information about motion effects: typically just the length of the effect and the new speed. It's also worth noting that it may not be possible to create certain motion effects optically with film. Specifically, it isn't possible to repeat frames (e.g., or even entire shots in a flashback sequences) without first duplicating the required

FIGURE 7-4 RE:Vision Fx's Twixtor Pro Software (shown here with Autodesk's Combustion Interface) enables you to retime digital footage in a nonlinear manner— in this case, compensating for interlacing and motion blur

frames. Video (and data), on the other hand, can be duplicated by the online-editing system.

7.1.7 Handles

In creating a production, it's inevitable that more footage will be shot than is used in the final edit. Typically the ratio of the total length of all footage shot to the length of the final cut (i.e., the shooting ratio) can be 10:1 or higher. This is mainly due to the number of takes and multiple camera angles used within a single scene. But even within a single take, it's rare that the entire duration of the filmed footage will be used. For every shot in a film, footage filmed before and after usually is edited out.

During post-production, editors like to allow themselves a margin of error—that is, at some point in the future, if they need to lengthen a shot by a few frames, they make sure that the extra frames are available on the editing system. These extra frames are called "handles," and for every event cut into the final picture, an extra number of these handle frames usually is available before and after. Editors normally have 4–15 handles per event during the final stages of editing, depending upon the requirements and needs (and budget) of the production.

7.1.8 B-Rolls

Before the days of nonlinear video-editing, editors (both for film and video) had to put all material needed for effects such as wipes and dissolves onto a separate tape (or film reel), which was known as the "B-roll." The first part of the effect (i.e., the outgoing shot) is cut into the program as usual (the A-roll). Both rolls also contain the extra frames for the overlapping section. When the time comes to create the effect, the A-roll and B-roll are combined onto a separate tape, which then has the completed dissolve or wipe. B-rolls are also used to hold the original-length shot prior to a motion effect. Though B-rolls are not necessary for modern nonlinear-editing systems, they're still a necessary stage for editing film, and as we shall see later, they may also be a requirement for digital-conforming systems.

7.2 DIGITAL CONFORMING

Digital-conforming systems, particular those used in the digital intermediate process, share many features of both nonlinear video online-
editing systems, while empowering film-based projects to utilize
many of the advantages of video-based projects.

7.2.1 Digital Conform Systems

Although many manufacturers of digital-intermediate-conforming
systems strive to include a high number of features, the actual requirements for a viable data-conforming system are very limited.
Basically, the fundamental requirement of a digital-conforming system is that it must be able to reorder a set of digital image files according to the final offline edit (although even this process may not be
necessary for certain situations) and output them without altering the
content in any way. A simple command-line computer program is
sufficient to satisfy these requirements, and in fact, this capability
might be integrated into the data management system used by a digital intermediate facility.[7] In practice though, conform systems are feature rich, incorporating an iconic or other graphical representation of
the conformed data, as well as providing many other options available to video-based online-editing systems.

In practice, the digital conform tends to be an ongoing process.
Throughout the digital intermediate pipeline, shots within the program are constantly being updated or replaced, and new material
constantly being acquired into the pipeline.

Digital-conforming systems can be separated into two broad categories: the "modular" system and the "integrated" system. A modular
digital-conforming system relies on other components of the digital
intermediate pipeline to perform various tasks. In a modular system,
data is input into the system (usually through the data management
system), which then conforms it and outputs the conformed data (or
specific shots and frames) to a number of other systems. For instance,
an external system might apply effects, such as a dissolve or a filter to

---

[7] A command-line computer program is one where a set of instructions is input
directly into the command window of the operating system and doesn't necessarily
provide any visual feedback.

a number of shots, to footage supplied to it by the conforming system (possibly via the asset management system), and supply the newly generated footage with the desired effect applied back to the conforming system (again making use of the asset management system if necessary). Similarly, the conforming system might be constantly bouncing shots back and forth between color-grading system (assuming color grading is being used on the production), as well as any restoration systems that may be being used, continually replacing original acquired material with color-graded finals. Perhaps the conforming module is the final stage in the pipeline, in which case, once everything has been completed, the conforming system sends the final, conformed data to an output module. This method provides some distinct advantages, particularly the ability to incorporate collaboration into the pipeline. One operator can be dedicated to a particular function, such as conforming the data, while another is responsible for the color grading, and so on. This also means that operators with particularly strong skills in certain areas can be more effectively utilized. There are a few drawbacks to using this method. First, it can be a slow process, because having to constantly transmit data between different modules requires time and computer resources, including additional disk space. By extension, this method is also more expensive to implement, because each subsystem is usually installed on a separate workstation. Finally, it may be difficult for the system to demonstrate a sense of priority so that the modules that require full, unrestricted access to the latest data always have it.

The integrated system takes the opposite approach to conforming data. Rather than assigning different tasks to specialized subsystems, the conforming station also provides the required controls for all the necessary tasks. For example, in addition to being able to assemble frames and shots in the correct order, the same system can also provide tools to color-correct and apply effects and other processes. It's still possible to incorporate networking and multioperator paradigms when using this method; it just means that each operator has all the required tools for performing any task. Successfully utilizing this approach usually requires incorporating strict access control procedures, to ensure that the right operators have access to the right data at the right time, and that the access privileges don't conflict with those of another operator. This approach tends to be best suited to smaller-scale digital intermediate

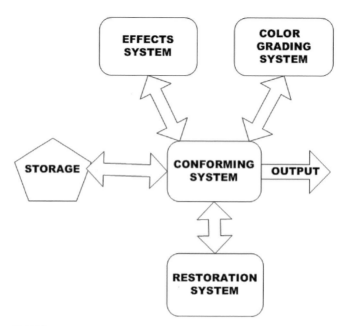

FIGURE 7-5 With a modular-conforming system, tasks such as grading are handled by separate systems

productions; each workstation required normally incurs considerable expense, due to the abundance of software-based tools and the high-performance hardware that might be needed to run them. But in using such a system, even a relatively small team, possibly in less time, can produce quality results just as those produced by a larger module-based team.

An extension of this paradigm is having a single all-in-one solution. For small or low-budget productions, it may be possible to complete the digital intermediate on a single system. As an extreme example, an editor who has completed the editing of a DV production has, in effect, conformed the data at the maximum resolution already (most DV-editing systems capture DV at full quality). The editor is usually able to use the same (offline) editing system to perform similar (if not as fully featured) operations to the footage, such as rudimentary color-correction and titling. Using this single system, an entire production can be edited from scratch, finished digitally, and even output to a variety of formats.

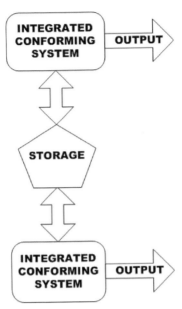

FIGURE 7-6 With multiple integrated-conforming systems, each system has a full set of tools for working with images

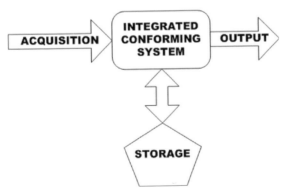

FIGURE 7-7 With an all-in-one system, a single workstation is used to finish a production

Clearly this approach isn't applied to larger-scale productions for good reasons. For one thing, it takes a lot longer and requires a highly skilled operator with a multitude of capabilities, but it demonstrates what is actually possible. In practice, the conforming system inevitably is some combination of the two paradigms, which may in turn depend upon the production's requirements.

A popular compromise is to combine the conforming system with the color-correction system, so that both systems take precedence over all other components in terms of resources. In addition, an operator is provided with the features of both and the ability to work with the most up-to-date versions of each shot.[8] For example, Autodesk's Lustre system (www.discreet.com) combines data conforming, color grading, and effects capabilities, with restoration and output. In addition it has the capability to directly acquire video into the system. Such systems typically can send data to external modules if required.

In addition to the specifics of the conforming system, consideration must also be given to how the data is to be conformed.

FIGURE 7-8 Autodesk's Lustre can be used as an end-to-end digital intermediate system

---

[8] In fact, the conforming system is often a subset of the color-grading system, rather than the other way around.

7.3   DIGITAL CONFORM PARADIGMS

Each of the many different methods for conforming data is typically best-suited to a certain scale of production. They're normally driven by EDLs or cut lists; it may be that simpler conforming systems require manually created edits, which isn't recommended for lengthy productions containing numerous events.

7.3.1   Fine-Cut Conforming

The fine-cut paradigm is the simplest to implement. It assumes that all the source material fed in is already in the correct, final-cut order. When this is the case, all the data is supplied without any handles, with each output reel matching exactly what has been supplied, cut for cut. Conforming a reel of this type merely involves loading the supplied data into the conforming system. Because the supplied data is already in the correct order, no additional operations are required. The conforming system effectively treats the entire cut as one long shot. Therefore, it may be necessary to divide the conformed data back into its original edits, particularly when more work has to be done on individual shots. When this is the case, the conforming system is responsible for distributing individual shots to other systems—for example, for color grading. Segmenting data back into original cuts may be done either manually, by inputting the cut points directly into the conforming system, or automatically, with the use of a production-supplied EDL of the final cut or the use of a cut-detection algorithm, which detects sudden changes in the contents of the picture and marks them as cut points.

For dissolves and other transition and motion effects, the cut points may have already been performed and included within the supplied data, in which case no additional work is required. However, any shot supplied that includes dissolves or wipes can't be separated into its constituent elements—meaning that the dissolve parameters (e.g., the duration or profile) can't be altered, and the two adjacent shots must be treated as a single shot. Similarly, motion effects can't be undone; they can be retimed, but it normally results in a reduction of temporal quality.

Alternatively, the fine-cut data may be supplied as an A-roll, with a separate B-roll containing the additional elements, in which case, the conforming system must either create the desired effect itself or include an effect completed by some other system—for example, a visual effects workstation. The inclusion of such effects can be managed by the use of EDLs, or it may be more convenient to make the inclusions manually.

Material is usually supplied as fine cut for film-based projects where the original negative has already been consolidated, or for video-based projects where the video has already been through an online stage (including situations where the offline-editing system works at maximum quality and is therefore able to output the final cut piece at maximum quality). The production may have been previously considered finished, but for some reason, it currently requires going through the digital intermediate process. A good example of this case is productions that are digitally remastered, meaning that the cut remains the same as the original but then undergoes the color-grading and restoration process digitally, before being output to the required formats.

However, the extremely limited amount of provided footage means that it isn't possible to add any extra footage (such as for a recut) without providing separate material (and hence incurring additional expense and requiring more time).

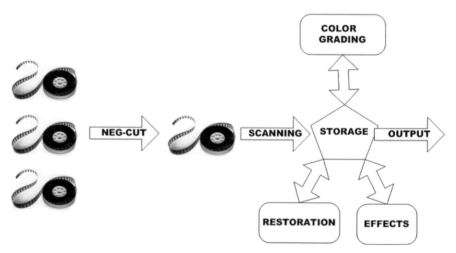

FIGURE 7-9   When conforming from fine-cut material, little or no editing is necessary

7.3.2   Conforming from Original Source Reels

An alternative approach is to conform a program from all the original footage that was shot. The original source reels (also referred to as "dailies" or "rushes") can be acquired into the digital intermediate system so that the material available to the conforming system matches the material available to the offline-editing system. Assuming the same naming conventions (reel numbers and timecodes) were used on both the offline-editing system and within the digital intermediate pipeline (which they should do), the EDL generated by the offline-editing system can be used by the conforming system to automatically and accurately select the correct footage from the source material and cut it together within the digital intermediate. One of the benefits of this approach is that the acquisition stage can begin as soon as the footage is created. As soon as any material is shot (and processed, if necessary), it can be acquired into the digital intermediate system, ready to be conformed once the editing is complete. Doing so also facilitates the creation of so-called "digital dailies,"—that is, digital copies of the filmed material for viewing purposes (e.g., output to video tape or transmitted via the Internet). However, it may be far too expensive to store so much footage, especially if it won't be accessed for a long time (typically the time required to edit the footage from the time it was shot can be several months). It need not all be acquired straight away of course, but by the time the edit is nearing completion, most of the original footage (around 90% of it) is redundant.

To solve this problem, it's possible to acquire only the needed footage, but this solution can still be time-consuming, because many reels of footage must be gone through, with each reel containing a small amount of relevant material. The act of physically changing the reels, combined with the potentially slow acquisition speed of the system (particularly in the case of film-based productions), largely contribute to the time requirements. On top of that, many issues are associated with physically storing the original footage at the digital intermediate facility doing the acquisition—issues such as insurance expenses to cover theft or damage.

7.3.3   Conforming from Master Source Reels

A good compromise between both of these situations is to create "master source reels," which are basically reels that contain a compilation of

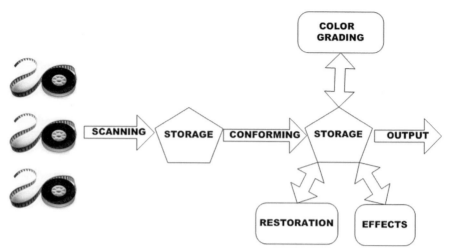

FIGURE 7-10 When conforming from rushes, the material must be edited to separate final shots from unused material

all the footage required for the final cut (and usually include some handle frames as well). Creating master source reels greatly reduces the total amount of footage to be acquired and managed, while retaining enough flexibility to allow some degree of recutting.

The difficulty in implementing this scenario successfully is that additional EDLs must be generated that reference the new master source reels as if they were the original material. When a new master source reel is created, the footage is given a new timecode (and reel number) to reflect the new location on a new tape (otherwise, a jumble of different timecodes would be on each new tape, and you would have no way of referencing the original reel numbers). This isn't necessarily true for film-based projects that are conformed using key numbers, because the key numbers remain intact even after being transferred to another reel. But most film-based projects are actually conformed using a timecode reference, and therefore they're subject to the same issues as video-based projects.

The new EDLs must be generated by taking the final (offline) EDL and replacing the source reel numbers and timecodes with the new reel numbers and timecodes as they appear on the new reels. This is a huge task to undertake if done manually; however, certain systems exist (in particular, those that can create the master source reels in the first place) to manage the EDL conversions automatically.

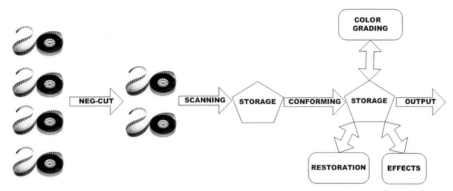

FIGURE 7-11 Conforming from master source reels requires scanning less material than working directly from rushes, and it affords more flexibility than fine-cut material

7.3.4 Conforming Data

As discussed previously, the preferred way to conform data is using an EDL. All the data within the digital intermediate system is indexed to distinguish each frame. A few methods can perform this process (they're covered in Chapter 6). The most common method is to assign each frame a source reel number and timecode. This way, if done correctly, the data can be referenced in exactly the same way as the offline-editing system references its own source material. Thus, the generated EDL is as valid on the digital system as on the offline-editing system. Therefore, the conforming system can process the data, locate the equivalent digital frames, and sequence them correctly.

Another method for conforming data is to organize the data on the disk according to the events in the EDL. Each EDL event corresponds to a different folder (which can follow the same numbering system of events as the EDL follows). The frames within each folder have to be ordered correctly, however, and managing handle frames might prove problematic. In addition, this method doesn't allow for program recuts or replacement EDLs to be supplied at a later date.

The other alternative is to manually assemble the shots. The benefits of such a system are that you don't need to maintain strict, consistent naming conventions, and in fact, this method can prove to be very fast in situations with a few events (e.g., where fine-cut material has

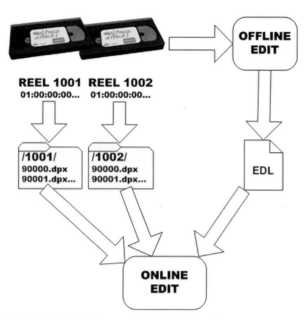

FIGURE 7-12 Data can be conformed by using an EDL to match the digital material to the offline edit by timecode and reel number

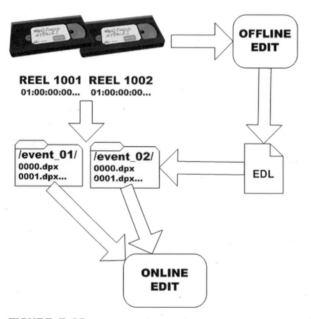

FIGURE 7-13 Data can be conformed by matching digitized shots to individual events in the EDL

been supplied), provided the conformist is familiar with the production. Unfortunately, this method is prone to inaccuracies and tracking problems, and it isn't suitable for a large-scale production. In any case, this method of conforming becomes too tedious to use for programs with many events.

Other options may be available. Systems that are configured to specifically allow it might be able to transfer data directly from the offline-editing system. If the data in the offline system is already at the maximum quality level, it may be possible to output the image data as a single file, "packaged" within an EDL of sorts. Loading this file into the conforming system automatically positions the images in the correct order, optionally including handle frames if necessary, as well as the ability to separately dissolve elements. The main reason this system isn't used very often is because there are many compatibility issues. In addition, it can take longer to transport the large amount of data than

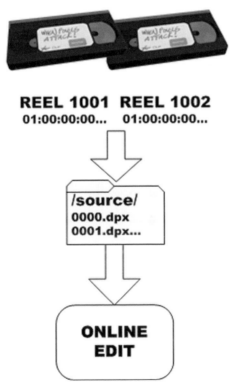

FIGURE 7-14 Data can be conformed by manually editing material together

to simply transport an EDL and thereby acquire the image data. However, software such as Automatic Duck's Pro Import line (www. automaticduck.com) allows the timelines created in offline-editing systems to be translated to finishing systems, rebuilding effects, transitions, and layers more seamlessly than when using EDLs.

7.3.5 Referenced Data

Because facilities tend to use different systems for each stage in a digital intermediate pipeline, particularly for large productions, a great deal of data transport and tracking is required, which can be slow and at times difficult to manage. The usual workflow is to designate a sequence within the conforming system that must be processed on a separate system, send it to that system, complete the effect, and bring it back into the conforming system, replacing the sequence that was there before. If further changes have to be made, the entire process must be repeated.

A much more powerful paradigm is to use referenced data. Using this approach, data isn't copied back and forth between separate systems, but instead, the conforming system uses pointers to the location of the desired footage. For example, let's say you have a separate system for creating dissolves, outside of the conforming system. With data referencing, you send the two parts of the dissolve to the external system, which then applies the dissolve. Rather than conforming the new data back into the conforming system, a reference is created, pointing to the location of the completed dissolve. During playback, the dissolve appears to be in the correct place, but if any alterations are made to the dissolve, the changes propagate back into the conformed program without having to do anything.

This concept can be expanded even further. It's possible for every system to rely purely on references. In the previously mentioned example, the dissolve system can obtain footage directly from the conform system as a reference, so if changes are made to the original footage, these changes are automatically reflected within the dissolve system and then passed on directly back to the conform system as a completed dissolve.

Though such a system can potentially reduce the overall disk space requirements of the pipeline, in reality, many of the files have to be

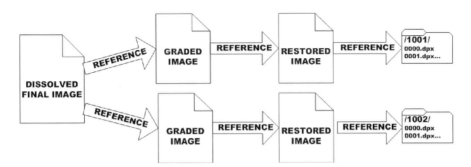

FIGURE 7-15 When using referenced data, complex shots can have many levels

cached. Therefore, no storage space benefit is obtained. Without a caching mechanism, the process could end up being very slow, especially when many levels of referencing are used. In addition, it requires careful management, because it is all too easy to delete footage that seems to serve no purpose, only to find out later that it was referenced by a different process.

Referencing systems tend only to exist in pipelines that have a common infrastructure, when facilities have designed their own digital intermediate systems themselves, or when facilities have bought a number of different systems from the same manufacturer who has included this functionality. Because no real industry standard for creating data references has been established, this capability is almost nonexistent among systems designed by different manufacturers; although occasionally, a third party steps in to supply software to bridge the gap between two systems.

7.3.6 Conforming Video Using Timecodes

Conforming video footage using timecodes is a fairly straightforward process. When an EDL is supplied to a capable conforming system, the system cross-references the reel numbers and timecodes in the EDL to the image data saved on the system. The precise mechanics of this process depend on the specifics of the conforming system and the data management paradigm. The most popular method involves storing footage within folders on the disk that correspond to the video reel the images were sourced from. Within the folder, each frame is assigned a frame number, from which a timecode can be derived using a simple formula (see Chapter 6). Because the offline edit is created using exactly the same timecode, the EDL produced can be input directly into the conforming system. (The EDL can't be directly input into the conforming system when master source reels have been created as an intermediate step, in which case, EDLs must be generated specifically for this purpose.)

SCENE EXTRACTION

Some digital video systems have the capability of performing scene extraction, which enables the system to somewhat automatically divide a video reel into cuts. The way that this process works is by comparing the recorded time of day against the timecode. Where a break appears in the time of day (or a break in the timecode), such as when the recorded time of day jumps from 12:13:43:21 to 12:17:12:10, but the timecode remains continuous (e.g., going from 01:00:13:12 to 01:00:13:13), the assumption is that recording was stopped (or paused) to provide an opportunity to set up a new shot (or new take), and the conforming system adds a cut point to the footage. This simple, yet highly effective technique will presumably continue to be used across a number of different imaging systems and provides an efficient way to quickly separate shots in a reel. Unfortunately, no equivalent system exists for film reels (at least, not yet).

7.3.7 Conforming Scanned Film Using Key Numbers

When conforming scanned film, it may be more convenient to conform the image data automatically by the film's key numbers, rather than another, more arbitrary parameter. Because each key number is unique, there is less chance that the wrong frame is loaded into the conforming system.

For this to work correctly, the digital-conforming system must be able to interpret an editor's formatted cut list (which lists the edits in terms of key numbers rather than timecode). The system must also be able to extract key number information from the digital images to be loaded in. Key numbers are either embedded into each frame's "header" or may be encoded within the filename.

At the present time, most film-based projects aren't conformed automatically using key numbers due largely to the limited ability for encoding key numbers into scanned images, coupled with the limited support for conforming key numbers within most digital-conforming systems. In addition, the accuracy of key numbers can't be guaranteed, particularly when the film is supplied as master source reels rather than an uncut, original camera negative.

7.3.8 Assigning Timecodes to Scanned Film

An effective, accurate method for digitally conforming film involves assigning a reel number and timecode value to each frame of film, as if it were a video tape. This process is usually as simple as assigning a reel number to each reel of film. Within each reel, a single "marker" frame is used as a reference point. This marker frame can be any frame on the reel, but for convenience, it's normally located just before the start of the picture. The frame is marked physically in some way, normally by punching a hole through it. This punch-hole frame is then assigned a specific timecode (for simplicity, it's usually assigned a timecode such as 01:00:00:00). The timecodes for every other frame on the reel can then be derived by counting forward (or backward) from the punch hole. The frame rate of the offline video-editing system must be taken into account so that both the offline and the conforming systems use identical timecodes.[9] Then, it's simply a matter of inputting the EDL produced by the offline system into the conforming system, in exactly the same way a video-based project is conformed.

The downside to this approach is that the timecode system must be implemented before a telecine of the film is made for offline-editing purposes. Where this isn't possible, or where master source reels are used for scanning (rather than using the original, uncut camera negative), the offline EDL must undergo a conversion process to correlate the telecine source timecodes to the new timecodes generated by the master source

---

[9] In fact, digital files are normally stored internally as frame numbers, which are independent of a frame rate, but the frame rate has to be supplied to derive the correct timecode from the frame numbers.

reels. This process can be a complex procedure. However the negative-cutting facility responsible for compiling the master source reels is often suitably equipped to automatically create the new EDL.

Ultimately though, this system works only when the timecodes used for scanning the film correspond directly to the offline EDL supplied by the editor (even if timecode conversions must be done first).

ACQUISITION EDLS

EDLs can be used for many operations in the digital intermediate pipeline, in addition to accurately conforming a program. EDLs are commonly used to designate the specific frames required for acquisition. For instance, a "capture EDL" for video, or a "scan EDL" for film can be input into the system, listing only the timecodes for the footage that is required.

Most video capture systems have a "batch capture" mode. Using this mode allows multiple shots across multiple tapes to be compiled into an EDL. When ready, all the shots listed in the EDL are captured into the system at once. This process can be performed unattended, with the operator only needing to change reels as required.

From within the conforming system, EDLs can be used to pick out specific shots or frames. Most commonly, an EDL lists frames that require restoration. The conforming or data management system processes the EDL and extracts the frames listed in the EDL (optionally including handle frames). After the frames have been corrected, they can be reintegrated into the conforming system.

EDL MATHEMATICS

On many occasions, an EDL has to be adjusted to solve a particular problem in the digital intermediate process, or to enable compatibility between separate systems. The simplest such operation might be replacing the reel number for all instances of the reel (e.g., changing all edits with reel 033 to 034). Other oper-

(continues)

ations might include adding an offset to particular timecodes, removing events, or even converting between frame rates. Another useful function is the ability to merge EDLs.

Many of these operations can be done by manually editing the EDLs, but some with lengthy and/or complex calculations might require using a computer system. This kind of functionality is often built into the conforming system, or it may be obtained through separate software solutions.

7.4 PLAYBACK

The conforming system is generally considered to be responsible for the playback of a finished production. This convention is used more because of convenience than necessity; the conforming system is the first place that the entire, full-quality finished film comes together. So isolating problems at this stage makes more sense than waiting until the data has been distributed to various other components. Similarly, the color-correction system is often combined with the conforming system, and the capability to view color-corrected changes to the production at the maximum level of detail, and at speed, should be considered essential.

Digital image playback systems are notoriously difficult to implement, especially at film resolutions (of 2k and higher). The sheer volume of data that has to be processed is enormous—three minutes of film data is equivalent to an entire DVD of data. The footage has to be viewed in real time at the same level of quality as the final output medium, so that you can see it as the audience eventually will see it, which means that three minutes of film data has to be played back in exactly three minutes—no faster, no slower, and without using any tricks such as dropping frames to maintain the frame rate.

With DV-based productions, inexpensive computer systems can process the associated data very reliably, and many high-end systems can play back HD video-quality data without any problems. Uncompressed 2k data playback, however, often requires a series of dedicated hardware and software components. Systems such as Thomson's Specter FS (www.thomsongrassvalley.com) can conform and playback 2k data from networked or local storage in real time.

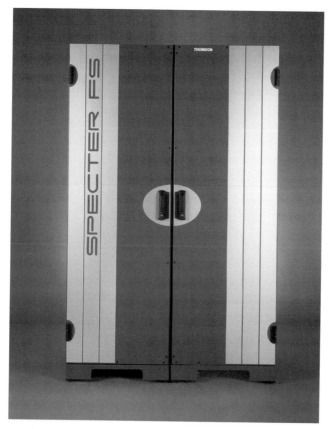

FIGURE 7-16 Thomson's Specter FS Is a hardware-based system for real-time playback of up to 2k image data

Some conforming systems work by displaying proxies (i.e., down-sized copies of the original images) rather than the full-size originals to increase the system's speed and responsiveness; such systems normally also have a method for switching to view the full-size images. Assuming this process has been properly implemented, one of the great strengths of a digital intermediate pipeline is its capability to instantly seek (i.e., go to) any frame in the entire production. Rather than having to search through stacks of tapes or reels of film and then spool through them to find the desired frame, this can be accomplished in a digital system simply with the click of a mouse. In addition, most digital-conforming systems provide many other features to increase productivity, such as timelines, resolution independence, vertical editing, and split-screening.

7.5   DIGITAL-CONFORMING INTERFACES

One of the main functions of a digital-conforming system is to allow manipulation of conformed material and provide feedback. Digital conforming can theoretically be achieved with very limited user input and without any graphical representation of the system's contents, but most systems provide at least some rudimentary display of their contents and current status.

The data that has been conformed can be represented in many ways, and different software solutions inevitably use different approaches. Perhaps the simplest type of interface is to use a storyboard display mechanism. With this method, each event is represented by a thumbnail image, showing a still of the event's contents. This method is similar to having a thumbnail of every event, in the order that the events occur, in the finished production. This is useful in ascertaining the production's overall progression, but it doesn't tell you whether a single event actually comprises several elements (e.g., in the case of an elaborate crane shot) or indeed the length of each shot.

A more useful option, therefore, is a timeline. Timelines are common in most nonlinear-editing systems. Basically, a horizontal timeline runs along the interface, representing the entire program. Each event is positioned on the timeline according to when it occurs, and the event is normally displayed as a small rectangle, its size indicating the length of the event. Sometimes thumbnails are drawn on top of the events in the timeline, but timelines normally don't include thumbnails, to increase the display speed. A position indicator usually shows the current frame being displayed.

Timelines are generally considered the most flexible and useful method of representation for a conforming system, and anyone who is familiar with a nonlinear-editing system (which most conforming systems operators are likely to be) will find using them intuitive. This system, though fairly simple, can be embellished further still. In applications such as Quantel's Qedit (www.qunatel.com), it's possible to zoom the timeline's display, to get an overall sense of the program's progression, or to focus on a specific detail (e.g., the timecode when a particular event occurred). It may also be possible to highlight events in a different color to distinguish certain features—for example, showing all events with attached motion effects, or even for project management purposes, providing the capability of highlighting sequences that haven't yet been approved by the production. Other options, such as the ability to attach notes or comments to specific events or timecodes, expand this interface further. The only disadvantage to this type of display is that it can be difficult to obtain detailed information about a specific event, such as the shot's source timecode.

A more advanced method is to display the raw data for the conform—for example, in an EDL-formatted list displaying a position indicator next to the event currently being viewed. A multitude of information can be derived from this type of interface, from the duration of each event, to information about the digital image format. The problem with this type of interface is that it isn't particularly intuitive for quickly browsing through a scene.

The different interface types can, of course, be combined together, so that an EDL-type interface might have thumbnails (thus expand-

FIGURE 7-17 Quantel's Qedit offers a detailed timeline for displaying information about conformed sequences

ing upon the storyboard interface), or it may be possible to "call up" detailed information for a specific event in a timeline environment. Alternatively, the conforming system may be designed to enable the operator to switch between different interface types.

7.5.1 Resolution Independence

Digital-conforming systems borrow a lot of functionality and ideas from nonlinear video-editing systems, but conforming data has several advantages over conforming video. One significant advantage is resolution independence. Unlike video formats, which are highly standardized, digital images can be of any dimension, which means that they can always (theoretically) be acquired at the optimum resolution. So, film images can be 4096×3112 or 2048×1556 pixels (or any other arbitrary value), while NTSC video frames can be captured at 720×486 pixels. With a resolution-independent system, these differently sized images can be mixed together without having to resize

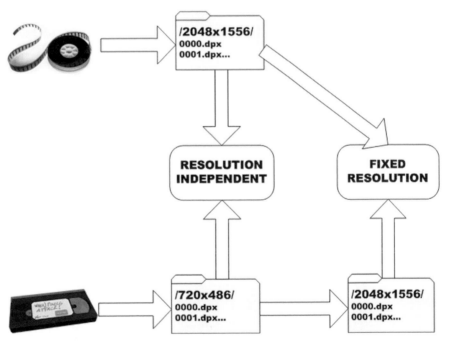

FIGURE 7-18 Resolution-independent conforming systems don't require images to be supplied at a fixed resolution

any of them (thereby retaining each frame's maximum quality level), until the frames are output, at which point the frames are resized (from the original image rather than one that has already undergone multiple resizing operations) to the desired output resolution. Conforming systems may choose to display differently sized images proportionally or show each image the same size.

It should be noted that not all conforming systems support resolution independence and may force the operator to nominate a "working resolution," to which all incoming data will be resized (or rejected) as necessary.

An extension of this method is the notion of format independence. As mentioned previously, digital images may be encoded in a variety of different image formats. Format-independent systems allow the combining of different format types with no ill effects. Other systems may require that images be converted to a common format. The same is also true of color spaces—for instance, it may or may not be possible to seamlessly mix images encoded in RGB color space with images in film color spaces.

7.5.2   Multiple Timelines

Rather than having a single timeline, containing the program's final cut, it can also be useful to have secondary timelines that are synchronized to the primary one. One of the possible applications for this option might be to store different cuts for a program. A common use for additional timelines is for reference material, perhaps scans of storyboards. Even more uses are possible, such as adding alternative camera angles to be included in a DVD release.

7.5.3   Vertical Editing

The concept of vertical editing is both simple and elusive. The basic idea is multiple timelines are stacked on top of each other, rather than running in parallel. When you're looking at any particular position in a sequence, the frame displayed is the one on the highest timeline (or track). In theory, this approach seems somewhat pointless, but in practice, it can be a very useful feature, especially for incorporating data from multiple sources.

Another option is to store different EDLs on different timelines. Corrections to a program are often made using a changes EDL, which is simply an EDL that contains just the elements that are different from the original offline EDL. Such EDLs can also be used for loading extra material, such as visual effects shots or footage that has gone through a restoration process. Loading each EDL onto a separate track can help to identify potential problems, as well as determine the origin of different material.

Vertical-editing systems allow rudimentary version control; newer shots are placed above shots that have been superseded but are still available for reference purposes. Many vertical-editing systems also allow individual tracks to be "turned off," meaning that the contents of that track are not displayed or that they're ignored at the output stage (or both), as if the track weren't there. This can be useful in situations where an EDL is loaded into the system, but the material isn't yet available to the system for viewing. Thus you can still load the reference to the events without affecting the picture. Another useful function is the ability to collapse several tracks, effectively merging their contents into a single track.

Conforming systems such as Thomson's Bones (www.thomsongrass-valley.com) enable you to simultaneously view multiple shots, using any of several different methods. The most common and intuitive way to view two (or more) tracks at the same time is to use a split screen. Using a split screen involves dividing the picture into two (or more) sections. Each part of the image displays the contents of a particular timeline. Generally, the overall picture corresponds to the whole image, but it may also be possible to display a complete image in each section. An alternative to this approach is to display a picture-in-picture, where one timeline dominates the display, while another timeline is displayed in a smaller window within the image.

Many conforming systems, in particular those that are combined with other systems (such as color grading), use tracks to add operations that affect the tracks below them. For instance, a track containing footage might lie underneath a track with a color grade setting, which in turn might lie under a track with a reposition operation. When you view the footage, you see it color graded and repositioned; however, by switching individual tracks off, you can view the footage without

FIGURE 7-19 Systems such as Thomson's Bones enable you to place shots on multiple tracks and to view separate shots at the same time

color-grading or repositioning or with any desired combination of operations.

Another function of vertical editing is to allow layering of footage.

7.5.4 Layers

In addition to stacking footage for organizational purposes, placing different shots on top of each other can be useful for creative purposes. The most common application of this approach is to superimpose one image over another. Certain shots use layering, similar to using a wipe or a dissolve, to give a split-screen or picture-in-picture effect to a particular sequence. Likewise, each layer can have transparency and other compositing parameters to enable the shots to be blended in a variety of different ways. Images that are in an appropriate format might already have individual layers stored within the file—in this case, the layers might automatically be separated onto different tracks. Similarly, image files containing alpha channel information can use it to automatically grant the images the desired level of transparency.

In addition to layering images, it's also possible to include text or 3D objects. Furthermore, each layer can comprise an element in 2D or 3D space, the latter being used to provide perspective to the layers. And this is only the beginning. Some conforming systems can automatically generate a number of effects based upon layers, such as adding drop shadows or reflections.

7.5.5 Placeholders

It's rare for all the required footage to be available to the conforming system when the final cut EDL is delivered. Therefore, early instances of the conforming system will invariably include gaps where footage is missing. However, rather than just showing a black screen for missing material, it's more useful to display a placeholder of some sort, typically a static image displaying the words "missing material" or some other indicator, such as a large "X". This approach is used to differentiate missing footage from footage that is meant to be completely black (e.g., for fade effects) and to ensure that the fact that the material is missing doesn't go unnoticed. Sometimes the footage might be available, but it hasn't been conformed correctly, and so a warning display is a useful indicator that something isn't right.

Certain shots tend to be delivered later than the majority of the footage. This is particularly true of visual effects shots, which can take many months to complete. To try to minimize the impact of the delayed delivery of such shots, many digital intermediate pipelines substitute missing footage with similar footage. In the case of visual effects material, the common procedure is to substitute the absent footage with "background plates"—that is, footage that has been shot (as part of the production shoot) to serve as the starting point of the visual effect. This footage might be of a literal background scene (as in the case of chroma-key effects, which combine a blue-screen element with a background element) or some other available element.

Because such background plates are already available, substituting them temporarily for the finished shot can provide a sense of fluidity to the sequence and, in addition, can provide the color grader with some preliminary footage to start with.

BLACK FRAMES

During editing, black frames are used for a variety of reasons. They're occasionally used for creative purposes—such as for fade effects, or where there isn't supposed to be any picture—but more often they're used as "spacers," to separate different elements, especially with vertical editing. EDLs can list edits explicitly as black (BK or BLK), and video-editing systems are usually able to generate a black signal internally.

For vertical-editing-conforming systems, black frames might have two different uses. A particular event might be designated black because it's supposed to be black, or because it's supposed to be empty (i.e., used as a spacer). The distinction is subtle but important. If the top track in a vertical-editing timeline contains black, it could be empty, meaning that the contents of a lower track are played instead, or a black track might actually display black frames rather than the footage below it.

Most conforming systems take the approach that the presence of black in a timeline indicates the event is empty, and when no footage is available on a lower track, the material is assumed to be missing. If black frames are actually required, an operator usually has to insert them into the timeline manually.

In some systems, black frames can be generated on the fly, as needed, but in other systems, they can't, requiring actual footage to exist in the form of black frames, which are then cut into the program in the same way as any other footage. Other conforming systems, such as those lacking support for vertical editing, might also require the insertion of black footage to create spacers between shots. Worse, some conforming systems might not correctly load shots with discontinuous timecodes numbering (as discussed in Chapter 6) and require black frames be used to fill in the gaps in the timecode. Under these circumstances, a large number of black

(continues)

frames might have to be generated that ultimately serve no practical purpose (but consume an inordinate amount of storage space). There are several solutions to this problem, however.

Format-and/or resolution-independent conforming systems can take advantage of their capability to mix images, creating black frames as very low-resolution (even 1 pixel) images, or the systems can use a highly compressed format, greatly reducing disk space requirements (and in this instance, not compromising quality because black frames inherently have no spatial or chromatic detail at all). Another option is to create a single black frame, and use the symbolic linking feature of the operating system (if available) to reference this frame for every required black frame. Since the link files use substantially less space than uncompressed black images, the disk space requirements are reduced substantially.

7.6   CONFORMING DIGITAL MEDIA

Conforming digital material (most notably computer-generated visual effects), should be a simple matter. Unfortunately, it can be more of a complicated matter than conforming scanned film. Digital media doesn't have a reference point other than a filename. It doesn't have equivalent timecode like video (or timecode that can be assigned to it as with scanned film), and it doesn't have a system such as the use of key numbers to make each frame unique. The problem is that the offline editor can cut a digital shot, such as a completed visual effect, into the final cut but have no convenient way of supplying the specifics of the edit to the conforming system. The edit will show up as an event in the EDL, but the timecodes accompanying it become largely meaningless and the process is certainly not automatable. Very often, each digital shot has to be manually inserted into the conforming system, which can be problematic for effects-laden productions, and it complicates the version-tracking process.

A viable solution can be borrowed from the way scanned film is conformed and involves assigning digital footage a reel number and timecode, just like all other footage in the pipeline. For this solution to work, a new tape (or several new tapes) is created and given a reel number. Next, the footage in question is output to this tape, and the timecode for each shot is noted. This tape can be given to the offline editor, who cuts it into the program and produces an EDL for each shot. Meanwhile, the footage on the conforming system is assigned the same timecode and reel number as the tape created. This way, the EDL will then correctly reference the data.

The specifics of the procedure aren't important, just as long as there is an accurate way to refer to the same shots in the same way on both the offline and the conforming systems. At some point in the future, the reliance on EDLs to correctly conform footage may be replaced by some other, more robust method for synchronizing the footage on both systems. Perhaps each frame of data might be given a unique number, and the same data (albeit at lower resolution) might be copied to the offline-editing system for editing, eliminating the need to use video tapes at all. At present however, EDLs are a popular and reliable method for ensuring that data is conformed automatically.

7.6.1   Re-editing

On some occasions, shots must be adjusted or re-edited even after the offline editing is complete. A member of the production team often sees something that requires a quick adjustment but doesn't neces-sarily warrant issuing a new EDL. In addition, at times the conformed timeline, for whatever reason, doesn't match the offline edit and must be adjusted manually. Most conforming systems provide basic tools for re-editing the footage.

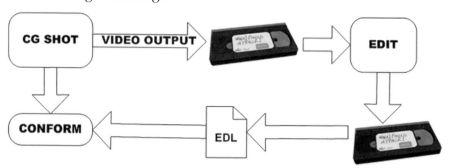

FIGURE 7-20   Digital media can be conformed by recreating it in the offline edit and generating an EDL

The simplest editing method is to take a source (e.g., a scanned reel of film), mark an in-point (i.e., the starting point of the edited shot), an "out-point" (the finishing point of the shot), and then do the same on the program's (the "record's") timeline, marking points for the footage's location. It's actually only necessary to mark three out of the four points, and the editing system automatically calculates the position of the fourth point based on the timing of the other points. Some editing systems automatically create a motion effect when the length of the source shot doesn't match the length of the record shot, speeding or slowing it as needed to make it fit. In some systems, you can also set a sync point, whereby a single frame in the source footage can be matched to a single frame in the recorded program.

New shots can be added to a sequence, either by being spliced in to the timeline at some point or by overwriting existing shots. Splicing in a shot adds the new shot without removing any of the existing footage. Operations of this type are known as "ripple" edits, meaning that the overall length of the program is changed. Performing ripple edits can cause sync problems with audio, multiple timelines, or tracks. On the other hand, overwriting a shot replaces the original footage with the new shot, which doesn't alter the program's length at all.

Similarly, events can be removed. "Lifting" a shot removes it, leaving behind an empty space (without altering the program's overall length). Extracting is another type of ripple edit; it removes the shot but doesn't leave a gap, instead making the previous shot cut to the following shot. This type of edit reduces the sequence's overall length. It's also possible to extract or lift just a few frames from a sequence, rather than removing entire shots.

In many cases, it can be necessary to divide a single event into two or more events, particularly when an effect is required for only a part of the shot. In this instance, a cut can be performed and is usually made at the currently displayed frame. Alternatively, a join edit can merge two adjacent events into a single one. However, this method usually works only when the shot's source footage is continuous (i.e., you can't join together two different shots).

Individual shots can also be slipped. Slipped shots change the timing of the footage without changing the lengths of any of the events in the sequence (and without altering the sequence's overall length), instead of just changing the required source frames. Transition points can be adjusted, too. Sliding a shot repositions it in the timeline so that it starts earlier or sooner. Adjacent shots increase or decrease in length to accommodate the process of sliding shots, and so the overall program length remains unchanged. Finally, trimming a shot makes it possible to increase or decrease the shot length. The adjacent shot is increased or decreased in length accordingly so that the overall length remains the same. A ripple trim alters the length of an event without affecting other shots, meaning that the program's length changes.

Making most of these types of edits usually requires additional footage. This extra footage may be covered by handle frames in the case of small adjustments; otherwise, more material may have to be acquired.

RE-EDITING LOCKED PICTURES

Given that the editing of most features is considered complete (or "locked") by the time it's conformed in the digital intermediate pipeline, it's remarkable how many last-minute changes seem to be necessary. In some ways, it's understandable—certain subtleties in the timing and picture can't be seen in the low-quality offline footage that editors work with. These subtleties become apparent only by watching the full-quality image on a big screen. But more than that, the production team tends to view the conformed pictures with a somewhat fresher perspective, and so an element of perfectionism sometimes comes into play. For the most part, re-editing a few frames here and there isn't much of a problem, particularly when the changes are covered by the handle frames. The real issue is that no paper trail of edited corrections is usually made on the spot. If anything were to happen to the data in the conforming system, it usually is a trivial matter to reload the offline EDLs back into the system and conform everything again. But small tweaks that were made might be forgotten and therefore lost.

(continues)

Trying to manually edit the offline EDLs to match changes that were made after the fact can also prove difficult or, at the least, tedious. Therefore, the most suitable solution is for the conforming system to output its own EDLs to reflect its contents at regular intervals. That way, if anything does go wrong, you'd still be able to revert to an up-to-date, accurate EDL.

7.6.2 Frame Patching

Many times, changes are made to individual frames outside of the conforming system, and such changes then must be included along with the rest of the conformed data. The most common reason for making these changes is "QC fixes." Throughout the digital intermediate process, facilities run "quality control" checks on the data to be conformed.

These checks inevitably reveal problems that have to be fixed—the problems usually are in the form of film damage or render errors. Because fixes are needed only for individual frames, as opposed to entire reels, just the frames in question are separated from the rest of the conform and output to the restoration system. Normally all the required fixes are completed together, and the frames output back to the conforming system. Rather than destroy the original frames by replacing them with the fixed version, the fixed frames are instead incorporated into a new "virtual reel," meaning that they're assigned a new reel number and source timecode, which don't actually exist in any physical form. The benefit of this method is that the original, unfixed frames still exist in the event that problems with the fixes are later revealed.

Within the conforming system, these fixed frames can be used to patch the original, conformed frames. In a vertical-editing environment, this process can be achieved by simply placing the fixed frames in the correct position on a new track within the timeline, above the previous versions. Alternatively, it may be possible to replace the original, unfixed frames with fixed ones in the timeline, without actually affecting the image data.

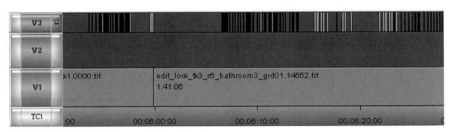

FIGURE 7-21 When using multiple tracks, it's possible to patch specific frames with repaired or otherwise corrected frames, by loading the fixed frames individually onto a higher track

7.6.3 Reconforming

One of the biggest logistical headaches in the entire digital intermediate pipeline is the having to reconform material. Reconforming is necessary anytime there is a significant change to the cut of the program. Any changes that require the program's soundtrack to be redone can be considered "significant." Inevitably, new offline EDLs must be supplied, either in the form of a changes EDL (for vertical-editing-capable conforming systems) where possible, or otherwise as completely new EDLs.

The reason reconforming becomes such a problem within the pipeline is because most systems and operations don't directly receive information from the conforming system, but instead from the actual data. For example, the color-grading system might receive frames from the conforming system in the correct order, but it doesn't "know" what each frame represents. It just "sees" a sequence of frames, which have previously been divided into individual shots, and each shot has separate color-grading settings applied. The crucial point is that whenever the cut changes, the color-correction parameters apply to the original cut, meaning that events may be in the wrong order, apply to the wrong shot, or more frequently, end on the wrong frame, creating "grading flashes" (i.e., a situation where the color shifts drastically in the middle of a shot). This applies to other systems as well. The most notorious issue concerns patched frames that are now out of sync with the new cut. These patches often have to be manually repositioned to match the changes to the conform, but sometimes it may be easier just to remove them and do the fixes again.

Similarly, when vertical editing is used, the track replaced by the new EDL (typically the lowest one) is now out of sync with all the other tracks, which have to be adjusted to match the changes.

Fortunately, some conforming systems include a reconform option, to manage such changes more intelligently. The reconform option works by examining every position in the timeline and assigning the reel number source timecode (from the original EDL) for that position to every frame (on all tracks). When the new EDL is input into the system, all the material already in the system is reassigned to the correct position, based upon the source timecodes. Any source material that doesn't recur in the new EDL is assumed to have been removed from the program and is removed from the timeline. New material not already present is then conformed in the usual way.

Other systems also must be able to perform a similar procedure to correctly incorporate the new cut. Many color-correction systems, for example, have a function to input old and new EDLs, and then a similar process is run to put the color-correction modifications in the right place.

If all the systems in the pipeline are able to automatically reconform data as needed, then the potential problems are reduced drastically. Still, regardless of the effectiveness of the reconforming software, the newly cut program will have to be checked thoroughly for other problems, such as missing footage or bad edits.

RESCANNING FILM

Even though one of the proclaimed benefits of the digital intermediate system is that film has to be handled only once—scanned and then stored away forever—in practice, film often has to be scanned more than once. Most reels of film have to be scanned only once, but rescanning is essential in several instances.

(continues)

RESCANNING FILM (continued)

If image data is damaged somehow, either through data corruption or an operation having gone wrong, it's often quicker and more convenient to simply rescan the image rather than try to repair the problem. The other time a rescan is necessary is when insufficient footage is available. If a reconform or re-edit requires footage that wasn't scanned in the first place, it's necessary to rescan the entire shot to include the missing footage. However, this presents a problem if the footage was supplied as master source reels, because it may mean that the additional footage isn't even available to be scanned. In this event, the remainder of the negative must be sent over separately, scanned, and then conformed in the correct place. At that point, the problem is that a difference between the original footage and the extended parts may be visible, because they were scanned under different conditions. These discrepancies can show up in the form of differences in color and image position, both of which can be an exacting and a time-consuming process to resolve.

These differences can also be visible with rescanned single shots. If the original shots have been patched, the patched frames may stand out from the rescanned footage. The most sensible solution in this case is to remove the patches from these shots and refix the footage.

ERROR REPORTING

One of the benefits of computer-based systems over other types of systems is that they can be designed to include a level of "intelligence." If you put a video in a player, or a reel of film on a projector, you can obtain a limited amount of information about that tape or reel of film. Load some digital images into a conforming system, however, and a wealth of information is potentially available. A conforming system can spout statistics on a multitude of factors, from the number of frames in the program, to the most frequently viewed image. This information need not be purely cosmetic however, and much of the information that conforming systems provide can save time and frustration.

ERROR REPORTING (*continued*)

Probably the most important thing the conforming system can tell you is which, if any, frames or shots are missing, without your having to play through the entire timeline to find out. A conforming system "knows" whether a shot is in a loaded EDL but the footage for it isn't available for playback. Dupe detection is used to determine whether the same source frame occurs twice in a production—another possible indication of something having gone wrong (except when flashback sequences are used).

Even more advanced options are possible. A conforming system can use motion-analysis techniques to determine, for example, whether any flash frames (i.e., single frames that appear at the

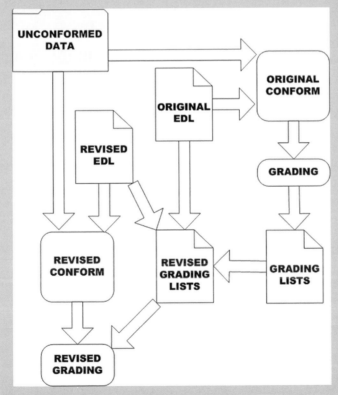

FIGURE 7-22 When significant changes are made to The Conform EDL, reconforming must be performed to preserve such settings, as those generated during grading

(*continues*)

end of a cut) are included or to look for tell-tale signs of render errors or video dropout.

Finally, it may be possible to use the same checksum files generated by the data management system to ensure that all the conformed frames are intact.

7.6.4 Offline Reference

One benefit of the video-based offline system (offline systems usually are video-based) is that it can quickly play out footage to video tape. Therefore, every offline EDL can be accompanied by an offline reference video. These videos can be acquired into the digital intermediate system and used as a reference for confidence checking.

Once all the data is properly conformed, the offline playout can be conformed onto a separate timeline or track (if available) and viewed in parallel with the conformed data. This method is one of the most effective ways to spot conforming problems, and some conforming systems even automate this process of confidence checking by comparing the picture contents of the conformed data with the equivalent offline playout frame, and marking any that appear different, indicating it should be checked. Other conforming systems have provisions for syncing the playback of a video tape (such as the offline playout) to the playback of the conform, so it may not be necessary to capture the tape into the system (thus saving time and disk space).

In addition, some conforming systems allow a digital audio track to be synchronized with the conformed picture, which can act as yet another test confirming that the footage is properly conformed.

EYE MATCHING

When all else fails, and EDLs don't conform frames in the correct place, shots can always be eye matched, which simply means

(continues)

positioning the shot until it "looks right." This eye-matched shot can be cross-referenced against an offline reference, or alternatively, the offline editor can supervise or approve this procedure. Eye matching can be a surprisingly accurate way of conforming footage, especially for shots containing a lot of movement, although it's a much slower process than using an EDL, especially for a large number of shots.

7.6.5 Back Tracking

As well as working out where a particular shot should go, a conforming system should also be able to work out where a shot came from. Very often, the only way of doing so is by looking at the reel number and source timecode of the footage in question. However, as the data goes through multiple incarnations and processes, it's possible that this information can be lost (especially in conforming systems that don't use a vertical-editing paradigm), in which case, it becomes a data management issue. Back-tracking data is often necessary, particularly for sequences with problems and that have to be reacquired.

7.6.6 Consolidation

The process of consolidation involves systematically replacing each frame in the conformed sequence with a new, single-layered (or flattened), unreferenced sequence, with all effects permanently rendered and all references to EDLs removed. After the consolidation, a string of individual frames are assembled. To all intents and purposes, the consolidated sequence looks exactly the same when played back as it did prior to consolidation. All the image data is normally moved to a single location, and all edits and effects are now committed and can't be undone. Consolidation is usually performed as a final stage prior to output, but it's sometimes applied to selected sequences to commit effects and prevent their being altered (e.g., for sequences that have been approved and signed off).

7.7 SUMMARY

In the digital intermediate environment, the conforming process is often a necessary step for marrying an offline-editing process that was done elsewhere, re-creating the production frame for frame, to the full-quality images. You can do this a number of ways, but the most common way is to use an EDL or cut list supplied by the editor, which enables the digital images to be matched to the footage the editors were working with, which typically includes the use of transition and motion effects.

A few things can go wrong during this process, because it isn't completely accurate, but most conforming systems offer the capability of re-editing conformed material to match the reference edit or to enable last-minute changes to be made. If significant changes are made to the edit, it may have to be reconformed to retain any work already started on the previous edit. With many systems, this process is automated, analyzing the original and revised EDLs.

Once material is conformed, it can be viewed to provide a sense of context, or any number of processes can be applied to it, either from within the conforming system or by being sent to other dedicated systems.

The following chapters look at the various creative operations that can be applied to the conformed images before they're output, starting with one of the most important: color grading.

8

COLOR GRADING

In Chapter 7, we looked at the different methods for ordering footage according to the cut produced by the editor. In this chapter, we'll look at one of the most important processes that can be applied to the material: color grading. This term encompasses both the act of processing colors to make them match, as well as of purposefully distorting colors from the original source for aesthetic purposes. Before we look at the various color-grading options available to the digital intermediate pipeline, we will first look at the issue of color management.

8.1 COLOR MANAGEMENT

Color science is a deep and complex subject. Most decisions concerning color are made from an intuitive point of view rather than a scientific one. For example, we decide which color clothing to wear by selecting an item of a particular color and trying it on, rather than by sitting at a desk with a calculator and performing a series of complex calculations. Color grading, even color-matching is also more of an intuitive process than it's an exact science. The most notable skill of a competent colorist is their ability to recognize when the colors look "right," rather than their ability to just operate the color grading equipment.

8.1.1 Color Perception

Our ability to perceive color is based upon physiological as well as psychological features of the human body. Color is really just an imagined concept. It doesn't exist in any real sense, but is a product of our brains interpreting the input from our visual system.

When each ray of visible light (light being a small part of the electromagnetic spectrum) hits a surface, part of it's reflected and part of it's absorbed (some of it may also be transmitted, if the surface happens to be transparent of translucent). The reflected light continues until it strikes another surface, which causes more reflections and absorptions, until it's completely dissipated (used up). Just as different sounds are a combination of vibrations on different wavelengths, light can be subdivided into separate wavelengths. Specific wavelengths represent specific colors, and the gradual transition from one wavelength (measured in nanometers, fractions of a millimeter) to another creates the entire spectrum, or rainbow of colors. As well as absorbing some or all of the overall energy content of light, some materials are better at reflecting or absorbing specific wavelengths of light. The combination of wavelengths reflected by different materials is what gives objects their color.

If observers are in the room, some of the reflected light will enter their eyes and hit their retinas where it is absorbed, producing a photochemical reaction in the retinal "photoreceptor" cells (a process similar to how photography works). This reaction forms the basis of our ability to see.

The human eye works in the same way as a camera (whether film, video, or digital). This is no coincidence—camera manufacturers borrow their basic designs from nature. Practically every component in a camera, from the focusing and aperture mechanisms to the light-detection mechanisms, has an equivalent in the human eye. The human eye has four different types of photoreceptor cells—a "rod" cell, which detects differences in luminance, and three different "cone" cells, used for resolving color, each responding to light of specific wavelengths. Each of these cells works in an analog fashion, meaning that an almost unlimited range of luminance levels are perceivable, unlike digital images, in which the number of levels are restricted (as determined by the format's bit depth). Of all the retinal cells, the rod cells are the most numerous. In fact, more rod cells exist than all the cone cells put together. The net result is that humans are better at perceiving differences in luminance than differences in color. Moreover, we perceive luminance as being far more important than the specific color content, which is why we can interpret black-and-white images without any problem but can't correctly interpret images that have no variance in luminance.

For instance, the amount of light entering our eye affects how bright we perceive a scene to be.[1] In actual fact, it's completely relative, affected by the scene's contrast ratio. In other words, we actually perceive that bright parts of a scene are based upon the darkness of other parts.

The same is true of color. People can perceive colors wrongly in certain situations. For example, studies have shown that people don't notice when a television's color control is gradually adjusted over the course of a film. The screen may be displaying blue skin tones by the end of the film, but the audience's perception continually compensates, and the color change goes unnoticed. This process is similar to our eyes adjusting when the lighting in a room is slowly adjusted. Context is important, too. A red square on a black background looks different than a red square on a white background, even though the color on each is measurably identical.

Don't believe me? Take a look at the images that follow. The image on the right appears brighter, although it isn't. And even though it's possible to train your eyes so that both images in fact appear the same, remember that the majority of people (i.e., the audience) who see them won't have trained their eyes in this way.

---

[1] The eye has a nonlinear response to light. We perceive a light source that only outputs 18% of the light of a second light to be half as bright.

FIGURE 8-1   In this example, the two images are identical but are perceived differently. Had color backgrounds been used, the colors in the image would also appear different in each image

All of these factors help explain why color grading has to be done intuitively rather than by manipulating numbers.

8.1.2   Colorimetry

Colorimetry is the science of color measurement. A color can be broken down into two measurable components: "luminance" and "chromaticity," and several other components can be derived from them. Luminance is a measurement of how much energy is inherent in the color, usually measured in candelas per meter squared (or in foot-candles).[2] It's similar to a measurement of brightness, except brightness is defined as being more relative, based upon a variety of factors, such as surrounding colors. "Lightness" is a logarithmic measurement of luminance, taking into account the eye's nonlinear response to light, which is a more intuitive measurement. In practice, each of these terms, while having subtle differences, are interchangeable. When talking about color in the digital intermediate environment, we refer more to changes in luminance and brightness (as in: "that's too dark!", "increase the luminance!", and "make it lighter!"), rather than discussing absolute values of light energy. Thus, the specific nomenclature amounts to the same thing. In broad terms, a lighter color is closer to white, while a less light (darker) color is closer to black.

---

[2] The actual measurement of luminance is biased toward the human visual system's response to light.

FIGURE 8-2 An image at different brightness levels (see also the Color Insert)

"Saturation" is the measurement of a color's purity, the color's strength in relation to its brightness. Because a color can be composed of light of several different wavelengths, the greater the variety of wavelengths in a particular color, the less saturated the color. The less saturated a color, the closer to gray in appearance it becomes. The concept is similar to adding more water to a juice drink. Saturated colors are perceived to be more vibrant and more artificial.

"Hue" is the measurement of a color's actual color component. It can be thought of as a specific, dominant wavelength of visible light in a color sample. It's typically measured on a color wheel where all the colors in the visible spectrum are positioned around a circle. The hue is found by measuring the angle from the top (which is usually red) of the color in question.

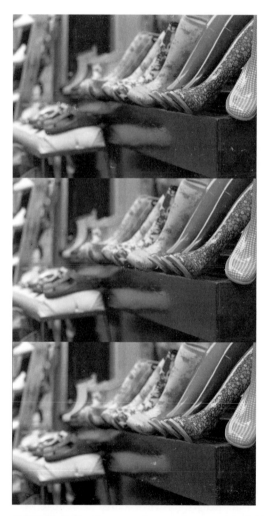

FIGURE 8-3   The same image shown with different saturation levels (see also the Color Insert)

Another method for measuring light is to use an "additive" color model that mimics the properties of light. White light can be formed by mixing red, green, and blue light. Because of this, any color can be formed by mixing these three components in different proportions. Black is the absence of any light at all. The different proportions define the color (i.e., hue and saturation) component, while the overall amount of light defines the luminance level.

A "subtractive" color model mimics the absorption properties of different types of material. Cyan, yellow, and magenta can be mixed in different proportions to make any color. The absence of any color leaves white, while a high level of each color tends toward black. This method is most transferable to the creation of printed colors, mixing inks for each of the colors (onto white paper) to generate any other color.

In practice though, black is very difficult to create using colored inks, and so a black component is often mixed in with the other three to improve the ability to form colors.

"Spot-process" colors, such as those created by Pantone (www. pantone.com), are strictly defined individual colors such as "8201" that represent the same color regardless of the format. Such colors are typically accompanied by a swatch book, a visual reference of the printed colors.

The CIE (Commission Internationale de L'Éclairage) model of color (also the variants "Lab," "XYZ," or "Luv") is the most widely accepted scientific method of describing a color. One luminosity component is combined with a chromaticity coordinate to derive the desired color. This method is independent of the medium containing the color (be it ink on paper, projected light, or a LCD display), and it can describe colors that are outside of the human gamut (i.e., colors that the human eye can't perceive).

Any of these methods might be used to represent a digital image, depending upon the file formats and software. Many of them can be applied to each other. For example, with an RGB-encoded image, it's possible to adjust the picture's hue content.

THE COLOR WHEEL

Many methods are available for creating or choosing colors within a computer, such as using solid-color swatches or entering values (say, for the red, green, and blue) components. One of the most intuitive ways for creating or choosing colors is through the use of a color wheel. A typical color wheel draws all the different hues in a circle; each color varies in some attribute, usually saturation, toward the center of the scale. Using this method, a colorist is able to quickly find the particular color desired. In fact, this method can be used to pick combinations of any two attributes of a color. However, a color is normally derived from (at least) three different parameters, and so a third value must be attached to the wheel. Most color-picking systems normally have this additional parameter in the form of a "slider," so that an additional lightness slider might be included in the hue/saturation wheel.

FIGURE 8-4   A typical color wheel (see also the Color Insert)

Alternatively, a 3D color cylinder plots the third parameter in 3D space. This method is less frequently used, because it's difficult to represent a 3D shape on a 2D screen, without presenting it from multiple angles (which would defeat the purpose of having such a compact interface in the first place).

8.1.3 Color Reproduction

Using the correct equipment, it's possible to obtain an accurate measurement for the color of an object in a scene. Photographers often use light meters to measure the luminance incident in a scene or reflected from a particular point. Density readings can be made for film samples, and a "vectorscope" can be used to measure different qualities of a video signal.

With digital images, it's very easy to extract color information for individual pixels in a digital image, using suitable image analysis software. In spite of this, it's extremely difficult to ensure that any given color is reproduced correctly on different media, or under different conditions. A large part of this is certainly a perceptual issue. As mentioned already, a color even looks different depending upon the surroundings. But it's also difficult to reproduce colors that are objectively the same—that is, ones that produce the same measurements.

One reason is due to differences in color-producing devices. Many different colors can be made using inks on paper, for example, that can't be accurately re-created using LCD crystals. A whole range of colors can be projected from film that can't be re-created using the phosphors that make up an image on a television screen. Each medium has a specific, limited range of colors that it can produce, known as the color "gamut" of the medium. For the most part, these gamuts overlap somewhat, meaning colors within the areas of overlap can be directly converted between different formats without any problem. But areas that don't overlap are said to be "out of gamut," and some other solution must be found to create the color.

What usually happens to out-of-gamut colors is that the closest match is found. This is a simple method, and works well in certain situations, such as where the gamuts of the two different mediums are reasonably similar to begin with. However, this method can produce "clipping" artifacts, where a range of colors in one gamut may be converted to a single closest match color in the new format, resulting in a single band of solid color.

It should be noted that the issue of out-of-gamut colors can only really be solved optimally by using a digital system. The system needs to have some degree of intelligence in order to ascertain which colors it can't re-create accurately. For example, when creating a print from photographic film, no options are available for controlling how out-of-gamut colors are handled. The only solution, aside from using a digital intermediate, is to perform some rudimentary color grading using printer lights, which affects the entire image rather than just the out-of-gamut colors.

But an even bigger problem arises when accurately reproducing colors: there's a high degree of variance in viewing conditions and display properties, even when viewing from the same source. For example, the same VHS video tape can be played in a number of different locations, and the color content will appear to be different, even though the tape's contents haven't changed. The ambient lighting in the room may be slightly brighter, causing the display to look "washed out" (or low contrast). The type of monitor may display the same colors differently from each other. Even two of the same make and model of television, playing the same source video side by side, might produce visibly different results. The reason for this is lack of calibration.

8.1.4 Calibration

Over the course of a few years, the colors on most display devices deviate from their original state. Phosphors wear down, LCD elements and light bulbs gradually burn out, and other components weaken. The net result is that lots of minor faults caused by hardware deterioration add up to a large drift in the displayed image.

Fortunately, most display devices have methods to adjust the image for different environment conditions, as well as for general wear and tear. Most televisions have controls to adjust the image's brightness and contrast, and its hue and saturation. Computer monitors also have methods for controlling the image, either through hardware (usually a control on the monitor itself) allowing the monitor display to be adjusted to better match the incoming picture signal, or through software, correcting the signal sent to the monitor instead.

The purpose of calibration is to ensure that two different devices display the same image the same way. It's also more than that though. Not only do two different monitors need to match, but they need to

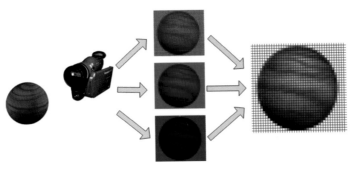

FIGURE 2-3 Color video images are formed by separating red, green, and blue components of the image and recording each separately.

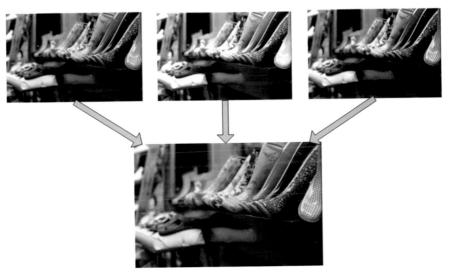

FIGURE 2-10 Color video images are made up of one luminance channel and two chromacity channels. © 2005 Andrew Francis.

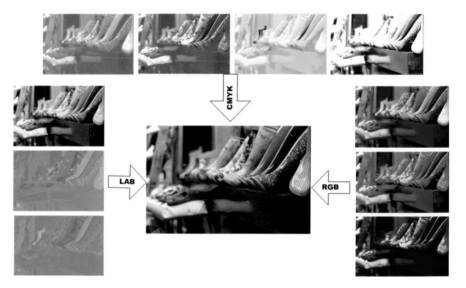

FIGURE 4-4 Digital images can use any of a number of different models to reproduce colors. © 2005 Andrew Francis.

FIGURE 8-2 An image at different brightness levels

FIGURE 8-3 The same image shown with different saturation levels

FIGURE 8-4   A typical color wheel

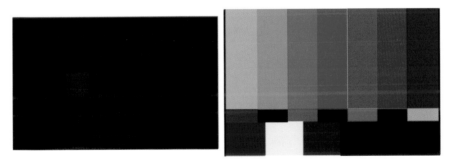

FIGURE 8-5   An example PLUGE (left) and a SMPTE color bar (right)

FIGURE 8-8 through 8.11 A digital intermediate pipeline provides endless possibilities for changing an image's color

FIGURE 8-9

FIGURE 8-10

FIGURE 8-11

FIGURE 8-13 Primary grading makes changes that affect the whole image

FIGURE 8-19 A gradient added to the sky gives it more texture. Note that the gradient also affects the lamppost, and so it has the same effect as placing a filter over a camera lens

FIGURE 8-20 Grading can be used to turn a daytime scene into a nighttime one. In this case, lens flare effects have also been added to the light sources

FIGURE 8-21 Grading can be used to apply relighting to a scene, making it appear as if the original scene had been lit differently. © 2005 Andrew Francis.

FIGURE 8-22 A simulated bleach-bypass look can be digitally applied to an image

FIGURE 8-23 The effects of cross-processing an image can be simulated digitally

FIGURE 8-24 A blue-green transfer is possible by simply swapping an image's blue and green components

FIGURE 8-25 Digital-grading techniques can be used to artificially add color to a black-and-white image

FIGURE 8-26 False color can be assigned to monochrome digital images, mapping different colors onto different pixel values

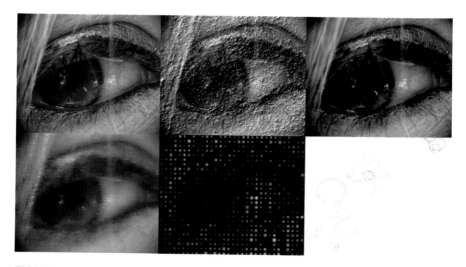

FIGURE 10-19 Using procedural filters such as Allegorithmic's Map I Time, it's possible to use an original image (top left) as the basis for new images or patterns

FIGURE 14-3 A polarizing filter can be used to polarize the incoming light in an image

FIGURE 14-4 Without using the filter when shooting, it's impossible to re-create the effect of polarizing the light

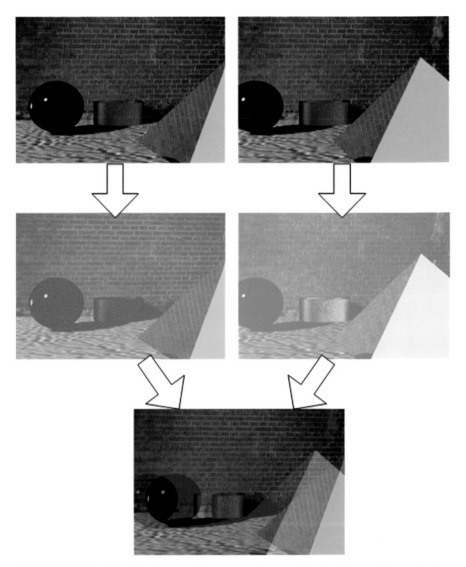

FIGURE 14-6 A left/right pair of images can be combined to form a 3D anaglyph

match an explicit standard. A properly calibrated monitor needs to match a specified set of parameters, so that every calibrated monitor matches every other calibrated monitor, regardless of location or make of device. The simplest and most effective way to do so is through the use of a test pattern such as a PLUGE (Picture Line-Up Generation Equipment) test pattern, or color bars.

Almost all broadcast-quality video tapes begin with bars. A bar is a standard signal containing a calibrated picture and audio reference that is recorded before the program starts. The idea is that the color bars recorded onto the tape are generated using equipment calibrated to SMPTE specifications, meaning they're standardized throughout the motion picture industry. It can therefore be assumed that the bars look correct on any calibrated monitor and produce expected results on any calibrated vectorscope. Therefore, anytime the bars don't display as expected on a calibrated system, it can be assumed that the signal on the tape must be adjusted.[3] The signal must be corrected, using controls on the video player, so that the bars on the tape display correctly. Once the bars display properly in a calibrated system, the accompanying footage also displays as intended.

The problem with this system is that it relies on everyone using properly calibrated equipment. If, for example, the digital intermediate facility creating the video tape didn't use a calibrated system, then it's entirely possible that the bars won't display accurately. Worse, it may in turn mean that the accompanying picture might be correct when seen onscreen but not when the bars are adjusted. In practice, however, most facilities, especially those working on large-scale projects, do work within a properly calibrated environment, and calibration issues rarely occur.

With film, color balance is mostly determined by the film stock and the type of lighting (filters and colored gels can also play a part however). Photographers and cinematographers usually record only a grayscale "wedge" to ensure correct luminance levels (or exposure settings). Color balancing is almost always done as a post-developmental process, and unlike most video transmissions, it's done subjectively, by analyzing the image (either using an automatic process or a

---

[3] This can be a problem with old or low-quality video tapes, and ones that have been through several format conversions.

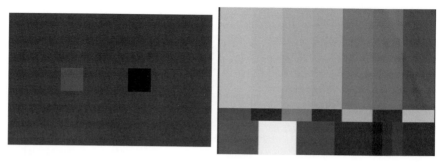

FIGURE 8-5   An example PLUGE (left) and a SMPTE color bar (right) (see also the Color Insert)

trained laboratory grader). For situations requiring some degree of objective reference, a standard Macbeth ColorChecker chart (www.gretagmacbeth.com) can be used.

8.1.5 Gamma

The digital world has no equivalent calibration system. Each digital image isn't accompanied by a set of bars to ensure proper coordination between two different displays. But this isn't really necessary. Digital images are specified mathematically, not by a signal that's subject to noise, deterioration, or interference. Every computer system reads the values from a digital image accurately regardless of how far the image has to be transmitted or how many times it has been copied. If a digital image looks wrong, it's normally because the display system has a problem, rather than because of an issue with the file.

That's not to say that calibration doesn't play a part, however. To calibrate a computer monitor, you typically adjust the "gamma" of the monitor until a test pattern looks (or is measured to be) correct. The gamma parameter is based upon the way monitors display images. The brightness of a single pixel displayed on a monitor is controlled by the amount of energy projected at it. This relationship between the pixel brightness and energy level is nonlinear—it takes more energy to make a dim pixel appear brighter than it does to make a bright pixel brighter. The exact nature of this nonlinear relationship is resolved by using "gamma-correction," which effectively controls how bright a particular luminance level is displayed. This is normally specified by a single value, where 1.0 represents a completely linear display. Typical values are between 1.8 and 2.2 for most computer monitors.

When monitors need calibrating, the gamma-correction is adjusted so that images display correctly. The simplest way to do this is to look at a test pattern, usually comprising several shades of gray, and adjusting the gamma-correction value until the image appears correct. There are also methods for taking measurements directly from the surface of monitors using specialized calibration kits, which is by far the most accurate method.

FILE GAMMA

Certain digital images (depending on the file format used) can have an associated gamma value saved within the image. This is usually the gamma-correction of the system that created the image. The idea is that when displayed on a different system, the file's value is compared to the display system's value, and the image's luminance values are automatically adjusted to compensate for differences between the two. In reality though, the value stored within an image is useless. A gamma-correction setting stored within a file is not necessarily an indication of whether the host system was properly calibrated. It can't possibly account for the multitude of differences in the perception of an image that aren't covered by the gamma-correction. The file can't record what the ambient lighting was like, nor what the manual controls on the display device were set to. In short, it doesn't prove that the system was calibrated properly. If both the original system and the current system are calibrated properly, the image displays the same on both systems, making the gamma value redundant. Worse, a system may try to compensate for a different gamma value stored within a file, which means that you may not see the image as it really is, even on a properly calibrated system. A far better option is to disable any file format gamma values and include a reference image acquired from each different source.

8.1.6 Correlated Color Temperature

White light is rarely pure white. The actual quality of the white light is termed its "correlated color temperature," measured in Kelvins.[4] Predominantly red light is said to have a lower temperature, while blue light has a higher temperature. Sunlight varies in color temperature throughout the course of a day, because of its varying angle to the earth. Sunrise and sunset are cooler, toward the red end of the spectrum (which is why sunrises and sunsets are often accompanied by red skies), while midday sunlight is much bluer. Artificial lights also have an inherent color temperature, varying from very low temperatures to very high ones, though these temperatures don't normally change over a period of time as sunlight does. The Appendix includes a list of the correlated color temperatures for different light sources.

Color temperature is important for monitor calibration. Monitors have different color temperatures for white depending upon their specification. For instance, the SMPTE specification requires that monitors in North America have a correlated color temperature of 6500K (although commercial televisions tend to have higher temperatures). A monitor's correlated color temperature affects the characteristics of the monitor's color gamut. If red, green, and blue light combine to create white at a particular temperature on one monitor, while another monitor has a different color temperature, then it's safe to assume that the color reproduction of the two monitors will be very different.

Color temperature also plays a role in shooting the scene. Video recorded during a shoot must be correctly "white-balanced," and a film camera must use a film stock appropriate to the lighting conditions and type of lights that are used. Otherwise, all the white light in the scene may be recorded with a color cast (or tint). For the purposes of color grading the digital intermediate, we tend not to worry about the

---

[4] The term "correlated color temperature" refers to the physical effect of heating a "black body" until it emits light. Different temperatures produce different colored light, and the relationship between temperature and colour is equivalent to the relationship between different light sources. So the color of a particular light source is not necessarily of a specific temperature, rather it can be correlated against this heated black body effect.

color temperature mismatches of the original shoot and instead focus on which adjustments (if any) have to be made to the result. So if a scene is shot on daylight-balanced film under fluorescent lights, the result, while not ideal, can be corrected by simply removing the green color cast.

8.1.7 Lookup Tables

One of the most efficient ways to convert images between different color spaces is to use a lookup table, or LUT. Very simply, a LUT is a table for converting values. Input values for different colors are "mapped" onto a set of output values, which is used to alter the image's color. For example, the color red might be mapped onto the color blue in the LUT. Then, for every occurrence of red in an image the LUT is applied to, it is replaced with blue. The practical use of LUTs is a little more subtle than that, however. LUTs are normally used to correct out-of-gamut issues. For instance, for an image saved in RGB color space to be printed onto paper, the file must first be converted to a CYMK color space. To do so, you can use a LUT to convert each RGB color into an equivalent CMYK color, or its closest match where colors are out of gamut. (The LUT can also use a scaling method to change all the colors by some degree, so that the image is perceptually the same as the original.)

The use of LUTs is not just restricted to converting image data, however. In the computer visual effects industry, artists often work with scanned film that has been encoded in a logarithmic format (which better emulates the response of film). To display the film as it would be seen when printed and projected, artists typically use a "display LUT" to display the image in an RGB color space, so that it can be displayed more accurately on their monitors. In this instance, the artists don't use the LUT to alter the image's contents, but to alter only the way it's displayed onscreen. This prevents unnecessary image degradation through the process of being converted through multiple color spaces (and lessens the impact of an inaccurate LUT).

LUTs are used for similar purposes in the digital intermediate pipeline. It's very rare (unless working exclusively with video footage) for a production to use only a single color space. Film-based projects use film footage (sometimes on a variety of different film stocks, each of which may have a different color space) that is scanned (each scanner has its own color space, according to the type of lamp or lasers and the CCD elements) to a particular format (which also has a specific color space), is displayed (on a monitor or projector, for example, each with its own color spaces), and color graded (although this process is usually a purely mathematical one and the internal color space of the grading system is normally exactly the same as the file format), before being output to a variety of different formats, such as DVD and recorded film (each with specific color spaces). Most digital film-grading systems work with images stored in a film color space, so that if you were to record scanned film directly back onto film (without any color grading), minimal difference between the recorded version and the original would be perceptible. This means that a typical facility has to worry only about converting the film color space to video color space for display and video output purposes. When no interactive color grading is to be performed on the images (or when some form of automated grading is performed), it's something of a trivial matter, because all operations are done mathematically and don't depend upon perception. However, in pipelines requiring interactive color grading, it becomes a major problem because the accuracy of the LUTs is paramount. That's because during interactive color grading, the colorist makes adjustments to the color, based on what he or she sees on the display. If, for instance, something looks "too red," the colorist reduces the amount of red. But if the actual color stored in the file, without any intervention, would have actually printed out without being too red, then the grader has actually made it worse, based upon inaccurate information from the display. Similarly, something that looks correct on the monitor may actually be in need of correction, once seen on film. This is currently the most significant problem plaguing digital color grading, but it's also the area where the most advancement is being made. Part of the problem is that it's just not practical to continually verify all grading decisions on film, and in addition, there's such a large difference in the color space of film and video. The other concern is that a simple LUT is based upon numerical approximations, primarily to correct specific tones, and doesn't take into account the complex dynamic of luminance and saturation within different color spaces.

A possible solution may be to use a 3D LUT. Rather than a single table of values, 3D LUTs (also referred to as "color cubes") contain entire mathematical models of the two color spaces in question. To overcome the color clipping issues associated with regions of out-of-gamut colors, some form of gamut scaling is used. A "linear compression" method takes the entire original gamut, and stretches and shrinks it so that all the colors fit within the new gamut. In many situations, images produced using this method are perceptibly indistinguishable from the originals, although many of the colors that were not out-of-gamut have also been altered. An alternative is to use a "soft clip," where only the colors close to the out-of-gamut regions are manipulated, so that the majority of colors "in-gamut" retain their values, although this can occasionally produce bizarre results.

The issue with 3D LUTs is that, ultimately the content determines how an image should be displayed (which is also why high-quality grading needs to be done subjectively rather than automatically). Strategies for gamut-mapping work well for certain types of images and not others. When comparing film to video, film tends to retain a lot of detail at the extremes of the luminance range. Film can have a large amount of detail in the highlight regions, whereas video, being a linear medium, has

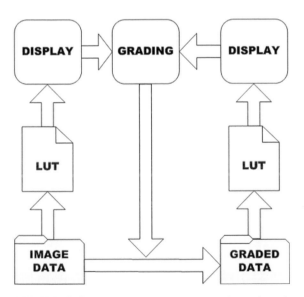

FIGURE 8-6 Although display LUTS don't directly affect the images, they're used as part of the decision-making process to determine how the images should be modified

detail distributed equally at all luminance levels. Factors such as this also explain why it's impossible to completely reproduce certain imaging methods on others. You can approximate or stretch highlight detail on a video display, but it will never look the same. With any gamut-mapping method, there will almost always be some trade-off, either in terms of color, brightness, or contrast.

8.1.8 Color Management Systems

A lot of perceptual factors are involved throughout a digital intermediate production. From the way a scene looks during shooting, through the way that it looks after it has been recorded and subsequently graded, until the film's premier, a single image can appear differently at these various stages. Much of the time this doesn't matter, because the way the image is perceived has little or no impact on how it looks at the end, nor any impact on the image quality. However, decisions are made at certain points based on how the image is perceived, and these decisions affect the final result.

Clearly a lot of elements must be considered to ensure that grading is performed under the best conditions, yielding the most accurate and highest-quality results. As with data management, perhaps the best option is to use an all-in-one color management system to integrate the issues of calibration and gamut conversion. Such systems are designed to eliminate the need to micromanage every aspect of a display device, instead utilizing a combination of preset parameters and periodic calibration for different situations.

The simplest of the all-in-one color management systems create a profile of each display device, based upon a calibration process. The system then compares the characteristics of any image to be displayed with the display profile and applies some form of display LUT to the image. Many of these systems rely on information embedded into each digital image though, which may be neither present nor accurate.

More sophisticated color management systems exist that build profiles based upon every step of the pipeline. For example, Filmlight's Truelight color management system (www.filmlight.ltd.uk) accounts for the characteristics of the film stock containing the original footage, the properties of the scanner, as well as the eventual output medium

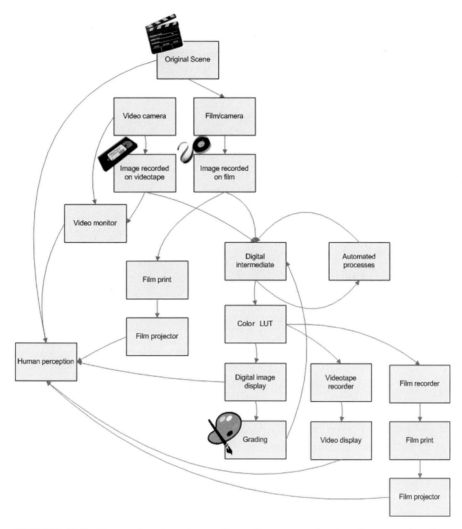

FIGURE 8-7 Perception is a factor throughout a production, but at a few key stages, it's critical to the appearance of the final image

(such as projected film, accounting for the characteristics of the film recorder, the output film stock, and even the projector); it then combines these characteristics with a profile of the display device using a 3D LUT.

Many processes in the digital intermediate pipeline rely on displaying images. Many processes affect the color of an image, some altering the image permanently (such as color grading), while others modify only the way an image is displayed (such as the use of a LUT).

Ultimately though, the only time color management is necessary is when color-grading an image or when viewing a color-graded image. None of the preceding stages (such as scanning film or copying files) usually require any alteration or selection of colors based upon what is seen on a monitor, and therefore don't require precise color reproduction.[5] In theory, the preceding stages can be done without the use of a color monitor. Digital images created by scanning film or by capturing video assign colors to pixels analytically, measuring film density or video signals respectively. Except in situations where image acquisition requires an operator to make adjustments to the color output, color conversion is handled automatically.

It can be argued that color management is not even necessary prior to the grading stage, providing that color-grading is done using a competent colorist and calibrated equipment, as one of the main reasons of performing digital color grading, indeed, one of the main reasons of using a digital intermediate pipeline, is that media with mismatched colors, from a variety of sources, can all be combined together, and processed so that they're all consistent. In theory at least, the colorist takes all of the footage and works with it until the output is suitable. However, superior image quality and faster turnaround may be possible with an-end-to-end calibration system.[6]

8.2 DIGITAL COLOR GRADING

Compared to every other method for color grading moving footage, digital color grading provides the most comprehensive set of options for altering color. Commercials and music promos have been taking advantage of these tools for many years, and film productions are now starting to as well. Whether you have a 120 minute, 35mm film production, or a DV short film on a laptop computer, you can enhance your footage in many different ways by using a digital-grading system.

---

[5] The exception to this is when a "preliminary grade" is performed during scanning.
[6] The true test for ensuring that the rest of the pipeline doesn't impact the quality of the material is to output it directly after acquisition, without applying any color-grading effects. For film material, this may mean scanning directly to a Cineon Printing Density (CPD) color space, depending upon the characteristics of the film recorder used for output.

ONE LUT TO RULE THEM ALL

It might be considered the "holy grail" of color management, but no LUT (3D or otherwise) is suitable for all possible situations. Different shots have different requirements. Certain shots might have a large amount of black, white, gray, saturated colors, or any combination. Each of these situations might require a different LUT for optimal results. Unfortunately, it isn't practical to spend time allocating different LUTs to different shots over the course of an entire program.

A good compromise might be to determine early on the production's overall "look" (e.g., "dark and moody," "bright and saturated," or "evenly balanced") and then creating a LUT suitable for shots falling into those categories. Shots that are potentially problematic can be tested by actually outputting them individually and viewing the results projected on film.

It's possible that using such a system may require continuous updating of the LUT throughout a production. If so, you must ensure that doing so won't cause grading inconsistencies. Typically, the creation of each LUT involves rechecking all the work done previously and having to re-render any images that have undergone a LUT transformation.

8.2.1 Painting by Numbers

Whether you change a red fish to a yellow one, turn a gray sky cerulean blue, or match the look of two shots filmed on different days, you are just rearranging numbers. All digital-grading systems, no matter how sophisticated, don't work in terms of specific colors, but just by performing mathematical operations. If you make something redder, the system increases the pixels' red component, while reducing the green and blue components. If you select all the green areas, the system searches for pixels with a strong green component. Granted, some of the mathematics used to perform some grading operations are highly sophisticated, but it's all simply math. For the purposes of interactive grading, it may not seem important to know

COLOR-SPACE INDEPENDENCE

By far the best option is to consistently record color in absolute color values—that is, in a way that doesn't rely on such relative scales as RGB. The "Lab" color model uses a luminosity value, coupled with chromaticity "coordinates" that provide absolute color values. This means that any color can be represented within the format, regardless of whether it can be displayed on a particular device. For this system to be used efficiently, you have to take into account the acquisition device's color space, because any colors that are out of the devices' gamuts may not be measured correctly. Further, if any alterations are made to the color, you also have to take into account the gamut of the display, because the operator may think that he or she is looking at a particular color but is actually looking at a color that can't be displayed correctly. Many color management solutions track colors that may be out of gamut and include an option for highlighting them.

The exception to this situation is computer-generated (CG) material. Provided that the creation of the material doesn't rely on any externally acquired images or color measurements, a CG image, encoded in Lab color space, can accurately record any color, even if it can't perfectly display it. For example, 3D software can render an image of a virtual ball made out of a shiny yellow-green material (which is a notoriously difficult color to reproduce on monitors) under simulated lighting. Every single shade of yellow on the ball's surface can be accurately recorded (with a precision dependent upon the system's bit depth) within the Lab color space. Unfortunately, displaying the image on a monitor or printing it on a sheet of paper subjects it to the limitations of the new medium's gamut, and some colors will be displayed incorrectly. However, the colors can be manipulated mathematically and output to different mediums with the maximum possible degree of accuracy.

COLOR MANAGEMENT EVERYWHERE

"It doesn't look like that on my monitor" is a frequent complaint heard throughout the digital intermediate process. Whether a studio executive is comparing the video copy to the film screening, or a cinematographer comparing the grade to a reference image on a laptop, or even two graders in disagreement, the statement is unavoidable. Most people assume that the same image is displayed in the same way on every device, but it isn't true. And aside from potential technical issues, such as out-of-gamut colors or contrast ratios, the majority of the time this problem is caused by lack of calibration. So it's important that everyone who is concerned about the grading process of a production ensure that they're viewing all material on a system that has been calibrated to a specification, which more often than not should be set by the digital intermediate facility in collaboration with the director of photography. The use of hardware calibration "probes," such as X-rite's MonacoOptix kits (www.xrite.com) can simplify the calibration process and allow monitors to be calibrated even when using laptops on location shoots.

this, and in fact, good grading is done intuitively. But digital-grading systems have limits, and those limits are imposed entirely by numerical constraints. Color-precision errors, clipping that occurs at the extremes of an image channel, and aliasing effects are all due to the mathematical nature of digital images (which are covered in Chapter 12).

Having said that, it's possible, with enough experience, to grade images simply by relying on the pixels' numerical information. For example, an experienced colorist can tell from looking at the pixel values how that pixel will probably print on film. Because color perception is affected by a multitude of factors, including diet and, in particular, the degree of fatigue the colorist is experiencing, many graders rely on the numerical information to ensure a high-quality grade, and most grading systems offer a wealth of statistical information about individual pixels or groups of pixels, including histogram distributions and vectorscope simulations.

8.2.2 Correcting Colors

Color grading (or "color-correction" or "color timing") is used for a variety of different purposes. Its primary use is ensuring each shot in a sequence maintains the same color balance as other shots, so a shot doesn't look out of place and distract the viewer. This process is known as "continuity grading." As is the case with many scenes in a production, shots may be filmed on different days, at different times of the day, or under different lighting conditions. Any of these situations can change the color balance, so when these shots are cut together, it becomes apparent that some shots have continuity with others while some shots don't. Using continuity grading can alter the colors of individual shots so that they all match. Then when the sequence is played back, every shot matches, as if they were all filmed at the same time.

Color grading can also be used to enhance a production's look. Colors can be altered so that they're deeply saturated, or they're dark and high key, to achieve a mood within the story. Colors can be removed, creating more of a monochromatic look, or they can be changed entirely. With digital-color-grading systems, these changes can be made to entire sequences, individual frames, or even just specific areas of a shot.

Figures 8.8 throgh 8.11   A digital intermediate pipeline provides endless possibilities for changing an image's color (see also the Color Insert)

FIGURE 8-8

Figures 8.8 throgh 8.11 A digital intermediate pipeline provides endless possibilities for changing an image's color (see also the Color Insert)

FIGURE 8-9

FIGURE 8-10

FIGURE 8-11

WHAT IS IMAGE QUALITY AGAIN?

Up until now, the main thrust of the digital intermediate pipeline has been on getting the best image quality possible, in terms of resolution and color. During color grading though, preserving image quality becomes only a secondary concern. That's not to say it isn't important though—it's just that one of the main reasons for supplying the digital-grading system with such high-quality images is it creates more possibilities for color grading.

Color grading is an inherently destructive process. Ranges of color values get stretched apart or squashed together, changed entirely, and even clipped or crushed at the extremes. But at this stage, it doesn't matter so much. Provided the grader knows the effects of each operation on the image and doesn't use destructive processes unnecessarily, then all the changes are ultimately being made for the better. You can make a shot extremely high contrast, ignoring the fact that the resulting image may lose a lot of color detail when such operations provide the look you desire. The point is that you're making choices that affect the image quality because you want to and not because you've been forced to by some limitation or oversight of the pipeline. Compressed video footage, for instance, while convenient to work with at other stages of the pipeline, can cause immense problems for color grading. If you stretch the colors apart too far, the compression artifacts that were previously imperceptible, now dominate the image, severely limiting the grader's options. Any compromises made with quality prior to color grading will reveal themselves at this stage.

Although artistic precedent takes control over image integrity during the grading process, it's still important to consider output requirements when making extreme changes to an image. "Selective destruction" caused by color grading is fine if no perceptible artifacts are the result, but some problems, such as "color banding," can occur when output to other media. One of the most common situations is that when highlights are lightened for film-based projects, they can look fine but will appear to "bloom" when viewed from a video source. The Appendix lists common image operations and their effects on image quality.

8.2.3 Anatomy of a Grading System

Various different solutions are available for digital color grading—solutions ranging from the inexpensive to those costing in excess of a million dollars. Despite the system's cost, several different paradigms are available to the digital intermediate pipeline.

The simplest option is to include grading controls as part of the conforming system. Most systems designed specifically for grading moving images are of this type. This way, the grader is always working with the most up-to-date version of the program and can watch it in the correct order. However, using such a system may prevent changes being made to the conformed data while grading is performed, or at least it may require additional licenses (at additional cost). On a smaller-scale production, when the offline edit occurs on the same system as the online, it may be possible to use color-grading tools within the editing application itself. For example, Avid's Xpress Pro system (www.avid.com) makes it possible to edit SD video uncompressed, color graded, and output directly without moving the data to another system.

A slight variant of this approach is a separate grading system that can access the data directly from the conforming system, usually by manipulating the output of the conforming system in real time. This way, the grading system has to focus only on providing color-grading tools, and not on playback and ordering. Systems such as Pandora's Pixi Revolution (pogle.pandora-int.com) can receive footage from another system and apply grading in real time.

An alternative option is sending individual shots to an external system, which then controls playback and has tools for color grading. This method tends to be cheaper to implement, but it makes the whole process much slower, because data usually has to be constantly transferred between various systems. This also means that the colorist has to know in advance which scenes he or she wishes to grade. There may also be compatibility issues between the conforming and grading systems.

Grading systems can make alterations to images directly, or they can employ a "grading list" system (also referred to as "grading metadata"), where the parameters for the changes are saved to a separate

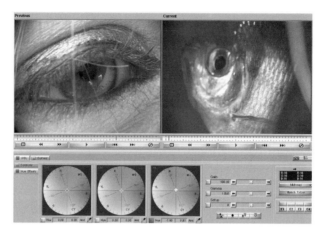

FIGURE 8-12 Digital-editing systems such as Avid Xpress Pro may also allow color grading to be used in an offline edit

file or database. This option is suitable for most situations, because it enables the grading parameters to be continually refined without committing the changes permanently. Once the changes are committed, further changes can severely compromise the image quality. The disadvantage of the list-based system is that the display of each image can be slower, because the grading system has to apply the necessary transformations to each frame before it can be displayed. When trying to view a full-size image in real time (as graders often have to do), it may not be possible to apply the changes to the image fast enough to display them in time. Many grading systems get around this issue by employing caching mechanisms, but they may still take time to generate and require additional disk space.[7]

Most grading systems apply the final grades prior to output during the process of "rendering." The rendering process involves applying the grading parameters to each frame separately and outputting the result, either as a new file, or overwriting the original. The process of rendering can be a slow one, and "render errors" can be introduced. (See Chapter 11 for more on the rendering process.) Sufficiently fast grading systems that can apply completed grades to the source image in real time can usually output graded material without the necessity of rendering.

---

[7] The other issue is that if the grading list files or database are deleted or damaged somehow, all the grading work is lost.

A typical grading system comprises two main elements—an interface containing controls for different operations, and a display for viewing the results. The specifics of the interface inevitably vary by product, and some extend the interface by providing an entire desk with buttons, dial, trackballs, and so on, to accelerate the grading process.[8] The display might be extremely simple, displaying only the graded results. It might include enhancements such as split-screens, showing the image before and after the grade has been applied. It may be possible to "zoom" the display in and out (without actually affecting the image in any way) for detail work. There may even be several displays, each showing different footage or versions of a grade. The grading system may also have a method for storing different versions of grades, as well as providing the ability to save and load presets, and a system for using reference images.

In addition to monitoring the graded image, it can also be useful to obtain analytical information about the image. To achieve this, the grading system might have the option to display tools such as vectorscopes or image histograms within the software, or it may be that these devices can be attached separately, monitoring the system's display output.

8.2.4 Global Grading

Regardless of the system's specifics, most digital colorists use a similar work flow. The first stage is to set the image's overall color balance, which is known as "global" (or "primary") grading. Typically this process involves manipulating the colors to remove any color casts or to compensate for contrast or exposure differences between shots.

Primary grading is normally a fairly straightforward process, using a simple set of tools. It can replicate all of the processes that are possible with film laboratory grading processes, which apply different intensities of light or different colored filters to an image to produce the desired result. Primary grading is normally achieved on a per shot basis: a representative frame from each shot is graded, and the results are applied to an entire shot.

---

[8] One of the benefits of working with such a control desk means that you can keep your eye on the image, rather than on the interface.

FIGURE 8-13 Primary grading makes changes that affect the whole image (see also the Color Insert)

Different grading systems use different methods to produce the desired effect; but using any system allows a wide variety of different looks to be achieved, whether the desired result is film noir or a pop video.

8.2.5 Secondary Grading

In many situations, primary grading isn't sufficient to produce the desired effect. Especially for detail work, it's sometimes necessary to apply grading to a single, isolated part of the image.

Many (but not all) grading systems allow selective (or "secondary") grading. In selective grading, specific parts of a shot are singled out (or "selected") for specific grading, normally using the same tool set used for primary grading.

There are two main methods for selecting part of a shot: "masking" and "keying." Masking involves using a shape (i.e., the "mask") to define a region that the selective grading is applied to. The simplest method is to define a rectangle or ellipse, or some other geometric, vector-based shape as the mask. Many systems allow the creation of "freehand" masks, which the operator defines to mask more complex shapes. Depending on the specific system, the masked area might be displayed with a border, in isolation, or using some other method (e.g., desaturating the unmasked region).

It may also be possible to combine multiple masks or to "invert" them (i.e., turn them inside out). Some paradigms allow masks with a soft (or "feathered") edge to more smoothly blend the transition between the selected area and the unselected area (particularly when significant grading differences exist between the two).

The process of keying selects a region of a shot based upon its color content. For example, keying purple in a shot selects all the instances in a shot that the color purple appears. Because it's likely that you want to select similar shades of color as opposed to limiting the selection to

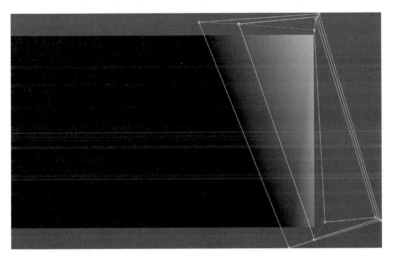

FIGURE 8-14 Areas of an image can be masked for selective work. In this case, only the masked area is shown

pixels containing exactly the same shade, most keyers also have the option to soften or adjust the "tolerance" of the keyed selection or to select a "color range." Different systems allow the keying of different parameters, such as saturation or luminance, while a more basic system works with just the hue or red, green, and blue channels. To make the system more interactive, the color to be keyed can usually be "sampled" (i.e., picked) directly from the displayed image. Again, the keyed area might be displayed in different ways, depending on the system.

With many systems, it's also possible to combine the two approaches, so that it's possible to mask a keyed area before applying a grade. Another method is to create masks based upon image properties—for example, the mask could be based upon each pixel's luminosity strength.

8.2.6 Dynamic Grading

Many shots are dynamic—that is, parts of the scene move, such as when a person walks across a room and cars drive on roads. Furthermore, the camera position may change during the course of the shot, with the view shifting considerably. Anytime any such movement occurs, the grade is affected, particularly if masks have been used to isolate specific elements in the scene. Because masks affect only the area they contain, and not specific elements, the mask could end up acting on the wrong part of the image in a dynamic

FIGURE 8-15 Areas can also be selected by keying colors in the image. In this case, the affected area is shown as a matte

GRADING SHOTS AND FRAMES

For most grading systems, the definition of a shot is somewhat arbitrary, and so a "shot" can be a shot as defined by cut points in an EDL, a single frame or an entire reel, depending upon grading requirements. Most graders prefer to define a shot by cut points in the EDL, and separate them into smaller sections if necessary. This should be done without affecting the way it appears in the conform system. In effect, the colorist should have an independent timeline from the conformed timeline, so that he or she can make edits for grading purposes, without making edits in the actual program.

It sometimes seems as though people working with still digital images have a much more elaborate toolset for editing colors than the motion picture industry does. However, there are good reasons for this. First of all, a trade-off will always exist between available time and detail. A digital image artist might have weeks to fine-tune a single image, while a digital colorist has the same amount of time to do maybe 2000 shots or more than a 100,000 frames. Thus, the digital-grading system tool set is normally designed to reflect that fact.

But perhaps more importantly, there must be continuity in the grading process, or there's increased risk of adding artifacts into the footage that are only noticeable when the footage is played at speed. Grading moving pictures requires a different approach to manipulating still images. You can't necessarily repeat a process that works for a still image across a series of frames and produce the desired effect.

The reason why no "magic wand" tool is available, for example, is because if you were to repeat that tool across several frames of moving footage, you would likely get different results (and hence get a different pixel selection) on every frame. (A magic wand tool is used in digital imaging to select an enclosed area of pixels similar to the one already selected.) The net result would be that the selection area would change erratically when played back, even if every frame looked fine when it was viewed in isolation.

FIGURE 8-16   In this instance, the ball has been selectively graded. However, as soon as the ball moves, the grading effect is revealed

FIGURE 8-17   This time, the selective grading has been keyframed so that it moves with the ball

GRADING FLASHES

One of the more common problems encountered during the quality control process is the issue of grading flashes. The ability to create a multitude of complex, dynamic grades, coupled with the sometimes constant changes that are made to the conformed program makes it easy for the grade applied to one shot to be mistimed and overrun onto an adjacent shot. The result is that the wrong grade is applied to one or more frames of a shot. When the grading is similar across both shots, it can be easy to miss the error, but often the grades are so different that the image appears to "flash," suddenly changing color. This problem usually can be resolved fairly simply by readjusting the grading timings, but grading flashes often aren't spotted until after final output. Many digital intermediate facilities opt to create a video playout prior to final output, to check for exactly this sort of problem. This problem may be easier to spot during playback (and is covered further in Chapter 12).

Grading flashes may be used purposefully as a grading technique to simulate lighting effects such as firelight, lightning, or explosions.

shot. Rather than enhancing the scene's visual quality, the mask reveals itself as a patch of color difference and looks like an error.[9]

Fortunately, most grading systems are equipped with "dynamic grading" options. The basic premise of dynamic grading is that certain grading parameters can be animated, modified over a period of time. So masks can move or change shape during a shot, or the parameters of the grades can be adjusted over time as needed.

Different grading platforms take different approaches to which parameters can be dynamic and how they can be animated. The most common method for animating grading parameters is through the use of keyframes.

Keyframing is a technique pioneered by traditional animators. Traditional (hand-drawn) animation is drawn a frame at a time. Clearly this process is very time consuming, so a new method was devised whereby the lead animators draw only a few of the important, or "key" frames. Other animators could then "tween," drawing the frames that go in between the key frames. Computer animation techniques adopt a similar work flow. Parameters can be set at specific key frames, and the computer interpolates the values for the in-between frames. Dozens of different interpolation methods can be used to create the in-between frames, but most of them work by plotting each keyframe as a point on a hypothetical graph and connecting the points to find the in-between frames' values.

These techniques can be used to create grades for dynamic shots or for special grading effects. Other animation techniques are also possible for more complex situations.

8.2.7 Rotoscoping

Sometimes the only way to achieve a desired effect is to create it a frame at a time. Often the case for complex moving shapes, masks have to be adjusted very accurately to match the part of the image they cover. The operator examines each frame, adjusts the mask to fit

---

[9] This is also one of the reasons why rescanning footage should be avoided, because each scan may cause the image contents to be in slightly different places, particularly with scanners that aren't pin registered.

the image and then moves on to the next frame. This process is known as "rotoscoping." It's a very time-consuming process, and facilities often have an additional operator (or team of operators) who are responsible solely for rotoscoping images.

Rather than using vector-based masks, it may be preferable to output "matte" images to accompany images. A matte image is a gray scale image (it may be embedded in alpha channels as part of the footage) that defines a selection area using pixels. Where the pixel is white, the pixel is considered to be masked. A black pixel indicates a pixel that isn't to be masked.[10] Gray pixels may be partially affected by the grade (e.g., in the feathered area of a vector-based mask), depending on how close the gray value is to black or white. Because mattes are defined by actual pixels rather than vector-based masks, they can be used to define a much more accurate and detailed selection area. However, in most cases, this level of detail is not necessary, and the appropriate selections can be made quickly by using masks. Even if the mask has to follow some highly complex motion, such as a buoy on a stormy sea, it can normally be accommodated through the use of feature tracking.

8.2.8 Feature Tracking

Humans are much more adept at analyzing moving pictures than are computer systems. A person can watch video footage of a sporting event, for instance, and be able to recognize different players and moving objects, regardless of camera movement. Even when the shot is switched between different cameras, we can still follow the action. Computers just can't do this. All a computer can perceive is a bunch of pixels that may or may not change color between frames, sometimes by a small amount, sometimes by a lot. An entire branch of artificial intelligence research is devoted to the study of "machine vision," which aims to simulate the ability to recognize objects and shapes when presented with a digital representation of a scene. Part of this research has resulted in the development of feature-tracking software, which can isolate a part of an image, a specific feature, and track its movement across following frames. A signpost in a street

---

[10] Sometimes the reverse is true, depending upon the specifics of the grading system.

scene, a pencil on a desk, or even the corner of a window are all examples of features that are trackable within an image.

Feature tracking works by first selecting a reference zone—an area (usually rectangular) containing the feature that is to be tracked. Next, a search zone is chosen, which is large enough to accommodate the movement of the feature between any two frames. The feature-tracking algorithm then examines the next frame's search zone, looking for a match with the reference zone. The specifics of how matches are identified vary between different algorithms, but once a match is found, the object's motion relative to the camera can be determined. The feature tracker then advances to the next frame, gradually building up data for the feature's motion across a range of frames.[11] The tracking data that is produced can then be applied to something, such as a grading mask, which then follows the movement of the feature. Successful feature tracking allows moving objects to be selectively graded using masks and other tools without having to resort to rotoscoping techniques for the majority of shots. Tracking data can also be used to stabilize a shot, smoothing out camera motion. Stabilization is covered in Chapter 9.

There are issues with feature tracking, however, and no one tracking algorithm is considered to be perfect. Lighting changes in a shot, perspective shifts caused by features moving closer to or farther from

FIGURE 8-18 A lamppost has been tracked across a number of frames

---

[11] Good tracking algorithms can track features on a "subpixel" basis, meaning that movement is more accurately recorded.

PRELIMINARY GRADING

With some digital intermediate work flows, it may make sense to apply some or all of the grading during acquisition. For example, certain film scanners have the ability to adjust the scanned film's colors. In many instances, this process can cause problems, because applying color adjustments prior to scanning can reduce the acquired images' color quality and limit grading options later on. However, some systems can achieve this without compromising quality, in which case, applying some degree of grading can save time during grading, as well as provide superior-quality images.

In these circumstances, it's advisable that full advantage is taken of such options. It should be considered to be no different than setting the correct exposure on a film camera, or white balancing a video camera when shooting in the first place. Some digital intermediate facilities perform the entire grading process at this stage, meaning that only the conforming and effects processes are needed after scanning, but relinquishing the ability to perform large changes later on.

the camera, image rotation, and occlusion by other objects can all produce errors in the tracking data. Much feature-tracking skill involves picking a suitable feature to track; inevitably certain shots have clearer and a greater abundance of suitable features. Many feature-tracking systems also can track multiple features, which can increase the accuracy of the data, as well as compensate for rotation and perspective shifts (e.g., by tracking two or more sides of an object). In some instances, it's even possible to approximate the results of rotoscoping by tracking multiple points and applying the data to a mask. For example, Autodesk's Lustre system (www.discreet.com) can track multiple points along a mask—for example, the mask can be used to automatically adhere to the shape of a person walking down a corridor toward the camera, something that might otherwise have required rotoscoping.

8.2.9 Changing Colors

For all of the different color models and file formats for storing digital images, there are as many ways to change the color of an image. Because an image can be represented in terms of hue and saturation, these parameters can be adjusted for the whole of an image (or selectively, depending upon the grading system).

Some of the more popular options for changing color are listed below:

TABLE 8-1 Options for Changing Colors

Operation	Result
Hue	Alters the hue component of a color, effectively rotating the color wheel.
Brightness	Affects the overall pixel values, resulting in the brightness being adjusted.
Saturation	Alters the saturation of a color.
Contrast	Alters the contrast of an image. Increasing contrast makes blacks blacker and whites whiter.
Gain	Alters the white point of an image.
Pedestal (or lift)	Alters the black point of an image.
Gamma	Alters the gamma of the image.
Exposure	Emulates an exposure change by altering brightness in a nonlinear way.
Tint	Mixes one color with another color, in variable proportions.
Channel mixing	Alters the relative strength of each component in color (typically RGB or CYMK).

Many solutions also have the capability to constrain changes to individual channels, so many of the above operations can be applied to a single channel (or part of a single channel), such as to the red, green and blue channels. It may even be possible to apply a gamma correction to a saturation channel for instance.

These operations can usually be adjusted gesturally by moving a slider or spinner on the grading system interface using a mouse or pen and tablet, or by adjusting dials or using trackballs, depending

GRADING VIDEO AND FILM

Many digital-grading systems feature separate modes for grading video and film. In general, when grading video material, the colorist is offered one set of controls (such as gamma, lift, and gain), and another set of controls when grading film (such as exposure, brightness, and contrast). The idea is that different controls are more suitable for grading different material. In addition, film material is typically stored in a logarithmic image format, and so the same parameters applied to both film and video material may produce different results. In the digital intermediate environment, it's possible to apply any type of alteration to any digital images, so brightness and contrast options could be used on video, or lift and gain on film. The primary reason for using a logarithmic format for film is that it's more suitable when the eventual result is output back on film.

upon the system specifics.[12] In other words, these operations can be applied to footage very quickly. However, many of these operations affect all colors equally, and it may be necessary to isolate specific regions without resorting to creating keys or masks.

8.2.10 Shadows, Mid-Tones, and Highlights

One of the simplest ways to divide the tonal range of an image is by separating the shadow (dark), highlight (bright), and mid-tone regions. With many grading systems, this separation is performed automatically based upon the luminosity content of each pixel, usually with some degree of overlap between the regions. With others, the region boundaries may have to be defined in advance.

Using these regions for grading is useful for making detailed changes to an image, without having to resort to time-consuming keying or masking. Many grading decisions are made that can be limited to one of these regions—for example, "the shadows need to be deeper"—

---

[12] Most colorists prefer to work with more tactile interfaces, especially those that allow them to watch the image, rather than the interface.

FIGURE 8-19 A gradient added to the sky gives it more texture. Note that the gradient also affects the lamppost, and so it has the same effect as placing a filter over a camera lens (see also the Color Insert)

and so being able to apply changes to just these reasons can accelerate the entire grading process.

8.2.11 Gradients

Most grading systems have some sort of tinting parameter to alter the image colors. For example, tinting an image red increases the image's red component, making it appear redder (or appearing with less cyan, if you want to think about it that way). The specific mechanics of this procedure depend upon the grading system, because increasing an image's red component may also have the side effect of brightening the overall image.

Tinting an image, as well as performing other operations, requires the operator to specify a color. Rather than tinting an image red, you may want to tint it yellow or purple, for example. But sometimes, it may be useful to apply a range of colors to a color operation. Perhaps you want the image to be tinted blue at the top, where the sky is, and green at the bottom, or perhaps the effect should be more pronounced at a particular corner of the image.

Gradients are a combination of two or more colors. The gradient starts at one color, and then smoothly blends into the other (as many times as there are colors). Many different methods are available for generating gradients (which may be linear or radial and may include transparency) to enable a color to vary in strength. Linear gradients are commonly used on outdoor scenes to add color to skies.[13]

8.2.12 Grading on a Curve

One of the most powerful methods that grading systems offer for changing the color content of images is the curve-based grading paradigm. With this system, a graph is presented to the operator, who is able to alter the shape of the graph to produce changes.

---

[13] In some applications, gradients are created by generating a mask with a soft edge, rather than a separate gradient entity.

The simplest version of this is the input-output graph. Some parameter, such as luminosity, is plotted with the input value against the output value. Typically, a straight line is plotted so that the input is mapped exactly to the output (0% input luminosity equals 0% output, 50% input is mapped to 50% output, and so on). Editing the curve can alter the image so that bright areas are darkened or brightened further with or without affecting the image's other regions. This can work for other parameters, so that, for instance, the saturation of highly saturated regions of color can be adjusted.

It's also possible to plot a graph of two different parameters. For instance, some grading systems have the ability to plot a graph of saturation against luminosity (among others). This means that the saturation of colors at a given luminosity (or luminosity range) can be increased or decreased as needed which can affect images in drastic or subtle ways with ease, and without visible boundaries where the adjustment begins and ends. Of course, in theory, it's possible to map most parameters against each other, so that for instance, a pixel's hue can be changed depending upon an image's red channel strength. Most systems provide instant feedback, displaying changes as they're made, which provides a lot of scope for experimentation, which in turn leads to a high level of creative possibilities that may not have been anticipated.

8.2.13 Manipulating Histograms

Video operators often refer to vectorscopes and similar equipment to ensure that images are properly color balanced. The digital equivalent is to use a histogram, which displays an image's luminosity distribution. Generally speaking, if the luminosity distribution stretches from the minimum possible value to the maximum possible value, then the tonal range is properly balanced.

Rather than making changes to the image color and then referring to the histogram to see how the changes affect it, it's much more convenient to make changes directly to the histogram and have them reflected in the image. For example, looking at the histogram can sometimes reveal where the peak white should lie, and the histogram can be adjusted to redistribute the pixel values correctly. Even more options may be available, such as the ability to edit histograms for different color spaces, or for individual channels.

8.2.14 Color Matching

Another unique feature of digital color-grading systems is the ability to automatically match two different colors. A computer system can compare the color information between two different color samples (a source and a reference), calculate the difference between the two, and then apply the difference to the entire image needing

FLESH TONES

Some colorists color balance an image by first setting white and black points and then identifying areas that should be neutral (close to 18% gray) and changing the grading parameters until the areas in question meet the required shade. Other colorists like to concentrate on making the flesh tones of people in the image correct, and then adjusting everything else to support this. The reasoning behind this is that audiences tend to "calibrate" their eyes based upon the flesh tones in an image, and so skin that is too green can cause the viewer to perceive a green cast to the entire image, even if the image is otherwise perfectly balanced. Some graders make use of a standard flesh tones color chart (such as those available at www.retouchpro.com) and grade flesh tones in an image to a reference color in the chart.

to be changed, making the source color the same as the reference. Because the changes are applied to the entire image, it can make other areas that were perfectly balanced look wrong however, and so the procedure is usually reserved for images that have a color cast.

The most obvious use of this process is to maintain grading continuity across different scenes, by picking specific colors that need to be the same in two different shots, and then matching one to the other. But color matching can be used for a number of different applications throughout the color grading process, such as to set neutral colors, or match colors in a scene to a reference color elsewhere.

Each grading system inevitably has a different method for performing color matching, depending upon the process that's applied to the image to shift the color components from the source to the reference color. For example, some paradigms may separately adjust the hue, saturation, and luminosity components, while others may make adjustments to the red, green, and blue components of each pixel.

8.2.15 Grading Priority

With the ability of applying many grading operations and processes to each image, the order of the operations becomes important. For example, tinting an image and then reducing the saturation produces different results than reducing the saturation and then tinting the image. To ensure that results of grading operations are somewhat predictable, most grading systems apply operations in a specific order. Some systems make it possible to adjust the priority of different operations, so that higher-priority operations are applied first.

8.2.16 Composite Grading

Regardless of the software used, digital color grading is merely a form of digital compositing. Masks, keys, and trackers are all features found in visual effects compositing systems, and the only

SURFACE-PLOT GRADING

Many of the grading operations, such as curve or histogram manipulation, work on two different parameters and are therefore easily displayed as 2D graphs. However, most color models have three or more parameters, which aren't easily reduced to a 2D graph. So, to plot changes in luminosity, depending upon the hue and saturation component of an image, requires a 3D surface-plot graph. Using such a paradigm, it's possible to brighten saturated reds exclusively, while darkening saturated blues and desaturated reds.

difference is that in the digital intermediate environment, those tools are largely streamlined for changing the color of hundreds of shots.

Even so, some grading systems lack some compositing functions that might otherwise prove useful. Some very effective color effects can be produced by compositing other images (or solid colors or gradients, or even the original images) onto the source images and using different methods to blend the images. For example, a technique long used by digital image artists is to "square" the image, multiplying all the image's pixel values by themselves. This technique has a similar effect to changing the contrast, and its visual effect is to create the appearance of an increase in the image's density.

Some systems, such as Da Vinci's Resolve (www.davsys.com), allow access to the operations being performed on each shot, to enable the creation of very complex grades. For example, a matte can be created that isolates an area for brightening. That same matte can also constrain another parameter, such as a blur effect.

8.3   GRADING PROCEDURES

Color grading is used for both practical and creative reasons. Grading can be used in many different situations to improve the visual aspects of a scene or sequence—e.g., drawing attention to specific features, correcting a lighting problem, or defining the mood of a piece.

8.3.1   Continuity grading

One of the most common tasks of the color grader is to balance two different shots so that no discernable difference in color or tone can be perceived in them. Many factors can cause these differences, some of which have been touched upon already, such as shooting a scene at different times of the day, but regardless of the cause, continuity grading is one of the most effective ways to minimize differences in the color or tone of shots.

Continuity grading involves using global grading to ensure that the overall brightness, contrast, and color balance of each shot are the same. This doesn't necessarily mean that the same grading parameters must be applied to each shot, but the end result is that every shot is visually consistent.[14]

Selective grading then adjusts individual elements within a shot so that it better matches other shots. For example, in a sequence featuring a red car driving among green foliage, global grading might balance the overall color, brightness, and contrast between shots; the car and tree elements might be separately isolated to perfectly match them between shots.

THE PROBLEM OF BACKGROUND PLATES

The digital intermediate process normally works hand in hand with the visual effects process. Occasionally, scanned footage is used to create a visual effects shot, while the conforming system simultaneously uses it as a "stand-in." In addition, the color grader simultaneously uses the visual effects shot as a "background plate," to set a grade for most of the image, and the grade setting is eventually tweaked upon receipt of the finished effect.

However, many visual effects departments request graded footage under the assumption that composites can be matched better to such footage. Sadly, this assumption is a myth. In practice, this kind of work flow accentuates differences in calibration between the two different departments and potentially exaggerates image artifacts by repeatedly performing operations on images. A far better option is to composite elements over the ungraded footage, matching it as if it were the final graded version. If required, mattes can be supplied along with the final shot to separate the foreground elements from the background, and then each can be graded separately if required. That way, the potential for degradation of the footage is minimized, while the level of control provided by the digital-grading process is maintained.

---

[14] In many instances, different shots require exactly the same grading parameters as a shot previously graded, particularly shots cut from the same take. Many grading systems accelerate this process by allowing grading parameters to be copied between two shots or even linked, so that changes to one shot affect the others.

Many graders also take advantage of the automated match-grading options provided by some systems, but the use of this feature usually depends on the requirements of specific shots.

8.3.2 Color Retouching

Grading is often used to repair "color damage," usually caused by the colors on the original material incorrectly recording color information, or by becoming degraded, for example where color has faded on old material (particularly if it was stored incorrectly). Other situations can cause the colors in an image to require such correction. Probably the most common issues concern exposure. Underexposed images tend to be too dark overall, whereas overexposed images tend to be too bright. Fortunately, many mediums, particularly photographic film, have a degree of exposure "latitude," meaning that detail is recorded even where the image appears to be peak white.

A further complication can arise where certain elements of a shot may each be exposed differently. For example, in a street scene, some well-lit buildings may be correctly exposed, while other poorly-lit buildings may be under-exposed, making the scene lack uniformity. Digital grading can help solve exposure issues by darkening over-exposed or brightening under-exposed images, both globally and selectively. Some grading systems have controls for modifying the exposure of an image directly, whereas others achieve the same results using a combination of different grading operations.

"Color casts," where an image is tinted by a particular color, are also common problems in images. Casts may be caused by significantly aged material (photographic film or printed material in particular), which has been degraded by chemical processes—similar to a newspaper turning yellow when it's left in the sun. Degraded materials also occur when the color temperature of the lighting in a scene doesn't matching the material—for example, when daylight-balanced film is used to photograph a scene lit by tungsten light, resulting in an image with an orange cast.[15] It's also possible that the

---

[15] This also applies to digital and video cameras, which require the white balance to be set to specify the type of lighting.

scene may have mixed lighting, in which case, some areas of an image may be properly balanced, while others have casts. These situations often are remedied by careful color grading, typically by balancing a region of the image that should be neutral (i.e., gray) or by ensuring the accurate representation of flesh tones, again using global grading to correct overall color casts and selective grading to tackle localized areas.

FIGURE 8-20 Grading can be used to turn a daytime scene into a nighttime one. In this case, lens flare effects have also been added to the light sources (see also the Color Insert)

8.3.3 Day-for-Night

Productions often choose to film scenes that are set at night during daylight hours, a process known as "day-for-night." There are many reasons for this, mostly practical and economic. Of course, a scene photographed during the day looks completely different than the same scene photographed at night, even when both are properly exposed. Because less light is available at night, our eyes (and cameras) must adapt—that is, they respond differently to light. So nighttime scenes tend to look much less saturated, have denser shadows (deeper blacks), and darker mid-tones. It's also common to increase the level of blue in a day-for-night image, because we're more susceptible to blue light under low-light conditions.

Day-for-night grading has been done as a chemical process on films for many years, and exactly the same processes can be replicated digitally, with a greater degree of flexibility. The scene is filmed during the day, and the image is color graded to look as if it was filmed at night—that is, the sunlight is made to look like moonlight, and adjustments are made to various aspects of the scene's color content to emulate nighttime.

It's worth noting, however, that practical issues are associated with shooting day-for-night scenes. Certain elements that are visible only during the day (such as the sun and flocks of birds) must be avoided during shooting (or may have to be removed digitally, which can be a time-consuming process), while elements that should be visible at night (such as lit streetlamps) have to be included or added later.

8.3.4 Relighting

Sometimes there isn't enough time (or money) to light a scene the way the cinematographer would like. Practical issues may be associated with lighting a building in the background with spotlights, for instance, or perhaps the correct gel wasn't available when the scene was shot.

Selective digital-grading processes enable scenes to effectively be relit, strengthening or diminishing the effects of photographed lighting, while simultaneously adding additional lighting effects not present earlier. Carefully placed masks can be used to brighten a spe-

FIGURE 8-21 Grading can be used to apply relighting to a scene, making it appear as if the original scene had been lit differently. © 2005 Andrew Francis. (see also the Color Insert)

cific region, making it look as if a spotlight was pointed at the area when the scene was originally shot.

It's possible to speed up the onset lighting process by anticipating the grading system's capabilities and limitations. In particular, backlighting effects may be difficult to reproduce digitally, while adding vertical wall lights might be fairly straightforward. Chapter 14 discusses the planning process for anticipating grading possibilities during production and preproduction.

8.3.5 Enhancement

Photographers, particularly fashion photographers, have been using digital and chemical processes to enhance images for years. Even the best photographer can only replicate reality, but he or she may want to enhance it. Fashion photographs usually are extensively retouched to remove a model's blemishes or imperfections, and the photographs also undergo any number of color enhancements. Eyes can be artificially brightened, make-up can be softened, colors saturated. With digital grading, many of these same techniques can be applied to moving images, making them look "better" than reality.

8.3.6 Color Suppression

Certain colors sometimes have to be removed, or "suppressed," from shots, usually for special effects purposes. Especially with commercials or corporate presentations that make use of particular colors in their branding, a photographer may want to suppress other colors, drawing attention to the product.

The digital-grading process allows this effect to be implement with ease, either to a range of colors across an image or to specific colors in a localized area. Digital grading provides the capability of photographing a scene in full color and then changing it to black and white. Such processes can also define a specific "look" for the production, as was done on the HBO miniseries *Band of Brothers*.

8.3.7 Lab Process Emulation

Chemical film processing has been around for decades now. Although few consumers use them, a number of different processing techniques are available for changing the look of footage.

"Silver retention" (also referred to as "bleach bypass" or "skip bleach") is a process used during film development, which retains the silver grains normally removed from the emulsion.[16] The resulting footage has higher contrast, reduced saturation, stronger highlights, and denser shadows. This process has been used on films such as *Seven*, *1984*, and *Saving Private Ryan*.

"Cross-processing" film involves developing a particular film stock using chemicals designed for different stocks (e.g., developing a color negative using "E-6" processing rather than the usual "C-41" process. The process changes an image's contrast and hues.

"Blue-green transfers" swap the green and blue layers during processing resulting in images with different color balances.

All of these can be replicated digitally, either by manually color-grading shots to emulate the effect, or through the use of specific software algorithms that mimic the chemical processes. For example, the blue-green transfer can be replicated simply by swapping the blue and green channels in an RGB image.

FIGURE 8-22 A simulated bleach-bypass look can be digitally applied to an image (see also the Color Insert)

---

[16] There are a number of different techniques for doing so, but the end result is normally the same.

FIGURE 8-23   The effects of cross-processing an image can be simulated digitally (see also the Color Insert)

LABORATORY ACCURACY

Compared to chemical grading processes, digital color grading affords a high level of precision. Laboratories usually assume a margin of error of around one printer light for each of the red, green, and blue components, whereas digital systems are accurate to within a fraction of a point. Putting calibration and color space issues aside, on a digitally graded production that is output to film, it's much more likely that differences in color between the graded image and the projected print are due to the more limited tolerance of chemical processing than the precision of the digital image. Certainly, chemistry can account for all the differences between several prints produced from a single negative.

8.3.8   Printer Lights

Photochemical color grading is achieved by varying the intensity of different colored light sources or by applying colored filters to a film being duplicated. Lab graders specify "printer lights" (or "points") as incremental grading units, so an image might be made greener by

FIGURE 8-24 A blue-green transfer is possible by simply swapping an image's blue and green components (see also the Color Insert)

"adding one green printer light," or darkened by "reducing by one point." [17] Many film color graders and cinematographers are used to thinking about color differences in terms of printer lights. In addition, many projects that will be output to film will inevitably go through some laboratory grading, to compensate for processing differences between different development batches. For these reasons, it may be useful for the digital-grading system to mimic the effects of applying different printer lights, rather than (or in addition to) grading using a more arbitrary scale, or one based upon the digital image format.

8.3.9 Colorization

One of the most impressive (as well as the most complex) capabilities of a digital-grading system is the addition of color to black-and-white images, substituting shades of gray for flesh tones, red roses, green foliage, and so on. As with the restoration of archival footage, this process is very laborious, but the results can be astonishing.

---

[17] Printer lights are a logarithmic unit, reflecting the response of photographic film to light, so doubling the number of lights won't necessarily result in doubling the image's brightness.

FIGURE 8-25   Digital-grading techniques can be used to artificially add color to a black-and-white image (see also the Color Insert)

FIGURE 8-26   False color can be assigned to monochrome digital images, mapping different colors onto different pixel values (see also the Color Insert)

Unfortunately, little automation is available to this process, so footage must be colorized through an intensive combination of masking and tinting (using either solid colors or gradients). Most of the time, it's done without affecting the luminosity information, so that the tonal range remains intact.

8.3.10 False Color

Another way to add color to black-and-white images is by using false color. This process is most commonly used on infrared imagery to define different regions. In the simplest form, a LUT is generated for the footage, whereby a specific luminosity (gray level) is mapped onto a particular color. So pure black might appear as bright blue, slightly brighter shades as yellow, and so on. Because it can be impossible to predict how the colors will be distributed, and because the end results often bear no resemblance to reality, these techniques are often relegated to scientific applications or special effects. However, it's possible to apply similar processes to full-color images to alter the results of such "false color" images through digital grading (applied either before or after the false color process is applied).

8.4 GRADING DAMAGE

As mentioned previously, grading is an inherently destructive process. Depending upon the source footage, and the amount and type of grading processes, the images might completely "break apart" visually or, more commonly, become subjected to increased levels of noise. Much of the time, these effects aren't noticeable until viewed under the target conditions (such as projected onto a cinema screen), and they're often difficult to resolve. Experienced graders know instinctively how different images hold up against different grading processes and which processes to avoid.

However, certain situations are unavoidable. For example, increasing the exposure of heavily underexposed images almost always increases an image's noise level, making it appear to "buzz" or "crawl" when played back.

Fortunately, the digital intermediate pipeline offers methods to combat this and other types of image degradation, helping to "restore" images to their intended state (these methods are covered in Chapter 9).

LOOK MANAGEMENT

Several new systems are currently emerging to tackle the issue of look management. With these systems, such as Kodak's "Look Manager System" (www.kodak.com), grading decisions can be made early on (i.e., "looks" can be defined), without compromising image quality. These grading decisions can be saved and loaded into the grading system during post-production to speed up the grading process.

However, the practicalities of such systems remain to be seen. First of all, one could argue that plenty of other aspects of the intermediate pipeline must be dealt with, rather than designing color schemes that may or may not be used later. Second, although many grading systems store grading information as "grading metadata," separate from the image data; they are largely incompatible. For look management systems to be successful, a common grading metadata standard has to be designed, one that is independent of the grading system. Finally, the largest problem may still be ensuring that every system in the production is properly calibrated; otherwise, the look management system becomes redundant.

8.5 SUMMARY

Many factors determine how we perceive color, and even the same color might be displayed differently on different devices. To minimize this effect, a digital-grading system should be calibrated to some standard viewing environment, as objectively as possible.

Color grading can be used to accurately replicate realistic colors, or to deviate from them, in order to create aesthetic images. Digital-grading systems offer a number of tools for controlling colors in an image, making overall changes to the content of an image, or isolating specific regions for more detailed work. Changes can also be made dynamically, with the properties of an effect being adjusted over time.

Grading can be used for several tasks, from ensuring color continuity across a number of shots, to changing a day scene into a night scene, and even to add color to a black-and-white image.

9

RETOUCHING AND RESTORATION

In the previous chapter we saw how color grading can be used to subjectively enhance digital images, by balancing tones and creating artistic looks for different kinds of footage. Color grading is also used to repair damaged footage, where colors may have faded over time, or lighting, exposure, or stock problems have caused the incorrect recording of color information.

Damage to images usually affects more than just the color content, however. Archival film stock can suffer from a range of defects, including scratches, dust, mold, and stains. Old video footage might have picture dropout or tracking errors. Even well looked-after, new film and video footage may suffer from any of these effects to some degree. Digital images, though immune to the effects of time, may nevertheless suffer from inherent noise or data corruption that can build up when the image undergoes multiple processes. Fortunately, the digital intermediate pipeline has options for tackling all kinds of image degradation.

9.1   IMAGE DAMAGE

Moving pictures can suffer from two different types of damage: intraframe damage and interframe damage. Intraframe damage can be seen on a single frame of the footage and includes dropout, chemical stains and so on. Interframe (or "persistent") damage lasts over a number of frames, and may only be visible when the sequence is played at speed. Picture shift, tramlines, and noise are all examples of interframe damage.

Most of the damage done to images is a function of the physical media used to record the images in the first place. Photographic film, being gelatine-based, is vulnerable to different types of fungi, not to mention scratches caused by frequent handling. Video tapes, on the other hand, are made from metal oxides (more commonly known as rust), which have a tendency to flake apart. Even digital images are subject to corruption, caused by failures in the storage devices.

FIGURE   9-1   This badly damaged film image exhibits a number of different problems

9.1.1   Optical Problems

Problems can also be caused by the optical system of the recording device. For example, lens aberrations can cause the picture to be distorted, such as when using a very wide angle lens, which can cause "barrel" distortion (where vertical lines curve outward). Vignettes are caused by a greater level of light "fall off" at the edge of the lens, causing the corners of an image to be darker and of lower resolution than the center. Focusing problems can cause images to appear blurry or "soft," which may not be intended, and "flare" caused by internal reflection of light on the lens can contaminate an image. However, optical problems are rarely corrected, because doing so is difficult, and to some extent, unnecessary.[1]

9.1.2   Film Damage

Film material is very difficult to store without exposing it to elements that can degrade it. Every time a reel of film (whether negative or positive) is duplicated or viewed, it becomes subjected to potential damage. Different types of damage affect the picture in different ways, and fixing them requires different solutions. The list that follows describes various kinds of film damage.

FIGURE 9-2   Barrel distortion bends vertical lines outward

[1] Some optical problems, such as lens flare, may actually enhance the aesthetics of an image and are sometimes even artificially added to images.

FIGURE 9-3   Pincushion distortion bends vertical lines inward

FIGURE 9-4   A vignette is caused by uneven distribution of light across the image, typically darkening the image's corners

FIGURE 9-5 Out-of-focus images contain little detail

- **Picture shift.** Picture shift (or bounce or weave) occurs when adjacent frames are projected with a slight positional change. All film stocks have small perforations (or sprockets) along the edge to enable the correct alignment of each frame before it's projected. But sometimes the sprockets may be damaged, and splices between frames may not be properly aligned. The result is that a sequence of images may not be perfectly positioned (i.e., lacking proper "registration"), and when viewed at speed, the image may appear to bounce vertically or weave horizontally. Such picture shift is an example of interframe damage, because it can be detected only when viewing a sequence; each frame viewed individually will appear to have no problems, and in fact the content of each image will be intact. This problem can occasionally be resolved by repairing the film damage, such as by rejoining a splice or redoing the sprockets, or it can be fixed digitally, using motion-stabilization techniques covered later in this chapter.[2]

---

[2] The same problem can be caused by mechanical failure during shooting or projection; even when the film is undamaged, if the projector or film camera can't accurately line up the film for each frame, the same problem may be visible. When the error is caused by a faulty camera, the problem is permanently recorded on the film, whereas when the projector is the cause, changing (or repairing) the projector solves the problem. The same problem may also be caused in digitally scanned material if the scanner doesn't use pin registration during scanning (i.e., locking each frame into place before it's scanned).

- **Chemical stains.** Film development is something of a messy process, requiring a number of different chemicals, and processes requiring accurate timings and measurements. Random factors (as well as poor storage or careless handling) can adversely affect the delicate chemical-development balance, resulting in a variety of different chemical stains, such as "watermarks," embedded on the film, distorting or obscuring the image underneath. Duplicating film with chemical stains copies the stain along with the underlying image, and the stain thus becomes part of the image.

  Although such problems might occur over a range of frames, they're intraframe problems and can be fixed on individual frames, either through physical or digital means.

- **Dust.** Tiny particles of dust, hair, and other fibers are constantly circulating through the air. Anytime film is handled (or even when it's just left out in the open), any of these particles can settle on it. Worse, because film is often run through machinery at high speed, static electricity can build up, attracting dust and other fine particles within range to stick to the surface. These tiny particles, when projected onto a large screen, become noticeable, and obscure image details. Even running the frame sequence at speed, the particles are a noticeable distraction, and a high volume of dust on a reel of film may render it unwatchable. As with chemical stains, dust is intraframe damage, and duplicating the film results in the defects becoming part of the copied image. During projection, dust that was on the negative usually shows up as white specks, whereas dust on a positive shows up black.

  Dust can be removed from film simply by cleaning it—for example, by using a dedicated ultrasonic film cleaner. During duplication, "wet gate" (or "liquid gate") printing methods can be used, running the source film through liquid to remove loose dirt. Both automated and manual systems can digitally remove dirt from scanned film. Note that "photographed dust," such as dust on the camera lens, may run across several frames and be much harder to fix, but these lens imperfections and others aren't usually very distracting to the viewer.

- **Scratches.** The several types of scratches that can occur range from minor, intraframe damage similar to a hair on a frame, to vertical running scratches (or "tramlines") that cover a range of frames. The majority of film scratches are caused by handling. The surface of film material is rather susceptible to friction, and running it through all kinds of equipment, from cameras to densitometers, can cause it permanent damage. Running scratches in particular are caused by small edges in contact with the film as it's pulled along, as when grit is in the camera's film gate. Scratches can be fixed digitally, but it can be a very involved process, particularly when fixing scratches across several frames.

- **Warping.** Damage to film, particularly damage caused by heat, can cause it to melt, shrink, stretch, or buckle. Although the surface of the film may be free of scratches, the image will appear to be warped—distorted, stretched, or shrunk in certain areas. Indeed, the effects might be small and not noticeable unless the sequence is viewed at speed. An additional problem is chromatic aberration, where each color-sensitive layer is distorted differently, resulting in color "fringes" in an image.[3]

  Warped images may be corrected digitally, either by replacing the affected areas or by using selective image-warping techniques (covered later in this chapter) to reverse the damage. Individual color channels can be warped to correct chromatic aberrations.

- **Tears.** It's fairly easy for film to be torn, by being mishandled or due to mechanical failure that excessively stresses the film. Tears usually occur at weak points (e.g., splices), and the damage is usually horizontal and affects only one or two frames. However, in some instances, it can affect an entire range of frames and may be difficult or impossible to fix. Tears can be fixed using splicing techniques, but in most cases, the tear is visible, even when the repair is complete. When working in a digital intermediate environment, torn film has to be scanned in separate parts, and the torn frames can be recombined digitally, either using dust and scratch repair methods or by discarding the bad frames and using motion-interpolation techniques to generate new frames. Digital sequences also require motion-stabilization techniques to compensate for any differences in the scanned picture positioning on either side of the tear.

- **Grain.** Film granularity isn't strictly speaking a type of damage, but it's an inherent property of the film itself. Different types of film stock, different exposure settings, and the amount of light in the scene all contribute to how much "clumping" of silver ions occurs within the film. This is seen visibly as the grain structure of the image. Larger grains are more visible, while finer grain structure

---

[3] This can also be an optical problem that occurs when lower-quality lenses are used—such lenses refract different light wavelengths by slightly different amounts.

results in greater image resolution. Grain structure in images can be both removed and added digitally.

- **Stock failure.** Film may simply fail to record images correctly due to problems with manufacture or development. Effects such as "reciprocity law failure" can produce unexpected results. Colors may reproduce incorrectly, images may be underexposed or overexposed, or the density of the film might be too high or low. Many of these issues may be solved by utilizing chemical procedures or with a combination of digital processes such as color grading (covered in Chapter 8) and digital paint (covered later in this Chapter) .

- **Light contamination.** Prior to development, a reel of film is constantly at risk from stray light. Film, by its nature, doesn't "know" when the image has been recorded, unlike video tape, which records a signal only when the recorder "tells" it to do so. For this reason, any light acting upon the film affects it. Ideally, light acts upon the surface of the film only for the duration that the camera shutter is open, focusing an image on the film for a fraction of a second, before advancing to the next frame. Once the film is developed, light doesn't affect it.[4] However, it's possible that light might "leak" through onto some or all of the film, and therefore "fogging" it, which results in overexposure of all or part of the film. A small amount of fogging may be recoverable through careful global or selective grading processes, but a great degree of fogging renders the film useless, either requiring the image area to be cropped to salvage intact regions or necessitating reshooting the scene.

DIGITAL REMASTERING

One of the most practical applications of the digital intermediate process for film material is the ability to remaster aged footage. An entire industry is devoted to the process of digitally remastering a film, rather than reprinting a damaged negative of an old film. Digital remastering typically involves going through the entire digital intermediate process (although conforming from original negative elements may not be possible, and digital remastering usually involves working from a fine-cut production

(continues)

---

[4] This isn't entirely true because continued exposure to light fades or bleaches developed film, but the effect takes a long time to build up and is analogous to leaving a magazine in the sun for a long time.

interpositive or internegative that already has correctly assembled all the elements), regrading it, and performing extensive restoration to damaged parts of the footage. The only pragmatic differences between a digital remaster of an old film and a digital intermediate of a new film is that much less flexibility is possible, in terms of editing and grading options, when working with aged film.

WHY USE FILM?

With all the potential sources of damage to film, it would appear that it's a very volatile format, constantly at risk from a multitude of different threats. This may be true for consumers, but the reality of film production is that many safeguards are in place to minimize damage to film. Most of the issues are caused by mishandling or incorrect storage, so most filmmakers go to a lot of trouble to ensure their film is handled carefully. Further, film tends to degrade gradually over time, whereas other formats, such as video, simply reach a point where they either work or don't, which makes them difficult or even impossible to recover. The majority of film damage can be corrected either chemically or digitally, and most of the damage is relatively simple to fix, especially compared to video. More recently, it has been suggested that due to a lack of standardization, no long-term storage solution exists for either video or data, whereas reels of film are in existence that are several decades old and are completely viewable.

9.1.3 Video Damage

In addition to problems caused by a video camera's optical system, video systems (and digital cameras) are subject to other problems caused by the CCD elements used to capture images. However, most of these problems vary by camera design, and like some optical defects, they may not require correction.[5] Some problems are related to the equipment used to play back a video, rather than being an inherent tape issue. For example, additional noise artifacts may be introduced by low-quality cables used to connect the video recorder to the monitor. Also, playing an NTSC tape in a PAL video system (and vice versa) can produce bizarre results. In such cases, problems can be solved by using the correct combination of video components for playback. Even when the problem is due to the video tape, different video players have different error-correction devices, some of which work better than others, that can compensate for the damage. Video damage may be caused by a number of different factors, but the types of damage are limited. Many of these problems are exclusive to (or at least more pronounced on) analog video formats; however, they may be seen in digital video formats such as HD and DV, which may also exhibit some of the problems seen in digital formats (discussed later in this chapter). The following list describes the types of video damage.

- **Dropout.** Tape "dropout" is intraframe damage (usually physical damage, to or resulting from deterioration of the tape) that causes part of the tape's signal to become unreadable. Part of the image is missing, and it's replaced either by random pixels, black, or even another part of the image, depending upon the video system. Dropout of this type can be fixed digitally using similar techniques to fixing dust and scratches on scanned film, covered later in this chapter.
- **Persistent dropout.** Sometimes dropout occurs in a fixed position across a number of frames. Fixing it digitally requires using the same techniques as used when correcting running scratches on scanned film, covered later in this chapter.
- **Noise.** Noise is caused by a variety of factors, and it results in the inaccurate recording of information. For every point of an image (or pixel) that is recorded, the associated level can vary from the actual (or measured) value for a number of technical reasons, depending upon factors such as the ambient temperature and the resistance of equipment's electronic circuits.

---

[5] Many video camera problems are caused by built-in features that overcompensate for certain situations. For instance, many cameras produce oversharpened or oversaturated images by default, to compensate for the consumer, assuming that he or she usually won't focus perfectly or light a scene before shooting it. In most cases, these problems can be avoided by disabling the respective controls on the camera.

The result is that individual pixels fluctuate in terms of color or luminosity. This fluctuation might be undetectable on a single frame, but when the fluctuation is viewed as part of a sequence, even minute fluctuations can be distracting or render a sequence unwatchable. One major cause of noise in a video source is generation loss, and so the best preventative measure to combat the effects of noise is to work from original material whenever possible, especially where quality is important. Noise may be introduced any time analog video signals are transported, as well as by gradual deterioration of video tape material. Noise can be corrected by using analog or digital noise-reduction techniques, covered later in this chapter.

- **Tracking.** Video signals contain synchronization information that ensures that the picture appears correctly and each frame appears at the right time. In the event of damage to this part of the signal, the picture can become unstable, even when the picture information is intact. VCRs use tracking systems to interpret the synchronization signals in the video, and these systems vary by design and video format. When the tracking signal is damaged, the picture might be distorted, or it may hold still for a number of frames and then "roll," as tracking is lost between sync pulses. Many VCRs include options to correct for tracking problems, and a number of digital techniques can sometimes correct tracking faults on digitized video footage.

- **Interlacing.** Most video formats (with the exception of "progressive scan" formats) are interlaced, which means that each frame is divided into two fields. Each field is recorded in succession, which means that fast-moving objects may exhibit artifacts when viewed as frames. Interlacing can be corrected using one of the deinterlacing processes (covered later in this chapter), or depending upon the project's output requirements, it may be safe to simply leave the frames interlaced.

- **Recorded transmission errors.** Although these errors aren't strictly caused by the video tape itself, several errors can affect a signal, and when it happens during recording, the errors become part of the recorded picture. "Ghosting" is a problem affecting pictures that are transmitted wirelessly, such as off-air (broadcast) material received by an antenna. Ghosting is caused by the transmission reaching the antenna and then reflecting off a hard surface (such as a tall building) toward the antenna. The reflected signal adds to the original signal, and the slight delay between the transmitted signal reaching the antenna, and the reflection reaching the antenna causes a kind of visual "echo" in the picture, with previous frames superimposed over the current one. Hum is caused by interference (usually magnetic) affecting the video signal in cables. The most common form of hum occurs when a power cable is alongside a video cable. The magnetic field created by the power cable, which is sinusoidal, modulates the video signal, causing rolling bars to appear over the picture. Both of these problems become part of the picture if it's being recorded, in the same way that using a VCR to record a channel that isn't properly tuned results in a poor recording, even when played on a different system. These issues can be corrected at the source, and when no other option is available, the impact of problems can be reduced. For instance, it may be possible to re-create the interference pattern embedded in a signal, invert it, and then apply it to the signal. (This technique is also used to clean up digital audio.) However, it's likely that the visual damage will remain to some extent, resulting in a signal that's far inferior to the original (transmitted) source material. Ghosting, in particular, is usually impossible to repair when it has been recorded as part of the picture.

- **Compression.** Different video formats use different forms of compression to encode video onto tape. Each compression method has associated artifacts that affect the image in certain conditions. For example, the 4:1:1 sampling compression used for DV NTSC video signals occasionally exhibits color "smearing" along the edges of an image's different colored regions. As with many other forms of video damage, these compression artifacts may be difficult to correct, necessitating the use of digital paint (discussed later in this chapter) and other techniques.

- **Timecode breaks.** Timecodes are recorded onto separate parts of the video tape, and timecode information can become damaged in the same way as the image information (or through problems during recording). Damage to the timecode track may cause a "break" in the continuity of the timecode progression. While these breaks don't affect the picture, they can be problematic when trying to edit the footage. Timecode breaks usually can be repaired fairly simply by regenerating the timecode information from a known starting point (although this approach may require copying all the information onto a new tape).

- **Distortion.** Damage or disruption to the video information can distort the picture. Less severe distortion can be corrected using similar techniques as those used to correct warped film images.

- **Clamping.** Video has a wide margin to define both the signal's black points and its white points. Anything that falls below a certain value is considered to be black, and lower values are considered superblack, although they're still displayed as black. With white values, anything above a certain value is considered to be "peak white." The advantage of this convention is that it allows room for error—for example when a signal drops uniformly (i.e., the values are decreased by a set amount), it's possible to simply increase the signal so that the image is restored to match the original. However, it's still possible for signals to exceed the maximum and minimum limits, causing the signal to be flattened or "clamped." Any signal that exceeds the black or white points (which can be seen using a vectorscope) can usually be corrected using controls on the VCR (or using digital grading, depending upon the video-capture method). However, signals that have been recorded clamped can't be corrected.

9.1.4 Digital Image Damage

Many of the factors affecting digital image quality are related to the material or processes that they were sourced from. Scanned film carries across all of the dust and scratches on the surface of the film, making them part of the image. Digital images can be copied without any degradation. However, manipulating digital images subjects them to a range of different problems, many of which can reduce the quality of the image significantly. These problems are described in the following list.

- **Corruption.** The only physical problem that affects digital images occurs when the storage device is damaged, making all or part of the data contained within it inaccessible. For small amounts of such data corruption, the effect is similar to video dropout on individual frames and can be treated using similar means. However, a large amount of corruption can destroy entire frames or sequences. In addition, even a small amount of corruption can destroy entire frames that use compression, or entire sequences that are encoded as single-file video streams. Of course, if an uncorrupted copy of the same file exists, it can simply be duplicated to replace the corrupted one.
- **Render errors.** Render errors can look similar to data corruption errors on images. They're caused by miscalculations or other errors

during the rendering process. They can usually be corrected by simply re-rendering the image, which should regenerate it.[6]

- **Clipping.** Peak white is achieved when a pixel's values reach the maximum, and pure black is achieved when the values are the minimum (usually zero). As mentioned previously, video has regions of superblack and peak white to allow a margin of error in the maximum and minimum levels. Most file formats however, don't have an equivalent region, and values can't be increased beyond pure white or below pure black (and everything in between is considered a shade of gray). Therefore, in the same situation where the image is darkened overall, black pixels stay black, and nearly black pixels become black. Then when you try to brighten the image to its original brightness, all the pixels are brightened, including those that were originally black. The originally black pixels are said to have been "clipped" (or "crushed"). For the sake of analogy, consider a jelly baby being pressed against a surface. With the video paradigm, the surface is flexible like a net, so the jelly baby can be pushed into it, and the original shape recovered later. With the digital paradigm, the surface is more like a hot stove, and pushing the jelly baby against it destroys part of the original shape, even after it's lifted off the stove.

  Many digital operations, particularly those color-grading processes that change the luminosity values of an image, can cause clipping. Because clipping is irreversible, its causes should be avoided. Certain high dynamic range file formats have superblack and superwhite regions like video and can be manipulated much more freely.

- **Posterization.** Stretching apart an image's luminance values (e.g., by modifying the contrast) tends to clump values together, causing similar problems to clipping colors. Regions of similar colors become the same, which can result in visible "steps" of color. As with clipping, it's irreversible but can be avoided by using images with higher bit depths.[7] Additionally, some processes can cause such posterization (or "banding") as a by-product. For example, certain noise-reduction techniques work by averaging groups of pixels so that they become the same color; however, posterization is usually visible only in extreme circumstances or when working with images of low bit depth.

---

[6] Interestingly, it's sometimes quicker to just use another restoration method, such as digital paint, to correct render errors than to re-render the sequence.

[7] But only the originals are resampled at a higher bit depth—simply converting an 8-bit image to a 10-bit image provides little benefit.

- **Aliasing.** By definition, pixels are rectangular. They're also hard-edged, meaning that a pixel can only be one single, solid color. This becomes a problem when trying to represent particular shapes using pixels, notably curves and diagonal lines, as the shape of individual pixels may become visible. When viewed at speed, a sequence of moving shapes may cause pixels to "pop," suddenly changing color as an edge moves across them. Certain image operations, such as sharpening filters, can also produce aliased images. This can be avoided by working at a higher resolution or by using "subpixel" or "anti-aliased" operations that are internally processed at a higher resolution and then averaged to produce a pixel. Aliasing can also be reduced by using blurring operations, although blurring can degrade or obscure small details in the image.

- **Moiré.** Because pixels are arranged in a regularly shaped grid, other regular patterns within the image can create interference. The resulting effect is sometimes seen on television, when people wearing clothing with fine lines move in front of the camera, causing the lines to separate into many colors or wavy lines. The effect is also seen when using a digital scanner to capture half-toned material, such as a magazine picture. Moiré can be reduced using specialized "descreening" techniques, or by rotating or blurring the image, all of which degrades the image somewhat.

- **Compression.** Lossy-compressed digital images are subject to the same problems that video compression causes. Many compression artifacts can't be easily corrected.

- **Noise.** Unlike video noise, digital noise isn't caused by making copies of the image. Digital noise is introduced by precision errors, and it exacerbates other digital artifacts, such as clipping and banding. Digital noise can be prevented to some degree by working with high bit-depth images, and the effects of noise can be diminished using digital noise-reduction techniques, which are covered later in this chapter.

9.2 DIGITAL REPAIR TECHNIQUES

The digital-restoration industry has been around for around two decades, although it has primarily been used to restore or enhance (or airbrush) individual scanned photographs. Certain techniques that are used to restore photographs can also be used within a digital intermediate pipeline, along with other techniques borrowed from the visual effects industry. Though some operations are sophisticated enough to allow for automation, many require a skilled operator (or team of operators) to achieve the best results. Some of the popular processes are highly developed, and different approaches are offered by different software manufacturers. Others are more theoretical but may be simple to implement.

THE CASE FOR UNCOMPRESSED DATA

Everything in this chapter assumes the source material isn't compressed using either lossy or lossless compression. Even a small amount of file corruption is enough to prevent the entire contents of the file being readable, let alone repairable. With uncompressed data, the majority of the picture content is intact, and the damaged areas can be fixed using other techniques.

Furthermore, lossy-compressed files may have discarded information crucial to repairing the files. Almost all of the operations listed in this chapter to repair certain problems work better with more image information available, even where the additional information is imperceptible. For example, sharpening a JPEG-compressed file can also sharpen the compression artifacts.

For these reasons alone, a pipeline favoring uncompressed file formats is preferable to one using any kind of compression, particularly when you intend to use restoration processes. However, in some situations, there's much less advantage to storing images without compression. For example, in a DV pipeline, the material is lossy compressed at the source; no uncompressed version is available. This is also true for material sourced from analog video formats that use compression. Converting files that have been lossy compressed to uncompressed ones still causes compression artifacts (e.g., those that occur when using sharpening filters), which in turn causes people to think that leaving the files compressed makes no difference, especially when the final output format will also be compressed. But along with the fact that compressed files are more susceptible to corruption, converting files to uncompressed formats (even if only for the duration of the digital intermediate process) makes sense because doing so avoids fur-

(continues)

ther compression errors being introduced into the images. Lossy compression is reapplied every time the file is saved. If no changes have been made to the picture content, the saved information should be identical to the original, because the compression will be exactly the same as before. But changing the picture content in any way, particularly by color grading or compositing layers, forces the compression algorithm to re-evaluate the data, discarding yet more information and degrading the image even further. In this way, it may help to think in terms of "generation loss" with lossy compressed images. Every time a compressed file is modified and saved, it effectively loses a generation. This isn't true for compressed files that have been saved uncompressed, because although the original image is degraded, it won't suffer from additional artifacts. Similarly, many people think that increasing a file's bit depth has no advantages, but they're wrong for the same reason. Increasing the bit depth reduces the likelihood of introducing errors in subsequent operations, even though increasing the bit depth doesn't in any way improve the existing information.

Ultimately, the practical reasons for sticking to a single compressed format may far outweigh the quality issues. Likewise, no value probably can be gained in converting files that won't undergo many restoration processes. For example, for news production pipelines, which constantly process a high volume of footage from a number of (mostly video-based) sources (much of which will never undergo any restoration processes), speed, performance, and storage capacity are much more important factors than quality. Thus, it makes sense to keep everything using a single, compressed format that is close to the perceptible quality of the original source material.

9.2.1 Image Averaging

Probably one of the simplest and most effective methods (not to mention underused) for eliminating or reducing problems is to use image-averaging techniques. The basic idea is that you have multiple copies of the same image, each copy with different degrees of damage. For example, when scanning old film, or digitizing tapes, several prints or tape copies of the same footage may be produced. Each copy is digitized and stored separately. The averaging process involves simply averaging each pixel's values at each point on the image across each copy. The idea is that deviations of specific pixels are caused by a random error—for example, noise or a speck of dust—and these errors are "averaged out" and don't appear in the final image. The more different copies are available, the better it works. "Weighted" averaging methods may take this approach further, analyzing the differences and biasing the average to the likely "correct" value for each pixel. This may be necessary to counter defects, such as dust on scanned film, that create such strong differences in luminosity that the averaged result still is distorted by the dust on a single image, even with numerous copies to sample from.

Averaging methods work for many different problems. For example, it can be used along with a beam splitter attached to a film camera during a shoot (a beam splitter splits the incoming light and sends it to different locations, such as several reels of negative) to compensate for differences in grain structure and processing variations of the negative, because each copy has had identical picture information sent to it, and any differences are due to issues such as these.[8] Furthermore, it can be used fairly easily to correct problems in a specific system. For example, if you have a video tape that has very little inherent noise, but the VCR and associated cables introduce noise to the signal during digitization, the tape can be digitized several times. The multiple copies are averaged, which reduces or even eliminates the additional noise (but the original recording retains the noise it contained). Similarly, a single reel of film can be scanned multiple times to eliminate the noise in the scanner's CCD element, as well as eliminating loose dust on the surface that changes position during each scan. (This process, however, won't eliminate problems such as scratches or mold, which will be present in every scan.)

The drawbacks to this process are largely practical. For example, there often isn't enough time to scan a reel of film or digitize a tape several times, particularly if the cost of doing so is more expensive than using other methods of correction. It may also expose the material to more damage—scanning a reel of film multiple times may add

---

[8] Doing so drastically increases the costs of associated lighting and film stock, however.

FIGURE 9-6 Multiple noisy images can be averaged to reduce or eliminate the overall noise

more scratches to the film and even risk tearing it. Secondly, there may not be multiple copies of the material available, and the copy that does exist might have significant damage that is inherent in the picture.

One of the other shortcomings is that this method can't correct problems that occur in specific positions, that exist in the original, or where the spatial information of each copy is different (such as with film bounce, badly tracked video, or film scanned without using pin-registration), without first correcting those problems.

9.2.2 Digital Paint

The concept of airbrushing photos has been around for a long time. It involves spraying a fine layer of paint onto an image to correct problem areas or enhance or otherwise alter some aspect of the picture. Most photographic retouchers now use a digital platform to perform the same techniques, because it affords a greater level of accuracy and flexibility. Rather than using an airbrush and paint, "digital paint" tools are used to perform the same (as well as many more) functions.

All of the tools used with still images can also be used on footage within a digital intermediate pipeline. Errors on frames can be corrected using "cloning" tools (which copy one part of an image onto another), or by applying solid colors, patterns, or gradients directly onto an image using shapes or paint-strokes. Even more options are available when working with footage because information can be obtained from any other frame. This allows, among other things, parts of the image from a good frame to be cloned onto a damaged frame, which can be one of the fastest and most accurate methods for repairing a number of problems. Different systems will inevitably offer different tool sets, usually designed for specific purposes.

There are caveats though. Use of digital paint on a sequence of frames can create interframe problems that are only visible when played at speed. Photographic retouchers have the luxury of making major changes to an image that won't be noticed (except in the instance when someone has seen the original image). When working with moving footage however, changes must be replicated exactly through the sequence. For example, to repair a shot containing a large vertical scratch running across a series of frames, you can individually paint each frame. But when played back, slight variations in the paint strokes will show up, causing a flickering artifact that is similar to watching hand-drawn animation. On the other hand, painting strokes that are exactly the same on each frame may result in the stroke appearing like a lens defect—a smudge of paint on the lens (which it effectively is). Successful use of digital paint, therefore, requires either the undetectable use of small amounts on a sequence's single frames (usually cloning from adjacent frames), or the use of animatable vector-based tools across a sequence, so that no random deviations are produced.

Digital paint is one of the few processes that isn't inherently degrading; any image that has been painted doesn't suffer any loss of quality, but of course, the quality of the painted area depends entirely upon the skill of the operator.

9.2.3 Dust-Busting

Removing dust, mold, scratches, and the like from scanned film is such an involved process that a number of different approaches are used. For many film-based digital intermediate pipelines, this process can be one of the most time-consuming and expensive, even though it at first may seem fairly insignificant. This process can also be used to correct dropout on video material, but the vast majority of video footage will contain far less dropout than the level of dust present on the equivalent film footage.

The presence of dust and scratches are generally accepted by a cinema audience, probably because there is a limit to how clean each individual print can be after being constantly handled. But on other versions, such as video or DVD, even a small amount of dust on the image can be distracting, especially because material directly shot on video won't exhibit this problem.

Spotting dust is the first part of the problem; it requires a trained pair of eyes (or several pairs) watching the footage in slow motion to find it. Many digital intermediate facilities run copies of the footage to be checked onto HD tapes, for the sake of convenience, from which a list (or even EDL) may be drawn up. Although HD resolution is somewhat lower than film (especially 4k scans), at higher resolutions, the dust is only better resolved, not more numerous. Any defects that can't be detected at HD resolution are usually imperceptible to the audience.[9]

Fixing the digital images derived directly from the scans is both difficult and extremely time-consuming. Every single frame of film must be checked and corrected. A typical, 90-minute film will consist of around 130,000 individual frames. On top of that, B-rolls and handle frames must be considered. Some digital intermediate facilities make a practice of dust-busting every single frame scanned, including those that may not make the final cut, which can mean fixing almost a million frames per film. However, the result is that each image is as close to perfect as possible.

An alternative approach is to fix frames only in the final conform. However, it's a less flexible approach, requiring careful management and can lead to problems if the material must be reconformed at some point in the future. A similar approach is to dust-bust material as a final step before output, although less time may be available to complete the dust-busting process.

---

[9] Note also that most QC checks are performed on HD material, even for film projects.

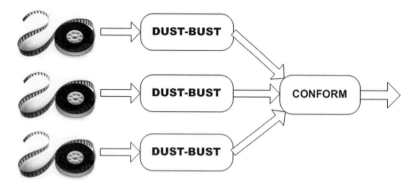

FIGURE 9-7 An effective approach, although time consuming, is to dust-bust film material as soon as it's scanned and then conform the cleaned images

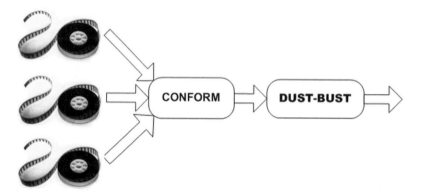

FIGURE 9-8 An alternative approach is to dust-bust only material that has been conformed, although doing so may complicate the reconforming process.

There are also other reasons for removing dust from scanned negative. Dust that has become part of the scanned image propagates to every print made from that point onward. Each speck of dust in scanned images appears in every projected print (along, of course, with new dust accumulated by successive printing and duplication processes). Because the digital scans are normally used to create the various masters (for video, Internet distribution, and so on), the dust also propagates to every other format created from the digital version. For this reason, it's always worth eliminating the dust as early in the pipeline as possible.

Fortunately though, two points make the whole process much easier: each frame of an image sequence is usually very similar to the previous one, and defects are usually randomly distributed with the frame area. Even at the relatively slow frame rate of film (24fps), it takes a lot of motion within the scene before a high proportion of the image is different than the previous one. Even panned or tracking shots normally contain areas of the image that are identical to the previous one (although possibly in a different location within the frame).[10] Coupled with the low probability of two adjacent frames containing damage in the same place (with the exception of certain types of scratches, which have to be repaired using different techniques), this means that dust can be removed simply by copying (or "cloning") the same part of the image over the defect from an undamaged frame. For example, in a sequence that contains a speck of dust over an actor's nose in one frame, the same area of his nose can be cloned across from the previous (or next) frame, which contains no defects. Provided the cloned information is accurately aligned, the sequence should look flawless when played back.

Similarly, motion-interpolation techniques (covered later in this chapter) can be used to analyze frames on either side of the damaged one and generate a new frame. A region of this new frame can be used to replace the damaged area.

Dust is commonly removed using techniques that fall into two broad categories: manual and semi-automatic processes. Manual processes are the simplest, requiring a digital paint operator (or team of operators) to go through each frame and literally "paint out" defects one at a time, typically by cloning picture information from adjacent frames or from elsewhere within the same frame. For example, Idruna's Speedduster (www.idruna.com) has a simple interface for quickly checking through frame sequences and painting out dirt as soon as it's spotted.

Automatic systems, such as MTI's Correct (www.mtifilm.com), require the operator to specify a set of parameters to control how the machine detects dirt. The software looks through each individual frame and compares it to the previous frames, using a variety of motion-estimation techniques and other algorithms (which vary among the different software programs), and unexpected changes in

---

[10] Many interframe compression techniques, such as MPEG, exploit this fact to dramatically reduce the amount of data stored for an image sequence.

FIGURE 9-9 Applications such as Idruna's Speedduster are designed for manually painting such defects as dust

picture and motion information are assumed to be defects. The parameters must usually be set separately for each new shot, because many factors within the images contribute to determining what constitutes dirt. For example, in an outdoor scene, raindrops in the scene might be incorrectly identified by the software as dirt. The software builds a "map" of defects on each frame, and then another process is run to replace all the defects with good image information, either copied from adjacent frames or generated using motion-interpolation techniques.

The automated processes have drawbacks, however; they can miss dirt (i.e., create "false negatives"), "repair" parts of the image that it wrongly interprets as dirt (create "false positives") such as sparkling highlights on a shiny surface, or create image artifacts when repairing a defect. For these reasons, it's often necessary for a human operator to verify all the changes made by the automated system.[11] However, for heavily damaged footage, such as archive film, an automated process can save many hours of work.

---

[11] Ironically, this process can often take as long as manually painting the dust!

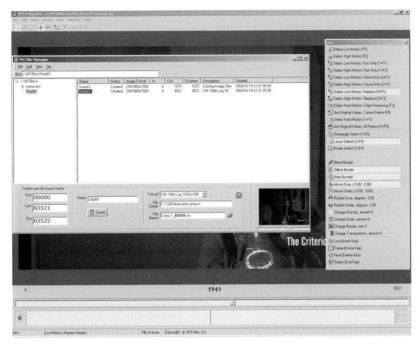

FIGURE 9-10 Applications such as MTI's Correct are designed to automatically remove a number of different defects

Successfully integrating dust-busting into a digital intermediate environment has other practical implications. Fixed images are either produced by overwriting the originals (which means that the changes may be irreversible and difficult to track), or by creating a new set of frames (which effectively doubles the disk space requirement for each shot to be fixed, and may require a separate rendering process, so introducing additional time and potential errors into the process).

One solution is to save a dust-bust layer for each image, containing data for each fix. These files can be losslessly compressed to reduce disk space requirements, and integrated with the original scans at the time of output. Finally, the system could be able to integrate with the other systems, such as the conforming system, so that for example, if the conform operator spots dirt on one of the frames, he or she can flag the defect to be fixed, and the information is instantly transmitted to the dust-busting operator.

A final approach is to store the changes as metadata (similar to how some grading systems store color changes), which are only applied (rendered) during final output. However, these may require significant computer resources to display the fixes prior to output, which can impact the performance of playback.

9.2.4 Scratch Removal

Running scratches and other persistent defects require different methods of correction. With persistent damage, the defects are not randomly distributed, so the odds of finding a "clean" area on an adjacent frame to clone from are very low. For small defects, corrections can sometimes be made by cloning from a similar area elsewhere in the same frame—a technique used to remove dust or dropout in fast-moving scenes.

For other situations, more complex (and typically more time-consuming) methods are required. The simplest, but still reasonably effective one is to generate clean pixels by interpolating between pixels on either side of the affected area. This method works better for narrow scratches (because less information has to be replaced) but can create artifacts along edges or artifacts that are visible only when the digital video is viewed at speed (particularly in fast-moving scenes). Some automated dust-removal systems have options for repairing running scratches using a combination of this method and motion interpolation, which can avoid artifacts created from fast-moving scenes.

Another method is to repair the defect by rebuilding one frame of the sequence (e.g., by using cloning techniques) and then using this good frame as the source to clone onto all other frames. Again, this technique can create motion artifacts (primarily in slow-moving scenes), but the major problem is in the images' grain (or noise) structure.

The problem arises because unlike original film material, cloned material doesn't have a random grain structure. Instead, it has exactly the same grain structure as the source area. This isn't usually noticeable (unless the image has been cloned so much that the grain structure is effectively eradicated) because the cloned regions themselves are somewhat randomly distributed. However, when cloning is used on a fixed area over a number of frames, the area stands out—because unlike the rest of the image, the grain pattern on the cloned area never changes. The result is that the cloned region looks like it was pasted on top of the moving images (which is essentially exactly what has happened). One solution to this problem is to use tools to strip all the grain from the original images prior to painting and then add grain back onto the image after cloning (see the sidebar "Texture Recovery," later in this chapter).

For certain scenes, however, the scratch might be so complicated as to require a visual effects artist to completely rebuild the entire sequence, typically by using wire and "rig-removal" techniques. This results in a highly accurate restoration of the scene but is a costly and time-consuming process. It's usually considered only as a last resort.

PHYSICAL RESTORATION

Sometimes the most effective method for removing dirt from film is simply to physically clean it prior to scanning it. In fact, many digital intermediate facilities recommend that all reels of film submitted for scanning are run through an ultrasonic cleaner first. This will remove much of the dirt, drastically reducing the time required to fix the digital scan files.

Additionally, "wet-gate" film scanners can be used to compensate for scratches on film. A film scratch consists of a depression on the surface of the film, which prevents light from being reflected or transmitted evenly across the film surface, distorting the image. Wet-gate scanners add a liquid layer (such as perchloroethylene, which has the same refractive properties as the film's gelatine) to the film while scanning, which effectively fills in the depressions. However, they don't necessarily remove dirt, which may instead float on the liquid layer while being scanned, causing long streaks to be recorded in the image. In addition, deep scratches that affect the film's dye layer still have to be repaired separately.

(continues)

> **PHYSICAL RESTORATION** (*continued*)
>
> A new technique currently being developed is to scan an infrared image for every frame scanned. This creates a matte that can be used to highlight defects on the surface of the film. Where no dust particles exist, the infrared light passes through (or is reflected back from) the film, whereas the presence of dust or other physical defects absorbs or scatters the light. These mattes might then be fed into an automated system that can quickly repair the highlighted areas.

9.2.5 Sharpening

A multitude of factors can contribute to the relative "softness" (or blurriness) of an image. For starters, the original footage might not have been well lit, properly exposed, or even properly focused. In addition, wear and tear of the material robs it of its former sharpness. Images on an old video tape may not have their former crispness, and film dyes might gradually spread or fade. Generation loss invariably reduces the sharpness of an image, as each subsequent copy introduces more defects and less accurate reproductions.

Digital processes can also reduce the sharpness of an image. In fact, with most digital images, softness is usually the result of a combination of destructive processes, such as spatial interpolation. This process is used when resizing (either increasing or reducing the image area) or rotating images, for example.[12]

Sharpening (also known as "aperture correction" or "unsharp masking") techniques work by re-creating hard edges from blurred regions. Each of the many different sharpening algorithms is suitable for different circumstances. Basically, digital sharpening works by analyzing groups of pixels and then increasing the contrast between pixels it detects lying on an edge. The result is that all the edges in the image look more pronounced and are perceived to be sharper. Digital sharpening techniques are by no means perfect. It's simply not possi-

---

[12] Although digital images can be rotated in increments of exactly 90 degrees with no loss in quality.

ble to reconstruct edges accurately from blurred images, because the information has been destroyed. Even the best sharpening algorithms are based upon estimates of the edges' locations, and the process of sharpening actually degrades an image. Oversharpening an image can lead to "ringing," where the edges are so pronounced that they seem to pop out of the image. Some algorithms even modify pixels adjacent to edge pixels to increase the apparent sharpness of each edge.

In the digital intermediate pipeline, sharpening techniques are to be avoided wherever possible, and when they're used, they should be applied to individual areas rather than entire images. Sharpening settings should be applied to entire shots rather than individual images (or at least, the sharpening effect should fade in and out over a range of frames) to ensure that the results are consistent and don't produce artifacts when viewed at speed. Also, sharpening should only be applied to the luminosity component of an image, because our eyes perceive details in terms of luminance rather than chromaticity.

It's important to note that sharpening can't "refocus" an image. Focusing a camera during a shoot adjusts many properties of the recorded image. Objects within the focal plane are sharp, while objects farther from the focal plane become increasingly blurred. Simply put, refocusing a camera both sharpens certain objects and blurs others. This process is very difficult to reproduce digitally using recorded footage, primarily because no depth information is recorded with the image. However, the blurring aspect, at least, is something that digital systems can do very well.

FIGURE 9-11 Digital sharpening can increase an image's perceptual sharpness, but it also increases the level of noise

9.2.6 Blurring and Defocusing

Blurring a digital image is done by averaging a group of pixels. As with sharpening, several different algorithms control exactly how the averaging is done, but the net result is that the more blurring that's applied, the fewer the visible details in an image. As with sharpening, blurring should be applied to a whole frame range rather than individual frames, so the effect isn't distracting.

Blurring can be considered to be highly accurate, as the process just destroys existing information. However, it doesn't accurately mimic the effects of defocusing a lens, which is a significantly more complex process than simply averaging the image area.

For example, defocusing a camera lens blurs the image but in such a way that bright regions "bloom" outward. In addition, the shape of this blooming is determined by the characteristics of the lens elements, creating, for example, circular or octagonal spots of light in the image.

Fortunately, several image-processing programs, such as GenArts's Saphire RackDefocus (www.genarts.com) mimic these effects, allowing scenes to be selectively defocused as required. Again, because digital images contain no depth information, it's difficult to accurately replicate the exact effects of defocusing a lens, but for most applications, defocusing processes work well.[13]

9.2.7 Image Warping

Manipulating digital images provides a wealth of options. Images can be cropped, resized, rotated, and panned fairly easily. In addition, it's also possible to stretch and squash images—that is, resize them in a particular direction. When you usually resize a square image, the resulting image is still square. But if you stretch the image horizontally, the vertical dimensions don't change, and the resultant image becomes rectangular. Of course, all the features within the image become distorted, but this result may be intended. For example, when

---

[13] Certain computer-generated 3D image formats have the capability to record depth information, which can be used to accurately simulate various focusing techniques.

FItgURE 9-12 Digital blurring doesn't produce the same results as manually defocusing a camera lens, although digital defocusing effects come pretty close (Genart's Sapphire Rackdefocus was used in this example). Note that manually defocusing a camera merely shifts the plane of focus, which may increase the focus of other elements

working with panoramic images that have been anamorphically squeezed to fit within a narrow image area, it may be necessary to stretch the image so that it looks realistic.

With a digital intermediate pipeline, it's possible to take this idea even further. In addition to stretching entire images, it's possible to stretch parts of the image. For example, a region within the image can be selected, and its contents stretched outward. Rather than replacing the surrounding image information, the rest of the image is squashed as required to accommodate the change, a process known as "warping." Although this sounds like something of a gimmick, it has many practical uses. For example, it can correct lens distortions, which stretch and squash specific places in the recorded image. Warping distorted images can reduce these effects dramatically. Because the warping process uses interpolation algorithms, warping is a destructive process, and the more warping is used on an image, the more degraded the image becomes. The use of warping should be kept to a minimum.

GLAMOR RETOUCHING

Photographic retouchers, particularly those working in the fashion industry, can spend weeks working on a single image, producing results that are effectively more perfect than reality. In addition to color grading and correcting dust, scratches, and other film damage, they routinely manipulate the subject of the image—for example, to remove stray hairs or skin blemishes, or even making more extreme adjustments, altering body shapes or facial features. This process adds a whole new dimension to fashion photography, effectively allowing for additional make-up or plastic surgery to be applied conveniently (and safely) after the shoot has been completed.

Although the digital intermediate pipeline shares many of the tools used by the photographic retoucher, much progress still must be made before such cosmetic enhancements can be applied to entire films. Probably the most important factor is the time it requires to perform such operations. In addition to the time required to apply such extensive processes to each individual frame, time must also be spent making sure that no motion artifacts are produced as a result. For example, simply removing a stray hair from in front of an actor's face on each frame of a sequence requires exactly the same methodology as removing a running scratch from a digital film sequence.

For now at least, certain shots, such as those without a lot of movement, might be viable candidates for such glamor-retouching processes, where the process parameters can be designed on one frame and then simply replicated across the sequence. Presumably the number of available options will grow in the future, as new technologies and hardware advances emerge.

FIGURE 9-13 Images can be selectively warped either to correct problems or to create a special effect

9.2.8 Texture Reduction and Addition

When you watch a film sequence, minute variations in the image structure are caused by the random distribution of grain across the frame. A "normal" amount of film grain isn't considered to be distracting to the viewer and, in fact, can even enhance the image. (Many cinematographers choose film stock on the basis of the type of grain it produces, thereby using grain as a creative tool.)

The same is true of video footage, which suffers from noise distributed randomly across the image. A small amount of noise is considered an actual improvement to an image sequence, making it appear perceptually sharper and more detailed than an equivalent, noiseless sequence.

Noise and grain (or other "image texture") should be considered a form of degradation, at least from a quality point of view. Image texture obscures or interferes with fine or subtle details, and the image is degraded as the noise or grain level is increased.[14] At some point in every sequence, noise or grain is more of a distraction than is pleasing to the eye.

---

[14] It's not really accurate to talk in terms of "increasing" or "decreasing" grain in an image, because the differences are due to the relative type and size of the film grains (and hence their frequency), which are in turn determined by the film stock and processing methods. The terms are used here for simplicity.

Digital methods can be used to add or reduce the amount of noise and grain in an image, but it's more likely that the levels will be reduced rather than increased to repair images (although they're often increased as a creative device). By its nature, grain addition and removal is more complicated than noise addition and removal, mainly because grain tends to be of a particular shape, whereas noise is typically distributed among specific pixels. However, certain noise reduction techniques can be used to remove grain patterns as well, usually by increasing the parameters.

The primary technique for reducing noise in an image sequence is to use a "median" filter. This simple process analyzes, for each pixel, the surrounding area of pixels, finds the median value (i.e., an average based upon how much a specific value recurs), and then sets the central pixel to that value. In doing so, the impact of noise within the image is reduced (because the small, random fluctuations are eliminated), but the process also destroys image information, particularly for fine or subtle details. This technique has other variations—for example, filters that process the chromatic information separately from the luminosity information, various proprietary filters, and targeting specific types of texture, such as the grain of a particular film stock.

Any type of texture-reduction process has trade-offs between the amount of texture removed and the resultant image quality. Each scene must be judged separately. In addition, because so many processes are affected by noise (while others may introduce noise), it becomes important to decide at which stage in the pipeline to implement noise reduction, with some digital intermediate facilities performing noise reduction early on, while others do it as the final stage prior to output.

A branch of processes are designed to add texture to images. These processes work best when the source image contains minimal texture and are usually used to add consistency between scenes—for example, increasing the level of film grain of one shot to match the level in the previous shot.

More creative effects are possible. Texture can be added to simulate a variety of materials. Film grain can be added to video footage to make it appear as though the footage originated on film. It's even possible, for example, to texture images to look like paint on canvas—though these types of texture operations usually have to be used in conjunction with color-grading operations and possibly digital filters to complete the effect.

TEXTURE RECOVERY

Almost all of the operations available in a digital intermediate pipeline can be applied to entire images or selected areas. However, many of these affect an image's texture properties, either reducing elements such as noise and grain, or else exacerbating them. This can become a continuity issue when applied to entire images (i.e., successive shots may have different levels of texture than other shots), which can distract the audience. Where the texture differs in images that have undergone selective processing, such as selective blurring, the changed areas may stand out from the rest of the image when viewed at speed. This problem can be compensated for by using texture recovery processes, which can rebuild the texture in images to match other areas. One such method is to apply grain or noise to the selected areas, adjusting the parameters until visual continuity has been achieved. Several commercial grain-emulation filters are designed to generate the correct grain structure when the operator chooses the particular film.

Another option is to simply remove all texture from footage upon acquisition and then add back the desired level and type of texture prior to final output. This method may also make processes such as scratch removal easier, but it requires more processing time. A quality implication must also be considered because all texture removal operations degrade the image to some degree. A good compromise, therefore, is to limit this procedure to shots that require some form of processing that affect the texture of the image and then add texture to match the unmodified images.

9.2.9 Deinterlacing

The majority of video footage is interlaced (as opposed to footage that is progressively scanned or is "full frame")—that is, each frame is divided into two fields, with each field occupying an alternate line.

Each field is typically recorded at a slightly different time from the other, meaning that a delay exists between fields. This means that the scene may have changed between fields.[15] Thus, each frame might have motion artifacts when viewed individually or on a progressive (noninterlaced) format (e.g., when projected on film). The artifacts are caused by the delay and are particularly likely to occur on fast-moving subjects. Provided the final output is also an interlaced format, the interlacing artifacts may not present any significant problems, and the footage can be left as it is. However, when progressive output formats or spatial operations (such as resizing or rotating the images) are required, the interlacing becomes part of the image, and the artifacts remain in the picture.

Fortunately, interlacing happens in a predictable way and can be corrected (or deinterlaced) digitally, using a number of methods. The simplest method is to discard one of the fields and regenerate the missing lines by interpolating from the remaining field. However, this approach dramatically lowers the image quality and can result in artifacts, such as smeared lines on the image.

A more advanced method is to use dedicated motion analysis software, such as RE:Vision Effect's Fieldskit (www.revisionfx.com), which calculates the motion of objects in a scene and uses that information to rebuild the image information. Methods such as these are slower but produce more accurate and higher-quality results.

For deinterlacing to work correctly, it must be applied before any other process, which might alter the position or size of the fields. No deinterlacing method is perfect, and the ideal solution is always to shoot using a progressive format wherever possible.

---

[15] It's entirely possible to have noninterlaced video material on an interlaced format and for it not to be interlaced. For example, one second of a PAL 50i tape might contain 25 progressive frames split into 50 fields. These fields can be used to perfectly recreate a 25p sequence without artifacts because the problem arises only when the scene is shot using an interlaced method. Throughout this book, it's assumed, for the sake of simplicity, that progressive material is stored on a progressive format.

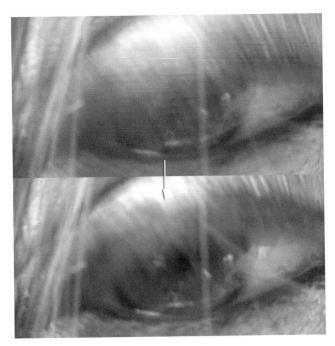

FIGURE 9-14 Motion analysis and image interpolation can be used together to deinterlace images while still retaining much of the original quality

9.2.10 Motion Stabilization

Audiences like smooth camera movement, particularly when the footage is blown up to cinema screen size. Unsteady camera motion, such as handheld camcorder footage can cause a cinema audience to suffer disorientation, vertigo, and even nausea in some cases. Most film and video productions usually ensure that all camera movements are as smooth as possible. Even handheld shots are typically made using special rigs (such as "Steadicam" rigs) to produce smoother motion.

Unfortunately, not all footage is as smooth as possible. Sometimes the image contains little bumps or vibrations that aren't noticed until after the end of shooting. In addition, lower-budget productions may not have access to the required equipment for smooth shots.

"Motion stabilization" (or "image stabilization") is a process where the motion of a sequence is analyzed and then smoothed or "stabilized." It typically works by the operator selecting a feature to be tracked (similar to the feature-tracking process covered in the previous chapter), and the motion of the feature is adjusted to the required level of smoothness. The downside to this process is that the edges of the image must be cropped, depending upon how much extraneous motion is removed. This isn't a problem if the active picture area isn't cropped—for example, when a larger picture area was shot than is actually used (as with Academy aperture 35mm film), and the cropped area doesn't intrude on this area. Otherwise, the resultant image may have to be resized to ensure the active area isn't cropped (which reduces the image quality), or the cropped region may have to be reconstructed, such as by using digital paint techniques. It also can't compensate for the "motion blur" smearing effect produced by a fast moving camera.

Similar to this is the concept of "reracking" a shot. Sometimes, misaligned scans or splices cause film footage to lose its vertical positioning. Visually, part of one film frame carries across to the next digital image (a similar effect is also seen sometimes when video signals lose their tracking information). Some digital restoration systems provide means to rerack the footage interactively, effectively resplicing images together. Often though, additional restoration processes are needed to correct other problems that are a side effect of misaligned framing (such as color differences, warping, or destabilized images).

9.2.11 Temporal Interpolation

One of the unique and most powerful tools within the digital intermediate pipeline is the ability to analyze and interpolate the motion of objects in an image sequence. Motion (or "temporal") interpolation can be used to increase or decrease the amount of motion blur within a scene (effectively emulating adjusting the shutter-speed control of the camera, even after shooting), regenerate an existing frame from others (such as for replacing damaged frames) and generate new frames for a sequence at a different frame rate (for creating slow-motion, fast-motion, or variable speed motion effects).

The mechanics of each motion-interpolation system varies by design, but in general they work by analyzing every pixel in each image (or groups of pixels), and comparing them to the pixels in other frames in the sequence, constructing a "map" of vectors of the motion of each pixel in the sequence. From this map, it's possible to estimate the position of each pixel at a sub-frame level (in-between frames). By blending regions of fast motion together, it's possible to simulate more motion blur (the blur effect produced when a fast-moving object moves in front of a camera with a slow shutter speed—the length of the blur on each indicating how far the object travelled while the shutter was open). It's also possible to reverse this process to some degree, effectively reducing the amount of motion blur, but this ability depends entirely on the image content, and in general, it's much easier to add motion blur than to remove.

Motion interpolation is accurate to a point. As a rule of thumb, the higher the frame rate relative to the speed (in pixels per second) of each moving object in the scene, the more accurate the results will be. The best results are produced by shooting at a high frame rate. Problems are also caused by, for example, lighting changes or objects that cross over each other, and the results may have to be adjusted with other processes—for example, to remove artifacts.

As with all forms of interpolation, motion-interpolated images are of lower quality than the originals. When using motion interpolation to generate frames to replace areas of other frames, it's sometimes worthwhile to generate the new frame and then replace only the required sections rather than the entire frame for better results.

9.3 SUMMARY

As we've seen, a lot of different tools are available to the digital intermediate pipeline. When utilized correctly, these tools can improve the perceptual quality of the image. However, the use of many tools requires a great deal of rendering time, and the opposite effect can be produced than intended, with some restoration processes actually reducing image quality. As stated, the dust-busting process of a digitized feature film is one of the most time-consuming and expensive parts of the process, yet in many ways, it's still a considerably faster process than attempting to use, for example, digital sharpening and blurring techniques on the entire film. Also, some scenes might need complex retouching procedures, requiring a visual effects artist rather than a digital intermediate restoration operator.

The next chapter looks at the use of digital processes, as well as other computer-generated material (such as text), that can be applied to images to modify them for creative effects.

10

DIGITAL EFFECTS AND TITLES

The previous chapter dealt with the various ways to repair damage sustained by various formats, as well as digital methods for subjectively improving the perceptual quality of footage. This chapter focuses on methods for adjusting images using various digital effects, as well as adding titles, watermarks, and logos to the footage prior to output.[1]

---

[1] The availability of specific effects, as well as the flexibility to adjust each effect, is determined by the type of software, as well as the specifics of the digital intermediate pipeline. Therefore, each pipeline may not offer all the effects and options listed in this chapter or may offer alternatives to produce the same result. The use of digital effects in the digital pipeline, with the possible exception of optical effects, should usually be considered as an additional expense, typically charged according to the amount and complexity required.

10.1   OPTICAL EFFECTS

The simplest and most common type of effect used is the "optical" effect.[2] This covers a variety of processes used to reposition and retime and to apply transitions to finished footage.

Many of these optical effects can be applied at the push of a button in the conforming or grading system, or are run as separate processes that generate new material to be brought into the conforming system. None of these processes take much time to process, though much time may be spent finessing them to achieve exactly the desired effect.

10.1.1   Flips and Flops

Sometimes it's necessary to reverse images in a sequence, so that, for example, an actor looks to the left instead of to the right. Problems such as these may be solved simply by "flipping" a shot, turning it upside-down, or "flopping" it, so that the left edge of the frame becomes the right edge, and vice versa.

In a digital environment, images can also be easily rotated in 90-degree increments. Note that rotating an image by 180 degrees is equivalent to flipping and then flopping it.

None of these operations affect the quality of the image, because all the image information remains unmodified; it's just rearranged.[3]

10.1.2   Transitions

Transitions between shots, such as dissolves and wipes, require new material to be generated from the source material. Simple transitions can usually be generated by the conforming system (and may be done

---

[2] The word "optical" used here is derived from the original lab processes, using combinations of lights and lenses, that were used to generate these effects on film

[3] This may not be the case for images with nonsquare pixels, and it's definitely not the case for rotations that aren't exactly 90 degrees.

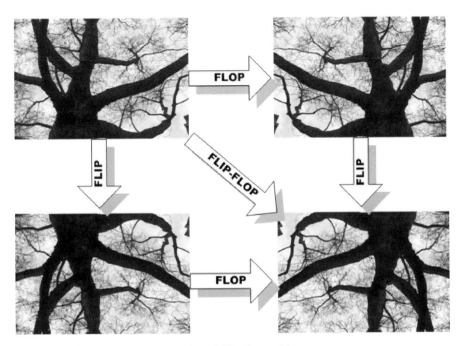

FIGURE 10-1   Flipped, flopped, and flip-flopped images

automatically, provided the necessary parameters are in the conform EDL), but more complex transitions, such as a 3-way dissolve (where the outgoing shot dissolves into a new shot, which in turn dissolves straight away into a third shot), or those that require specific attention, may have to be done using a separate system.

A dissolve transition simply constitutes fading one shot out while fading another in during a specified duration, and a wipe effect uses the image area to control the amount of each shot that is visible—controls it by a predetermined pattern and applies it over a fixed duration, as covered in Chapter 7.

In a digital system, even these transitions can be modified in a variety of ways to produce nonlinear transition effects. For example, a shot may start to rapidly dissolve into another one and then slow down, maintaining some of the previous shot, while the new shot dominates. A wipe might slowly grow from one corner of the image and accelerate toward the end of the transition duration. Alternatively,

FIGURE 10-2 An image rotated in 90-degree increments

a wipe could be combined with a dissolve, so that the dissolve effect is distributed unevenly across the frame. They can also be combined with other effects—for example, a drop shadow.

Many digital intermediate systems can produce many of these non-linear effects, with many adjustable parameters, although the exact types of modifications vary among digital intermediate pipelines.

Many systems allow the use of effects at every stage of the process. For example, Thomson's Bones (www.thomsongrassvalley.com) allows effect nodes to be added to any shot, in any order.

10.1.3 Motion Effects

The speed of a shot can be adjusted (or "retimed") within the digital intermediate pipeline for practical or creative purposes. It can be as

FIGURE 10-3 Effects can be applied to transitions, which themselves can be nonlinear

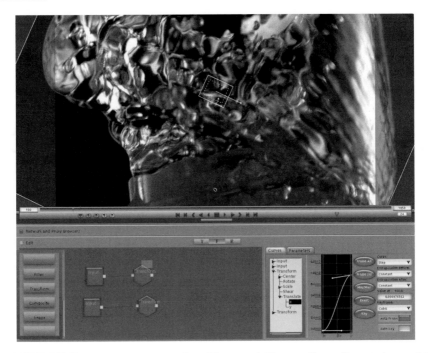

FIGURE 10-4 Some systems, such as Thomson's Bones, allow effects to be used in conjuction with any other tool

simple as speeding up a shot by removing a proportion of the frames (for example doubling the speed of a sequence by removing every other frame), slowing down a shot by repeating a proportion of frames (halving the speed by showing every frame in a sequence twice), or creating a freeze-frame effect, by repeating a specific frame for the desired duration.

As with transition effects, motion effects can be listed in the conform EDL and may be performed automatically by the conforming system. Even more, nonlinear speed effects are possible with the digital pipeline. For example, the fashionable timing effect often seen in

FIGURE 10-5   The original image sequence

FIGURE 10-6   The sequence at double speed, achieved by discarding alternate frames

FIGURE 10-7   The sequence at half speed, achieved by duplicating every other frame

FIGURE 10-8   The sequence with a freeze frame

trailers, where a shot runs at high speed before suddenly slowing to a crawl, is possible using motion-interpolation systems that can selectively increase or decrease a shot's speed, usually by plotting an acceleration or speed graph.

THE USE OF B-ROLLS

The creation of B-rolls, covered in Chapter 7, may be necessary for certain optical effects, particularly those that modify the duration of a shot. Dissolves, for instance, require footage from both the outgoing and incoming shots to cover the duration of the dissolve.

(continues)

FIGURE 10-9 A dissolve uses overlapping A-roll and B-roll material

THE USE OF B-ROLLS *(continued)*

The extra material is usually created as a B-roll, effectively becoming an additional reel as far as the conforming system is concerned. This allows the B-roll to be sent to separate systems that can then generate and render the required effects as a new sequence.

For the sake of continuity, and to reduce the likelihood of errors, it may be necessary to incorporate the rest of the transitioned shots as part of the transition effect, which means that individual shots are only separated by cuts and that the pipeline treats a long sequence of dissolves as a single, long shot. This approach can reduce the chance of errors, such as duplicate frames, being created at the join between the rendered effect and the adjacent material. However, it requires additional space and can take longer to re-render.

An issue often arises concerning the order in which effects and grading are applied. For instance, it's much more convenient to apply grading to rendered dissolve material, rather than rendering the dissolve using graded material. This is because the dissolves are less likely to require changes, whereas grading tends to undergo constant revision. In addition, several different grades may be needed for different output formats, which then means that multiple rendered dissolves have to be created for each output format.

On the whole, grading can be applied to rendered dissolves by selectively mixing together the two grades on either side of the dissolve and applying that to the dissolved region. However,

(continues)

THE USE OF B-ROLLS *(continued)*

with certain shots and grading types, this method can create artifacts, where the grading of the incoming shot may be visible on the outgoing shot (or vice versa). In this case, it may be necessary to first apply the appropriate grading to the incoming and outgoing shots and then create the dissolve material from the graded sequences. Note that attempting to regrade, or applying additional grading to a previously graded, rendered image, will degrade the image. To successfully change the grading of an image, the original grade must be adjusted and reapplied, and the dissolve re-rendered.

Occasionally, insufficient B-roll material is available to create a transition at the desired duration. This is especially common with dissolves, where an "empty" or black frame may be included in the offline edit but isn't noticeable until the sequence is viewed at full quality, where it may be seen as a flash frame. This situation can be remedied by retiming or freezing the B-roll or by adjusting the transition duration.

10.2 RESIZING AND REPOSITIONING

Another useful feature of the digital intermediate pipeline is the ability to alter the composition of a sequence after it has been shot. This can be achieved through a combination of resizing and repositioning the images. Clearly, this is limited by the picture area of the source footage, as well as the output requirements. In fact, different compositions are often made for different output formats, particularly for different "widescreen" and "fullscreen" releases, which is covered in Chapter 11. These processes can be also animated to create a zoom or panning effect, months after photography has wrapped.

Although repositioning images doesn't degrade the images (it does, however, crop, or remove the edges of the images), the resizing process does degrade the images to some extent because it relies on interpolation methods to generate new images. Images that have been resized and positioned (or "recomposed") are less visually sharp and may exhibit artifacts such as aliasing or banding. In addition, for film-originated material, repositioning resizes the grain structure, which is locked to the image content, possibly resulting in continuity problems between scenes.

CAMERA SHAKE

One of the uses of digital repositioning tools is to simulate camera shake, a small oscillation of the picture in the frame, creating a similar effect to trying to hold a photograph still when sitting on a bus. This is often used as a creative device, such as to present an enhanced sense of impact for sped up action scenes, or to lend the camera a feeling of weight, for example in a scene with an explosion.

As with many options provided by the digital intermediate, this effect can be produced during filming, but adding it later on instead allows more room for changes and experimentation to get the desired effect.[4]

10.2.1 Interpolation Methods

Many of the processes in the digital intermediate pipeline, particularly those that alter the spatial content of the images, rely on some form of interpolation. Interpolation is a mathematical process whereby new information is generated to fill gaps in the original information. The process is similar to the effects of stretching a woolly sweater. When the sweater is unstretched, the pattern on it appears as designed. But when the sweater is stretched, the gaps between threads grow bigger, and the pattern becomes distorted. The function of interpolation is simply to try to fill in the gaps between pixels, just as the function of the "tweening" process in animation is to create the frames in between key frames in a sequence.

---

[4]These methods can't be used to reliably simulate the effects of actually moving a camera through a scene because it won't provide any sense of perspective.

FIGURE 10-10 Digital images can be resized and repositioned. With some systems, it's also possible to rotate the images

Digital images use interpolation processes for increasing the size of an image, as well as for decreasing the size of an image. Perhaps one of the most important uses of image interpolation in the digital intermediate pipeline is the video-to-film transfer, where video material is resized to film resolution (requiring an increase in the number of pixels by a factor of 9).

Many different algorithms are used for image interpolation, and some are more useful in certain situations than others. Software such as Shortcut's Photozoom Professional (www.trulyphotomagic.com) allow images to be resized using specific algorithms. Some of the most common algorithms are described in the following list.[5]

- **Nearest-neighbor interpolation:** Simply duplicates the closest pixels from the original positions to create additional pixels. This method is very fast, although it produces aliasing and edge artifacts, which make it easy to tell it has been resized.
- **Bilinear interpolation:** Analyzes a 2×2 area of pixels from the original image and then generates new pixels based on averages of the analyzed pixels. This method isn't as fast to process as the nearest-neighbor method, but it produces smoother, more natural results.

---

[5] While it isn't correct to describe certain methods as more accurate than others—after all, interpolation by definition, can't re-create unavailable information—the fact is that some methods seem to produce more perceptually pleasing results than others.

However, the entire image appears less sharp than other methods and may result in edge artifacts and a loss of edge sharpness.

- **Polynomial interpolation (or quadratic interpolation) methods:** This includes, for example, the bicubic method, which analyzes a larger 4×4 area of pixels to create each new pixel. Specific algorithms produce slightly different results, typically varying in smoothness and sharpness. This method is slower to process than bilinear methods, though it sometimes may produce better results, particularly along edges. However, where a lot of interpolation is required (e.g., when increasing the size of a small image to a very large image), other methods may be more suitable.

- **Spline interpolation methods:** This includes, for example, the b-spline method, which re-creates the pixel information as points on a spline (similar to those used for spline-based computer animation). By measuring new points on the generated curve, in-between values can be determined. This process can be fairly slow, and prob-

FIGURE 10-11 An image resized to 400% of its original size using nearest-neighbor interpolation

FIGURE 10-12 An image resized to 400% using bilinear interpolation

FIGURE 10-13   An image resized to 400% using bicubic interpolation

lems can arise when trying to interpolate areas of high contrast mixed with areas of low contrast.

- **Frequency-based interpolation methods:** This includes, for example, "Fourier" or "Lanczos" interpolation methods, which convert the source image into a set of frequencies, apply various filters to the information, and then convert the frequencies back into a larger image. These methods can be slow to process and can also introduce noise into the image.

- **Fractal interpolation methods:** Reconstruct images as fractals—that is, complex mathematical equations. Fractals, by definition, are resolution independent, so they can be rendered at any resolution, although this process may take some time. While this type of processing can create very large images relatively well, it may introduce significant amounts of noise or other artifacts.

- **Adaptive interpolation methods:** Combine two or more other interpolation methods, each of which is applied to different parts of

FIGURE 10-14   An image resized to 400% using B-spline interpolation

FIGURE 10-15   An image resized to 400% using Lanczos interpolation

FIGURE 10-16   An image resized to 400% using shortcut's Hybrid S-spline inter-polation method.

the image. One of the drawbacks of many other methods is that they're applied to the entire image in the same way. In most images, this approach isn't the best one to take, because some parts of the image (e.g., those that are distant or out of focus) require a smoother result, while others, such as those with a high degree of detail, require a sharper result. Adaptive interpolation uses algorithms to determine which type of interpolation is more suitable for each area, which results in a more pleasing result.

Interpolation can occur transparently for many of the systems and processes that use it, in that the operator doesn't have to worry about using them, (or may not even be able to select which ones are used). For example, if a pan and scan operator recomposes an image, he or she usually wants to work interactively with the image, adjusting the size of the picture intuitively, rather than having to adjust numerous parameters for each shot. Further, most of the

FIGURE 10-17 An image resized to 400% by re-imaging the source at a higher resolution

research into image interpolation quality is concerned with still images rather than image sequences, so some interpolation methods may be better for still images than moving images. Similarly, most tests are concerned only with the effects of increasing image resolution, although interpolation must also be used to some degree when rotating or decreasing the size of an image. Some interpolation methods may also be better suited to specific operations, such as rotation or warping, than others. Currently, no interpolation method uses interframe sampling to read pixel values from adjacent frames to provide a more accurate interpolation, although this would undoubtedly be a lengthy process.

Perhaps the most useful way to integrate different interpolation methods into a digital intermediate pipeline is to use a faster interpolation method for display and previewing purposes, and a slower but better quality method during rendering for final output. Ultimately, there is no substitute for imaging at a higher resolution.

10.3 FILTERS

One of the staples of digital imaging, be it digital photography or digital movie post-production, is the use (or occasional overuse) of digital filters. A filter is a process that is applied to an image, part of an image, or an image sequence to modify the content. Some filters are designed to remove dirt and scratches, others to create halos or glowing effects within the image, and still more to make an image, for example, look as though it was painted by Van Gogh.

Image filters, such as those in GenArt's Sapphire range of filters (www.genarts.com), can create lighting effects or emulate filters on the camera lens, such as star-shaped highlights. They can be used to reposition the image in a variety of ways, to create a kaleidoscope effect, or to emulate different materials, such as embossed stone or a sketch on a sheet of paper. Procedural filters, such as those in Allegorithmic's Map|Time product (www.allegorithmic.com), allow various mathematical procedures to be strung together to create a diverse range of effects.

All filters degrade the image in some way, but usually these effects are desired, making the images perceptually better. However, certain filters can create artifacts, particularly when applied to a sequence and viewed in real time, and the output must be carefully checked.

10.3.1 Computer-Generated Material

An increasing number of productions rely on computer-generated (CG) material for certain shots. These are normally supplied by departments or facilities external to the digital intermediate pipeline and may be in the form of complete shots or "elements" to be composited onto existing shots in the program. Invariably, these shots will be in a variety of different file formats and color spaces and may therefore require grading to maintain color continuity. However, certain CG shots may carry certain advantages over filmed footage. For example, 3D CG images may carry "depth-channel" information, which is used to determine the distance of each pixel from the camera. This can then apply additional effects, such as simulated depth of field, lighting effects, and even atmospheric effects such as fog.

3D CG images may also carry automatically generated mattes, for example, to isolate specific objects, which can then be used in conjunction with a number of different processes. These processes generally don't account for effects such as reflections (note that the reflections in the pyramid shown in Figures 10-20 through 10-22 are not correctly affected by the effects).

FIGURE 10-18 A source image (left) can be passed through a software-filtering process (in this case, GenArt's Sapphire Effects) to produce a radically different image. Original image © Andrew Francis 2005

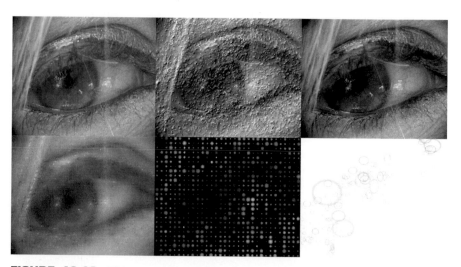

FIGURE 10-19 Using procedural filters such as Allegorithmic's Map|Time, it's possible to use an original image (top left) as the basis for new images or patterns (see also the Color Insert)

FIGURE 10-20 The original 3D image, saved with depth information

FIGURE 10-21 A 3D blur effect applied to the image simulates a focal point

FIGURE 10-22 A 3D fog effect applied to the image simulates fog in the scene

10.4 PARTICLE SYSTEMS

A special type of CG imagery, "particle systems," can create a variety of effects. Particle systems are a mathematical model of particles (i.e., points), each of which may be assigned various properties, such as color and shape, that can change over time. Particle systems can model a number of different phenomena. For instance, a particle system can model weather patterns, fire, and smoke.

As well as creating effects in their own right, particle systems can also be used to modify other parameters. For example, a particle system can generate a transition effect or control other features, such as text placement. Note that the implementation of particle systems within a digital intermediate pipeline is by no means mandatory, and the capabilities of each pipeline will vary.

THE OPEN FX PROJECT

With all the different digital image-editing systems, there was a need to unify the way that third-party effects software (i.e., plug-ins) could easily be used with any number of the systems. Such is the idea behind the Open Effects (OFX) system, which has already been adopted by a number of digital intermediate systems manufacturers. More details can be found at openfx.sourceforge.net.

10.5 TEXT

Several different types of text commonly appear in productions. Titles and subtitles are types of text that appear onscreen, usually to provide translation of dialog or establish a scene's location or time frame. Traditionally, subtitles to translate dialog are placed in the lower half of the screen, whereas other titles can be placed anywhere. Titles and subtitles typically use simple, static text that either cuts or fades in and out.

Many productions have opening credits, which list some of the people who worked on the production, as well as the title of the film. Although some productions use simple titles for this purpose, many use more complex, animated text with specific styling.

End rollers (or simply credits) provide a more extensive list of individuals who worked on the production, as well as copyright and similar notices. Traditionally, the credits appear at the end of the production as white text scrolling up a black background.

Captions (or closed captions, which are captions that don't appear as part of the picture), are used for distribution purposes to enable the hearing impaired, for example, to read the words being spoken in the scene, as well as to be informed of important sounds. Captions are normally supplied as raw text (or timed text) data rather than image data and are used with specialized equipment.

Text can be stored digitally in a simple ASCII text file.[6] These files tend to be very small (1 million words of text requires approximately 6MB) but don't carry any information about how the text is to be displayed. Other text file formats, such as extensible markup language (XML) or rich text format (RTF) files, contain parameters for certain stylistic attributes of the text, such as the size and typeface.

However, the majority of text that appears onscreen is usually encoded as part of the image. The reason for this is simple: rendering text directly onto the image guarantees that it appears exactly as intended. Generating text in this way by imaging applications usually allows a greater degree of control, especially in terms of creating a specific style.

10.5.1 Text Styles

Text can appear in many different ways and has several different attributes. The most common attributes are described in the list that follows.

- **Character set.** The "character set" is used to distinguish between different alphabets—for example, to differentiate between the Roman character set used for languages such as English and

---

[6] ASCII (American Standard Code for Information Interchange) defines standards for machine-readable hexadecimal codes that represent each letter of the alphabet, numbers, punctuation symbols, and other symbols.

French, and the Cyrillic character set used for Russian, Ukrainian, and Hungarian languages. Each character set also defines other symbols such as punctuation marks and numbers where applicable.

- **Typeface.** The typeface (or font) is used to describe the styling of each character. Use of a specific font ensures that each time a particular letter is used, it has the same shape, whereas different fonts render the same characters slightly differently. Some typefaces even provide symbols rather than letters.
- **Size.** The size of a specific typeface can be measured using a number of scales. The most common measurements in typography are "points," which are 1/72 of an inch, and measure the height of the typeface from the top of the highest letter to the bottom of the lowest letter, and the "em space," which considers the area of the font, rather than just the height. However, such units are less meaningful in a digital intermediate context because the images themselves

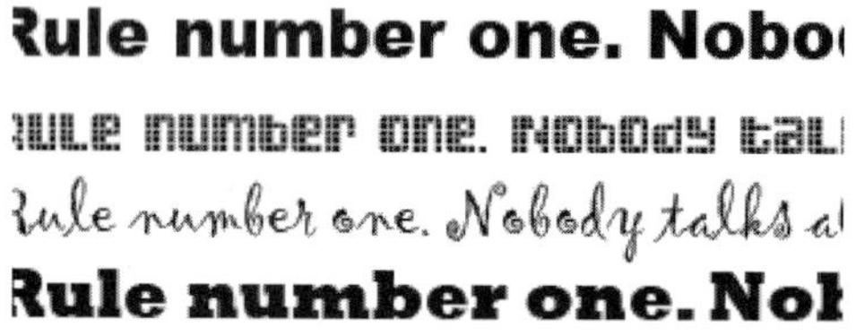

Rule number one. Nobo

ꓤULE number one. Nobody tal

ꓤule number one. Nobody talks a

Rule number one. Nol

FIGURE 10-23   Text in Different Fonts

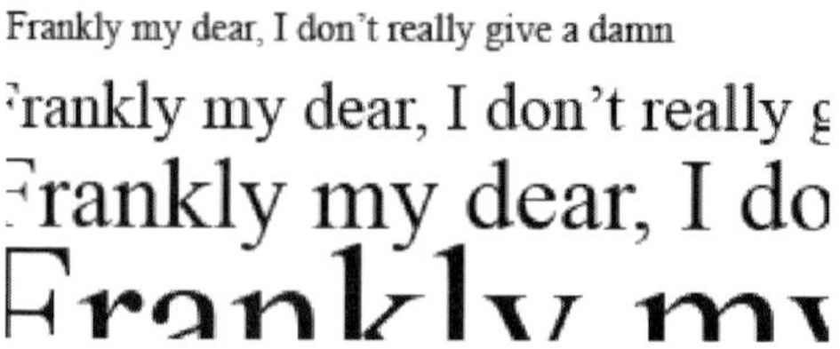

Frankly my dear, I don't really give a damn

ꓛrankly my dear, I don't really g

ꓛrankly my dear, I do

ꓶrankly my

FIGURE 10-24   Text in Different Sizes

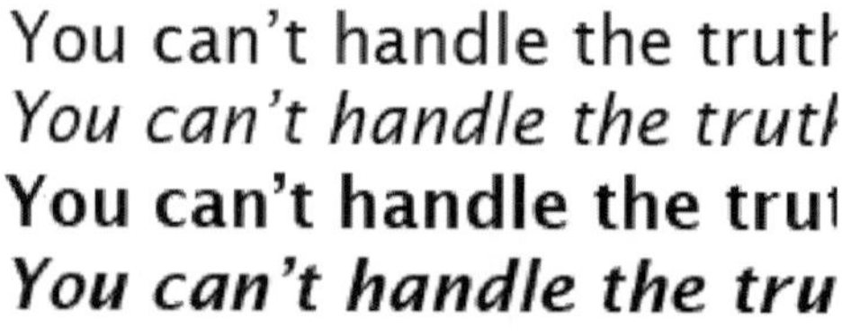

You can't handle the truth

You can't handle the truth

You can't handle the trut

You can't handle the tru

FIGURE 10-25   From top: regular, italic, bold, and bold italic styles

have no inherent physical size and rely on the output medium to determine size. Therefore, font sizes tend to be expressed in terms of the number of pixels in height from the top of the highest letter to the bottom of the lowest letter.[7]

- **Variations.** Different typefaces often come in several variations. For example, the thickness or "weight" of each font may be varied, so that there is a thin variant of a particular font, or a "bold" (thicker) typeface. "Italicized" (i.e., slanted) fonts or "condensed" (narrower) fonts also have variants.

- **Kerning.** The amount of kerning determines the relative space between each character in a word, the amount of space between each word, and the amount of space between each line (although in many applications, these values are split into three separate parameters). The amount of kerning is usually expressed as a percentage, relative to the area of the font characters.

- **Color.** Each character may be a specific color. In addition, with many applications, the outline of each letter can be colored independently from the rest of it. In addition, some applications allow these colors to be in the form of a gradient, a CG pattern, or even sourced from another image.

- **Depth.** Certain applications create text in 3D to allow the surface to be shaded or to cast shadows. They may also have other properties to define reflectivity or shininess. Specifying a depth parameter determines the virtual thickness of the letters in terms of distance from the lens and is relative to the font size.

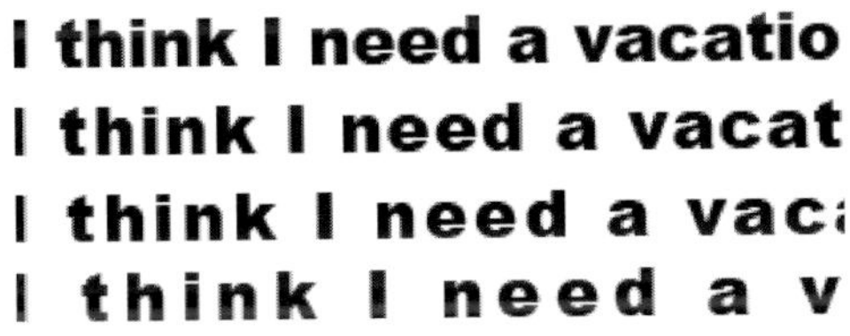

I think I need a vacatio
I think I need a vacat
I think I need a vac
I think I need a v

FIGURE 10-26 Different kerning can be used to compress or expand the text's horizontal size

---

[7] Sometimes points are used within a digital environment, although the relationship of points to pixels isn't standardized, meaning that a font set to 12 points in one applications may have a different size (relative to the underlying image) to the same type settings in another application.

As with all CG material, text generated within the digital intermediate can easily be accompanied with automatic matte generation, so that the text can be isolated for further effects, such as glows, blurs, or semi-transparency.

10.5.2   Text Positioning

Just as important as the visual attributes of the text, the positioning of words can be adjusted to suit specific requirements. This also has practical uses as well as creative ones and is particularly important for various output formats that may compose shots in different ways. Almost all formats require text to be positioned within a "title-safe" margin, to ensure that it's visible on a wide variety of display devices. (The topic of title-safety regions will be covered in Chapter 12.

The position of text need not be static, it can "roll" (i.e., move up or down the image), "crawl" (move from side to side), or follow complex paths. Further, text can fade in and out and use any of the same transitions used with conformed footage.

Applying text to an image is best done just before final output, because as soon as the text becomes part of the image, any changes that have to be made to the footage also affect the text. In addition, where text moves across an image, it's advisable to apply some degree of motion blur so that the movement looks smoother and less artificial.

END ROLLERS

Unfortunately, generating a large amount of text at film resolution is a fairly expensive process. Credits, which can be several minutes long, require many frames to be generated at great expense, even though they're relatively simple to create, the only requirements being a long list of text that rolls upward.

For the time being at least, it's often economically better to create credits optically on film and then splice the film into the digital internegative or interpositive, or scan it along with the other footage.

10.6 WATERMARKS

It's sometimes desirable to stamp a visible watermark (i.e., an image such as a company logo) across an entire production. This is common practice for many television and Internet broadcasts, for example, which put "bugs" (i.e., small animated logos with the originating channel information) across all broadcasts. Although this process is usually a separate one performed automatically during the broadcast, it sometimes may be necessary to add such logos at the digital intermediate stage. Another use for watermarks is to label certain copies of the production. For example, some productions create advance screening or preview copies of the program prior to final release, and it may be useful to have a special notice or other visible image stamped onto the footage.

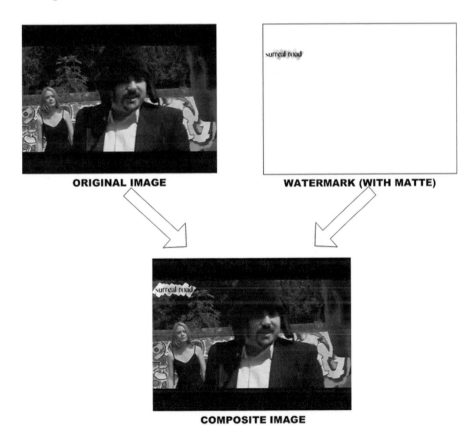

ORIGINAL IMAGE WATERMARK (WITH MATTE)

COMPOSITE IMAGE

FIGURE 10-27 A watermark applied to an image

Visible watermarks may be static, meaning that a single-frame image is applied across a number of frames, or they may be dynamic, meaning that a looping animation lasting a number of frames is applied to the sequence. Either way, the watermark image, or image sequence, may be accompanied by mattes to allow accurate compositing. For the sake of continuity, as with text, watermarks of this type should be applied as a final stage.

Another type of watermark is the "invisible" watermark, which makes very small adjustments to the image data that can later be detected by appropriate software. Invisible watermarks are almost exclusively used as a copyright-protection device. A number of different algorithms are available, and they work by subtly altering the image data to create a digital "signature" (or "fingerprint") that can be read back from the file at a later time. Watermarks won't prevent the file from being accessed or modified; all they can do is provide an image's proof of ownership. However, they can be used for tracking purposes, such as to locate the origin of an illegally obtained copy of the production. Most invisible watermarks are designed to survive transformation. Resizing or blurring an image slightly won't disrupt the watermark information, and some watermarks are retained even when converting the images to other formats, such as when printed on paper.

One issue of the different digital-watermarking algorithms is their robustness. As the details of many of the algorithms are kept secret, it can be difficult to discover what makes them fail. This is fairly sensible, because if an abundance of information on how to break the watermarks was available, they would quickly become useless. But at the same time, it's questionable as to how early in the digital intermediate process watermarking should be employed. It may be that if watermarks are added to the images directly after acquisition, subsequent processes such as grading and restoration may inadvertently remove them. The degree to which they degrade the image is also a consideration. As with any operation that degrades images, watermarking is probably best left until the end of the pipeline.

10.7 SUMMARY

A number of digital effects can be used throughout the digital intermediate process to change the appearance of footage. These effects range from subtle effects that are only noticeable on a moving image, to full-blown effects that can't be replicated practically. Although most are inherently destructive to the image, as with color grading, their use can help to create stunning imagery.

Digital text tools can be used to add words to the images, and the properties of the text can be controlled to a great degree. Finally, it's also possible to add hidden or visible digital watermarks to an image, to identify the material's owners.

11

OUTPUT

The previous chapter looked at the uses of digital effects and titles for putting the finishing touches to conformed and graded productions. The digital intermediate process has a significant advantage over other paradigms for creating productions because it can easily and simultaneously output the same data to a number of different mediums, such as video tape, DVD, 35mm photographic film, and streaming web servers. This chapter discusses the different options for outputting the finished production to several different mediums.

11.1 RENDERING

With many of the different systems and processes in the digital intermediate pipeline, changes, such as color grading, made to the acquired footage are saved as metadata and don't permanently affect the original images; they are just used to modify the way the images are presented to the viewer. Keeping the original image data separate from the modifications allows greater flexibility in making revisions, without having to compromise quality. If changes were integrated with the images at the time they were created, later revisions would have to be based upon the revised material. Therefore, the images would suffer from a generation-loss effect similar to the effect that photographic film and video tapes are prone to.

Every single frame in the production therefore can require several processes be run to generate the images for the final production. This procedure is usually known as "rendering." Depending on the specifics of the digital intermediate pipeline, each frame may require several rendering "passes"—for example, one to resize an image, another to

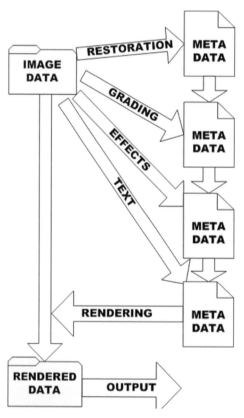

FIGURE 11-1 A rendering process is required to make changes to images' permanent output

remove defects such as dust or dropout, another to apply the color grading, and several others to add optical, text, and other effects.[1]

Rendering consumes an incredible amount of computer processing. Calculations are required for each of the millions of pixels on each frame. Because the total frames per production usually number several hundred thousand, the total number of calculations required to fully render a production are in the trillions. For the production to be rendered within a reasonable time frame, either the rendering system must process each calculation very quickly or the task must be divided among several systems.

11.1.1 Dedicated Rendering

Some digital intermediate facilities use specially configured computer systems solely for rendering purposes. Others may harness the processing power of the playback or grading system to render the files once the final version is "locked." Either way, such configurations rely on these systems' speed to render the required files.

The advantage of the dedicated rendering setup is that it can be very cost effective, particularly for medium-sized facilities that render only one production at a time. On top of this, it's easy to make predictions as to the time frame of each rendering process because few factors affect the processing speed, which is fairly consistent. Furthermore, such systems tend to be fairly robust, in that they are less prone to compatibility issues and other render-related problems. The downside is that dedicated rendering is a case of putting all the proverbial eggs into one basket: if the rendering system fails, deadlines might be missed. Similarly, while the system is rendering, it can't be utilized for other tasks, such as grading another production.

11.1.2 Distributed Rendering

An alternative method is to distribute the frames to be rendered among a number of systems. For example, in a rendering "pool" (or

---

[1] In a pipeline using a layered image paradigm, where each version is stored in the original file as a separate layer, a rendering process must still be made to flatten the layers, compositing them or discarding unused layers as necessary.

render "farm") consisting of 10 rendering systems, every 100 frames having to be rendered may be divided equally among the rendering systems, so that each renders 10 frames out of every 100. This approach can be even more sophisticated, with render "wranglers" assigning more frames to faster machines and less to slower ones.

This system can be extremely efficient, particularly for large pipelines, because each rendering system can be used as necessary or removed from the pool when needed for other tasks or other productions. Additional expense is required to provide enough rendering systems (although most of the time, plenty of existing systems used for other purposes can be adapted), as well as to provide the required infrastructure to facilitate the rendering and management. Such configurations must be continually monitored for problems, because they're prone to network errors, disk failures, and other sporadic glitches. Two separate systems occasionally produce different results. This problem occurs with very complex images, when mathematical errors are made or when part of the rendering process utilizes a system's GPU (graphical processing unit) rather than the CPU; any of these situations can lead to continuity problems or grading flashes.

11.1.3   Background Rendering

A third approach is to harness other computer systems' idle time. Most modern computer systems rarely use their maximum processing power at any given time. For example, digitizing an hour of video footage might use a fraction of the available memory and no network bandwidth. Thus, these resources aren't being used (although the display resources may be used to provide feedback about those frames being digitized). Rendering processes, on the other hand, typically use all the available memory, processing power, and network bandwidth, while not having to provide a display of the frames being processed. Likewise, many systems are sometimes left completely unused while waiting for the next job to be processed. Rather than monopolizing the resources of a single dedicated rendering system, or of a pool of systems, it's sometimes possible to harness the idle systems' "spare" resources and put them to work rendering some of the frames. As soon as the resources are needed again by the host system, the rendering is suspended until the resources become available again, a process known as "background rendering."

The benefits of background rendering are that it's an extremely economical method of rendering frames and enables the use of the systems for other processes. Thus, background rendering is suitable for smaller facilities, which may not have access to a large pool of computers or be able to afford a dedicated system. However, this method is the slowest of the three, because it must share rendering resources with other processes. Furthermore, this method can be prone to render errors, caused by miscalculations or software failures.

In practice, most digital intermediate facilities don't stick to a single rendering paradigm and usually turn to different approaches for different rendering requirements. For example, background rendering may be used throughout the production, while distributed rendering is used toward the end to ensure maximum speed, with dedicated systems used for specific processes, such as reformatting images for specific output mediums.

The required amount of rendering varies by the production, digital intermediate pipeline, and the pipeline subsystems. Some configurations, particularly those for video productions, are able to process and render all frames completely in real time, meaning that rendering time doesn't even have to be considered.

11.2 VIDEO OUTPUT

Output of digital footage to video-based media is a fairly straightforward process. After all, most of the viewing devices used throughout the digital intermediate process require some form of analog video signal as an input. So, in theory at least, video output requires merely attaching a VCR to the output signal, providing that the system can play back the production in real time. This process is commonly referred to as "crash" recording (or "live" recording) and effectively dumps the incoming signal onto tape as it's received, with no particular concern for adhering to specific timecodes.

However, most pipelines require a much greater degree of control over this process. First of all, the output has to be synced to very specific timecodes, particularly when using "insert" editing to precisely overlay particular shots and sequences into exact positions on the tape. For this to work, the output or playback system must be given the ability to directly control the VCR, which is usually facilitated by adding a control cable to suitably equipped systems.

Because different video formats have different requirements (e.g., a 1080p24 HD video records at a different picture size and frame rate than a 525 SD video), separate renders of the production are necessary for each required format. Some playback systems, such as Thomson's Specter FS (www.thomsongrassvalley.com), can perform the necessary calculations in real time while outputting the video, so no extra rendering time (or storage space) is required for video output. However, for many systems, time must be allocated between the completion of the production and the output to video to accommodate this additional rendering.

The only factors affecting the quality of the recording (provided the output system is of maximum quality) are the VCR deck, the type of video tape, and the cables connecting the deck to the output systems (i.e., gold-plated and low-capacitance cables minimize the introduction of noise into the signal). So a digital Betacam can provide a better recording than a VHS, for example, despite the fact that they record an identical signal.

Digital video systems (e.g., HDV or DV) usually directly record a digital signal, such as through a Firewire cable. This results in the maximum possible quality, although the footage may first have to be "transcoded" to the proper digital format, which requires additional time and storage space. Most digital video decks also have analog video inputs, and so for the sake of simplicity and speed considerations, many digital intermediate facilities choose to output video by analog means.

VCRs usually require some "pre-roll" time (usually several seconds) to get the tape up to speed before beginning the recording. At the end of the recording some "post-roll" time allows the tape to speed down. Many distributors have specific requirements for how the tape should be formatted, with specific timecodes for slates and test patterns. Audio for production is usually created separately; the video and audio components are on different "tracks" of the video, and thus can be recorded at different times in different places if need be.

Video tapes vary in length, and productions either are recorded in their entirety onto one tape, or they're split into several reels of around 20 minutes each. The material is output in real time so that an hour's worth of footage takes just over an hour to output to tape (allowing for setup time and other necessary operations). Every tape the system outputs usually undergoes a lengthy "quality control" check for a number of defects and issues (covered in Chapter 12). Because of the QC process, a digital intermediate facility usually outputs only one tape per format, which becomes the "master" tape; the facility outputs an additional tape as a backup, which is usually stored within the facility. If corrections must be made, the corrected shots can be inserted onto the master tapes.

Because each tape's output can be a lengthy and expensive process overall, especially for film or HD-based projects, it's often preferable to generate a single tape on a high-quality format and then just "dub" this tape across to the other formats. The typical method is to output an HD master at 50i, which is then used to generate all other 50 Hz formats (such as 625 PAL SD tapes), and an HD master at 59.94i or 23.98p to generate all other NTSC formats. Progressive-format-based productions (such as film or 24p HD projects) normally also output an HD master at 24p for posterity. Providing that the frame rate remains the same, "downconverting" (i.e., copying a video from a higher-quality or larger video format to a lower-quality, smaller one) is a viable alternative to re-rendering and reoutputting the finished production to a number of formats.

11.2.1 Frame-Rate Conversion

One characteristic of video formats is that each has different frame-rate requirements. Most productions stick to a single frame rate throughout. At the time of output, therefore, a decision must be made as to how to convert the program to match the output frame-rate requirements.

One of the simplest, and most common methods is to play out each sequence "frame for frame," meaning that one frame of footage in the digital intermediate equals one frame of video. Of course, this approach results in different playback speeds, because if images are shot at 24fps and played back at 25fps, for example (e.g., images shot on film and played back on PAL video), then the footage will playback slightly faster than it was shot. This also means that the audio must be sped up or slowed down accordingly so that it doesn't become unsynchronized. For small adjustments, such as from 24fps to 25fps (i.e., a difference of 4%), the frame-for-frame method usually suffices. However, for larger differences, such as film to NTSC, some other method must be used. The common solution is to apply a pull-down (as described in Chapter 7), which repeats some frames at pre-determined intervals. This results in footage that plays back at the same speed as the original, although motion won't appear as smooth as with other methods. An additional solution is to apply a motion effect (as described in Chapter 10) to the entire production, to generate a new set of frames for playback at the desired speed. This approach usually results in smoother motion, but it requires significant time and storage space to generate the additional frames. Depending on the method, some visible motion artifacts may be produced.

11.2.2 Video-Safe Colors

Video has a slightly different color space from the gamma-corrected RGB spaces used by computers. Thus, some colors that appear on a computer monitor won't show up correctly when broadcast; and such colors are termed "illegal" colors. Therefore, it's usually a requirement that all video footage output from the digital intermediate process be "legal" (or "video-safe") within the respective video color space.

Most digital intermediate video output systems perform this check automatically and adjust the color space as needed. In some cases, it may be impossible to output video that contains illegal colors. Where this isn't the case, video can usually be output using a LUT to convert the colors so they fall within the correct color space, or software or hardware may be available to re-render all the footage so it's safe. Sometimes this process can be done in real time on the output system; otherwise, additional time and storage space must be factored in.

11.2.3 Aspect Ratio

Different formats have different aspect ratios or picture shapes. For example, some high-definition video formats have an aspect ratio of 1.78:1, whereas the majority of standard definition video formats have an aspect ratio of 1.33:1, which is much narrower. It's possible to convert between different aspect ratios fairly easily, using any of a number of methods.

When converting a wide image to a narrower one, the wider image can be "cropped" vertically, trimming the image's left and right edges to achieve the desired shape.

FIGURE 11-2   A 2.35:1 image

FIGURE 11-3   The 2.35:1 image cropped to 1.33:1

FIGURE 11-4 The 2.35:1 image squeezed to 1.33:1

Alternatively, the image can be "squeezed," squashing the image to fit the narrower shape, although doing so distorts the image and isn't generally recommended.

Finally, the image can be "letterboxed," resizing the picture so that it maintains its original shape and filling the top and bottom of the adjusted image with black.

FIGURE 11-5 The 2.35:1 image letterboxed to 1.33:1

FIGURE 11-6   A 1.33:1 image

FIGURE 11-7   The 1.33:1 image cropped to 1.78:1

FIGURE 11-8   The 1.33:1 image squeezed to 1.78:1

FIGURE 11-9   The 1.33:1 image letterboxed to 1.78:1

The same options are also available when converting a narrow image into a wider one, cropping the top and bottom of the image, squeezing or letterboxing it, or filling the sides of the image with black.

Cropping an image affords the greatest flexibility (although part of the original image inevitably is lost) because the picture can also be resized to enable the shot to be recomposed as part of the process. Where the image is cropped, it may be desirable to perform a "pan and scan," to best select how to crop the image on a shot-by-shot basis.

11.2.4   Reinterlacing Video

Although it isn't a particularly common request, it may be necessary in some circumstances to "reinterlace" progressive footage to reconstruct fields, which is usually the case for projects that were originally shot on interlaced video systems and subsequently deinterlaced as part of the digital intermediate process. When frames are output to video normally, the odd lines of each frame are used to construct one field, and the even lines are used for the other. Thus, no intervention usually is required.[2]

---

[2] The field order is usually determined by the video format. For example, NTSC DV video specification stipulates that the lower field (even lines) be output first. The Appendix lists the most common video formats along with their respective field order.

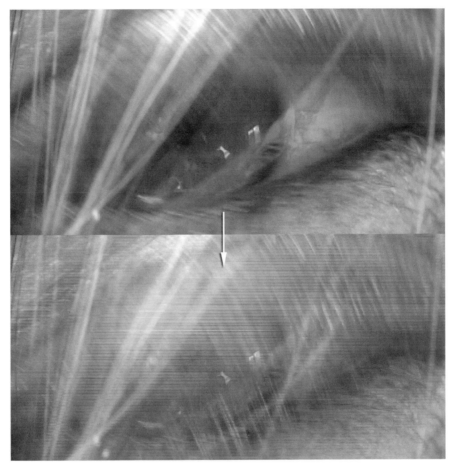

FIGURE 11-10 Images can be reinterlaced to break them back into fields

The options for subsequently reinterlacing footage are much the same as those for deinterlacing footage (as described in Chapter 9)—that is, a frame may simply be split in half and duplicated so that it appears once for every frame, or you may perform sophisticated motion analysis on the frame to separately reconstruct each field. A rule of thumb is to simply reverse the method used to deinterlace the footage in the first place.

TEXTLESS ELEMENTS

Occasionally, distributors may require that the deliverables include "textless" elements, which means that the shots with titles in them must be output separately again without the text, usually as a separate sequence of shots (e.g., right at the end of the tape). For this reason, it's advisable to always retain copies of the original shots (with color grading and so on applied) for any shots that have to be "texted" (i.e., had text elements composited on them) at some point.

11.3   FILM OUTPUT

Digital images can be output to film using a straightforward process. Unexposed film (usually a negative stock with very fine grain) is exposed a pixel at a time, firing three lasers at the surface of the film (one for each of red, green, and blue) which are at varying intensities depending upon the RGB values of the image's source pixel. This process is repeated for each pixel in the digital image until the entire frame has been exposed, and the film is advanced to the next frame. When the entire reel has been exposed, it's sent to a lab for development and printing.

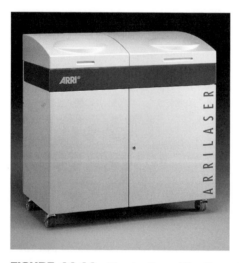

FIGURE 11-11   The Arrilaser Film Recorder

Film recording is currently a fairly slow process. Arri's popular Arrilaser Speed Performance recorder (www.arri.com) takes approximately 2 seconds to record a frame from a 2k image or around 4 seconds to record a frame from a 4k image. Productions are usually recorded using lasers (or "filmed out" or "shot") in reels of up to 2000 feet (up to 22 minutes of footage). A 2000-foot reel of film, comprising up to 32,000 frames, can take around 18 hours to record at 2k or 36 hours at 4k resolution, depending upon the recorder. This means that a typical film might take several weeks just to complete the recording.

Most facilities get around this bottleneck by using multiple recorders, simultaneously recording several separate reels on each recorder. Another option is to stagger the film-out of reels throughout the post-production process, so that as soon as a single reel is approved, it's sent to the recorder, while the facility completes other reels. Reels must be processed separately, and each reel should end on a scene change, to minimize continuity errors caused by differences in each reel's development. Other recorders, such as the Celco Fury (www.celco.com), can output to other formats, such as IMAX.

To ensure the graded digital version matches the final film output, correct calibration of the film recorder is crucial to the digital intermediate pipeline. The recorder is usually calibrated to a standard, and the calibration of the digital-grading system is manipulated to match the output of the calibrated recorder. That way, the recorder can be calibrated quickly and independently from the grading system (of course, this step must be done before grading begins).

Each digital image to be recorded must be "mapped" to each frame of film to match a particular format (or "aperture"). For example, Super-35 images usually fill the entire frame, while Academy aperture occupies a specific region of each frame. Predefined standards specify the size of digital images (in pixels) depending on the output aperture, and many digital intermediate facilities use these standards to determine the working file size used throughout the pipeline. In other cases, the digital images have to be resized to match the standard. Film recorders also output each frame individually, so footage sequences have to be output as individual images (i.e., one for each frame), which again is standard for most facilities but may require separate rendering for the others.

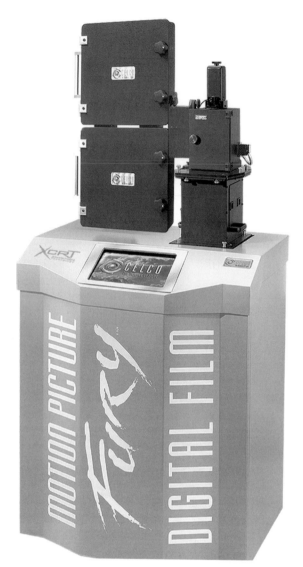

FIGURE 11-12   Celco's Fury Film Recorder

Once the recording process has started, it can't be interrupted without loading a new reel of film. If the system breaks down, it may be possible to recover the frames recorded until that point and start a new reel from the start of the last shot. However, this requires that the two reels be spliced together later to create the complete reel.

At the end of the film-out process, a "digital internegative" or a "digital interpositive" is created. These are equivalent to the internegative or interpositive produced by a traditional (nondigital) chemical lab process to finish a film, which would then be duplicated to make the distribution prints. Because generating each reel digitally requires such a long time, productions normally generate a single digital interpositive, which is then used to create several internegatives. The latter, in turn, are used to create the thousands of distribution prints for cinemas. Clearly this approach leads to more image degradation, because it introduces an additional generation into the process. Some digital intermediate facilities have sufficient film recorders to be able to offer multiple digital internegatives, which can then be used to create the distribution prints directly, resulting in superior quality pictures. As the recording technology improves and becomes less expensive, more facilities will offer this approach.

It's interesting to note that, of all the output formats, photographic film is widely considered to be the most suitable for long-term storage. Digital file formats and storage devices change so frequently that anything used today probably will be unreadable in 50 years. Video tapes don't have the necessary level of quality or the longevity of film. On the other hand, film originally shot almost a century ago is still viewable today. For this reason, even productions that aren't likely to have a cinema release might still benefit from digital internegative output.

DIGITAL FILM AND THE LAB

It's unfortunate that the last step in the digital intermediate for film-based projects is a chemical one. A lot of work goes into ensuring that a film's digital version is of the highest possible quality, but at the end of the pipeline when it's on film, it becomes prone to all the factors that affect physical film, such as dust and scratches, chemical impurities and the like. Unlike digital versions, every film loses a generation of quality every time it's copied. The lab process for film isn't as consistent as that for digital, and one of the reasons that digital color grading can't accurately predict the way

(continues)

DIGITAL FILM AND THE LAB (*continued*)

a particular film print will look onscreen is because it depends, to some degree, on the chemical balance used to process the final print, which itself isn't an accurate process. Therefore, chemical labs often use printer-light grading on the internegative when creating prints to compensate for differences in chemical balances and to ensure that the final print is as close as possible to the intended result. Digital intermediate facilities usually supply the lab with a standard calibration image, such as color bars or a "Marcie" image, used to guarantee correct color balance.

The creation of the digital internegative is also prone to the problems and concerns associated with shooting film on a set, such as ensuring that the digital internegative isn't contaminated by light before development and protecting each reel from damage. However, if anything happens to the digital internegative, some comfort is afforded by knowing that creating a new one is always an option. At the very least, whenever problems are encountered with the digital internegative, it may be possible to film out just the shot having to be replaced and then splice the replacement negative into the original digital internegative.

11.4   DIGITAL MASTERING

Without a doubt, the most convenient and highest-quality output can be obtained by generating a digital master. This can be done for archival purposes, to allow conversion to other output digital formats, such as DVD or streaming Internet video, or for digital cinema distribution.

A "digital source master" is a finished production in digital form from which all other formats can be created. No standards to speak of currently exist for creating digital source masters, and thus the final rendered output usually serves this purpose. The digital source master can be a number of individual digital images stored inside one or more folders (such as one image per frame, and one folder per reel). It can be a single digital video-encoded file, such as for DV-based pro-

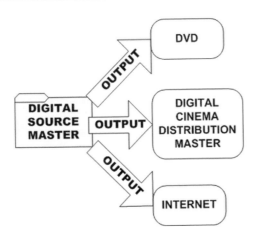

FIGURE 11-13 The digital source master can be used to output a number of different formats

ductions, or it may be a more complex, proprietary format devised by the digital intermediate facility.

Regardless of the specifics of the digital source master, outputting to other digital formats includes three stages: transcoding, compression, and encryption.

11.4.1 Transcoding

A digital image file consists of two components: the image data (the "essence") and data concerning the organization of the image data (the "metadata"). Each image format organizes the image data in a different way, even when the image itself is the same. For example, a TIFF file and an SGI file might display an identical image, right down to the individual pixels, but the image would appear completely different when comparing the raw data saved on disk. For this reason, converting between different formats, even those that use the same color space and so on, involves reorganizing the data. For formats that aren't directly compatible (such as converting a 10-bit format to an 8-bit one), not only must the data be reorganized, but changes must also be made to the image data to make it compatible with the new format.

This process of transcoding can be very time consuming, particularly for most productions with large number of frames. Transcoding is also used when converting between still images and digital video streams (such as a QuickTime file). In addition to reorganizing the data, it may be necessary to resize, retime, and alter the colors of the footage.[3] For this reason, the transcoding process may degrade the images somewhat, depending upon the specific differences between the formats, but the degradation is usually a factor of the new format's limitations of and can't be avoided. All transcoding should be done from the original digital source master to maximize the quality of the transcoded footage.

11.4.2 Compression

As discussed previously, the two types of compression methods are lossy compression and lossless compression. At this stage in the digital intermediate pipeline, lossless compression might be utilized more because storage space may take precedence over other considerations. Lossy compression probably will be used too, especially when transcoding to other formats (such as for DVD versions).

Using lossy compression, in particular the so-called "visually lossless" compression methods, at this stage is acceptable because even though the image quality is degraded, most such compression methods are designed so that the quality differences are imperceptible. Because lossy compression is performed at the very end of the pipeline, the images won't usually undergo any operations that rely on the imperceptible information and that would otherwise introduce compression artifacts (such as color grading).

Lossy compression techniques fall into two main categories: intraframe and interframe methods. Intraframe compression methods, such as M-JPEG compression, analyze each frame separately,

---

[3] Retiming methods used during transcoding are the same as those used to alter the video frame rate.

compressing the image by discarding data that's imperceptible (which is the same as compressing a single digital image to a JPEG file). This process is repeated for each frame. The result is a single frame of footage, when viewed, appears no different than the original frame. However, it's possible that motion artifacts may be visible when the compressed footage is played back at speed.

Interframe compression methods, such as MPEG compression, compare each frame to the previous one and discard parts of the image where no change is visible between frames. This can result in much smaller files, particularly as the vast majority of footage doesn't change very much between each frame. However, sometimes the compression method (or "codec," short for "compressor decompressor") can be fooled by subtle changes in the scene, which can lead to smearing and other artifacts. The amount of file-size reduction is determined by the compression method in conjunction with the threshold, which determines the level of minimum quality (i.e., deciding how much of the footage can be thrown away).

One problem with compression is that it can be difficult to estimate the amount of file-size reduction that will be achieved for a given program. Compression is often used to ensure that a certain amount of footage, such as a 90-minute production, will fit on a specific storage media (such as a DVD). The most common way around this difficulty is to specify a target bit rate for the compression method. For example, for 100 seconds of footage that must fit on a 150MB device, a bit rate of 1.5 megabytes per second might be specified to ensure that the final compressed version will fit on the device. The codec analyzes the footage a second at a time and aims to provide sufficient compression to meet the target level of compression. This technique is often used for DVD, videos, and streaming video on the Internet. However, it results in scenes containing a lot of motion (thus requiring less compression to be perceived at a high level of quality) looking inferior to those with less motion, and it may even produce visible artifacts. One solution to this problem is to make use of variable bit-rate codecs, which adapt to the requirements of the footage, increasing the bit rate for scenes with a lot of motion and reducing it for scenes with much less motion, while aiming to maintain an overall target bit rate. Though this approach can produce superior results, it may be impractical for certain applications, such as streaming video, which must be delivered at a constant rate to ensure smooth playback. Another option is to perform multiple analysis passes on the footage, to more accurately interpret the footage content.

Even for a specific codec with a standard bit-rate requirement, the quality of the final, compressed footage is determined in part by the software that performed the compression. For example, DVD video requires footage that has been compressed using an MPEG-2 codec at a specific bit rate, but several different algorithms and compression systems can be used to process a digital source master into the MPEG-2 file format. Each method can produce a different result, according to the image evaluation, in terms of factors such as sharpness, color, motion smoothness, and artifacts. For this reason, many compression systems provide the capability of tailoring many of the detection parameters affecting these factors to the specific requirements of each production, although this process can require lots of time and expertise.

11.4.3 Encryption

Data encryption methods can restrict access to the contents of a digital file or storage system. It's normally used to prevent piracy or leaked copies of images, or even the entire film, prior to release. It's commonly used in a digital cinema environment, where data is prone to interception, but in theory, it could be used throughout the entire digital intermediate process as an added security measure. However, it can increase the processing time and make the files more vulnerable to corruption. Thus, it's typically used at the end for transmission or long-term storage.

Methods for encrypting data range from password-protected file storage, to quantum cryptography, each of which varies in terms of security, expense, and practicality.

Data encryption works by scrambling the contents of a file (or an entire storage device) in a manner similar to randomly rearranging all the letters in a book. When the correct credentials are supplied, the contents are put back in the correct order—that is, the file is decrypted. These credentials can be provided in the form of a password, a digital "key," or even something like a swipe card used at the workstation, which then "unlocks" the file, allowing access to its contents.

11.4.4   Digital Cinema Distribution Masters

Digital cinema works by projecting images directly from a digital file. A projection system's specific workings vary between cinemas, and they're determined in part by each distributor. In general, the various projection systems share some similarities in terms of requirements.

From the digital source master created at the end of the digital intermediate process, a digital cinema distribution master (DCDM) must be generated. A DCDM is a set of data that conforms to a specific standard in terms of formatting and storage. The DCDM is then duplicated to several central servers within the digital cinema network, each of which is then distributed to each cinema for playback.

The specifications for the DCDM, as outlined by the Digital Cinema Initiative, lean toward an uncompressed, color-space-independent format, which should guarantee that the creation of the DCDM doesn't result in any degradation of the digital source master. Individual cinemas interpret the DCDM based on the characteristics of their projection systems, so that, for example, a projector's specific color space will determine the color calibration or corrections (if any) that must be applied to the DCDM during playback.

The current DCDM specifications are covered in detail in the Appendix.

11.4.5   DVDs

One of the most important output media, particularly for commercial productions, is DVD (Digital Versatile Disc) output. DVD is currently the best-selling consumer-grade medium for film and television productions. It offers several significant advantages over video-tape-based media, such as VHS, including higher-quality pictures and audio, the absence of degradation or generation loss, the ability to instantly seek to any part of the program and switch between audio and caption formats and languages, all in a more compact package.

Because DVD is an inherently digital format, the digital source master can create the DVD master directly. DVD is a relatively new format and, very simply, is, like CD-ROM, a set of digital files stored on a write once read many (WORM) optical disc.

Each of the several different DVD specifications is for a different purpose, which can lead to some confusion. For example, a DVD-ROM disc can be used as a digital storage medium (under the "Book A" specification), similar to a flash drive or a floppy disk, by recording the desired files directly onto it, which perfectly preserves the data but makes it accessible only to other computer systems. For set-top DVD players to display the DVD content, a DVD video (or "Book B" specification) disc must be created. This format has an explicit file structure, requiring that audio and video content conform to a detailed specification. Video must be compressed to the MPEG-2 standard and split into separate files, with a typical single disc capable holding an hour of high-quality audio and video.[4]

The DVD video-mastering (or "authoring") process involves transcoding and compressing the digital source master to an MPEG-2 format file before assembling the other elements (such as audio and caption streams and menu elements) into a DVD master. For large distributions, the master is then usually sent to a replication center that creates a glass master for stamping thousands of discs to be sold. More limited, low-budget distributions can simply use DVD writers to copy the master to writable DVD discs (such as DVD-R or DVD+R discs), which can then be played on most set-top players.[5]

---

[4] Most commercial DVD video discs actually have two separate layers of data, meaning that a single disc can hold two hours of footage.
[5] Recordable DVDs are not as robust or widely supported as pressed DVDs, which are compatible with all set-top DVD players.

11.4.6 Other Digital Formats

New formats are introduced on a regular basis. In addition to DVD video, there's CD-ROM-based video formats, such as Video-CD (VCD) and Super Video-CD (SVCD), each of which has variants. Shorter productions can be mastered in the same way as DVD video, but they require the storage capacity of only a CD-ROM, giving rise to mini-DVDs and other hybrid formats.

New display devices, such as cellphones and handheld digital video viewers (e.g., Sony's PlayStation Portable (www.us.playstation.com), will no doubt give rise to other new formats; the introduction of new storage media such as HD-DVD, HVD, and Blu-ray discs will enable the distribution of content of higher quality and increased quantity. And new compression methods and codecs such as MPEG-4 (also called "H.264") and Windows Media High Definition Video (WMVHD) will make it possible for higher-quality footage to be transmitted across limited bandwidths.

For now, at least, digital formats have no widely adopted standards (other than DVD video), and so most digital formats are targeted for playback on specific systems, rather than for wide-scale distribution.

11.4.7 Streaming Video

Digital files can be transmitted across the Internet using several different methods; one such method is to place them on a website, and another is to establish a secure network connection between two connected systems. Any of these methods can send digital footage of any type, whether as a series of still images, a compressed MPEG file, or even an entire DVD video structure.

Such methods, however, are not generally useful for viewing footage "live"—that is, as soon as it's received. Transmission of data across the Internet occurs at a variable rate. The same file, transmitted several times across the Internet, requires a different length of time to complete the process each time it's sent.

Compounding this issue further, it can be very difficult to calculate with any degree of accuracy the length of time required to transmit a given file from one location to another. Transmission durations depend on a number of factors, including the quality of the route between the two systems, Internet traffic, and the network bandwidth of all points along the route. Trying to view footage as it's received can result in dropped frames or stalling, or the playback can suffer from lag.

A couple of ways can be used to get around this issue, employing a process known as "streaming." Streaming a video means transmitting it from the host system to one or more client systems, at a rate that enables it to be viewed while it's being transmitted.

The simplest method for streaming video is "buffering." With buffered video, the host system transmits all data to the client as fast as possible, usually through simple HTTP (web-based) or FTP protocols. The client playback system stores the locally received material and analyzes the average rate that data is received. It uses this information to estimate how long the transfer will take to complete. Once a point is reached where the estimated time remaining is less than the duration of the video, playback begins. Provided that the analysis was correct, the video will finish playing just after the last of it has been transferred. This process relies on several factors, however; first, the transmission rate can't drop below the average once playback begins, and the video is encoded in such a way that each second uses the same amount of storage space. This method requires client systems with appropriate playback software to handle the buffer timing, although the host system doesn't require any specific software.

A more advanced paradigm is the dedicated streaming server that controls the rate at which data is transmitted to the client. Such a system enables the host to adaptively vary the bit rate to compensate for discrepancies in transmission speed, so the client experiences a much smoother playback (although the image quality will vary). Installing and configuring such a server requires a significantly higher cost than the buffered method and is therefore unsuitable for limited distribution of material.

At the present time, streaming video output is considered low quality, even with the widespread availability of broadband Internet connections, particularly for long feeds that take a long time to buffer. Streaming video is usually reserved for short promotional videos, commercials, or trailers. In the future, it may be possible to transmit full-length, DVD-quality video using streaming techniques without experiencing much delay, which will serve a new distribution market.

11.4.8 Archiving

The digital source master has different requirements for long-term storage than output targeted for playback on specific systems. The aim of output in the long term is to create files that can be used to generate more output at some point in the future. The simplest and most common form of archiving is to simply copy the digital source master onto a long-term storage device, such as a tape or optical system.

Many digital intermediate facilities also retain digital copies of each different output format, such as a standard-definition PAL video, and a high-definition 1080i59.94 video, in addition to the digital source master. Other facilities may choose to archive the original elements, such as the scanned footage, the grading lists, restoration layers, and so on. These elements will usually require a lot of storage.

The problem with archiving is that it can be difficult to predict under which circumstances the archive will be needed. In the short-term, an archive may be needed to generate duplicates of certain output formats, which means that it would be much more convenient to just archive the digital versions of each format. The archive may be needed to allow output to other, newer formats at some later date, and in that case, it would be useful to keep the digital source master to generate new formats. In the long term, the archive might be required to regrade or re-edit elements, in which case, saving all the original elements is much more useful.

The ultimate aim is to create a single format that is stored at the maximum resolution (or is, in some way, resolution independent), is color-space independent, and contains information to relate the data back to the original offline EDL, perhaps even including handle frames. Although this can be achieved to some degree through specific file formats and the use of metadata, the prevailing problem remains: ensuring that anything archived today is useful in the long term.

Digital image file formats that were widely used 10 years ago, such as the TrueVision Targa format, are less popular now and, in some cases, are not viewable using modern systems. This trend doesn't seem to be going to change. Even the popular Cineon format used throughout the industry already seems to be beginning to lose out to the next generation of high-dynamic range formats such as JPEG 2000 and Extended Dynamic Range (OpenEXR).

This is compounded by the inevitable changes that will be made to the file structure of the host operating systems and to hardware interfaces. Chances are that the hardware used to archive files today won't be compatible with future systems, rendering their contents unreadable. This is, in turn, made worse by physical decay of the storage media—for example, many consumer-grade recordable CDs that were created ten years ago are now unreadable, despite the fact that the hardware used to read them hasn't changed very much. Tape-based archiving systems have a life of around 5 to 10 years, which means that either the tapes have to be regularly regenerated (i.e., the data restored and rearchived to new tapes) to increase the data's longevity or online storage must be used.

Use of online storage simply means that the data is stored on systems that are operational and powered. For example, a digital intermediate facility may have 100TB of online storage, of which 90TB is devoted to ongoing projects and 10TB to archiving previous projects. The archived files can be easily monitored for disk errors, and individual disks replaced as needed. Having instant access to the images for viewing or transfer is an additional benefit; in contrast, tape-based archiving systems have linear access, meaning that the tape must be spooled along to find the desired file, and the file must be restored to an online system before it can be accessed. Using online storage is expensive, particularly because the overall capacity must be increased with each new project.

Standard definition video-based pipelines may resort to using a DV25 or DV50 format for archive because these archive formats store the footage in a digital format, and the DV codecs are the most likely to be around for another decade or so (particularly because of all the consumer investment in them). DVD is also suitable, although the quality is inferior to DV.

The individual components of the digital intermediate pipeline are constantly updated. New versions of grading systems, for example, tend to be released on a yearly basis, and ten years from now, many of the most prominent ones won't exist, meaning that reading the project files created by the original system will be impossible. So the chances are that many project files created for use within a specific pipeline won't be usable in a few years' time and might even become outdated within a year or two, especially if major changes are made to the host system.

All of this amounts to a great deal of uncertainty as to how best to ensure archives are readable. Some standardization is certainly required—standardization of image file formats in the long term but also of various components within the pipeline. Most conforming systems rely on the CMX 3600 EDL format, which in turn is supported by all major editing systems. Thus, it should be possible to correctly interpret these EDLs on different systems, even in a few years' time. Color-grading systems, on the other hand, tend to have proprietary project files, formatted in such a way as to make them unreadable by other systems. So, although it's possible to archive an EDL to preserve the details of a film's final cut, it's unlikely that the settings for the color grading applied to each shot can be preserved in a useful way.

The only way to completely guarantee perfect preservation of the digital intermediate is to store, not only the associated data, but also the physical systems, network cabling, display devices, and so on. Clearly, this approach is preposterously impractical (not to mention that physical decay of the components probably could cause the failure of the systems when they're reactivated anyway), but it's indicative of the process's volatility. A much more feasible, though time-consuming and costly, method is to archive the digital source master, periodically updating it by transcoding and rearchiving whenever changes are made to the pipeline—changes that threaten to make the archived data redundant.

DIGITAL ARCHIVING TO ANALOG MEDIA

A novel approach to digital archiving has arisen through the use of nondigital media. It can provide benefits in terms of the amount of physical space required to store a given amount of data. For example, Autodesk's Fire (www.discreet.com) has the capability to save all project data (video and nonvideo) to an analog tape, such as a Betacam tape, allowing for complete recovery of the project state at a later time. Similarly, Crsitalink's Firestreamer utility (www.cristalink.com) allows any digital data files to be stored on miniDV video tapes, through a VCR connected to the PC. This allows a high volume of data to be stored on a small tape. Future digital-archiving systems may rely on photographic film (perhaps high-contrast lithographic film) to allow very great amounts of data to be stored digitally for long periods of time.

11.5 MULTIPLE VERSIONS

It's rare that a production will require a single version of the final project to be output, especially for larger productions. Often a feature is re-cut to satisfy the needs of different distribution outlets—broadcast television and airline versions of films are often created which censor certain scenes (such as airplane crashes in the cases of airline versions), or cut down to fit a particular time slot. DVD may be output in several versions, such as a theatrical version (to match the version on film) and one or more extended or recut versions (e.g., for a special edition release). These versions can be output in addition to those output to different media, such as film.

Although additional versions such as these share much of the same footage, it's common practice to output each version separately, in its entirety. This greatly simplifies project management, although it

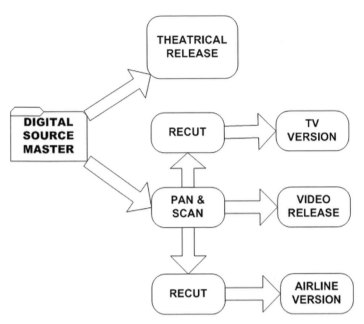

FIGURE 11-14 Managing multiple output versions can be a lot of work

requires additional storage space and version checking. In some instances, the changed scenes are output on their own as separate elements (usually with a guide frame before and after to show exactly where in the picture the new scene belongs), although this approach means that the output version must be re-edited separately to incorporate the changes.

Multiple versions may be output for additional reasons. For example, it's common practice to output a "widescreen" version (i.e., formatted to fit a screen with a 16:9 aspect ratio) and a "full-screen" version (formatted to fit a screen with a 4:3 aspect ratio). A separate 2.35 aspect version can also be output (although it would normally be letterboxed to fit within a 4:3 or 16:9 aspect display) to match a theatrical release. Finally, versions may be output for different locations—for example, replacing titles and other text with other languages. Creating each of the separate versions can be time consuming, particularly from an organizational point of view because each shot must be cross-referenced against the particular version to be output, with changes added as necessary.

Systems such as Thomson's Bones software (www.thomsongrassval-ley.com) streamline this process somewhat, enabling different opera-tors to be linked to different outputs, so that, for example, a title may be added to the rendered film output but not to the video output.

11.5.1 Panning and Scanning

In some instances, outputting a finished production to different for-mats may destroy the original composition. For example, outputting a 4:3 formatted picture to a 16:9 medium (or vice versa) results in hav-ing to crop part of the image (assuming that the picture isn't letter-boxed). In such situations, it may be necessary to "pan and scan" the new output.

FIGURE 11-15 A 16:9 image

FIGURE 11-16 The 16:9 image panned and scanned to a 4:3 image

With panning and scanning, the picture is resized to fit within the new format (usually ensuring that the aspect ratio of the original image remains unchanged) and then repositioning the shot to create a new composition.

You must avoid some pitfalls during this process. One of the most frequent problems is with shots of two or more people talking. The original composition may have a person at each edge of the frame, which means that inevitably one of the people will be cropped out of the panned-and-scanned shot. One solution is to pan the image, moving the image within the frame dynamically throughout the shot. This process can be difficult to achieve because poorly timed panning can be distracting to the viewer or can impair the visual style created by the original camera work.

Sometimes it might be desirable to omit the person who's talking from the recomposed frame and focus instead on another element in the scene. Having to make these kind of decisions is why it's prudent to perform the panning-and-scanning phase with a synced audio mix of the final cut, to determine which parts of a shot have to be viewed and which can just be heard.

11.5.2 Captions

Captions, subtitles, and other "timed text" elements are words (typically a transcript of spoken and audio effects) that appear onscreen for the hard of hearing or in foreign-language films.[6] The captions are normally stored in a simple text file, with a timecode (usually either a frame count or a SMPTE timecode) to set the temporal positioning and the duration followed by the text to be displayed. In the case of "closed captions" (or subtitled DVDs), the text isn't printed over the image, but instead is displayed when requested, superimposed over the image (in the case of TV, video, DVD, and various digital formats), or transmitted to a portable receiver (in the case of cinema releases). Subtitles for cinema releases, on the other hand, are usually

---

[6] Captions for the hearing impaired and subtitles for foreign-language films differ very subtly because captions must include audio elements, such as door slams, whereas subtitles require only spoken words to be transcribed.

embedded into the image during the release printing process, appearing onscreen as part of the image.

With digital cinema distribution, it is possible to keep all caption and subtitle material separate from the image, with the text rendered over the image during display, negating the need for making prints for specific regions, as different languages can be selected on a per-screening basis. In theory, some provision would allow more control over the display of subtitles, such as associating different typefaces or colors with different characters or events, and the ability to reposition and animate text, such as having the words crawl along the bottom of the screen.

11.6 COPY PROTECTION

Digital imaging allows each copy of an image to be identical to the original, thus preserving the overall quality. Throughout the digital intermediate pipeline, this fact is a boon for maximizing the visual quality of the finished production. However, it also means that it can be very easy for pirates to run off a copy that is in every way identical to the original. This is good news for the pirates, who would have previously been selling inferior quality video dubs, or material re-photographed from a cinema screen, but bad news for distributors selling genuine, licensed material. Piracy may take the form of nonprofit file-sharing, where users connect to a large online database and transfer films to each other digitally, or professional duplication, where pirates aim to sell replicas of commercial DVDs and videos, even those which may not yet have been released.

There are several methods for dealing with piracy, such as litigation, although this approach has a tendency to target the wrong people and create a sense of disdain with consumers, as has happened to some degree with the music industry.

Other methods include embedding visible or invisible watermarks in the images or utilizing rights management and image scrambling or digital locks. The use of watermarks, discussed in chapter 10, doesn't prevent copies of a production being made, but it does allow copies to be traced back to a source, information which can then be used to prevent future piracy.

Digital rights management systems assign ownership or licenses of material to each file. When a consumer attempts to copy a file, the system verifies the user's credentials to ensure that they permitted to make the copy before proceeding. The problem with such systems is that they are dependent upon the hardware and software running on the display system being set up correctly for digital rights management. So far at least, no standard has been established for digital rights management, meaning that it's usually limited to proprietary devices, such as Apple's online music store iTunes (www.itunes.com), which allows purchased music to be played on a single system with Apple's own iTunes software or on a single iPod music player. Clearly such a situation can cause problems: if the same type of system was used to handle DVD playback, for example, DVD rentals would be impossible, and different DVD releases would be required for each digital rights management system, causing unnecessary confusion.[7] In fact, Sony recently abandoned a new copy-prevention system for music CDs amid claims that the system made the CDs incompatible with certain players and prevented legitimate copies being made.

Similarly, the media might be protected by digital locks, whereby the content is encrypted and can be decoded only by the correct digital "key" supplied by the playback system. This is the reason that commercial DVDs can't be copied digitally using normal DVD writers.[8] An extension to this solution is to incorporate a pay-per-view type scheme into each production. The file can be encrypted, and therefore copied freely, but is unwatchable or scrambled until the digital key is supplied to temporarily unlock it. This functionality is somewhat more standardized within future digital formats such as MPEG-7 and

---

[7] In addition, most digital rights management systems don't have a built-in provision to handle each item's expiry of copyright (at which point it becomes public domain and may be copied freely).

[8] Some DVDs also have "regional" coding that prevents them from working on systems in other regions. This is designed to prevent people obtaining DVDs from other countries but, in reality, causes more confusion among consumers. Many DVD players are now sold that are "region-free," bypassing the region locks altogether.

MPEG-13. Although digital locks can ultimately be broken, the process can be a difficult one, sufficiently complicated to deter the average consumer.

Finally, it's also possible to create distribution media that "self-destruct," such as Flexplay's ez-D discs (www.flexplay.com) that expire after 48 hours. Although it's not an ideal solution for consumers wishing to buy DVDs of a production, they're suitable for generating preview or screening copies or commercial DVD rental copies. However, the process can be very expensive and is unpopular with the majority of consumers.

11.7 SUMMARY

The digital intermediate paradigm offers a wide range of options for producing finished productions in a form appropriate for viewing by consumers. With many pipelines, all the footage has to undergo a rendering process, to make all the changes to the images permanent, although this process can require significant time. The images can then be output to a number of different media, including both film and video, although the prerequisites for each are slightly different. It's also possible to output to other digital formats, such as for digital cinema distribution, which generally maintains a high level of quality.

A digital intermediate pipeline may also offer other advantages for output, such as the capability of adding watermarks or encrypting footage. In the long term, no clear solution exists that specifies which storage method is most suitable for archival purposes, although a suitable method will likely evolve.

The next chapter focuses on ensuring the output has attained an acceptable level of quality, covering the types of problems that can arise, as well as methods that can be used to correct them.

12

QUALITY CONTROL

The previous chapter described different methods for outputting a finished production to a variety of media. In many cases, the production then undergoes a technical quality control (or QC) check to ensure that it meets the required technical standard for broadcast or theatrical release. The QC process is necessary because of the many links in the production chain. Material is supplied from multiple sources and run through many separate processes, and a number of different companies may have handled it. The QC process is essential in ensuring that an acceptable level of quality is maintained, regardless of the processes used until this point.

During the QC process, any number of problems may be spotted, ranging from barely noticeable minor issues to severe ones that threaten to make the program unwatchable. The problems may be technical, meaning a problem with the media (such as a faulty video signal); they may be visual, meaning a problem with the image content (such as an out-of-focus shot); or the problems may be editorial (such as a shot starting at the wrong timecode). QCs are usually performed at an external location, to prevent bias, and a QC report is generated (either by human inspection and testing, or by an automated system), with issues typically graded on a five-point scale that indicates the problem's severity, with a grade 1 problem considered severe and a grade 5 problem considered imperceptible.[1]

QC requirements vary depending upon the output medium—for example, aliasing may not present significant problems for digital release (particularly when the source master's resolution is higher than the final digital resolution) but will be noticeable on nondigital formats, or on digital formats with a higher resolution than the source master. Different distributors may also have specific requirements, such as designating particular timecodes for different elements on video masters. For example, the British Broadcasting Corporation (BBC) requires that program content start on 10:00:00:00 and be followed by a minute of black (among other requirements). In addition, various distributors may differ in their interpretation of the severity of a particular issue. Local news channels, for example, might have, out of necessity, a much lower standard for an acceptable level of quality than other channels.

Video (both analog and digital video) formats have the most well-defined technical QC specifications, whereas film distributions focus more on visual quality and digital QC specifications range from the entirely subjective to nonexistent, depending upon the specific output and distributor.[2]

12.1 TECHNICAL VIDEO CONSIDERATIONS

Technical problems that are flagged in a video material's QC report may be the most difficult to decipher but are usually the simplest to fix. Many problems are caused by a fault somewhere in the output path—such as with the VCR used to record the footage on tape or perhaps an incorrect configuration of a parameter—and they are usually remedied by re-outputting the material. The facility originating the

---

[1] This scale is taken from CCIR Recommendation 500.
[2] This undoubtedly will change as the digital cinema industry gains more prominence.

material can detect many problems before resorting to the external QC, particularly when the facility is equipped with correct monitoring equipment, such as vectorscopes, waveform monitors, and graphics cages.

12.1.1   Video Standard

PAL, NTSC, and SECAM are different video systems with individual specifications. Therefore, each video system is incompatible—for example, you can't play back a NTSC video in a PAL VCR.

Using the wrong video system isn't strictly a flaw, but it has more to do with the distributor's delivery requirements.[3] Video standards issues can be solved by simply outputting the material once again but at the correct standard, which may require the use of a different VCR, or a changed setting somewhere in the output path (although a QC still must be carried out on the new tape). Be warned though, different video systems also differ in other properties, particularly the frame rate and image area, and even the color space. Many digital intermediate pipelines transparently handle different output formats and can be re-output without any problems. In other situations, however, it may be necessary to re-edit, reframe, or regrade the production for different video standards. Otherwise, a faster option is to run the video through a "standards converter," recording the output to a new tape using the correct standard, although the results may be inferior in quality to re-outputting directly from the digital source.

12.1.2   Illegal Colors

While the use of illegal colors probably won't lead to an arrest, it may prevent the show from being broadcast. Different video standards have their inherent color spaces, and colors created that fall outside of that color space (such as those that might be created in an sRGB color space), are termed "illegal," meaning that they won't

---

[3] Some distributors' guidelines also require that a particular video format be used in conjunction with a video system, such as a 625 Digital Betacam or a 1080p24 HDD5.

display properly when viewed on standard monitors. Many digital output systems automatically curb the output of illegal colors to specific video systems, but for those systems that don't, it may be possible to apply a "video-safe-color" digital filter to the final material that will render the footage without any illegal colors. Otherwise, it may be necessary to regrade the sections with illegal colors and then re-output them.

Although video allows for headroom in terms of luminance ranges, specific black points (the "black level") and white points (the "video level") should be adhered to when outputting to specific video formats. The minimum pixel value (i.e., RGB 0,0,0) of a sequence should be output at the video's black point, and the maximum pixel should be output at the video's white point. Waveform monitors are typically used to detect regions where this may not be the case, by superimposing the luminance signal over a calibrated graph.

Scenes that don't meet the required luminance ranges may have to be regraded, or re-output onto video. Since many VCRs have controls for correcting the black level and video level during a recording, it's usually possible to adjust the levels for each recording rather than

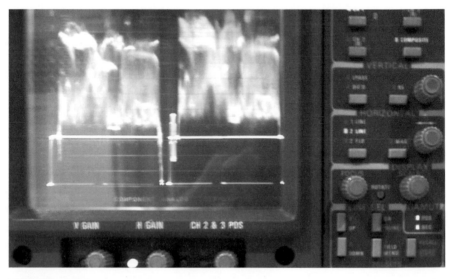

FIGURE 12-1 A waveform monitor can be used to inspect a video signal's properties

having to regrade entire sequences, especially if the graded version is correct in terms of luminance ranges. Likewise, if an entire video tape has consistently wrong luminance ranges, it may be possible to dub the tape onto a new one using the VCR's controls, saving time and expense.

Similarly, problems may arise with the chromaticity (or "chroma,"—a video signal's color component), where colors may be recorded incorrectly—for example, where blues display as greens. Incorrectly recorded colors can be harder to measure objectively except when checking a known reference (e.g., bars or another standard reference image) using a vectorscope. Otherwise, an experienced operator may see problems subjectively (e.g., with flesh tones) on a calibrated monitor. In general, properly color-graded productions should encounter chrominance problems only due to some fault on the output path, with regrading necessary only when the original grading was flawed. Again, the quickest option for correcting chromaticity issues on entire videos is to make use of the "chroma level" controls on the output VTR.

12.1.3 Aspect Ratio

The "aspect ratio" of a production denotes the shape of the picture area—quite simply, the ratio of the width of the picture to its height. Various formats have strictly defined aspect ratios—for example, most standard-definition videos (as well as "full aperture" 35mm film) have an aspect ratio of 4:3 (also referred to as "fullscreen"), whereas high-definition videos normally have a 16:9 aspect ratio (also referred to as "widescreen"). Other ratios may be used, depending upon the distributor's requirements. For example, some broadcasters transmit a 14:9 aspect ratio image, which is cropped and letterboxed to fit a 4:3 screen.[4]

The aspect ratio is usually defined at the start of the production, and the output matches the production. Sometimes the picture may have to be reformatted for a different aspect ratio, which can be done by cropping and resizing the images (a process called "center

---

[4] Although they may still require a 16:9 deliverable.

cut-out,"—cropping the sides of a 16:9 image to get a 4:3 image) or by using the "pan and scan" techniques discussed in Chapter 11. The latter techniques require more interactive control. Alternatively, it's possible to quickly reformat a video signal by passing it through an aspect ratio converter and recording it onto a new video tape. Simply resizing the picture area to fit a different aspect ratio results in a distorted picture, with shortened or fattened, or taller or thinner, actors in a scene.

12.1.4 Safe Areas

Consumer-grade televisions don't display the entire active picture area. Instead, they crop the edges of the picture by some amount— either electronically cropped or cropped by the casing of the set (which is also true, to some degree, for film projection, where small differences in the size of the film gate may crop the edges of the picture).[5] For this reason, the content at the edge of a frame is usually not visible, which means that it's vital not to put specific details close to the frame's edge, including such details as action elements (events that occur in a given shot) and graphics elements (such as titles, logos, or "bugs").

To ensure that the vast majority of viewers can see the relevant content, each format has established "safe" areas for both action and graphics. It's generally accepted that any action appearing in the action-safe zone can be seen by the audience, and any graphics and text within the graphics-safe (or "title-safe") region will be readable on most television sets. The action-safe area represents the inner 81% of the total image area (or 95% of the width), while the graphics safe area represents the inner 64% of the picture area (or 90% of the width) for 4:3 formats. For 16:9 formats, the definition becomes a little complicated; refer to the Appendix for more information. Safe areas can

---

[5] The reasons are largely historical. A degree of "overscan"—that is, picture area cropped from the display—was created so that during power fluctuations, which used to shrink the picture onscreen, the resulting, shrunken picture would still fit the screen. Today, television manufacturers use overscan to compensate for productions designed around this limitation, which in turn gives rise to the need to compensate for the overscan....

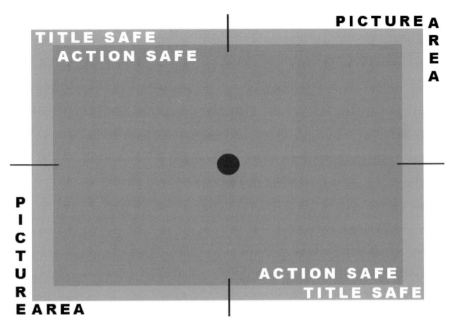

FIGURE 12-2 An example line-up chart, showing the safe areas

be measured using special character generators (or "cages") that overlay the boundaries over the video image. In addition, a "framing chart" image can be placed at the front of a video playout to help diagnose incorrect framing.

The reverse of this is also true: on every shot, pictures must extend beyond the safe areas to the frame edge to avoid unnecessary cropping of displays that can show the entire picture area.[6] When these boundaries are breached, especially in the case of text, it may be necessary to return to the original elements (i.e., the footage and text layers) and reposition and recompose them to fit the safe area.

---

[6] Sometimes material is output to video with the assumption that a certain crop will be applied (i.e., the entire picture is output but is framed for a particular image area—anything outside of this area should be ignored). However, in these situations, it's recommended that material always be output already cropped to avoid potential confusion.

12.1.5 Frame Rate

The frame rate is almost exclusively determined by the output standard. For film, this means a frame rate of 24 or 25fps. For NTSC video, it's 29.97fps, and for PAL video it's 25fps. Likewise, each high-definition format has a specific frame rate. For example, 1080p24 is 24fps (progressive frames) and 1080i50 is 25fps (interlaced, 50 fields per second). A comprehensive list of the frame rates for the most common formats can be found in the Appendix.

When a frame rate must be changed, it can be done digitally, using any of the temporal interpolation processes outlined in Chapter 10 or by passing the signal through a standards converter.

12.1.6 Fields

Many video formats (i.e., those that are interlaced) have two fields for every frame of picture. Because each field represents half the frame, one field carries picture content for lines 1, 3, 5, and so on (and is referred to as the "upper" field), while the other field carries picture content for lines 2, 4, 6, and so on (and is referred to as the "lower" field). Unlike progressive formats, each field in interlaced video represents a different moment in time, having been photographed separately. If the first field (i.e., the "dominant" field) photographed is output after the second field (but within the same frame), movement in playback can look erratic (although no problem is apparent when looking at a single frame of the sequence). This can happen, for instance, when shooting onto a format (e.g., PAL Betacam) that stores the upper fields first and then recording out onto a format (such as PAL DV) that stores the lower field first. To avoid this, either the frames can be deinterlaced completely during the digital intermediate process (see Chapter 9), making them progressive, or the field dominance can be reversed by removing the first field, either digitally or through a standards converter (although it can result in cut points occurring on a field rather than a frame). A second option is to reposition each frame vertically by one line, although doing so removes one line of the image on one side and creates a blank line on the other (which is usually replaced by duplicating the adjacent line).

Similarly, some errors can occur that are caused by fields appearing in the wrong place in a frame—that is, a lower field becomes an upper field, and vice versa. In this instance, playback looks erratic, whether or not it contains movement. Solving this problem requires fields be swapped, though it may then necessitate the need to reverse the field dominance, too.

Progressive material may require that footage be supplied an interlaced format. Normally this doesn't require reformatting the footage and doesn't have any associated quality loss. For example, a project mastered at 30fps with progressive frames may be output to a 1080i60 (high-definition interlaced video format at 60 fields per second), and each frame divided in half so that alternate lines are stored in each field. Thus each frame remains identical to the source material. In the (somewhat rare) event when progressive footage must be encoded so that each field represents a separate instance in time, it may be achieved by using a digital "reinterlacing" process on the footage (as described in Chapter 11), although it will likely result in some image degradation.

12.1.7 Timecodes

In most cases, the video timecode should run continuously without breaks. However, recording errors or incorrect settings on the output system or VCR can cause timecode problems, such as jumps in the timecode (e.g., when the timecode suddenly goes from 01:00:00:00 to 12:54:17:05), which may not be visible in the picture content. Fortunately, most timecode problems can be fixed by replaying the material onto tape (or a new tape if you suspect that the fault is in the original), dubbing the tape to a new one or even just re-recording the timecode track, leaving the picture and audio untouched.

Many timecode problems are caused by lengthy or multiple recordings; therefore, most facilities make it a common practice to record to a "prestriped" tape (one with a black video signal and timecode track already recorded onto the tape), simply inserting the video and audio content without modifying the tape's timecode.

12.1.8 Signal Faults

Any number of technical signal faults can occur during a video recording (or indeed, during playback). Problems such as line blanking, control track damage, flicker, and dropout are all related to the mechanics of the VCR and video tape and may be remedied usually by outputting a new tape, possibly using a different VCR. Where this isn't possible, it may be possible to repair the damage digitally by digitizing the faulty tape and using restoration techniques before outputting the corrected material). For example, video dropout can be treated in a similar way to dust and scratches on scanned film.

RECORDING LOGS

Many guidelines also require all supplied video material to be accompanied by a "recording log." This log is simply a listing of the contents of the tape, usually including the following elements for each recorded item:

1. The timecode on the tape of the beginning of the item.
2. The timecode on the tape of the end of the item.
3. The title or description of the item.
4. The recording date.

It may also be useful to note other pertinent data for reference—such information as the output system or VCR and the name of the operator.

It's also good practice to record a "slate" (i.e., a still frame with shot information) before each item and to label each tape with details such as the production name, as well as the type of output (such as, the "master" or "dub"), and to set the tape permissions to write-protected to prevent accidentally erasing the contents. Some digital intermediate facilities may also use barcode or RFID (radio frequency identification) tags to aid tracking.

FLASHING AND REPETITIVE PATTERNS

People with photosensitive epilepsy (or PSE) are vulnerable to strong light pulses of high frequencies, which can trigger seizures. Under certain conditions, these seizures can be triggered by watching video content that contains bright, flashing images or fast-moving patterns. Individuals with PSE can also be affected by fast cuts, bright spinning spiral patterns, strobe lighting, or other fast-moving, high contrast content, in particular with a high red color component. Each distributor offers its own interpretation of exactly what can and cannot be displayed safely, in terms of the maximum frequency (e.g., the BBC allow pulses at intervals of 360ms or longer), but in general, any flashing sequence shouldn't last longer than five seconds. In certain circumstances, a warning may be placed at the start of a program that contains content that might be unsafe in this regard.

12.2 FILM QUALITY CONTROL

In the usual production pipeline, once the digital intermediate has been recorded to film negative and developed, an "answer print" is made, which may or may not include sound. The answer print is suitable for previewing the "release prints" (i.e., the prints distributed to cinemas).

Producing film releases involves less technical issues than producing video, in part because far fewer variables are involved in film processing than with video recording. Film-processing laboratories work to achieve a specific, standardized level of quality control and perform the necessary checks on developed material themselves, such as ensuring the proper development of each reel and checking that the sprockets are in the right place. This relieves much of the production and post-production teams' burdens, and they instead can focus on more subjective issues.

As with video formats, the aspect ratio is important, but different film formats have explicitly defined dimensions for the image area for

35mm (a list of them can be found in Appendix), which must be adhered to. The film should be visually inspected for damage, such as scratches, and to determine whether it's free from splices whenever possible. Film can be regraded optically, if necessary, to make overall changes to the prints' color component.

Labs provide "timing reports" to accompany each answer print. The timing reports contain details of the "printer light" settings used to generate the print. Every print is made from a negative using a combination of red, green, and blue light, and the amount of light can indicate potential problems. A perfectly exposed negative, in a perfectly balanced chemical process, would be exposed with printer lights of 20-20-20. Because of differences with different processing runs, most digital intermediate facilities also supply a standard test pattern as part of any filmed-out material, which is used to match-grade the processed film and ensure the correct result.

12.3 DIGITAL ERRORS

Although a digital pipeline offers the filmmaker many wonderful creative possibilities, a multitude of issues can arise within the digital intermediate environment. Digital problems are fairly rare, but given the sheer volume of data and individual files being processed on a given production, the likelihood of a problem affecting some of the data increases. Many of these problems can be detected visually, while some can be detected by automated processes.

12.3.1 Render Errors

For various reasons, renders of digital images can sometimes fail, resulting in a corrupt file, signs of corruption within an image (typically seen as randomly colored pixels in uncompressed images), images with no content, or images with missing or faulty compositing (e.g., in images with text composited over a background, the text may disappear for no apparent reason part way through a shot). Anything that compromises the actual file structure of the images (namely, file corruption) may be detected fairly easily using a number of automated file processes. However, these problems may also be introduced simply by transferring the files, such as across a network, and can be resolved by recopying the file in question from a good copy (or re-rendering when no such copy is available).

All other problems may be detected only by visual inspecting each frame, which can be a tedious process. For this reason, the majority of digital errors (particularly the subtle ones) are detected during the video tape QC (assuming one is performed), or ideally, during a digital QC prior to output. Render errors may always be solved by simply re-rendering the shot in question. Note that the entire shot (cut-to-cut) should be re-rendered to avoid introducing flash frames.

12.3.2 Flash Frames

A "flash frame" (or "timing shift") is a generic term that can be applied to any sudden change in the content of a shot. It might be a wrong frame inserted into the middlze of a sequence, or an abrupt stop of a digital effect, such as when a particular grade applied to a scene accidentally carries over into the first few frames of the next scene.

The causes of flash frames may be editorial, such as when a cut-point is set incorrectly on one of the systems or when data is accessed from the wrong shot, or a flash frame may be the fault of the rendering system or output path. For the latter, the problem can be resolved by simply re-rendering or re-outputting the scene, otherwise, the problem must be corrected, such as by adjusting the shot list on the relevant systems.

Similar problems can arise with duplicate (repeated) or dropped (missing) frames appearing on the output, which can occur through rendering, output, or editorial problems, necessitating re-rendering,

FIGURE 12-3   In this sequence, the wrong grading parameters were applied in the last frame. When played real time, the sequence appears to flash at the end

re-outputting, or reconforming, respectively. If the original material is damaged or unavailable, the restoration techniques outlined in Chapter 9 may be used to rebuild frames.

12.4   DIGITAL ARTIFACTS

By definition, many digital processes are destructive to the image. Digital grading may stretch the colors too far for a particular output, resulting in "posterization," or "clipped," or "crushed" colors, while resizing images may leave undesirable "aliasing" artifacts (both issues are covered later in this chapter). Each different digital process carries the risk of introducing more artifacts, whether it's oversharpening the image (which causes "ringing") or using lossy compressing (which carries a whole host of potential artifacts), and so the entire digital intermediate process must strike a delicate balance between minimizing the visual impact of such artifacts and enabling such processes to improve the image's subjective quality and creative content. Clearly, maximizing the image quality throughout the pipeline is one of the best ways to do so, but there is always going to be a limit to the effectiveness of such preventative measures.

Anytime artifacts are found, they can usually be traced back to a particular problem, and a decision can be made as to the method you want to use to reduce the impact. For example, when trying to correctly balance a scene's luminance, you might introduce a high level of noise into the shot by using digital grading on underexposed footage. If too much noise is present, a decision should be made either to reduce the amount of grading applied to the original shot (which may impair the scene's subjective quality) or to use digital noise-reduction techniques (which may cause the scene to lose sharpness). The Appendix lists the most common destructive digital operations and the types of artifacts they can introduce.

12.4.1   Spatial Artifacts

Spatial artifacts are caused by the "space" of an image—the shape, size, and distribution of pixels. The most common artifact of this type

FIGURE 12-4 Aliasing can be seen along diagonal or curved lines

FIGURE 12-5 With a higher-resolution image, the effects of aliasing are less pronounced

is "aliasing," which is a jagged appearance of an image's curved or diagonal edges. Because pixels are just squares, it's easy to accurately draw horizontal or vertical straight lines just by stacking them next to each other, but when you try to represent a curved or diagonal line or edge with too few pixels, the corners of the pixels stick out, making the curve appear jagged. One way to reduce this effect is to redigitize the image at a higher resolution, so that the edge can be represented with more pixels.

Redigitizing the image isn't always an option, particularly by the time you get to the QC stage. Many practical or economic reasons may account for the necessity of working with lower-resolution images in the first place. However, aliasing can be reduced in part by employing "anti-aliasing" mechanisms. These work by averaging regions with edges, altering the aliased pixels to give the impression of a smoother line, but possibly resulting in a loss of sharpness. Many interpolation methods use similar techniques (as discussed in Chapter 10), but for the purpose of fixing QC problems, reducing the impact of aliasing may be possible by using a combination of blurring and sharpening effects, or even by using sophisticated interpolation methods to artificially increase the resolution.

Another effect prevalent in digital images, particularly those originating from CCD-based devices, is "blooming," where a point of light "spills" into an adjacent pixel, which can blur parts of the image. Blooming typically occurs when shooting a brightly lit source. Blooming problems are typically resolved by "edge enhancement" or "sharpening" techniques (see Chapter 9), which increase the contrast along detected edges.

12.4.2 Chromatic Artifacts

When an image contains too few colors to fully represent the subject (as when an image's bit depth is too low), chromatic artifacts can occur. You can see this problem primarily in regions of gradual color change—for instance, a shot of a sunset. With insufficient color information, regions of graduated color appear to have "steps" where one color abruptly changes into another.

FIGURE 12-6   If all else fails, it may be possible to reduce the effects of aliasing with a combination of interpolation and restoration techniques

This stepping is caused when the color difference between two adjacent shades of color (or channel values) is too far apart. The most common cause of banding is from stretching colors too much during the digital-grading process. Working at as high a bit depth as possible can prevent the occurrence of banding; otherwise, it may be necessary to regrade the images. Perhaps using a combination of blurring, sharpening, and noise-addition techniques can correct such a problem, but in most cases, it only degrades the image further.

12.4.3 Noise

"Noise" in an image refers to random errors in the accuracy of the information in a digital image. The errors aren't strictly a product of digital images, but are common because they're inherent in most imaging methods (except CG imagery). For instance, in shooting a perfectly gray surface, you would expect an image in which every pixel is the same shade of gray. In reality, however, some pixels might

FIGURE 12-7 In this image, banding produces discrete delineations between areas of different tones

be slightly too dark; others too light. These errors likely are distributed fairly randomly across the image and are caused by errors within the capture device itself. Some digital image operations can add or increase the level of noise in an image, such as sharpening or color grading.

Several methods are available for reducing the noise in an image. The best way is to capture the same image several times and then create an "average" of all the images. This can be time consuming (or otherwise impractical), however, and doesn't account for less random and more localized noise effects (e.g., caused by a faulty CCD element). Another method of reducing the noise is to use a noise-reduction algorithm, which works by performing a statistical analysis of the image and calculating probable areas of noise. Some common noise-reduction techniques are covered in Chapter 9.

Noise can be insignificant in still images, where a highly detailed scene might contain a small amount of noise that is undetectable when viewed. However, the noise can become a larger problem when present in a sequence of frames and is visible as tiny fluctuations in color.

12.4.4 Temporal Artifacts

Just as with color and space, motion is segmented into evenly spaced discrete units (i.e., frames). Digital moving pictures typically work the same as other moving-picture formats—that is, a running sequence of still images. The major problem that can arise is when this rate of display (i.e., the "frame rate") is too low, the viewer becomes aware of the individual images, and the illusion of motion is lost. The sequence is said to "strobe." This strobing effect isn't unique to digital media, and in fact, the film and television industries' own solutions are equally applicable here. The human eye is unable to detect most changes that are faster than one-fifteenth of a second in duration (peripheral vision can detect changes in motion faster than the center of vision). Therefore, cinema and television standards dictate that when the frame rate is higher than one-fifteenth of a second, the strobing effects won't be visible. In fact, cinema standards assume a frame rate of 24–25fps, while broadcasters typically use a rate of 25–30fps (depending on the regional standard). Digital media can be played back at any frame rate, but for the sake of simplicity (and to avoid affecting the audio sync), the same frame rate is typically used as the output format. It's also a logical assumption that the frame rate for playback is the same as the rate that the imagery was acquired;

FIGURE 12-8   A fast-moving object exhibits a lot of motion blur with a slow shutter speed

otherwise, the motion may look unnaturally fast or slow (unless that effect is desired, of course).

"Motion blur" is an effect caused by an object's movement during the length of a single frame. In an extreme example, a ball being photographed might move across the whole screen in the space of one frame, causing it to be imaged along the entire path, and resulting in a long "smear" or blurred image of the ball.

Motion blur is controlled, to some degree, by the length of time the imaging device records a frame. Most imaging devices have moving parts and, therefore, can't record continuously. For example, video cameras have a shutter that closes (i.e., blocking all light out of a scene) when advancing from one frame to the next one. (Film cameras run the shutter at a fixed speed, instead varying its angle, but the principle is the same.). Thus, any movement that occurs during the brief period that the shutter is closed won't be recorded. Conversely, all motion that occurs when the shutter is open is recorded onto a single frame. The two ways of reducing the amount of motion blur are either to increase the frame rate (which isn't always practical because it could cause playback or compatibility issues later on) or decrease the shutter speed (or shutter angle) of the imaging device.

Interestingly, although motion blur can be considered an artifact, many people prefer watching footage containing some amount of motion blur, and it's more of a creative issue than a quality one. For this reason, the degree of motion blur in a scene is normally controlled at the time of shooting, although it's much easier to add simulated motion blur than to remove motion blur than has been recorded in-camera later on.[7]

Many other motion-related artifacts can occur. All of them are caused by changes to some aspect of the images between frames (e.g., mis-

---

[7] This can be controlled by shooting at a very high frame rate and then combining a proportion of frames to produce a desired frame rate. The method used to combine the frames affects the amount of motion blur and has the added benefit of reducing random noise (when used in conjunction with image-averaging methods). This topic is covered in greater detail in Chapter 14.

FIGURE 12-9   Less motion blur is seen with a faster shutter speed

registration or color flashes), but all motion-blur effects are a product of the equipment or methods used during shooting and aren't a product of digital media.

12.5   VISUAL CONSIDERATIONS

Maintaining high-quality footage isn't just about preventing processing defects (whether digital or otherwise). In addition, subjective factors affect the visual quality of an image.

12.5.1   Sharpness

Audiences respond well to sharper images with visibly strong edges, and to important features (particularly human faces) within the focal plane. The sharpest images can be obtained in the digital intermediate environment by acquiring source material at the highest possible resolution (usually the source format's native resolution), and avoiding any processes that feature interpolation or smoothing algorithms, before outputting at the same resolution as the source was captured.

In reality, it's difficult to avoid using processing that doesn't affect an image's sharpness in some way. However, in most cases, the overall loss of sharpness may be negligible when compared to the benefits achieved, as when reducing the level of noise on a particular shot. By far, the most significant way to ensure sharp images is to achieve the maximum possible sharpness when shooting, which means using high-quality, carefully focused lenses.

When image sharpness is a concern during the QC process, it may be possible to use digital-sharpening techniques outlined in Chapter 9, although these techniques may present undesirable side effects.

12.5.2 Exposure

Broadly speaking, properly exposed footage has bright highlights, dark shadows, and easily discernible pertinent features.[8] The color-grading process (if adopted) of the digital intermediate pipeline should ensure that the output footage is balanced as desired, and the color balance doesn't change much during the rest of the digital inter-mediate process. The ability of color grading to change the exposure of a given shot, particularly without introducing significant artifacts into the footage, is somewhat limited. The general rule is that digi-tal grading can change the recorded exposure by about 20 printer lights (about one stop) without introducing noticeable artifacts into the process. By far the best guarantee of correct exposure is to cor-rectly expose the material when shooting, which means using suf-ficient illumination in the scene, in conjunction with correct filters and camera settings (and film stock for film shoots, not to mention an appropriate development process). In cases where the source footage exposure can't be guaranteed (e.g., archival footage), digital grading may be used to correct the exposure (possibly with a number of other processes for extreme exposure differences).

12.5.3 Color Rendition

To maximize audience comprehension (as well as audience empa-thy), colors in a given scene should be accurate renditions of their real-life counterparts. A tomato is much easier to recognize when it's red than when it's orange (it may get mistaken for an orange in the latter case). This is particularly true of flesh tones, as people can dif-ferentiate between realistic flesh tones and those that are off color.

---

[8] This description is somewhat oversimplified; entire books are devoted to defining proper exposure.

During a shoot, color balance is controlled through careful lighting and camera settings, and with filters and recording media, but the fine details of color in the digital intermediate pipeline are entirely controlled during the color-grading stage, typically with the digital colorist working in conjunction with the cinematographer. For this reason, the best way to ensure accurate color rendition is by using an experienced cinematographer, a competent colorist, and correctly calibrated equipment.

12.5.4 Continuity

The term "continuity" covers many aspects of producing a production. It encompasses scene continuity—for example, a person sunbathing in one shot normally won't be drenched with rain in the next cut; story continuity—actors in a production set in the Middle Ages shouldn't be wearing wristwatches and television sets shouldn't be part of any shot; and visual continuity—a scene of darkness and uncertainty won't normally include a bright and sunny shot. The visual continuity can also be disrupted by factors such as varying degrees of certain digital processes, such as inserting a shot with a strong glow effect into a scene with more subtle glow effects (or none at all). Visual continuity issues can sometimes be corrected by adjusting the properties of the rogue shot, using those processes at the disposal of the production team—such processes as darkening an overly bright shot. In other cases (and this is true of other continuity issues), a visual effect or reshoot may be necessary.

12.5.5 Smooth Motion

One factor that distinguishes amateur productions (e.g., home videos) from ones of broadcast or film quality is the unsteady motion visible in the former. By contrast, professional productions, for the most part, feature smooth camera movements, even in frantic handheld scenes, through a combination of specific equipment geared for this purpose and the skill of the cameraman who operates it. Along with the difficulty in trying to watch a shaky scene, unsteady motion is largely avoided because it can cause motion sickness. In situations when the camera motion isn't as smooth as desired, either because of the way the shot was filmed or of faulty camera equipment, you can use digital stabilization techniques (covered in Chapter 9) to smooth it out.

SOURCE MATERIAL QCS

There's a lot to be said for performing the same standard of QC checks on the source material acquired into the digital intermediate process, as you would on the output material. In the long run, problems, such as improperly fixed film stock, can be treated much easier (and much cheaper) if they're caught early, rather than using digital methods when trying to correct problems later down the line. Particularly during shooting, faults intercepted with material already shot may be reshot, which isn't usually an option by the time the material is conformed and can be viewed. In addition, if other problems are noticed early on, such as excessive dirt and scratches on a reel of film, you might be able to treat them first, saving time (and possibly money).

12.6 EDITORIAL ISSUES

Editorial issues include such problems as countdown leaders starting on the wrong frame, synchronization issues, and bad cuts.

Each distributor generally has requirements for every output element—for example, a requirement for the starting timecode of the production (i.e., the "first frame of picture") or for the location of textless elements. If such elements are in the wrong place, it may be necessary to re-output the elements.

Sync problems can occur for a variety of reasons. Perhaps the production has been conformed incorrectly, or it contains duplicated or dropped frames somewhere. An outdated EDL might have been used, or a number of other problems might be encountered. Similarly, "bad edits," (such as a cut in the middle of a shot, or the wrong shot inserted into the middle of a sequence) may exhibit symptoms that are similar to sync problems. Sync problems are usually detected by running the audio track with the finished production (audio sync problems generally manifest as a delay between when speech is heard and when the speaker's mouth moves). Alternatively, running a copy of the offline edit, if available, alongside the finished output version normally reveals both bad edits and sync problems, as well as the starting location of the problem and hence its cause.

Depending upon their specific cause, these problems are usually resolved by correcting the edit and re-outputting the sequence. In the event that the sequence "drifts," becoming increasingly out of sync, then it's likely that a mismatch in frame rate has occurred, either because of the way the material was conformed or an incorrect setting on the output path. When the production has been conformed at the wrong frame rate, it can result in a lot of work to correct it.

12.7   THE DIGITAL QC PROCESS

It goes without saying that throughout a production, every digital image should be checked for problems. However, a thorough QC check should be made prior to final output (from the digital source master, if available). Performing the QC requires watching the material at the correct speed, as well as using slower speeds to check details. It may be possible to use automated processes to check for some problems, such as illegal colors or damaged frames. The use of analytical devices, such as waveform monitors or digital histograms, may also provide a more accurate examination during the QC process. Ideally, a digital system that can quickly fix problems should be used for checking material, without having to switch back to other systems. Systems such as Assimilate's Scratch (www.assimilateinc.com) enable the QCer to play back and compare images, and it provides tools to correct problems.

12.7.1   Comparing Digital Images

Many systems allow the simultaneous display of multiple digital images, which is useful for making detailed comparisons. For

FIGURE 12-10 Systems such as Assimilate's Scratch provide a digital playback system suitable for the QC process

CREATIVE DECISIONS

There's a caveat to the entire discussion of visual QC issues: in many cases, certain shots were intended to look the way they do. That's not to suggest people can't be bothered to ensure a high level of quality, but that sometimes they are trying to create a visual style for the production that devites from convention. For example, a deliberately out-of-focus human face might intentionally prevent the audience from viewing the actor's expression. Similarly, the color rendition of an object or person might be unrealistic in order to stylize it. The digital intermediate process provides an unprecedented degree of stylization and it gives rise to a host of creative potential. For this reason, it may be safe to ignore QC report notes that point out visual issues (not to mention, certain editorial issues, such as single-frame edits), providing those visual effects were intentionally created.

FIGURE 12-11 Although two images may look the same, a difference matte can be created to highlight the differences

example, it may be possible to sync the digital playback system with a video playback system, to cross-reference the edit in an offline reference video with the final output. Such systems can also be used for visual comparisons of an image's different versions—for example, comparing a graded image to an ungraded image. To make this process easier, you can use split screens or some sort of interactive wipe process to compare images. The ability to create "difference mattes" can also be important. A difference matte is an image mathematically generated by comparing two images. For every pixel that isn't different, the resulting pixel is black. The greater the difference, the brighter the pixel becomes. This approach can be very useful in ensuring that changes made to an image don't significantly affect the image content.

12.8 SUMMARY

A number of technical considerations must be made to ensure that material is output at an acceptable level of quality and that it will be viewed in the manner intended. Fortunately, the digital intermediate pipeline offers a number of tools for checking for potential problems and for correcting problems that are found.

With the successful completion of the QC process, the digital intermediate process comes to an end. The following two chapters look at ways the digital intermediate process might develop, starting with a look forward to new technology and developments.

13

THE FUTURE OF DIGITAL FILM

Almost everything in this book so far covers actual working practices in use today. But the digital intermediate is a rapidly evolving field. Within a year or two, new techniques and systems will be in use, giving rise to new methodologies and paradigms. For this reason, it's useful to look at the possibilities of digital film mastering in the future, to try to anticipate where this technology might go, and where it has to go to overcome key issues.

Speculation on future trends is an inaccurate process by definition. So many things can change in a short space of time, and one small change can rapidly affect the bigger picture. However, we can make certain projections about the near future of the industry—predictions based on trends that have emerged in associated fields, namely computer and digital technology.

Hardware will become cheaper and more powerful. This single assumption, based on "Moore's Law," has a drastic effect throughout the digital pipeline.[1] Traditional mastering is relatively unaffected by changes in the cost and power of digital technology, because the majority of the components are mechanical or chemical. However, a drop in cost and increase in performance is intimately tied to the performance of the digital lab. Consider storage media: not only will the disk space necessary to store a feature film soon be affordable to individual desktop computers, but it may even make the sometimes tedious procedure of data management more . . . manageable. This trend has been observed in the last few years, where the average digital storage capacity of a digital intermediate facility has increased from several terabytes to several tens of terabytes, requiring digital intermediate facilities to concurrently handle multiple productions.

As CPU power increases, relative to price, we can do more with the technology, achieving higher levels of quality, as well as having the ability to offer more intensive processes, such as filtering. Where once film images required custom-made hardware to display and process scanned film footage in real time, this capability can now be found on a number of off-the-shelf desktop PCs. A four-fold increase in available storage space, CPU power, bandwidth, and RAM is the difference between the current 2k mastering systems and future, higher-quality 4k film mastering.

The industry will grow. The digital intermediate process for film inevitably will gain momentum over traditional labs, for a number of reasons, but probably the overriding factor is that eventually, finishing a film chemically will be simply more expensive than finishing a film digitally. Smaller companies will offer innovative ways to perform parts of the digital-mastering service at much lower cost. For example, a small facility could offer color-grading services for a film, without offering a comprehensive film-scanning and recording service. The facility could opt to "farm out" those services to scanning boutiques.

13.1 THE FUTURE OF IMAGING

Digital imaging methods are already starting to replace other methods. At the consumer level, digital cameras already outsell film-based cameras by a large margin. Filmmakers are already experimenting

---

[1] Moore's Law states that computer systems double in power every eighteen months.

with using high-definition digital video cameras for film production rather than the traditional 35mm pipeline. Some of them enjoy the increased freedom to experiment and the faster production turn-around, while others lament the inferior picture quality. Certainly no video camera currently on the market can match the 35mm format in terms of picture quality. However, new advances are slowly improving image quality and creating solutions for a number of other problems.

13.1.1   High Dynamic Range Imaging

High dynamic range (HDR) images were originally conceived to solve problem in digital photography and 3D imaging simulations. One of the frequent complaints of professional photographers who use both digital formats and film formats is that digital images simply don't have the dynamic range of their film-based counterparts. Take a photo of a scene using a film camera, and compare it to a digital image of the same scene, and the differences in color become apparent.

Many details in the color of a photograph aren't even visible in such a straightforward comparison. For example, consider a photograph of a direct light source, such as a bare light bulb. The photograph and the digital image may look identical in terms of how the images appear, but in fact, the contents will be very different. If you were to decrease the brightness of the digital image, the light source would turn gray. However, if you were to decrease the brightness of the photographic image, the element would become visible, as does the scene beyond the bulb.

Digital intermediate facilities can replicate this result to some degree by using logarithmic image formats, such as Cineon or DPX files. Unfortunately, these files are typically limited to 10 bits of luminosity, providing a range from 1–1024, which is lower than film's range by a factor of ten.[2] Even without this limit, the vast majority of monitors that display digital images are themselves limited to around 100 steps of luminosity. In the digital intermediate pipeline, this isn't an inher-

---

[2] The human eye is thought to have a dynamic range of around 10,000:1 under suitable conditions.

ent problem, because it's possible to scan film and output it directly to a new piece of film with marginal loss in visible tonality. However, anytime the luminance of an image is modified (which is a frequent occurrence during digital color grading), decisions are made that affect the color—decisions based on feedback from the digital image display. Images are darkened and brightened, contrast increased or reduced, based upon the image's appearance on a digital device (although major modifications are usually checked on a test film print). A combination of careful color calibration and an experienced colorist ensures that the desired effect will ultimately be achieved in the film version, but it's still a destructive process, reducing the quality of the image. An additional problem concerns long-term storage. How is it possible to guarantee an image will display correctly on devices that may not exist yet?

As we've seen throughout this book, one of the difficulties in working with color images, particularly those that originate from one type of media and are destined for another, is that it's difficult to guarantee that a given color in one media will display as intended in another. The simple act of scanning a frame of film for video output moves it through three different color spaces—the original film color space, the color space of the scanner, and the color space of the video. Provided the same types of film, the same scanner, and the same output device are used, it's possible to "reverse-engineer" the process to determine exactly which colors are transferred accurately and which aren't. This process is currently used by most facilities to complete a feature film digital intermediate, where the source material is film and the output is a combination of film and video. But as the number of different input and output formats increase, which is likely to happen over the next few years, this process becomes much harder to control.

HDR images aim to solve these problems by encoding colors using physical values, in terms of their electromagnetic wavelengths (also known as CIE or XYZ color spaces) and a more "absolute" measurement of luminance.

HDR images have the potential of recording arbitrary numbers (similar to density readings) for pixel values, rather than on a fixed scale. With this paradigm, each pixel is instead given a floating-point number (e.g., 0.9 or 3.112), and the bit depth instead relates to the precision of the number (i.e., the number of decimal places it's accurate to). Images of this type are also referred to as "floating-point images." This means, in practical terms, that film might then be sampled for density at each pixel, rather than as a fraction of the maximum and minimum brightness allowed by the system. This, in turn, means that different film stocks will be more accurately represented digitally, and it relieves much of the burden on the scanner operator in manually setting the dynamic range.

Furthermore, it has great implications for the color-grading process because it provides a useful set of data to work with. Finally, HDR images aren't prone to effects such as clipping or crushing of luminance levels, because the information isn't destroyed. In the same way as it's possible to push a video signal outside of viewable limits and then recover it later, floating-point numbers can be increased beyond a viewable limit and reduced later if necessary.

Working with images in the HDR format achieves two distinct aims. First, it ensures colors are recorded more accurately. Second, the HDR format can more effectively mix images that have different native color spaces, and it can output to any number of different media, provided the color space of each device is known. For example, video could be digitized and stored as an HDR image. Given the color space of video, each YIQ (or YUV) value could be encoded as an XYZ value. Having done so, the video could be output to a variety of media, such as film, paper, video, and digital projection by converting the XYZ values as needed for the particular output requirements (a process known as "tone mapping"). For example, the film and digital color spaces may encompass all of the encoded XYZ values, meaning they could be output without modification, while the others could use a conversion process to approximate the desired result.

Encoding chromaticity information in this way would also immensely aid the color-grading process. Experienced colorists could check colors based on their physical values, rather than relying on feedback from the monitor. Color-grading software could account for the color space of the display used to make grading decisions and compensate for the limits of the display when altering the image colors. In addition, the image could be displayed in a variety of different ways without

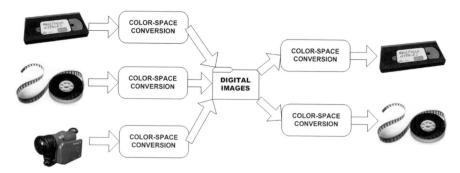

FIGURE 13-1 With conventional image formats, a number of color-space-conversion processes are used

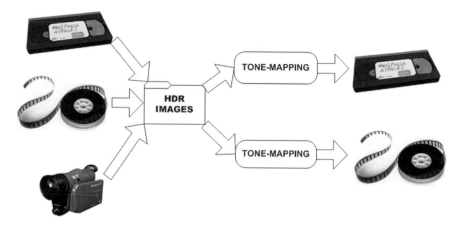

FIGURE 13-2 With HDR images, the native color space is retained, requiring tone mapping for output purposes

affecting the content. For example, it's possible to simulate exposure changes in photographs that have been converted to HDR images.

Several file formats already exist that can take advantage of this extended color space. TIFF files can be encoded using a 24-bit or 32-bit LogLuv method (i.e., logarithmic luminance values against U and V CIE coordinates) or the Pixar 33-bit specification. Two new types of file formats—Industrial Light & Magic's OpenEXR specification (www.openexr.org), and the images native to the Radiance lighting-simulation system (radsite.lbl.gov/radiance)—are also in widespread use and offer similar functionality. In addition, the camera raw files created by some digital cameras may also qualify as candidates for HDR imaging, although these files inevitably vary by camera design and manufacture, making compatibility problematic. In time, Adobe's recent Digital Negative (DNG) open file specification may help to unify the different raw formats, ultimately resulting in future digital and digital video cameras having the ability to output to a single format.

Using digital technology also allows images to be combined to increase the effective dynamic range. For example, an image of a scene recorded onto a typical piece of photographic film has around 5–8 stops of latitude. It's possible to increase this latitude further by taking an additional picture of the scene at higher levels (or lower levels, or both higher and lower) of exposure, capturing detail in areas that were

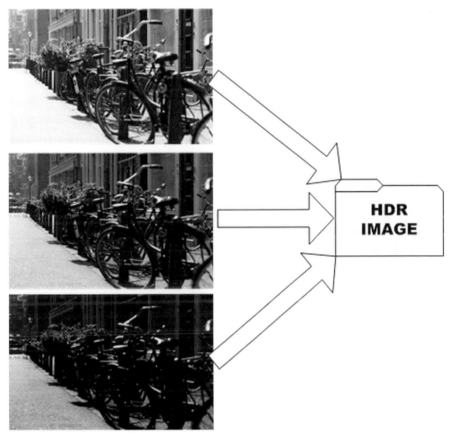

FIGURE 13-3 Multiple exposures can be combined to create a high dynamic range image

outside this range in the original image. Provided the image content is exactly the same (i.e., the lighting or composition of the scene hasn't been changed), and knowing the exposure setting of each picture, the images can be combined digitally, creating a new image with a far greater dynamic range of even the original film image.

Several systems are already designed to accommodate some HDR formats—such systems as Idruna's Photogenics HDR image-editing system (www.idruna.com) and may also make it possible to combine images of multiple exposures to create a digital image of extremely high dynamic range.

In the future, any of these HDR formats might become the digital intermediate standard, providing increased color accuracy and compatibility with a range of output media, and ensuring greater longevity of archives.

13.1.2   Future Displays

Many digital intermediate facilities have been aware of the limitations of conventional CRT computer monitors for a while now, in terms of luminance, dynamic range, and color space—and also in

FIGURE 13-4 Idruna's Photogenics HDR software enables you to edit high dynamic range images

psychological terms. Viewing images on a small screen is a completely different experience than viewing the same image projected onto a much larger screen (which is one reason why people still go to the cinema to watch films). It can be important to replicate these more theatrical conditions to get a better idea of how the final program will be presented. Even when the final output is video, viewing the footage on a larger screen can be very beneficial.

The current trend is toward digital projectors as the primary method of display. Digital projectors, until recently, were of inferior resolution when compared to HD video monitors, and the projectors lacked accurate color rendition and luminance power. The latest digital projectors provide resolution that's at least equal to HD video, with the added benefit of a larger color space and greater dynamic range. Future projectors, such as the Sony 4k SXRD (www.sony.com/professional), which can display images in sizes up to 4096×2160 pixels, should be able to play digital images with a level of quality that's close to that of a first-generation film print.

13.1.3 The Future of Photographic Film

Many people refer to the "imminent death" of photographic film as a capture medium. The truth is, film is unlikely to die any time soon

FIGURE 13-5 Sony's 4k SXRD projector is able to display high resolution images

for a number of reasons. First of all, it still remains the highest-quality medium for image capture today. Second, and perhaps more importantly, many filmmakers simply enjoy the process of working with film. It's a robust format, the pitfalls are well known, and experienced cinematographers can anticipate the results of a shoot before the film is even developed.

Eventually, the increased quality and convenience of digital capture methods may indeed make film redundant (although even then, undoubtedly, many will still use it as a format). When film actually becomes redundant depends as much upon advances in film stock as on advances in digital imaging. New film stocks may emerge to better bridge the gap between shooting on film and taking advantage of the digital intermediate process.

Film stocks such as Kodak's Vision 2 HD super-16mm stock (www.kodak.com/go/motion) are designed to ease the process of transferring and matching the color and look of 16mm film in an HD environment with film and imaging technology designed specifically for that purpose. Future film stocks may continue to expand upon this idea, perhaps even making film a more viable capture format for video advocates.

13.1.4 The 4k Problem

So-called "4k" digital intermediates are the current "holy grail" (or one of them, at least) of most film-based digital intermediate facilities. Images of 4k (i.e., those that contain approximately 4000 pixels per line) are thought to closely match the spatial resolution of most film stocks and therefore can facilitate the migration from 35mm film formats to digital ones without audiences being able to detect any quality difference. Many distributors are therefore waiting until 4k digital intermediate pipelines become commonplace before adopting the widespread use of the digital intermediate process.

The problem with 4k images is that they are very difficult to manage. It's only relatively recent that working with 2k (i.e., containing approximately 2000 pixels per line, roughly the same resolution as the high-end HD video formats) digital images is convenient. Even so, resources are often stretched to the limit. Images at 2k consume huge amounts of disk space and processing power, and they require a long time to copy or edit, especially compared to SD video images.

Working with 4k images quadruples the processing, timing, and storage requirements, because they have four times the number of pixels of their 2k counterparts. For the vast majority of facilities, this amount is simply too much data to handle. For a start, these requirements necessitate a choice between doing four films at 2k or one at 4k. Since 4k mastering doesn't generally pay four times that of 2k mastering, it becomes an economic issue as well. Second, 4k data can't be moved fast enough to maintain the level of interactivity and feedback of 2k pipelines. Many systems can play 2k images in real time, whereas they can't play 4k images at that speed. While it may be possible to view 2k proxies and apply changes to the 4k source data, this approach, to some extent, defeats the purpose of using 4k images.

In the march of progress, 4k pipelines will become more feasible and therefore more available. However, it's likely that this change will be brought about by improved technology rather than the desires of distributors.

13.2 FUTURE DI PIPELINES

Changes will be made to existing pipelines, and new work flows and methods will be developed to take advantage of the improved technology and the new features. It may well be that the industry changes from being facility-based to a more production-centric approach: digital intermediate teams will be freelance, and they'll be assembled for a specific production. All the necessary equipment will be leased for the duration of the production as opposed to the current trend of facilities providing all the services for the production. It may be that the large studios will establish their own digital intermediate departments and will use those departments for every production they produce.

New work flows should help to better standardize the process—such as by introducing well-defined QC chains throughout each production and possibly even tagging every shot with information (i.e., metadata) that's updated throughout the process.

13.2.1   Storage Devices

One problem with digital storage devices is that they aren't intrinsically visual. A piece of film can be placed on a lightbox, or even simply held in front of a light, to display its content. A video can be put into a VCR for convenient viewing on a television or video monitor. With a digital image, it must first be copied across to a suitable system and then viewed on a monitor using an appropriate software package. This requirement makes it very difficult to quickly identify the contents of a tape backup that was made a few weeks previously. Of course, some asset management systems can maintain thumbnail images of the contents of different storage devices, but such systems (i.e., ones capable of storing the thumbnail images) can't always be accessed. Instead, it's possible that the storage devices themselves will be able to display content.

This functionality is already possible with lower-capacity portable storage devices. For example, the Archos AV4100 (www.archos.com) is able to (among other things) store and display 100GB of images. Of course, this product isn't necessarily designed for storing the images typically used in a digital intermediate environment, and it's much more expensive than a regular 100GB portable disk drive. In time, however, other storage manufacturers may follow Archos's lead.

Alternatively, such devices can be used to maintain the reference material of all the rushes. After a scene has been shot and transferred to a digital format, it can be copied, compressed, and placed on the device. Filmmakers can then use the device to check rushes, or perhaps even rough cuts, while away from the screening rooms.

13.2.2   Portability

As technology improves, it tends to shrink as well. Smaller equipment is more portable and therefore can be used on the set. This situation, in turn, gives rise to accessing new options during filming. First of all, more immediate feedback is available. A colorist can apply quick grades to some of the footage, which may help determine whether complex shots should be relit and rephotographed to obtain higher-quality results. The same is true of any other aspect of the digital

FIGURE 13-6   The Archos AV4100 can be used as a model for more visual data storage devices

intermediate process—effects can be applied to shots for quick pre-views, and the footage QCd (or quality checked) for problems. Of course, the fast pace of most production sets may prevent the use of such work flows because they could slow down the production, but at least, the option will be available.

13.2.3   Ease of Use

As advances to the hardware are made over time, the software and the various component's user interfaces have also improved. Each new version of a particular software product tends to bring about improvements aimed at a wider audience, and the new product is usually easier to operate than previous versions were, making it possible for crew members to be trained to learn certain aspects of a system. At the least, images and other digital media can be easily displayed on the set, without requiring specific operators to perform this process.

Other equipment will be introduced that provides more intuitive interaction with digital media. For example, Wacom's Cintiq graphics tablet (www.wacom.com) enables the user to interact with a computer system simply by drawing on the screen with a stylus.

13.3 DISTRIBUTION

One of the most important aspects of creating moving pictures is ensuring people can see them. At the present time, films are distributed to cinemas, made available for rental, sold on DVD, and even broadcast on TV and airplanes. Other types of productions may be shown on television or the Internet. Industry developments may bring about new methods and types of distribution and may make existing distribution methods more accessible.

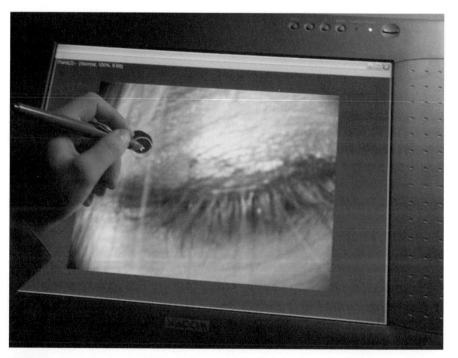

FIGURE 13-7   Wacom's Cintiq product range makes for a very intuitive interface device

13.3.1 Digital Cinema

Perhaps the next significant change to the industry will be the widespread adoption of digital cinema. At the moment, digital cinemas are rare, and so outputting to a digital cinema format is not often requested. Probably the most established body in this area, the Digital Cinema Initiative (DCI), a cinema distributor consortium is in the process of compiling guidelines for the digital cinema format. These guidelines will cover compression, frame rates, and image sizes. (For information on these guidelines, refer to the Appendix.) Once these specifications have been finalized and published, a natural shift in many digital intermediate pipelines will occur to better accommodate them, more so once digital cinema starts to gain prominence.[3]

Creation of output for digital cinema involves taking the digital source master, created at the end of the digital intermediate process, and using it to create a digital cinema package (DCP) that combines visual, aural, and verbal components within a compressed, encrypted data set. The facility creating the digital intermediate (and hence the digital source master) may be capable of creating the DCP, or perhaps an external facility can use the digital source master to create the DCP.

Once completed, the DCP is ready for duplication, and then it's transported, using physical media, satellite feeds, or networking as required, to each cinema. It may then be combined with other elements, such as forthcoming trailers and advertisements, into a playlist, which can be displayed.

13.3.2 Internet Distribution

The Internet is bound to become an important distribution channel in the long-term. Right now, each user's average bandwidth is too limited to transmit footage of acceptable quality in a reasonable time. The problem is complicated somewhat by the fact that transmis-

---

[3] At the time of writing, Ireland announced plans to install approximately 500 digital projectors in cinemas throughout the country, becoming the first country to actively adopt digital cinema; current estimates predict that the majority of DCI-compliant cinemas should be ready during 2006 or 2007.

sion speed tends to vary, making it difficult to accomplish real-time playback from a server. Other pitfalls will be encountered, too: footage has to be encoded to work specifically with different playback software that users may or may not have, and no one is entirely sure how to effectively prevent material from being pirated. However, for some, these issues aren't important—the casual user, creating freely viewable content for a website, isn't concerned about pirated copies, nor is such a user troubled by the fact that certain people may not be able to view the encoded footage.

One benefit of using Internet distribution methods is that it allows schedule-independent viewing. At present, cinemas are efficient only when every screening is fully booked. To improve the odds of this happening, each film is shown according to demand. Popular films are shown regularly, even on multiple screens. But from the audience's point of view, a moviegoer may want to see a less-popular film, and such films are shown at inconvenient times (which, then, of course, results in the film becoming even less popular and a vicious circle ensues). Similarly, television broadcasts are programmed for specific times, so when viewers miss a broadcast (and they didn't set their VCR to record it), they won't get to see it. With the Internet, on the other hand, this issue becomes much easier to deal with. The program is always available to watch, and requires resources only when it's being watched (aside from the space required on the distribution server), making it a far more efficient distribution method. Further, programs on the Internet are accessible within the home, which provides an added layer of convenience.[4]

New developments are also improving the speed of data distribution across the Internet. For example, the Bittorrent protocol improves speed during high-traffic periods by using a data-swarming approach. When many users access a single file, rather than each of them transferring it from a single location (which places a lot of strain on the originating server and significantly slows transmission), the users access parts of the file from other users. With very popular files, the transmission rate may even be higher than the maximum bandwidth of the originating server. Moreover, such a system is easily implemented, with freely available systems such as Downhill Battle's Blog

---

[4] The Internet loves to count things too, so accurate statistical information, such as how many times a particular production has been watched, can be easily obtained.

Torrent (www.blogtorrent.com), which features a simple means of installation on any website.

Internet distribution probably won't mature until it becomes more accessible to the casual user. Therefore, for example, set-top boxes that can connect to the Internet will simplify the downloading and playback processes. However, it's unlikely that the average user bandwidth is going to be increased dramatically any time soon, which means that material must either be of low quality to be played as soon as it's requested, or that higher-quality material takes several hours to transmit before the user can view it. Sony has recently announced plans to create a downloadable service, whereby people can pay for films to be downloaded to their cell phones, which may well serve to kick-start a whole new era of distribution.

13.4   THE BUSINESS MODEL

Many individuals involved in establishing independent facilities specializing in the digital intermediate process want to know how to make it work from an economic standpoint. The only real need for independent digital intermediate facilities at the present time is for producing telecines, feature films, online videos (perhaps) and for converting video to film. These processes require specialized equipment and technical expertise. The facilities can usually handle, rather easily, other pipelines and other aspects of establishing independent facilities.

The paradox is, of course, that such equipment and expertise costs a great deal of money, and thus it's difficult to price competitively to recover working costs, particularly when, as with feature film production, it isn't a strictly essential process (at least not until the rise of digital cinema). However, money can be made, and income may be generated from by-products of the process, rather than the sale of the digital intermediate process.

13.4.1   Visual Effects

Many facilities that offer a digital intermediate process also have separate visual effects departments for compositing and animation (this also applies to the use of optical effects and retouching processes). A production that selects a particular facility to do its digital intermediate often ends up also diverting the production of many visual effects shots to the same facility, partly out of convenience but also out of proximity. For example, when certain shots are seen in context for the first time in the digital intermediate environment, the filmmakers may decide that additional effects are required, particularly when they can be produced right down the hall.

13.4.2 Deliverables

One of the most profitable options within the digital intermediate environment is the creation of additional deliverable material. For example, it may cost a great deal of money to digitally master a film and produce a film print for distribution, but additional copies can be produced very quickly, easily, and cheaply. Furthermore, most facilities are equipped to produce video masters (such as HD video versions) with negligible additional expense. And of course, this can be extended to the creation of DVD masters and re-edited versions (such as for television broadcast or airlines). On the other hand, distributors tend to budget separately for each deliverable format, so a facility supplying all the relevant formats should just about break even. Incidentally, deliverable requirements can also involve the production of theatrical trailers, which are typically comprised of elements that have already been scanned and finished in the final product. Therefore, creating trailers simply requires re-editing and outputting.

Finally, once digital cinema becomes more prominent, creating separate digital cinema packages may be required for each production. A facility could specialize in DCP creation for projects that have undergone a digital intermediate process elsewhere, or even for those that haven't. These projects may only require being transferred and prepared for digital projection.

13.4.3 Digital Dailies

With suitably equipped facilities, every recorded frame can be digitized as soon as it's available. This capability makes it possible for digital "rushes" (or digital "dailies") to be generated, so that all the footage requiring editing and viewing can be copied and output to any required formats. This capability will eventually accelerate the digital intermediate process, and produce images of higher quality. In addition, original material will be less likely to become damaged (because it will be handled less).

The problem is that the facility in question must have adequate storage space (around ten times the space required by a cut-together production) to accomplish this process, because most scanned material is never used. In addition, the production will occupy this space for a much longer time than it would if it had been transferred after editing was completed. The concept of digital dailies is covered in Chapter 5.

13.4.4 Production Supervision

As filmmakers become more aware of possibilities of a digital intermediate process, there's more of a need for supervision during the production. This supervision must be provided by someone from the digital intermediate facility who can advise the production team as to the available options when the digital intermediate process begins. The supervisor is also needed to ensure that images are lit and shot in a suitable way that enables processing later on.

13.5 SUMMARY

At present, the most immediate problem possibly is the lack of standardization. One way this can be remedied is through the widespread adoption of a common image file format, especially one that is color-space independent, as are several HDR image formats. Tagging each scene and shot with information that can be continuously updated throughout the production will aid the QC process immensely because problems can more easily be traced back to a point of origin. Improved quality of the final output will be produced by generating more masters from the digital source, rather than through the more traditional methods of duplication, which degrade the quality with each generation. These improvements will become more feasible as hardware advances to the point where additional copies can be generated much quicker than they can at present, or as the price of each system decreases so that multiple systems can be used to simultaneously produce output.

Regardless of future changes, the digital intermediate process has a lot of untapped potential for creativity and flexibility, and some of these options are covered in the following chapter.

14

VIRTUAL CINEMATOGRAPHY

As a filmmaker, by deciding early on (ideally during pre-production) that you're going to finish the production using a digital intermediate pipeline, you can gain an incredible advantage. Until recently, most digital intermediates typically were designed as a direct substitute for chemical laboratory processing and didn't take full advantage of the available digital options. But as technology advances, and as filmmakers become more knowledgeable of the various possibilities, digital intermediate pipelines will move toward virtual cinematography.

14.1 WHAT IS VIRTUAL CINEMATOGRAPHY?

Many definitions of "virtual cinematography" describe it as the ability to create a shot or sequence entirely with a computer, using a number of digitally created elements to compose it. However, it's much more than that. It's a paradigm for shooting to maximize the range of options afforded by a digital pipeline during post-production. Or, to put it another way, virtual cinematography enables filmmakers to make creative cinematography decisions during editing, rather than having to commit to those decisions when shooting. This level of control can vary from making simple lighting adjustments to potentially altering camera placement after shooting, techniques demonstrated in films such as *The Matrix* trilogy.

Why would you want to do this? Because it means that a scene can be lit in a much simpler (and therefore faster and less-expensive) way and then later, tweaked to the same aesthetic level when far more time is available (and external factors are less influential), and, in some cases, with an unprecedented level of control.

The downside is that many lighting strategies work extremely well when used practically (on the set), and they don't have a simple digital equivalent. Second, many cinematographers are much more comfortable creating a lighting effect when shooting rather than estimating how the effect might look at a later date. Further, the purpose of creative lighting is to evoke a sense of mood within the scene. It's reasonable to assume, therefore, this sense of mood is transferred directly into an actor's performance on set.[1]

In many cases, however, the advantages of digital cinematography far outweigh the disadvantages. Take, for instance, the stylized "bleach bypass" chemical-processing effect. In a bleach-bypass process, the silver halide crystals aren't removed from the film negative during development. The net effect is that a monochrome layer (the silver crystals) is superimposed over the color image. When printed, the picture benefits from increased contrast and reduced saturation. In the digital intermediate, this process can be emulated by simply reducing saturation and ramping up the contrast at the color-correction stage. However, the process can also be taken much further in the digital realm than its chemical counterpart. First, the level of the bleach-bypass effect can be adjusted. Digital colorists have complete and independent control over both the level of contrast, and the level of image saturation. In the traditional process, it's possible to limit the bleach-bypass effect to some degree by adjusting the ratio and timings of the chemical baths, but it can't be achieved with the

---

[1] This phenomenon has been witnessed on several occasions; actors often give better performances on the physical set than in front of a green screen.

same level of accuracy and the interactive feedback of digital systems. Second, the effect can be applied selectively—that is, to a specific part of an image—in the digital process. With a digital grading system, different grades can be applied to selected areas of the image and adjusted over time. With a chemical process, selective grading requires extensive masking and duplication processes, which can reduce the image quality and lack the accuracy of the digital equivalent (to say nothing of being extremely difficult to do). A digital system, on the other hand, can produce a bleach-bypass effect limited to a single part of a shot, such as a single character or part of the background, processes that are either unachievable or else highly difficult with chemical processes.

Ultimately, when embarking on a virtual cinematography methodology, it's imperative to know in advance the techniques that can, and those that can't, be replicated accurately and easily later. This chapter attempts to cover many of the more common strategies, as well as to outline some yet unexploited effects that are possible with a digital pipeline.

THE LIMIT OF FACILITIES

Up until recently, facilities and post-production houses that offer a digital intermediate service don't cater to the virtual cinematographer. The majority of the digital intermediate market has offered an equivalent of a lab process that focuses almost exclusively on providing more comprehensive grading and mastering services than provided by chemical labs. It's somewhat ironic that the market has overlooked many real strengths of a digital pipeline, but then the industry is still in its infancy. The primary concern has been the accuracy and integrity of matching monitor color to film projection color. Presumably this focus will shift as the potential of virtual cinematography is realized.

14.2 DIGITAL PRE-PRODUCTION

The majority of productions begin with a script. And the majority of those scripts are written using (or at least exist on) computer systems.

Interestingly, what happens next is that the scripts are printed onto paper, with hundreds of copies handed to various people, pages updated as necessary, notes scribbled on them, requiring careful, meticulous tracking of exactly which copy of a given page of the script is the correct, up-to-date one. A lot can be said for paper, especially when comparing it to using computer systems. Paper doesn't run out of power, it's easy to modify, and it doesn't randomly crash at the most inconvenient time. In fact, many pre-production phases are achieved almost entirely without the use of any digital systems.

However, a good case can be made for keeping at least part of the pre-production phase digital: collaboration. Take the script, for example. The most up-to-date, complete version can be stored digitally, accessible to those who need it. Updating the script can notify all the recipients of the changes straight away, highlighting them, possibly with notes as to why particular changes were made. Older versions can be archived, available when needed for reference. During shooting, more notes can be added to the script, notes describing dropped shots or camera notes about particular takes. Further down the line, the script can be fed into editing systems, allowing editors to more efficiently organize shots and assemble sequences. When outputting, lines of dialog can be extracted from the script and used to generate captions.

The same is true for other pre-production material, such as storyboards (which can be scanned and used as placeholders for shots in the editing system). Furthermore, digital "pre-visualization" systems can test shots and create lighting plans before shooting begins.

14.2.1 Pre-Visualization

Pre-visualization encompasses the use of storyboard sketches to plan shots and directions in an iconic format, resulting in a plan of a film that closely resembles a comic book. With the use of a digital system, it's also possible to compose "animatics"—animated storyboards that impart a sense of motion as well as composition and framing. Many filmmakers create animatics by using cheap cameras to shoot test scenes, and then they roughly cut them together for appraisal.

With the use of computer-generated material, 3D shots involving simple or complex cinematography can be planned in advance, taking into consideration such factors as set design, costume, and lighting. Software such as Antics Technology's Antics (www.antics3d.com) enables the filmmaker to quickly create scene mock-ups, complete with furnishings and virtual actors and then make adjustments to the position of the camera.

Filmmakers may ultimately use a system that includes a variety of pre-visualization—from storyboard sketches, photographs, and video footage, to 3D models created by the visual effects department—to create a visual plan of the film before on-set shooting begins.

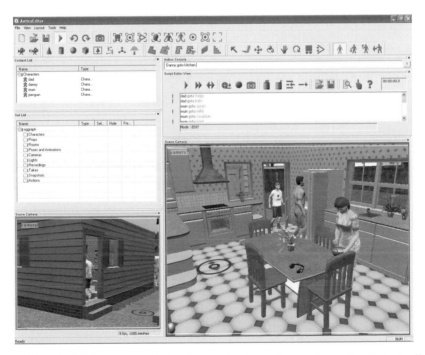

FIGURE 14-1 Antics Technology's Antics Software is a simple but effective previsualization tool that enables you to position actors, cameras, and other elements before you begin shooting

14.3   SHOOTING DIGITALLY

There are many advantages to recording to a digital format as opposed to analog ones, such as video or film. The most obvious advantage is the easy transfer of material when using a digital intermediate pipeline, allowing immediate editing and copying of footage.

Many additional benefits are available. When you shoot a scene digitally, you can monitor the footage with much greater flexibility than with other means. Multiple copies of the camera output can potentially be viewed simultaneously and across great distances. In addition, a number of analytical processes can be run to check the output for potential problems. Systems such as Serious Magic's DV Rack (www.seriousmagic.com) provide a whole host of monitoring options, such as vectorscopes, waveform monitors, and audio monitors to run as software modules that intercept recorded data. This process costs a great deal less, and the result occupies much less space than its real-world counterparts.

Prolonged recording is also possible. When you're recording straight to a central server, the recording can continue until the disks are full, which may take several hours, depending upon the system's capacity.[2]

FILM VS. VIDEO AS CAPTURE MEDIA

The question of whether to shoot on film or video is quite an old debate. Historically, it's an easy question to answer: if you want your production to be shown in a cinema, you should shoot on film. Even when the aim isn't a cinema release, shooting on film and then transferring to video can result in superior quality images than if you just shoot on video. However, this process tends to be somewhat more expensive.

With a digital intermediate environment, and with the current prevalence of HD video cameras, the debate has become re-

(continues)

---

[2] Most digital-imaging systems record to removable digital media at present and frequently must be replaced.

energized. On paper at least, HD video has many of the same characteristics as film. Sony's HDCAM SR video format is uncompressed, meaning that it captures a wide range of color with a high level of precision, and its working resolution is very close to that of 2k film. In addition, it can record scenes in a logarithmic color space, which provides a response to light that's similar to film. Another obvious benefit is the ease of transferring any video format to a digital intermediate pipeline (compared to the difficulty of transferring film), and conforming using timecodes is much easier. Finally, much effort (and money) can be saved by not having to process entire reels to remove dust and scratches.

The difficulty of replacing film with any video format is that many filmmakers simply enjoy working with film. A quality issue is involved as well. 35mm film is thought to have an inherent resolution of at least 4k. Therefore, until video cameras can capture the same level of detail, film will simply look much sharper. Coupled with this consideration is the fact that video pixels are regularly arranged rectangles, whereas film is made up of randomly shaped grains, which are much easier on the eye and create the illusion of even greater resolution.

14.3.1 Photographic Emulation Filters

Certain shot setups and certain lighting effects require different photographic filters, or chemical processes. Many of these filters and processes can be successfully replicated digitally. Some can be emulated to some degree, and some are impossible to achieve without hiring a team of visual effects artists (and even then, they may not be possible). If you know that you definitely want a specific effect, then it's probably a good idea to shoot it that way on the set. If you want more creative control later, or it will take too long to set up the shot, then it's probably best to assume that you're going to do it later. But it's always best to get the post-production facility to provide test examples of the kinds of effects you want to achieve, so that you can make a more informed decision.

FIGURE 14-2   Serious Magic's DV Rack offers a vast array of video tools that can be accessed with a single laptop

It's also worth noting that many digital filters can be used with extreme parameters, or in conjunction with others, to create altogether new cinematographic effects, such as applying a barrel distortion effect and then a star-burst effect. It's also worth noting that some filters are impossible to replicate digitally. For example, a polarizing filter works with incoming light (i.e., filtering out light of certain polarity), which is impossible to reconstruct from a photographed image.

FIGURE 14-3 A polarizing filter can be used to polarize the incoming light in an image (see also the Color Insert)

FIGURE 14-4 Without using the filter when shooting, it's impossible to re-create the effect of polarizing the light (see also the Color Insert)

The Appendix contains a list of common digital filters and their availability and ease of use when compared to practical filters.

14.3.2 Panoramic Images

Panoramic images cover a wide field of view. There's a very subtle difference between a panoramic image and one that simply has a wide aspect ratio (e.g., anamorphically squeezed images). Panoramic images might have an 180-degree field of view, whereas a wide aspect ratio image has a much narrower horizontal field of view, and the vertical field of view is narrower still.

Panoramic images are created either by using an optical system with a very wide-angle lens or by using multiple cameras. The problem with using an optical system is that the images suffer from optical distortion. It's possible to correct the distortion, but the result is often a poor-quality image. When using multiple cameras, they are positioned so that each overlaps the others by some amount. The shots are then combined digitally to form a complete image, correcting for differences in exposure and scale. This technique has been used for a long time in digital photography, but it can be applied to moving pictures as well.

14.3.3 Stereoscopy

"Stereoscopy" (or "stereoscopic imaging") is a photographic method that creates the illusion of a 3D image. When you see a 3D image, your left eye receives one image, while your right receives another image, taken from a slightly different viewpoint. Many different techniques can be used to create stereoscopic images, but the most practical one for moving pictures is recording a scene with to two identical cameras positioned slightly apart (or using a special stereoscopic camera that comprises two lenses).[3]

---

[3] The separation distance between the two lenses determines the apparent depth of the scene when viewed, with the optimum result obtained when the distance is 1/30 of the distance of the closest object to the lens.

FIGURE 14-5 Multiple images can be combined digitally to form a panorama

Presenting the image to the viewer is somewhat trickier. The best results are obtained when each member of the audience wears special goggles that project the images directly into their eyes. A much cheaper method is to rely on "anaglyphs." Anaglyphs are composite images, with one image put through a red filter, and the other through a green or blue one. The viewer then wears eyeglasses that have a red filter over one eye and a green filter over the other, corresponding to each viewpoint's color. Although the eyeglasses are fairly cheap and the composite images are easy to generate, especially in a digital environment, the viewer sees a monochromatic image.

An alternative option is to use polarized light, where each image is separately projected onto a screen, using two projectors, each of which polarizes the light in a different way. The viewer wears eyeglasses with polar filters over each eye that block the light from the projector. A new advancement of this technique is to use a special cellophane layer over a laptop or cell phone screen to separate the screen into two halves and polarize each half separately.

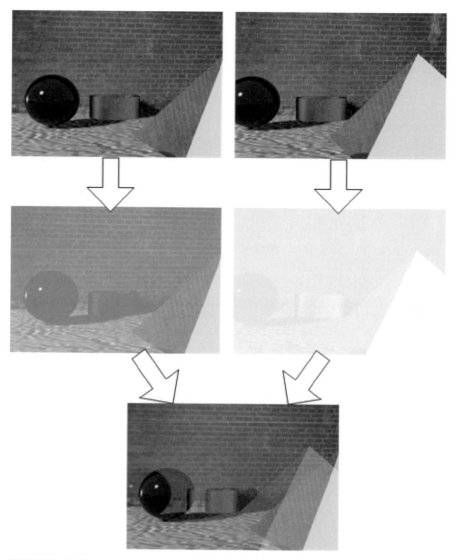

FIGURE 14-6   A left/right pair of images can be combined to form a 3D anaglyph
(see also Color Insert)

WIDESCREEN VERSUS FULLSCREEN

One consideration that you might have to make during pre-
production is whether to shoot material to a "widescreen" format (e.g., 16:9 or 2.35:1 aspect ratio) or to shoot to a "fullscreen"

(continues)

format (4:3 aspect ratio). From a cinematography perspective, the decision affects the shot composition and a whole host of other choices that you will make. But within the digital intermediate, the distinction is somewhat irrelevant. Widescreen images can be cropped to create fullscreen ones, and vice versa. It's important to use the option that makes best use of the picture area. If you shoot a widescreen format on 35mm film, for example, it's best to compose the shot at the aspect ratio you desire, but you might as well expose the top and bottom of the image because doing so has no disadvantages. The extra image information you get by making these exposures may be useful in other ways, particularly if the production has to be panned and scanned to produce a widescreen version later on.

Clearly, one deciding factor is the intended output format. People with widescreen televisions prefer to watch fullscreen content cropped top and bottom rather than letterboxed left and right, and people with traditional televisions prefer to watch widescreen productions cropped left and right rather than

FIGURE 14-7   Shooting in 16:9 but protecting the 4:3 area. © 2005 Andrew Francis

(continues)

WIDESCREEN VERSUS FULLSCREEN *(continued)*

letterboxed top and bottom. For this reason it's important to consider the widescreen composition within a fullscreen frame, and vice versa—a process referred to as "shoot and protect."

FIGURE 14-8   Shooting in 4:3 but protecting the 16:9 area. © 2005 Andrew Francis

14.3.4   Depth Recording

Without a doubt, the single most important advancement to digital production will be the ability to capture depth (i.e., distance from the lens) information from the camera. This capability will open up a multitude of possibilities, as well as make compositing much easier. Elements can be isolated far more intelligently than with the existing methods of rotoscoping, keying, and tracking. It will be possible to enhance the sense of parallax (i.e., the illusion of distant objects moving slower than closer ones) and will provide a new range of effects. Atmospheric effects such as fog, lighting, and shadows can be applied much easier with more convincing results than by using existing methods.

At the present time, there's no reliable system for capturing a scene's depth information. Part of the problem is that depth must be captured through the same lens that's used to photograph the scene to ensure that the depth information corresponds to the captured image. The capturing of depth information must occur at the same moment as the image is photographed; otherwise, motion artifacts are introduced. Further, for best results, the resolution of the depth information has to be almost equal to the image resolution.

With photography, it's very difficult to record depth information to this degree. The closest method to achieving it is recording stereoscopic images and then processing them, using numerous mathematical operations to extract depth information for each frame.

With computer-generated 3D images, the depth information is already available and can be encoded as an extra channel for later extraction. For example, Autodesk's 3D Studio Max (www.discreet.com) software can encode such depth information in the image, which can then later be extracted and used in conjunction with certain effects, as seen in Chapter 10.

14.3.5 Virtual Sets

Chroma-key backdrops have been used in productions for many years. A foreground element (such as an actor or object) is positioned in front of a background of solid color (such as a blue screen or green screen) and photographed. Special chroma-key software or hardware is then used to remove the background, which makes it possible to position the foreground elements in front of completely different footage. This process is easier to describe than to do, however; creating an end result that looks natural requires a great deal of planning, and skilled compositors are needed to seamlessly blend the background and foreground elements.

This relatively simple concept can be expanded dramatically to a "virtual set" paradigm, whereby the entire scene, except for foreground elements, is created artificially (either from stock footage or computer-generated material). Such virtual sets may be less expensive to film than hiring real ones, and virtual sets are especially popular with low-budget or corporate productions. Other films, such as *Sky Captain, The World of Tomorrow*, and *Sin City*, use virtual sets to achieve more stylistic control. For example, *Sin City* filmed certain scenes in front of a green screen so foreground elements would have a colorful appearance, while the backgrounds could look more *film noir*, as they were drawn in the original comic book series.

SHOOTING CHROMA KEY

Chroma key is traditionally the domain of the visual effects department; however, it can be a useful tool to any filmmaker and is quite simple to do properly. More adventurous cinematographers might choose to integrate chroma-key elements into a scene for the purpose of adding grading effects later on. For instance, painting a wall in bright green allows easy chroma-keying of the wall later on, and therefore, any color can be assigned to it during grading.

When shooting for chroma key, you are separating foreground elements (those elements, such as the actors, you want to keep in the shot) from the background (the area that effectively becomes transparent). Successful shooting for chroma can be achieved by following a few simple rules: Any bright color can serve as a "key." It's a myth that blue or green make the best chroma-key colors; most digital chroma-keyers will accept any color as a key.

- Choose a key color that doesn't appear in any foreground elements to any degree. One reason that chroma keys tend to be blue or green is that skin tones contain a lot of red coloring but very little blue or green.

- Light the background as evenly and strongly as possible (but expose as if you were lighting foreground elements). The lighting should always be objectively verified, for example, with a light meter. Similarly, no shadows should be on the background.

- The physical distance between the chroma key and the foreground elements should be as great as possible. This distance will reduce the effects of "spill" (e.g., light reflected from the chroma key reflects off the foreground elements, contaminating them with colored light).

(continues)

- All foreground elements should be as sharp as possible to ensure that the chroma-keyer can extract a hard edge later; otherwise, the foreground elements will have a colored edge, contaminated by the chroma key's color. You may have to select an exposure and a lens combination that affords a high depth of field.

- Use an imaging device with high resolving power to help produce a good, hard edge on finely detailed areas, such as hair. It is also vital to use an imaging device that does not perform any color compression on the image.

- Avoid any reflective material in the foreground because this material may pick up reflected light from the chroma key.

- Compose the foreground elements in the center of the shot, so they're completely surrounded by the chroma key. Doing so will provide greater flexibility when compositing the shot, which will allow the foreground elements to be repositioned anywhere on the screen, except where a foreground object crosses the edge of the screen when shooting.

- Be aware of the usable picture area. In a typical chroma-key shot, you can imagine an area, such as a square, enveloping the desired elements. Everything in this area should be surrounded by the chroma key (and no foreground elements should stray from this area). Anything outside this area can be ignored (e.g., bits of scaffolding or crew members) because they will be cropped out.

- The camera should not show any movement. Integrating camera movement into a chroma-key shot invariably involves using a motion-control camera or, at the very least, tracking markers. Otherwise, the shot becomes subject to the effects of parallax.

- Ultimately, remember that you want a solid area of a single color (i.e., "single color" is defined much more stringently than being "perceptually the same").

14.4 DIGITAL POST-PRODUCTION

This book has covered many of the techniques that are frequently used in all sorts of digital post-production environments, from the application of effects and titles to color grading. But there are more techniques that haven't been fully exploited.

14.4.1 Image-based Lighting

In 3D computer animation, one of the ultimate goals is to create a "photo-realistic" rendering of a scene, one with accurate lighting and surface interaction. One way to achieve this is to use a physical model for the interaction of light on surfaces, such as "radiosity." With certain implementations of this technique, it's possible to use an image of the lighting in a real-world scene (for example, an HDR image of a reflective sphere within a scene), which then becomes the basis for a "map" of the scene's lighting.

With this approach, different images can be used within the same scene to create different effects. For example, it's possible to use a lighting map obtained from a nightclub, or one from a rain forest, to produce different lighting effects in the scene. At the present time, this functionality is rarely seen in the digital intermediate environment, but perhaps one day, it will be possible to just load in images of lit environments and apply them to shot footage to quickly generate appearances for the footage.

MAKING VIDEO LOOK (MORE) LIKE FILM

No technique can make video footage, especially formats such as DV, look as the scene would look if it were originally shot on film. The best you can hope for is the scene looking as if were shot on film and then telecined to video. The distinction is important because the majority of video formats are so limited in such factors as dynamic range and color space (not to mention resolution), that they can't possibly compete with film.

(continues)

As always, the best option is to shoot whenever possible on film in the first place. If it's not possible, you can shoot a scene with a video camera and then run processes on it to make it look more like film.

Several so-called "film look" software packages may work but are either so simple that they can't be used for every situation (or they look artificial), or are too complicated to be used to optimum effect.

The following tips serve as a starting point for making your video look more like film:

- Choose certain options during shooting. Make sure the scene is well lit and properly exposed. Turn off automatic exposure and automatic focus options because they aren't normally available on film cameras, and sudden changes in exposure or focus look artificial. Disable any digital filtering options (e.g., digital sharpening). Open the aperture as wide as possible. Video cameras require less light than film to be properly exposed, meaning that film footage tends to have a much shallower depth of field than the equivalent video image. To compensate for a wider aperture, the video camera has to increase the shutter speed, producing less motion blur on each frame, although it can be simulated later.

- Take reference stills of the scene using a photographic camera with the same settings that are on the video camera. The developed pictures can help match colors later.

- Capture the footage to a set of frames, using an uncompressed, 10-bit format.

- Deinterlace the footage according to the requirements of the video system.

- Color-grade the footage, matching the digital image to the reference photograph.

(continues)

MAKING VIDEO LOOK (MORE) LIKE FILM (*continued*)

- Filter the result to remove noise, sharpen edges, and add grain.

- Speed-change the result to 24fps. If possible, use a method that combines a speed change with motion blurring.

- Stabilize the result if necessary.

14.4.2 Virtualized Reality

"Virtualized reality" is a method of repositioning cameras after footage has been shot. The premise is that you film a scene using numerous fixed (and identical) cameras. Later, the data from each camera can be collated and interpolated (in terms of space and time) to re-create the position of a camera at any time. Using such a system is similar to working with 3D animated scenes, where cameras can move to any position at any time, following paths that are impractical or even impossible to follow with real cameras. Currently, the technology is in its infancy, although it was used to a limited degree in filming the 2001 Superbowl. In this production, a number of carefully positioned cameras were used to create dynamic replays across the pitch. Similar effects have been created in films such as *The Matrix* trilogy, which used multiple cameras firing in sequence to create a camera move in very slow motion (a technique also referred to as "timeslicing"). All virtualized reality shots require careful planning and elaborate setups, and thus they are mainly for special-purpose effects. However, as the technology develops, we may see more productions take advantage of the benefits, perhaps to the degree that cranes and tracks are needed less during filming.

THE LINE BETWEEN VISUAL EFFECTS AND THE DIGITAL INTERMEDIATE

It's important to remember that the digital intermediate team generally doesn't share the same skill set (or equipment) as dedicated visual effects artists. With time, the definition of "visual

(continues)

effect" (and therefore the requirement of a specifically trained artist to implement it) will be more complex. In addition, the expectations of the digital intermediate pipeline's potential will also be more complex. As noted earlier, the current trend is that colorists are becoming more knowledgeable of editing operations, so that they can make on-the-spot adjustments during grading, if needed. Another trend is editors knowing more about visual effects, from compositing elements together, to manipulating and animating 3D data. So the questions are: what constitutes a visual effect requiring a dedicated team outside of the digital intermediate environment, and what should be expected from digital intermediate artists?

First, a team of visual effects artists are required to create highly complicated, and/or time-consuming visual effects. More often than not, it depends upon the discretion of the facility to define these boundaries, but in general, the following rules of thumb determine what constitutes a visual effects shot:

- **Creating from scratch.** This includes inserting new objects into a scene; it also includes replacing (or even "rebuilding") an element of a shot, such as repairing heavy damage to a range of frames (e.g., a tear in a piece of film).

- **Character animation.** Animating in 2D or 3D to imbue an element with a sense of "personality."

- **Complicated tracking effects.** Tracking moving features can vary in complexity. However, trying to track subtle movements, or partially or wholly obscured features, or attempting to replicate effects such as motion blur, are best left to specialized compositors.

- **Changing a fundamental characteristic of a shot.** For instance, altering the motion of a moving object independent of other elements (or adjusting the motion of the camera) or changing the composition of elements in a shot.

14.5 SHOOTING FOR THE DIGITAL INTERMEDIATE

In general, shooting for a digital intermediate pipeline is analogous to shooting in other ways. However, a number of techniques can be used to maximize the efficiency of the process down the line with the current, commonly-available tools.

- Shoot at the highest possible quality. The quality of the source material translates directly into the quality of the final production. Even VHS video masters look better when they originate from 35mm film material rather than VHS footage.
- Maximize the contrast ratio of every scene. Doing so ensures more data to work with during the digital intermediate process.
- Get as much color onscreen as possible. Colors can be changed to a degree during digital grading, but having strong colors in original footage makes it easier to pull "keys" for different elements to make adjustments. Be aware of "spill" from overly bright colors, which may reflect onto other surfaces. Even if the shot is destined to be a black-and-white image, shooting color actually provides greater control over the look of the final image because of the ability to selectively mix the red, green, and blue color channels individually to provide a monochrome image.
- Concentrate on the scene's action. The performance is one of the most critical elements of a production, and it's also one of the only elements that can't be adjusted during post-production.
- Get correct exposure and focus. Good exposure translates into higher-quality source images and reduces the level of noise in the final output. Focusing can't be easily corrected; although digital-sharpening techniques are available, they don't compare to a correctly focused image and, in some cases, do more harm than good. If a shot is destined to be out of focus, sometimes it's best to shoot in focus and use digital defocusing tools later.
- Avoid the use of photographic filters. Many filters, particularly color ones, can be replicated digitally, although some filters (such as polarizing filters) have no digital equivalent. Unnecessary use of photographic filters may limit options later.
- Keep shots steady. Although digital-stabilization processes can correct a little bit of wobble in the footage, they degrade the image to some degree and, at the very least, result in some cropping of the image.

- Fill the maximum shooting area. Even when composing shot for a specific region, the extra picture information outside of the "active" picture area can be used for digital processes.
- Keep material in good condition. Although digital restoration is very sophisticated, correcting faults such as dust, scratches, and video dropout is a very laborious process.
- Shoot at a high frame rate to provide more options. With more frames in the source footage, you have more options for retiming, restoration, and even interactive control of effects, such as motion blur, during post-production. Be warned though: a higher frame rate directly equates to higher production costs.
- Keep it wide. It's possible to zoom into shots during post-production to emulate a narrower camera angle but not a wider one. If you have any doubt about the desired focal length of a shot, aim to shoot wider rather than narrower. Beware that digital zooms only work up to a point and can sometimes result in larger film grain and a loss of sharpness. Also, remember to "shoot and protect" where needed (see the preceding section).

14.6 SUMMARY

Currently, the digital intermediate process offers a number of possibilities to the filmmaker. For those comfortable working with film, it offers benefits in editing, effects, and color grading. For those working with video, it provides a complementary process, providing high-quality duplication and a streamlined work flow. And for the more experimental filmmaker, many as yet untapped techniques are available for filming in new and unique ways, imbuing a production with stylization that would be very difficult to achieve through other means and providing more options (and perhaps more time) for experimentation after shooting has completed.

A number of pitfalls must be avoided throughout the digital intermediate process, but knowledge of where things can go wrong and why some things are done the way they are, combined with careful planning, can result in higher-quality, more controllable, and possibly more stylized results. To paraphrase one of the digital intermediate producers I've worked with, "The digital intermediate isn't just a process; it's a complementary art."

APPENDIX: REFERENCE SOURCE

A.1 VIDEO-DATA SIZES

The following table lists common video formats, their specifications, and standard, and the parameters of their equivalent digital counterparts.

TABLE 1

Format	Resolution	Frame rate	Field order	Sampling	Bandwidth	Compression	Image aspect ratio	Precision	Native digital resolution	Pixel aspect ratio
HD Digital										
HDCAM SR	1080	23.98p, 24p, 29.97p, 30p, 50i, 59.94i	Upper first	4:4:4 (log or linear)	880 Mb/s	4.2:1 (MPEG-4)	16:9	10-bit	1920 × 1080	1.0
HDCAM SR	1080	23.98p, 24p, 29.97p, 30p, 50i, 59.94i	Upper first	4:2:2	440Mb/s	2.7:1 (MPEG-4)	16:9	10-bit	1920 × 1080	1.0
HDCAM	1080	24p, 25p, 30p, 50i, 60i	Upper first	3:1:1	143Mb/s	7.1:1	16:9	8-bit	1440 × 1080	1.33
HDD5	1080	24p, 25p, 30p, 50i, 60i	Upper first	4:2:2	250Mb/s	4:1	16:9	8-bit	1920 × 1080	1.0
HDD5	1080	24p, 25p, 30p, 50i, 60i	Upper first	4:2:2	250Mb/s	5:1	16:9	10-bit	1920 × 1080	1.0
DVCPRO HD100	1080	60i, 50i, 60p	Lower first	4:2:2	100Mb/s	6.7:1	16:9	8-bit	1440 × 1080	1.33
DVCPRO HD100	720	59.94i, 59.94p	Lower first	4:2:2	100Mb/s	6.7:1	16:9	8-bit	1280 × 720	1.0
HDV	1080	50i, 60i	Upper first	4:2:0	25Mb/s	22.5:1 (MPEG-2)	4:3	8-bit	1440 × 1080	1.0
HDV	720	25p, 30p	n/a	4:2:0	25Mb/s	22.5:1 (MPEG-2)	16:9	8-bit	1280 × 720	1.0
SD Digital										
Digital8 (NTSC)	525	29.97	Lower first	4:1:1	25Mb/s	5:1	4:3	8-bit	720 × 480	0.9

Format	Lines	Frame rate	Field order	Sampling	Bit rate	Compression	Aspect	Bit depth	Resolution	PAR
Digital8 (PAL)	625	25	Lower first	4:2:0	25Mb/s	5:1	4:3	8-bit	720 × 576	1.067
DV25 (NTSC)	525	29.97	Lower first	4:1:1	25Mb/s	5:1	4:3	8-bit	720 × 480	0.9
DV25 (PAL)	625	25	Lower first	4:2:0	25Mb/s	5:1	4:3	8-bit	720 × 576	1.067
DVCAM (NTSC)	525	29.97	Lower first	4:1:1	25Mb/s	5:1	4:3	8-bit	720 × 480	0.9
DVCAM (PAL)	625	25	Lower first	4:2:0	25Mb/s	5:1	4:3	8-bit	720 × 576	1.067
DVCPRO (NTSC)	525	29.97	Lower first	4:1:1	25Mb/s	5:1	4:3	8-bit	720 × 480	0.9
DVCPRO (PAL)	625	25	Lower first	4:1:1	25Mb/s	5:1	4:3	8-bit	720 × 576	1.067
DVCPRO 50	720	29.97	Lower first	4:2:2	50Mb/s	3.3:1	4:3	8-bit	720 × 480	0.9
DVCPRO-P	525	30p	n/a	4:2:0	50Mb/s	5:1	4:3	8-bit	720 × 480	0.9
Betacam SX (NTSC)	525	29.97	Upper first	4:2:2	18Mb/s	10:1 (MPEG-2)	4:3	8-bit	640 × 480	1.0
Betacam SX (PAL)	625	25	Upper first	4:2:2	18Mb/s	10:1 (MPEG-2)	4:3	8-bit	768 × 576	1.0
DVD (NTSC)	525	29.97	Upper first	4:2:0	9.6Mb/s (Max)	Variable (MPEG-2)	4:3	8-bit	720 × 480	0.9
DVD (NTSC)	525	29.97	Upper first	4:2:0	9.6Mb/s (Max)	Variable (MPEG-2)	16:9	8-bit	720 × 480	1.185
DVD (PAL)	625	25	Upper first	4:2:0	9.6Mb/s (Max)	Variable (MPEG-2)	4:3	8-bit	720 × 576	1.067

(continues)

TABLE 1 (*continued*)

Format	Resolution	Frame rate	Field order	Sampling	Band width	Compression	Image aspect ratio	Precision	Native digital resolution	Pixel aspect ratio
DVD (PAL)	625	25	Upper first	4:2:0	9.6Mb/s (Max)	Variable (MPEG-2)	16:9	8-bit	720 × 576	1.69
Digital Betacam (NTSC)	525	29.97	Upper first	4:2:2	8Mb/s	2.3:1	4:3	10-bit	640 × 480	1.0
Digital Betacam (PAL)	625	25	Upper first	4:2:2	8Mb/s	2.3:1	4:3	10-bit	768 × 576	1.0
D1 (NTSC)	525	29.97	Lower first	4:2:2	27Mb/s	1:1	4:3	8-bit	720 × 486	1.0
D1 (PAL)	625	25	Upper first	4:2:2	27Mb/s	1:1	4:3	8-bit	720 × 576	1.067

A.2 FILM-DATA SIZES

The table that follows lists the physical dimensions and equivalent digital sizes of different film formats.

TABLE 2

Format	Width (mm)	Height (mm)	Aspect ratio	Native pixel resolution	Pixel aspect ratio	Approximate file size (@10-bit log)	Approximate bandwidth (@24fps)
16mm	10.26	7.49	1.37	1712 × 1240	1.00	9 MB	216MB/s
Super-16	12.52	7.42	1.69	2048 × 1744	1.00	12MB	288MB/s
Academyaperture	21.94	16.00	1.37	1828 × 1332 (2k) 3656 × 2664 (4k)	1.00	10MB (2k) 39MB (4k)	240MB/s (2k) 936MB/s (4k)
Cinemascope	21.94	18.59	2.35	1828 × 1556 (2k) 3656 × 2664 (4k)	2.00	11MB (2k) 45MB (4k)	264MB/s (2k) 1080MB/s (4k)
Full aperture	24.89	18.67	1.33	2048 × 1556 (2k) 4096 × 3112 (4k)	1.00	13MB (2k) 51MB (4k)	312MB/s (2k) 1224MB/s (4k)
8-perf VistaVision	37.71	25.17	1.5	3072 × 2048 (3k) 6144 × 4096 (6k)	1.00	25MB (3k) 101MB (6k)	600MB/s (3k) 2424MB/s (6k)

A.3 RELATIVE FORMAT QUALITY

The following table is a rule-of-thumb guide to the relative quality of different formats. Some debate is still questioning the quality of HD video compared to 16mm film., Certainly other factors such as compression play a role in the resulting quality of any medium.

Highest quality	IMAX film
	65mm film
	8-perf VistaVision film
	6k digital image
	35mm film
	4k digital image
	2k digital image
	HD video (progressive)
	16mm film
	HD video (interlaced)
	SD digital video (progressive)
	SD digital video (interlaced)
	DVD
	SD analog video
Lowest quality	Internet streaming video

A.4 RELATIVE PICTURE SIZE

The following diagram shows the relative size of different digital formats, by resolution.

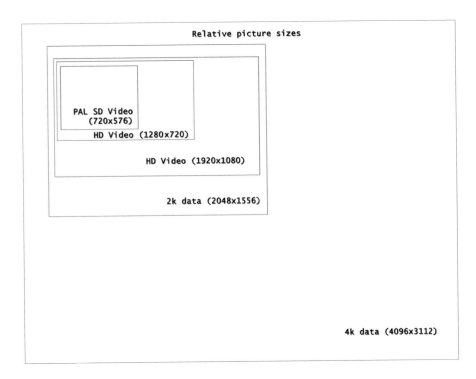

A.5 DATA STORAGE

The following table lists the typical capacity of different storage media. Note that factors such as transfer speed, reliability, and cost should also be considered when choosing a data storage device. In addition, certain formats may require the use of separate readers/writers.

Device	Capacity (GB)	Equivalent NTSC DV footage (mins)	Equivalent 2k/10-bit footage (secs @ 24fps)	Equivalent 4k/10-bit footage (secs @ 24fps)	Quantity required for 100 minutes of DV footage	Quantity required for 100 minutes of 2k footage	Quantity required for 100 minutes of 4k footage
CD-R (74 minute)	0.63	2.9	2.20	0.55	35	2,723	10,890
CD-R (80 minute)	0.68	3.2	2.41	0.60	32	2,490	9,957
DVDR (single layer)	4.7	21.8	16.57	4.14	5	363	1,449
DVDR (dual layer)	8.5	39.4	29.97	7.49	3	201	801
HD-DVD (single layer)	15	69.5	52.89	13.22	2	114	454
HD-DVD (dual layer)	30	138.9	105.79	26.45	1	57	227
Blu-ray disc (single layer)	25	115.8	88.15	22.04	1	69	273
Blu-ray disc (dual layer)	50	231.5	176.31	44.08	1	35	137
Flash disk (1GB)	1	4.6	3.53	0.88	22	1,702	6,807
Flash disk (8GB)	8	37.0	28.21	7.05	3	213	851
Firewire disk (200GB)	200	926.0	705.23	176.31	1	9	35
Firewire disk (500GB)	500	2315.0	1763.09	440.77	1	4	14
Firewire disk (1TB)	1024	4741.1	3610.80	902.70	1	2	7
Sony DTF-1 tape	42	194.5	148.10	37.02	1	41	163
Sony DTF-2 tape	200	926.0	705.23	176.31	1	9	35
DLtape VS1	80	370.4	282.09	70.52	1	22	86
DLtape IV	40	185.2	141.05	35.26	1	43	171
Super-DLtape I	160	740.8	564.19	141.05	1	11	43
Super-DLtape II	300	1389.0	1057.85	264.46	1	6	23

A.6 CHARACTERISTICS OF STILL IMAGE DIGITAL FILE FORMATS

This table lists the specifications for different file formats.

Format	Bit depth (per pixel)	Color model	Compression	Additional features
Adobe Digital Negative (DN6)	Various	Various	Lossy, lossless, or none	Supports all the features of the TIFF specification
Adobe Photoshop	Various	Various	Lossless	Supports image and "adjustment" layers, multiple channels, layer masks, vectors, color profiles, other metadata.
Cineon	30-bit	Log or linear RGB	n/a	Ability to store key numbers.
CompuServe GIF	8-bit	Indexed RGB color	n/a	Supports animation, keyed transparency.
DPX	24-bit or 30-bit	Log or linear RGB	n/a	Ability to store key numbers and timecodes.
DV Stream	24-bit	YUV or YIQ	Lossy	Contains multiple frames in a sequence, along with timecode and other metadata.
JPEG	24-bit	Linear RGB	Lossy	
JPEG 2000	Various	Various	Lossy or lossless	Supports color profiles, transparency, masks, other metadata.
LogLuv TIFF	24-bit	Log HDR	n/a	Covers 4.8 orders of magnitude with 1.1% precision.
LogLuv TIFF	32-bit	Log HDR	Lossless	Covers 38 orders of magnitude with 0.3% precision, allows negative luminance values.
OpenEXR	48-bit	Log HDR	Lossless	Covers 9.6 orders of magnitude with 0.1% precision.
Pixar TIFF	33-bit	Log HDR	Lossless	Covers 3.5 orders of magnitude with 0.4% precision.
PNG	24-bit	Linear RGB	Lossless	Supports transparency.
Radiance	32-bit	Log HDR	Lossless	Covers 76 orders of magnitude with 1.0% precision.

(continues)

(continued)

Format	Bit depth (per pixel)	Color model	Compression	Additional features
Targa	24-bit	Linear RGB	n/a	
TIFF	24-bit or 48-bit	Linear RGB	Lossy, lossless, or none	Supports layers, multiple channels, color profiles.
Windows Bitmap	8-bit or 24-bit	Linear RGB	n/a	

A.7 DIGITAL IMAGE OPERATIONS

Several common digital image operations are available to most pipelines. The operations may be reversible even after they're applied, and they may or may not degrade the image. Many have an optical equivalent; some don't.

Operation	Purpose	Reversible?	Image degradation	Optical equivalent	Notes
Sharpening (e.g., aperture correction, edge enhancement, unsharp masking)	Exaggerates fine detail	No	Medium	n/a	Can potentially cause "ringing" in image.
Blur (e.g., defocus, smooth, soft focus)	Removes fine detail	No	Severe	Defocus	Not exactly the same as defocusing an image or scene.
Upsampling (aka uprez, scale)	Increases the pixel resolution of an image	Yes, usually by down-sampling using same method	Low	Enlarge	Quality dependent on algorithm used; can result in edge artifacts' doesn't compare to re-imaging original source at higher resolution.
Downsampling (aka downrez, scale)	Decreases the pixel resolution of an image	No	Severe	Reduce	Quality dependent on algorithm used; can result in edge artifacts; can produce better results than re-imaging at lower resolution.
Noise reduction (e.g., median)	Reduces noise level in an image by removing fluctuations	No	Severe	Vaseline on lens	Can produce results similar to blurring image.
Rotation	Rotates the image	Yes	None to severe	Rotation	Increments of 90 degrees result in no degradation on square pixel images; otherwise, quality dependent on algorithm used.
Cropping	Removes part of the image	No	None	Cropping	

(continues)

(continued)

Operation	Purpose	Reversible?	Image degradation	Optical equivalent	Notes
Panning	Repositions an image	Yes	None to severe	Reposition	If image is panned by a whole number of pixels, no degradation occurs; otherwise, quality dependent on algorithm used; may result in cropped image.
Desaturation	Removes color from the image	No	Severe	Transfer to black-and-white film	
Primary color grading	Changes the overall color of the image	Yes, with HDR image	None to severe	Printer lights / colored filters	Excessive color correction can lead to banding, clipping, or crushing.
Elective color grading	Changes the color of parts of an image	No	Low to severe	Masking	Tends to introduce noise into images' images suffer same consequences of image undergoing primary color-grading process.
Warping	Stretches part of the image	No	Medium	Distorted lens	Quality dependent on algorithm used.
Vignette	Adds a faded or darkened border	No	None	Vignette	

Effect	Description		Severity		Notes
Lens flare	Simulates the effect of flare on the camera lens	No	Medium	Flare	Tends to look inferior to real lens flare.
Chromatic dispersion (aka color diffraction)	Produces a "rainbow" effect	No	Severe	Diffraction grating	Difficult to replicate digitally impossible to replicate digitally.
Polarization	Polarizes incoming light	n/a	n/a	Polarizing filter	Impossible to replicate digitally.
Glow (e.g., halo, bloom)	Exaggerates bright colors	No	Medium	n/a	
Retime (aka motion interpolation)	Changes the speed of a shot	Yes, when speed decreases; no, if speed increases	None to severe	Varispeed	Quality dependent on algorithm used; may result in motion artifacts.
Digital paint	Applies paint to the image	No	None	Paint	
Invert	Reverses the colors in an image	Yes	None	Print/reverse	

A.8　COMMON COLOR TEMPERATURES

The following table lists the correlated color temperature of some common light sources.

Light source	Correlated color temperature
Candle	1500 K
Warm-white fluorescent	3000 K
Early/late sunlight	3200 K
Tungsten	3400 K
Xenon lamp	5000 K
Noon daylight	5500 K
Daylight-balanced fluorescent	6000 K
Overcast sky	6500 K
Northlight (blue sky)	10000 K

A.9　CMX 3600 EDL FORMAT

The following illustration is of a typical CMX 3600:

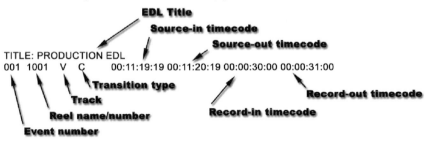

Although it's optional, the first line of the EDL usually contains a title. The second line, and all the subsequent lines, consist of the following components:

1. **The event number.** Differentiates between different lines in the EDL. Problems arise, however, when the lines are incorrectly ordered or when duplicate event numbers exist.

2. **The reel number (or reel name).** Identifies individual source reels and can usually consist of both numbers and letters. However, it's generally safer to use numbers only, if possible, and to avoid using names longer than six characters.
3. **The track.** Video only (V), in most cases; however, numerous audio channels may be included (e.g., A12).
4. **The transition type.** Usually a cut (C), but dissolves (D followed by the duration), wipes (W followed by the wipe SMPTE number and the duration), and motion effects (M2 followed by the duration) may also be present.
5. **The timecodes.** A pair of source timecodes (i.e., in and out points) are mapped onto record timecodes (also in and out) for every event.

Note that the frame rate isn't intrinsically specified in the EDL, which may lead to problems.

Conversion between EDLs of different frame rates involves converting all timecodes to frame numbers, typically using a sync reference frame—a timecode at which both EDLs line up (usually 00:00:00:00)—and then converting the frame numbers to the new timecode.

A.10 KEY NUMBERS

A typical key number reads as follows:

IS 00 9123 1234•

The first two digits contain the manufacturer code and film type, the following 10 numbers are the serial number for the particular reel, repeated every foot with the frame zeroed at the dot. This is repeated every 16 frames (i.e., 1 foot) for 35mm film, and so individual frames are counted as the zero frame key number + number frames. In this instance, 5 frames from the zero frame is key number IS 00 9123 1234+05, and so on. It's also possible to do this as negative numbers, so that 4 frames before the zero frame, in this case, is IS 00 9123 1234-04 (or IS 00 9123 1233+12). The same is true of 16mm film, except that it has 20 frames per foot.

A.11 WIDESCREEN SAFE AREAS

Image	Horizontal action safe	Horizontal title safe	Vertical action safe	Vertical title safe
16:9	3.5% from edge	5% from edge	3.5% from edge	5% from edge
16:9 protected for 4:3 (4:3 center cut-out)	15.13% from edge	16.25% from edge	3.5% from edge	5% from edge
4:3 protected for 16:9 (16:9 center cut-out)	3.5% from edge	5% from edge	15.13% from edge	16.25% from edge
1:1.85	3.5% from edge	5% from edge	3.5% from edge	5% from edge
1:1.85 protected for 16:9 (16:9 center cut-out)	5.3% from edge	6.7% from edge	3.5% from edge	5% from edge
1:1.85 protected for 4:3 (4:3 center cut-out)	16.57% from edge	17.65% from edge	3.5% from edge	5% from edge

A.12 CIE CHROMACITY DIAGRAM

CIE chromacity diagrams, such as the one provided later in this Appendix, map all colors in the entire visible gamut (enclosed by the curve on the graph) as points on a graph. For every visible color, an x and y coordinate can be found on the graph (luminosity is treated separately and normally denoted as of a z value). Furthermore, you can use the diagram to determine the boundaries of different color spaces (e.g., sRGB or NTSC video) by plotting the maximum value for each component (i.e., the maximum values for red, green, and blue output). Where color spaces overlap, the enclosed colors may be accurately reproduced by each color space. Otherwise, the colors are out of gamut and must be altered before they can be displayed.

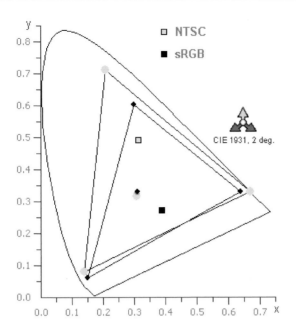

A.13 DIGITAL CINEMA MASTER SPECIFICATIONS

The following guidelines are based on version 5.1 of the DCI's specifications, as pertaining to the image content of a Digital Cinema Distribution Master (DCDM).

- Images may be encoded in one or more reels, which are later digitally spliced together.
- Images should be 12 bits per pixel JPEG2000 format images, encoded in an X'Y'Z' color space (i.e., gamma-corrected CIE color space coordinates).
- Spatial resolution should be 2048x1080 (2k) or 4096 × 2160 (4k) pixels, or an image area letterboxed to fit these areas, depending on the aspect ratio. For example, a 4:3 image at 2k would have an image area of 1440 × 1080 pixels, and a 16:9 image at 4k would have an image area of 3840 × 2160 pixels.
- 4k images should be accompanied by 2k counterparts.
- Frame rate must be 24 or 48 Hz for 2k images, 24 Hz for 4k images.

- The data must then be compressed, encrypted (using AES 128 encryption), packaged in an MXF container file, and finally combined with audio and other elements to form a Digital Cinema Package (DCP), the size of which should not exceed 500GB.
- Images must have a pixel aspect ratio of 1.0.

For more information on these specifications, visit the DCI's website at www.dcimovies.com.

GLOSSARY

2k   An image that is roughly 2000 pixels along one edge.

4k   An image that is roughly 4000 pixels along one edge.

Academy aperture   An aperture used for film material.

Access rights   See "file permissions."

action safe   The safe area defining where the picture content is visible.

aliasing   The effect in which the edges of pixels are clearly visible; the process of creating this effect. See also "anti-aliasing."

alpha   Transparency information; an image channel not normally displayed.

analog   A continuously variable signal; not digital.

anamorphic   A type of lens for compressing an image; an image that has been compressed, typically along the horizontal axis; a format using anamorphic compression.

anamorphic squeeze   The process of distorting an image to an anamorphic format.

answer print   A film print for generating release prints.

anti-aliasing   A technique for minimizing aliasing effects.

aperture   The part of an imaging device that controls the amount of light received into the device; the area of a frame used for an image.

aperture correction   See "sharpen."

artifact   A defect in an image.

ASA   See "film speed."

aspect ratio   The ratio of an image's width to its height.

authoring   The process of combining elements, typically when creating DVDs.

background plate   A shot serving as background for another element, typically for a visual effect; a placeholder for a shot.

banding   See "posterize."

bandwidth   The data transfer rate, usually measured in bytes per second.

bit   binary digit, the smallest unit of computer data.

bit-depth   The possible range of color information that can be encoded. See also "precision."

bitmap   A raster image; an image containing only black or white pixels; a Windows bitmap-formatted image.

bit rate   A measurement of bandwidth.

bluescreen   See "chroma-key."

broadcast-safe color   See "legal color."

burn in   To encode information directly into an image.

byte   A data measure consisting of 8 bits.

cache   A store of data, which can be accessed rapidly; a copy of an image held in the store for fast display or processing.

cadence   The ordering of frames in a pulldown sequence. See also "pulldown."

cathode-ray tube   A device that uses an electron beam fired down a vacuum tube to create an image.

CCD   See "charge-coupled device."

CDL   See "color decision" list.

center cut-out   A method for converting an image to another aspect ratio by cropping the picture around the center.

CG   Computer-generated—images that have been generated by a computer.

channel   An individual component in a digital image.

charge-coupled device   A device that detects and measures incident light, typically arranged in an array to allow image recording.

checksum   A file value calculated by adding up all of its binary digits; a signature used to identify a digital file.

chroma   See "chromaticity."

chromaticity   The color component of light.

chroma-key   A method for creating a key based on a certain color; a screen of solid color; the process of shooting foreground elements in front of such a screen.

CinemaScope   A specific anamorphic aperture used for film material. See also "anamorphic."

Cineon printing density   (CPD) is a digital image color space designed to mimic the response of film.

client   A computer system that receives data from a server.

clone   To make an exact copy of a video tape using digital means.

closed-caption   A text element that doesn't form part of the recorded image.

cluster   A group of computer systems that combine resources to perform a single task.

CLUT   Color lookup table. See "lookup table."

CMYK   A color model combining proportions of cyan, magenta, yellow, and black.

color cube   See "lookup table."

color decision list   A portable list containing grading parameters to be applied to footage.

color space   An imaging system's reproducible color range.

color timing   See "color grading."

color correction   See "color grading."

color grading   The process of altering an image's colors.

component video   A video signal that separately encodes every color component.

composite   An image that contains composited elements.

composite video   A video signal that encodes color components together.

compression   The process of reducing image dimensions or color ranges, either by discarding or by reorganizing information.

conforming   The process, usually performed automatically, of assembling source material into a program.

consolidate   To move elements to one location, often combining them; to remove all extraneous material from a program.

contrast ratio   The ratio of the brightest color to the darkest color in an image.

corruption   A fault in a digital file.

CPD   See "Cineon printing density."

crop   To remove one or more edges of an image.

CRT   See "cathode-ray tube."

cue   To spool to a specific point in a video sequence or on a tape.

cut   A version of an edited program; a transition between a frame of one shot to a frame of another shot; to copy and remove a shot.

cut list   A list of edits within a sequence or program. The edits are usually specified in terms of key numbers.

cut point   A frame number or time code position where a transition occurs.

dailies   Raw, unedited footage from a shoot; the process of watching such footage.

data   Information, typically in digital form.

day-for-night   A technique for shooting a scene during the day and using various processes to make the scene appear to have been shot at night.

DCDM   See "digital cinema distribution master."

D-cinema   See "digital cinema."

DCP   See "digital cinema package."

decrypt   To rearrange encrypted data so that it can be viewed correctly.

deinterlaceing   The process of removing interlacing from a frame or sequence.

density   The level of developed grains at a specific point in film material.

detective quantum efficiency   An objective measurement of image quality, combining MTF measurements with signal-to-noise ratio measurements. See also "modulation transfer function"; "signal-to-noise ratio."

DF   See "drop-frame timecode."

difference matte   An image showing the difference in pixel values between two images.

digital   A signal consisting of discrete units of information.

digital cinema   Motion picture theaters that use digital material rather than film material; the process of providing digital cinema.

digital cinema distribution master   A DCDM is the digital output used for digital cinema exhibition.

digital cinema package   A collection of elements for digital cinema projection.

digital dailies   The process of watching dailies in a digital environment.

digital source master   The digital master created at the end of the digital intermediate process.

digital versatile disc   A DVD is an optical disc-based digital storage medium; consumer-grade digital video format.

digital video   Video material encoded in a digital format; moving images encoded in a digital format; consumer-grade digital video format.

digitize   To make digital, usually by sampling an analog signal. See also "sampling."

directory   See "folder."

dissolve   A transition from one shot to another using a blend.

D-max   The maximum density level in a film image.

D-min   The minimum density level in a film image.

downrez   See "downsample."

downsample   To decrease the number of pixels, usually by interpolation, in an image.

DQE   See "detective quantum efficiency."

drop-frame timecode   A method whereby certain frame numbers are omitted from the timecode to synchronize playback to real-time clocks.

dropout   A fault on a video signal where picture information is missing or damaged.

dropped frame   An individual frame that is omitted from a sequence, including during playback.

DSM   See "digital source master."

dub   To copy—usually applies to video tapes.

dust-bust   The process of removing dust, scratches, and the like from scanned film.

DV   See "digital video."

DVD   See "digital versatile disc."

dynamic   A parameter that varies over time; an effect utilizing varying parameters.

dynamic range   The response of a system to various luminance levels; the system's capacity for encoding a range of different luminance levels. See also "luminance."

edit   To manually assemble footage to form a sequence or program.

edit decision list   A portable list of edits, usually specified in terms of reels and timecodes, making up a sequence or program.

EDL   See "edit decision list."

EI   See "exposure index."

encode   The process of storing data in a particular format.

encrypt   To alter data so that it can be accessed only by someone with the proper credentials.

enlarger   A device used to increase the size of a photographic image.

event   A shot in a sequence; a shot in an EDL. See also "edit decision list."

exposure   A measurement of the amount of light incident on a particular point over time; the act of exposing a sensitive material to light.

exposure index   A method for recording film speed, accounting for other factors. See also "film speed."

exposure latitude   The potential range of exposure recordable by a given material.

extract   To remove a shot from a sequence so that the adjacent shots cut together.

eye-match   To visually match two images.

false color   A method for applying color to a monochrome image.

field   Half of a video frame. Each field is usually recorded when no other field is recorded., Fields are usually recorded in an interlaced manner.

file attributes   Data attached to files and folders by the operating system that may contain additional parameters or information about the file.

file extension   The suffix at the end of a filename, usually to denote the file type.

file permissions   Data attached to files and folders that denote who has access to perform certain functions, such as viewing or editing the files.

file security   See "file permissions."

file header   The metadata contents of a file.

film negative   Film material containing images with reversed color. A negative must be printed before it can be viewed normally.

film positive   Film material containing images that can be viewed directly, such as by projection.

film print   See "film positive."

film scanner   A device used to digitize film images.

film speed   A value for the sensitivity of film material to light.

film stock   A type of film material with specific characteristics, such as sensitivity to light.

film-out   The process of recording material onto film from a digital source.

filter   A device, attached to an imaging system, to modify images during recording; a digital process used to modify images.

firewire   A data transfer technology defined by the IEEE1394 specification.

flare   An effect caused by light reflection on the lens; a process mimicking this effect.

fog   Light contamination, usually from stray light; an effect to add depth to an image.

folder   A structure on a disk that can contain files.

footage   A collection of moving pictures.

FPS   See "frames per second."

frame   A single image within a sequence; to position and compose an image; the area containing a viewable image.

frame patch   The method of replacing a shot's individual frames with other frames; a frame used for this purpose.

frame rate   The speed at which individual image frames are displayed to form a moving sequence, usually measured in Hertz or frames per second.

frames per second   A unit of frequency used to describe the rate of picture images shown every second in a moving picture sequence.

full aperture   An image-recording method, usually for film material, that uses the maximum imaging area.

fullscreen   A 4:3 image format.

gamma   the relationship between a pixel and the corresponding point of light displayed on a device such as a television; a value describing the amount of gamma correction used; a method for altering the brightness and contrast of an image.

gamma-correction   The process of modifying a pixel value for display on a device with a nonlinear response.

gamut   See "color space."

gate   The part of an imaging device that crops an image, usually to constrain the image to a particular format.

gauge   The size of a film image.

GB   See "gigabyte."

generation   A copy, usually of analog material.

generation loss   The loss of quality that occurs when a new generation is created.

gigabyte   A measure of 1024 megabytes.

global grading   See "primary grading."

grading flash   A discontinuity in color in a sequence.

grading list   See "grading metadata."

grading metadata   Data concerning the grading to be applied to an image or sequence.

grain   A light-sensitive region in film material; a the smallest part of a film image.

graininess   A subjective measurement of the amount of grain in an image.

granularity   An objective measurement of the amount of grain in an image.

greenscreen   See "chroma key."

gray scale   An image without chromacity.

handle   Additional frames of a shot that extend beyond the cut points.

hard cut   A cut within source footage.

HD   See "high definition."

HDR   See "high dynamic range image."

HDTV   See "high-definition television."

header   See "file header."

headroom   The region of an imaging system above the maximum or below the minimum displayable brightness value.

high definition   A video format with increased resolution.

high-definition television   A video signal that carries high-definition video suitable for television; a television that can display this signal.

high dynamic range image   A digital image format capable of encoding color in an objective way, typically as coordinates on the CIE chromacity chart.

histogram   A method for displaying the distribution of pixel values in a digital image.

HLS   A color model combining hue, luminance, and saturation.

hue   The angle of a color's wavelength, as measured on a color wheel.

in-place edit   The process of making changes to a file directly without creating new files or rendering.

interlacing   A method of combining two fields in a frame, by encoding lines of alternate fields to each frame.

inter-neg   See "inter-negative."

inter-negative   An intermediate film negative.

interpolate   to estimate intermediate values, usually in terms of pixel values

inter-pos   See "inter-positive."

inter-positive   An intermediate film positive.

inverse telecine   The process of relating an edited pulldown sequence to the original film footage. See also "pulldown."

ISO   See "film speed."

jog   To progress through footage, usually a frame at a time.

KB   See "kilobyte."

key   A region of transparency or selection, usually based on a color range; the method used to create transparency or selection; the color used to do this.

key number   A code that uniquely identifies a frame of film.

keycode   See "key number."

keyframe   A frame that specifies a particular setting at a particular point in time, usually for dynamic effects or animation purposes; the process of creating keyframes.

kilobyte   A measure consisting of 1024 bytes.

Lab   A color model combining luminance and chromacity coordinates.

lag   An effect that's created when frames aren't delivered fast enough for real-time display.

LAN   See "local area network."

latent image   The invisible image formed on exposed photographic film that is developed to form a visible image.

layer   An individual image in a composite image; a process applied to an image, such as a "grading layer;" a single track in a vertical editing system.

leader   Frames that precede a program or sequence.

legal color   A color, typically in video formats, within a particular color space.

letterbox   A method for converting an image to another aspect ratio by filling the missing area with black.

lift To remove a shot from a sequence without altering the timing of the sequence, usually leaving a gap; to adjust the black level in an image.

line spread function See "spread function."

local area network A group of computer systems that are able to communicate with each other, usually through cables or wireless transmission.

log See "logarithmic."

logarithmic An exponential numbering scale; measurement on this scale; an image encoded using values on this scale.

longitudinal timecode Timecode information that is encoded to a specific part of a video tape.

lookup table A lookup table (LUT) is a method for replacing stored colors with other colors; a LUT is typically used to convert between different color spaces. More sophisticated LUTs may use "color cubes," or other 3D mathematical models.

lossless compression Compression that doesn't result in a loss of information.

lossy compression Compression that results in a loss of information.

LTC See "longitudinal timecode."

luma Gamma-corrected luminance.

luminance The intensity of a particular color; the component of an image pixel or signal measuring the intensity. "Luminance" is synonymous with "brightness" and "luminosity."

LUT See "lookup table."

mask A shape that constrains an effect applied to an image.

master To create a final production for a specific format; the media containing this material.

matrix See "video-switching matrix."

matte An image used to constrain an effect applied to another image.

MB See "megabyte."

megabyte A measure consisting of 1024 kilobytes.

megahertz   A unit of frequency in the order of millions of cycles per second; see also "millions of instructions per second."

megapixel   A unit of measurement of digital image area; one megapixel consists of one million pixels.

metadata   Data concerning other data; typically data that can be encoded that doesn't contain image information.

MHz   See "megahertz."

millions of instructions per second   A measurement, typically used with computers, to denote the number of calculations that can be performed in one second.

MIPS   See "millions of instructions per second."

modulation transfer function   MTF is an objective measurement of a system's response to different frequencies.

monochrome   An image consisting of a single color.

motion control   A programmable motorized unit, allowing for precise and repeatable motion of a device, typically a camera.

movie   A film production; a moving picture sequence; a digital moving picture sequence file.

MTF   See "modulation transfer function."

NDF   See "non-drop-frame timecode."

nearline storage   Storage whose contents are accessible but at a slower rate than online storage.

negative   See "film negative."

NLE   See "nonlinear editing."

noise   Random fluctuations in a signal.

non-drop-frame timecode   A timecode method whereby frame numbers are counted in a continuous fashion.

nonlinear editing   Editing footage in any order.

NTSC   National Television Systems Committee; a video standard used in most of North America and parts of east Asia.

offline edit   An editing phase performed without permanent changes, usually without working with original, full-quality material.

offline storage   Storage whose contents are not immediately accessible.

one-light grading   To apply simple, overall color grading to an image, usually for viewing purposes.

online edit   An editing phase that replicates to the original, full-quality source material the changes made in an offline edit.

online storage   Storage whose contents are immediately available.

operating system   Software used to control the basic hardware functions of a computer system.

optical   Pertaining to a lens or an image-recording system; an effect applied to an image; an image or shot that has had an effect applied to it.

OS   See "operating system."

overscan   The region of an image outside of the safe area. See also "safe area."

overwrite   To replace a file with another one; in non-linear editing, to replace all or part of one or more shots with another shot.

PAL   Phase-Alternate Lines; a video standard used throughout most of the world.

pan and scan   The process of repositioning and resizing material to fit different aspect ratios; footage that has undergone this process.

panorama   An image that has a wide field of view; an image formed by placing multiple images side by side.

parallax   An effect in which distant objects appear to move at a slower rate than closer ones.

perf   See "perforation."

perforation   A hole, in a series of holes, along the edge of a strip of film, which is used to position images.

Picture line-up generation equipment   A device used to calibrate a display.

pin registration   A feature of some film scanners that for registering film scans more precisely.

pixel   Picture element; the smallest spatial component of a digital image.

pixel aspect ratio   The ratio of a pixel's width to its height.

platform   See "operating system."

PLUGE　See "picture line-up generation equipment."

point spread function　See "spread function."

positive　See "film positive."

posterize　A digital image artifact caused by low color precision. A posterized image displays steps in color. Also, a process used to exaggerate this effect. See also "precision."

post-roll　The amount of time required by a linear system to decelerate from real-time playback speed to a stop.

precision　The degree of accuracy in reproducing colors and in recording colors; a measurement, usually in bits per pixel or bits per channel of this degree of accuracy.

pre-roll　A period used by a linear system to accelerate from a stop to real-time playback speed; the amount of time required to do so.

primary grading　Color grading that affects an entire image.

printer light　A measurement of grading film chemically; a light used for making film prints.

printer point　See "printer light."

privileges　See "write-once read-many."

program　A collection of shots making up a complete production.

progressive scan　A frame that doesn't consist of fields; a method of recording video without recording fields.

progressive segmented frames　A method of storing progressive scan video material using fields.

proxy image　An image copy, usually downsampled, to which changes can be made that are later applied to the original image.

PsF　See "progressive segmented frames."

pulldown　A method of translating film frames to video frames; a sequence that has undergone this process.

punch hole　A frame used as a sync point; a hole punched into a frame of film.

RAID　See "redundant array of inexpensive disks."

RAM　See "random access memory."

random access memory　A non-permanent memory store used by computer systems, typically for performing calculations.

raster   A digital image consisting of regularly arranged pixels, usually rectangular.

rasterize   The process of converting a nonraster image to a raster image.

raw scan   The unmodified image data, as created by a film scanner; any unmodified acquired image.

real time   Footage shown at the rate it was recorded.

reconform   To apply changes (usually automatically) to an existing conformed sequence. See also "conform."

redundant array of inexpensive disks   A specification for combining multiple digital storage devices together to act as a single high-capacity device, optionally with some form of data protection.

reel   A single unit of footage, such as of film or a video tape; a collection of shots; a part of an output production.

registration   The positioning of an image within a frame.

release print   A film print used by cinemas for projection.

remaster   To create a new master from a program that has already been mastered. See also "master."

rendering   The process of applying changes to an image; processing image data; outputting digital images.

render farm   A number of computers used for rendering.

resample   To upsample or downsample an image; to redigitize an image from its source, usually at a different resolution.

resolution   An image's spatial detail; the number of pixels in a digital image; the number of lines in a video image.

resolution-independent   An image that can be of any resolution; a system that conforms images of different resolutions.

resolving power   The measurement of an imaging system's resolution.

reversal film   Film material that records a positive image directly from a source.

rewritable   A type of media that can be recorded onto multiple times; a device used with such media.

RGB   A color model combining proportions of red, green, and blue.

ringing   The effect produced when images have been artificially sharpened too much.

rotoscope   The process of generating masks or mats for every frame in a sequence; the result of this process.

rushes   See "dailies."

safe area   A region within an image where elements are generally guaranteed to be visible across different display devices.

sampling ratio   The ratio of different color components, typically Y:U:V or Y:I:Q, in video.

SAN   See "storage area network."

saturation   The purity component of a color.

scanner   See "film scanner."

scene   An environment used for filming; a collection of shots within a particular location or time frame.

scrambling   A type of encryption that modifies all or part of a visible image, typically obscuring details.

SD   See "standard definition."

secondary grading   The process of adjusting color in selected parts of an image.

seek   To go to a specific point in a timeline or in data.

selective grading   See "secondary grading."

sequence   A collection of shots and/or individual images.

server   A computer system that sends data to a client.

sharpen   A process of exaggerating the edges of an image.

shoot and protect   A method of shooting onto a particular aspect ratio, which ensures that other aspect ratio images can be extracted later.

shot   A collection of moving pictures, typically of continuous action without transitions; having photographed an image.

shuttle   To progress through footage at a rate that's a multiple of real time.

signal-to-noise ratio   The ratio of image information to inherent noise within a system.

silver halide   The light-sensitive crystals within film material.

slate   A description of a sequence—typically in the form of an image at the start or end of the sequence.

Sneaker Net   A method of transmitting data, by physically relocating storage derices.

soft cut   A transition that includes a very brief dissolve.

splice   To insert a shot between two other shots; a method for joining two pieces of film; the point on film material where a join has been made.

spread function   An objective measurement of image sharpness.

sprocket   See "perforation."

stabilize   The process of removing random motion in an image sequence so as to steady it.

standard definition   A video format with low (i.e., standard) resolution.

standards conversion   The process of converting between different video standards.

still image   A single image, which can be part of a sequence.

storage area network   A group of storage devices that communicate with other computer systems.

streaming   The process of transmitting data for instant viewing.

sync   synchronization; two or more sources are said to be "in sync" when their timings are precisely the same.

sync pulse   Part of a video signal that indicates the end of a line of picture; part of the video signal that indicates the end of a field.

tape-to-tape   The process of transferring material from a source tape directly onto a record tape.

TB   See "terabyte."

telecine   The process of transferring film material to video.

terabyte   A unit of measure consisting of 1024 gigabytes.

thumbnail   A miniature copy of an image for fast previewing.

timecode   A method for identifying and counting individual frames in a sequence, typically dependent on frame rate to provide values applicable in real time.

timecode break   A discontinuity in timecode within a sequence.

timeline   A method for displaying an edited program; a sequence or program.

timestamp   The date and time properties of a file.

time warp   The ability to adjust the speed of a shot; a shot that has undergone this process.

title safe   The safe area of an image that defines the position where titles can be viewed.

tone mapping   The process of converting an HDR image to a specific color space. See also "HDR"; "color space."

tracking   The process of tracking the motion of a feature in an image sequence, usually to attach other elements to it.

tracking marker   An object placed in a scene during shooting to allow tracking at a later time.

tramline   A persistent scratch typically vertical, across a number of film frames.

transcode   Modifying the encoding of image data to change the image to a different format.

transition   A method of moving from one shot to another.

unsharp mask   See "sharpen."

uprez   See "upsample."

upsample   To increase the number of pixels in an image, usually by interpolation.

variable bit rate   A data stream with varying bandwidth requirements; a compression method using varying bandwidth requirements.

VBR   See "variable bit-rate."

VCR   See "video tape recorder."

vector   A mathematical shape.

vectorscope   A method of displaying an image's chromacity content; a device that displays this information, usually for video signals.

vertical interval timecode   A method of recording timecode as part of the video signal.

VHS   See "video home system."

video cassette recorder   A device that records and plays video tapes.

video home system   Consumer-grade analog video format.

video tape recorder   See "video cassette recorder."

video-safe color   See "legal color."

video-switching matrix   A device that routes video to many different places at one time.

vignette   An effect caused when light is distributed unevenly across a lens; a process mimicking this effect.

VITC   See "vertical interval timecode."

VTR   See "video cassette recorder."

WAN   See "wide area network."

warp   To alter the shape of all or part of an image.

watermark   A visible image, typically a logo, placed over all images in a sequence; information embedded imperceptibly into an image.

waveform monitor   A device display used to an image's luminance content, usually for video signals.

wide area network   A group of computer systems that communicate with each other over long distances, such as through the internet.

widescreen   An image format with a wide aspect ratio, typically wider than 4:3.

wi-fi   Wireless fidelity, see also "wireless network."

wipe   A transition that reveals one shot over another.

wireless network   A group of computers that communicate with each other without using cables, typically by using radio transmissions.

WORM   See "write-once read-many."

write-once read-many   A type of media that can be recorded onto once, but the recorded data accessed multiple times, such as a compact disc; a device used with such media, such as a computer disc recorder.

YIQ   The color space used by the NTSC video format, encoding luminance and two chromacity components.

YUV   The color space used by the PAL video format, encoding luminance and two chromacity components.

ACKNOWLEDGMENTS

"Le cinema e un'invenzione senza avvenire."
(The cinema is an invention without a future.)
—*Louis Lumière*

I want to thank a number of individuals who are as much a part of this book as the paper and ink.

The complementary artist Claire McGrane and Steve Parsons of Framestore CFC; Andrew Francis (also responsible for many of the beautiful images throughout this book), Simon Cross, Luke Rainey, Gavin Burridge, and Peter Lynch; Aviv Yaron, Kevin Wheatley, Courtney Vanderslice, Mitch Mitchell, Peter Robertshaw, and Colin Brown of Cinesite Europe; Stuart Fyvie of Lipsync Post; Neil Robinson of Filmlight; and Aaron James of NBC News Universal London: thanks for teaching me this stuff in the first place.

Howard Lukk of Walt Disney Studios; Walt Ordway of the DCI; Dave Bancroft of Thomson; Paul Debevec, Greg Ward, Flemming Jetmar, many members of the Telecine Internet Group (tig.colorist.org); and the numerous manufacturers and PR agents: thanks for answering a multitude of questions for me.

And finally, to my friends and family for moral support, to Joanne Tracy, Lothlorien Homet, Becky Golden-Harrell, Angelina Ward, Marie Hooper, and the others at Focal Press, without whose efforts you would just be holding a stack of blank paper right now.

INDEX